The Faber Book of the Turf

John Hislop has reached the top in the racing world as an amateur rider, writer and the owner–breeder of the great Brigadier Gerard. Since 1971 he has been an active member of the Jockey Club. David Swannell was senior Jockey Club Handicapper for ten years and Clerk of the Course at Beverley, Wetherby and Thirsk. A long-term student of turf literature, he has been concerned in the creation in 1983 and the running of the National Horseracing Museum at Newmarket.

THE FABER BOOK OF

THE TURF

—

edited by

John Hislop and
David Swannell

faber and faber
LONDON · BOSTON

First published in 1990
by Faber and Faber Limited
3 Queen Square London WC1N 3AU
This paperback edition first published in 1992

Phototypeset by Input Typesetting Ltd, London
Printed in Great Britain by
Clays Ltd, St Ives plc

A CIP record for this book is available from the British Library

ISBN 0-571-16625-3

2 4 6 8 10 9 7 5 3 1

CONTENTS

List of Illustrations ix
Introduction xi

PERSONALITIES

The Jockey Club – *Roger Mortimer* 3
Caroline, Duchess of Montrose – *Richard Onslow* 6
Fred Archer – *The Hon. George Lambton* 10
The Fifth Earl of Lonsdale – *Douglas Sutherland* 12
The Hon. George Lambton – *Michael Seth-Smith* 15
The Sixth Earl of Rosebery – *John Hislop* 18
Mrs Vernet – *Caroline Ramsden* 25
Fred Darling – *Sir Gordon Richards* 28
Cecil Boyd-Rochfort – *P. T. Beasley* 33
Jim Joel's Racing Reminiscences – *H. J. Joel* 36
The Hon. Dorothy Paget – *Caroline Ramsden* 43
Aly Khan – *Quintin Gilbey* 51
The Maktoum Family Business, 1989 – *Michael Seely* 52
A Small-Scale Owner – *The Hon. William Douglas Home* 59

TRAINING AND BREEDING

The Choice of a Broodmare – *Count Lehndorff* 65
The Training of Racehorses – *The Hon. George Lambton* 68
Training – *H. S. Persse* 72
Breeding to Win the Derby – *Peter Burrell* 83
Some Thoughts on Racing and Breeding – *Sir Noël Murless* 89
Messieurs Mathet and Pollet – *Peter O'Sullevan* 96
On Horses and Training – *Henry Cecil* 100
Great Breeders and Their Methods – *Abram S. Hewitt* 106
The Royal Studs, 1989 – *Tony Morris* 109
All in a Day's Work – *Susan Gallier* 112

HORSES

Origins of the Thoroughbred –
The Hon. Captain Rous, RN 125

The Darley Arabian – *Thomas Darley* 127

Gimcrack (1760) – *Paul Mellon* 129

St Simon – *Peter Willett* 131

Scapa Flow, Fairway and Walter Alston –
The Hon. George Lambton 135

Death of a Derby Winner: Humorist – *Sir Alfred Munnings* 142

Easter Hero – *B. J. O'Sullivan* 146

The End of a Long Life: Hyperion – *The Earl of Derby* 147

Brigadier Gerard on Newbury Racecourse – *John Hislop* 149

The Horse of the Decade – *Simon Barnes* 151

When the Horse was King – *John Hislop* 153

EIGHT OUTSTANDING RACEHORSES

Alycidon (1945) – *Roger Mortimer* 159

Abernant (1946) – *Roger Mortimer and Peter Willett* 165

Ribot (1952) – from *Timeform* 172

Petite Étoile (1956) – from *Timeform* 174

Sea-Bird II (1962) – from *Timeform* 175

Nijinsky (1967) – from *Timeform* 177

Mill Reef (1968) – from *Timeform* 179

Brigadier Gerard (1968) – from *Timeform* 182

JOCKEYS

Genius Genuine – *Samuel Chifney* 187

'Jocked Off' a Derby Winner – *Anon.* 188

Fred Archer – *In Memoriam* 189

Tod Sloan – *The Hon. George Lambton* 191

The Night before the Grand Prix – *Quintin Gilbey* 192

Piggott and Sir Gordon – *John Hislop and Others* 195

The Strength of an Acrobat –
Lester Piggott and Kenneth Harris 199

The Jockeys' Championship 1987 – *John Oaksey* 204

Peter Scudamore's Record 1989 – *Alan Lee* 207

Wasting to Ride – *'Ellangowan'* 210

The Whip: Use and Misuse – *Anon.*   211
Advice to Amateur Riders – *Harry Brown*   212
The Amateur Rider – *A. B. Paterson*   215

VICTORY AND DEFEAT

An Unusual Double, Ascot 1881 – *Sir John Astley, Bt*   221
The Two Thousand Guineas, 1910 –
The Hon. George Lambton   225
The 1913 Derby – *Michael Seth-Smith*   226
The Derby, 1934 – *John Welcome*   229
The Queen Alexandra Stakes, 1934 – *R. C. Lyle*   239
'20–1 and Not a Pal On' – *Colin Davy*   240
The Grand National, 1935 – *Basil Briscoe*   244
Anthony Mildmay and Davy Jones – *Roger Mortimer*   248
A Wartime Interlude – *John Hislop*   252
The Derby, 1949 – *Roger Mortimer*   259
Mandarin and Fred Winter – *'Marlborough' (Lord Oaksey)*   262
The Cheltenham Gold Cup, 1964 – *Ivor Herbert*   265
The Derby, 1986 – *Racehorses of 1986*   268
Desert Orchid – *Simon Barnes*   270
The Melbourne Cup – *Adam Lindsay Gordon*   272

A MIXED CARD

Lady Florence Paget: The Pocket Venus – *Henry Blyth*   279
The Changing Pattern of Racing – *John Hislop*   296
Making a Handicap – *Geoffrey Freer*   299
Rule 153 – *David Swannell*   304
Selling Races, 1884 – *Sir George Chetwynd, Bt*   307
The Time Factor – *'Donovan'*   308
A Pacemaker – *John Skeaping, RA*   311
The Gentle Art of Tipping – *Geoffrey Gilbey*   312
Ecclesiastical Wrath – *John Radcliffe*   315
A Racing Bore – *Geoffrey Gilbey*   316
A Cautionary Tale, 1898 – *Arthur M. Binstead*   318
The Thoroughbred Sportsman: George Osbaldeston –
Anon.   319
Rainbow's Race – *Rolf Boldrewood*   320

The Joys of Multiple Ownership –
Michael Thompson-Noël 327
How to Bet – *Jack Leach* 331
The Charms of Newmarket –
Newmarket Journal, November 1875 333
As We are Now – *John Hislop* 337

Sources 343
Acknowledgements 347
Index 349

LIST OF ILLUSTRATIONS

Plates between pages 116 and 117 and 244 and 245

1 Oaks Day at Epsom, 1934. King George V and Queen Mary arrive on the course.

2 Mr Jim Joel leads in his Derby winner, Royal Palace, at Epsom, 1967.

3 The Hon. George Lambton, *c.* 1903, at Bedford Lodge, his first training establishment on his appointment as private trainer to the 16th Earl of Derby.

4 Henry Cecil, an outstanding trainer of the 'eighties.

5 Jack Jarvis, with two of his patrons, Lord Rosebery and Sir Laurence Philipps.

6 St Simon (1881), a mature stallion, at Welbeck.

7 Hyperion (1930). Nine years old, at the peak of his stud career.

8 Brigadier Gerard after winning his last race, the 1972 Champion Stakes.

9 Sea Bird II (1962). At three years old.

10 Brigadier Gerard (1968). At three years old. J. Mercer up.

11 Nijinsky (1967).

12 Gordon Richards on Pasch after winning the 2,000 Guineas, 1938.

13 Harry Brown, the last amateur to head the list of National Hunt riders, at Aintree in 1935.

14 Pat Eddery. At the top of his profession and Champion Jockey for the seventh time in 1989.

15 Lester Piggott. Ten times Champion Jockey and rider of twenty-nine Classic winners.

16 Steve Cauthen, the first American since Danny Maher to be Champion Jockey.

17 Peter Scudamore, five times top National Hunt rider, who broke the record of 1,138 winning rides set up by John Francome.

18 Steve Donoghue (1884–1945), winner of fourteen Classic races, in the colours of Lord Derby.

19 Charles Smirke and Palestine, winner of the 2,000 Guineas, St James's Palace Stakes and the Sussex Stakes.

20 Golden Miller (1927).

21 Becher's Brook first time round in the Grand National of 1934. Won by Golden Miller (centre), ridden by G. Wilson.

22 L. Piggott, in the classic position in the field at Tattenham Corner, on Crepello, winner of the Derby, 1957.

23 Prince Khalid Abdulla's Dancing Brave, winner of the 2,000 Guineas, the Coral Eclipse Stakes and L'Arc de Triomphe.

24 Desert Orchid (Simon Sherwood) at Sandown, 1988. A national hero of the eighties.

Illustrations in text

Fred Archer, the greatest jockey of the nineteenth century, with his wife, sister-in-law and father-in-law.   1

H. S. (Atty) Persse, trainer of the brilliant, unbeaten The Tetrarch.   63

Easter Hero (1920). A truly great chaser.   123

Mill Reef (1968). At three years old. Geoff Lewis up.   157

Danny Maher, the finest jockey of the era, who headed the list of flat race jockeys in 1908 and 1913.   185

The Cheltenham Gold Cup, 1964. Arkle jumps the last fence on his way to victory.   219

The Marquess and Marchioness of Hastings, *c.* 1864, at the start of their four years of marriage.   277

INTRODUCTION

Our aim is to present a selection of turf literature and items of interest which, so far as it has been possible to discover, have not appeared in a previous anthology.

Personal choice in such a collection is always open to criticism of inclusions and exclusions, and is bounded by the length of the book; so we, as compilers, hope that the reader will bear with us in this respect and find some entertainment in our offering.

The several excerpts from George Lambton's *Men and Horses I Have Known* and John Hislop's writings are due in the former case to our admiration of this classic, and in the latter to persuasion from his partner in the enterprise.

We are extremely grateful to all those living authors who have so kindly given permission to include their work and to the relevant authorities in other cases. We would like to acknowledge with special thanks the faultless work of our patient secretary, Sally Hendry. Without her we could not have entered the stalls, let alone started.

John Hislop and David Swannell
Newmarket, 1990

PERSONALITIES

Fred Archer, the greatest jockey of the nineteenth century, with his wife, Miss
Annie Dawson and G. Dawson, respectively his sister-in-law and father-in-law.
(*Sherborn, Newmarket*)

The Jockey Club

The concept of government by an hereditary aristocracy was discredited beyond redemption in England when the follies and ineptitudes of those responsible for the conduct of the Crimean War became generally known.

In the hundred years that followed, the power, the privileges, and the prestige of the aristocracy gradually diminished and were finally swept away in the gale of two terrible wars. Democratic ideals spread, and a way of life that would have been unthinkable in 1914 was an accepted fact forty years later. Few important institutions remained untouched. Almost alone the Jockey Club stands out as a fortress of the old order that the forces of democracy have not so much failed to capture as chosen to bypass.

The list of members shows how little the basis of the Club has altered during the 200 years of its existence. The self-elected governing body of English racing remains fundamentally aristocratic and conservative. The names of men prominent in business or in industry, who patronize racing, are for the most part missing. On the other hand there is clearly no anti-Semitic bias. With the exception of Sir Winston Churchill, there is no statesman of great influence among the members, but it must be remembered that the aristocracy no longer plays a leading part in the government of the country. The names of a high proportion of the members are totally unknown to the man in the street.

That the Jockey Club continues to hold its position is all the more remarkable since the redistribution of wealth means that members of the aristocracy no longer dominate the field as owners and breeders. Moreover, racing, through force of economic circumstances, has tended to become for those actively participating in it less of a sport and more of a business. As the cost of maintaining a single horse in training for a year at a fashionable Newmarket stable is roughly equivalent to educating a couple of boys at Eton over a similar period, even the richest owner has to try and make his racing pay. To own horses without being compelled to back them substantially when they are fancied is a luxury that singularly few can contemplate today.

Of course the Jockey Club has its critics, particularly during a spell of hard weather when there is no current racing to write about, and racing correspondents traditionally fill in space by instructing the rulers of the Turf in the way to run their business.

The most common criticism is that the Club draws its members from too narrow and exclusive a circle; that it is, in effect, a closed shop, the members of which are hopelessly out of touch with the feelings and desires of the average supporter of racing. It is also said that the ingrained conservatism of most of the members, some of whom look back to the Edwardian age with nostalgic affection, impels them to cling to the past and to set their faces against reasonable and progressive reform.

Few would deny that the criticisms contain a substantial grain of truth, but as often as not the reputation of the Jockey Club as a whole has suffered because of the offhand arrogance or the obvious incapacity of a single member. Institutions are apt to be judged by their worst representatives rather than their best ones, and one selfish or foolish action by a Club member is remembered while the solid hard work that is often done usually passes with no observation at all. A few seasons ago the Stewards visited every racecourse in the country, paying particular attention to the cheaper enclosures, interviewing racegoers to obtain suggestions from them, and recommending improvements to the executives concerned. Only a few people know how much was accomplished in that particular year.

Sometimes it is alleged that the Club applies disciplinary measures in a manner that is arbitrary and unjust and that certain owners and trainers are permitted to run their horses in a manner that at least would be the subject of inquiry if perpetrated by persons of less distinction. Whatever may have been the case in the past, the fact is that the greatest possible care is taken in disciplinary cases, particularly those which may involve a man's livelihood. Furthermore there have been cases when a timely and unofficial word of warning has probably been instrumental in saving a young man's career.

Criticism of the Jockey Club as an institution is not, however, of sufficient proportion or influence to place the authority and status of the Club in serious jeopardy. All who are engaged professionally in the sport, and in fact all who pass through the gates of a racecourse, continue to submit themselves in greater or lesser degree to its authority with only an occasional feeling of resentment.

There are two main reasons for this. The first is that most fair-minded people will agree that, with all its faults, the Jockey Club has served racing so well and has the best interests of the Turf at heart. In particular there is considerable admiration for the wise and tactful manner in which the sport was kept alive during two world wars, despite strong opposition that was frequently, though not invariably, inspired by motives of unquestioned sincerity.

Secondly, the Jockey Club enjoys, by and large, the loyalty and support of the Press. Co-operation between the two has grown appreciably closer in the past thirty years, and though mutual irritation is anything but uncommon, serious clashes are happily few. Press criticism of the Club is usually concerned with some aspect of administration rather than with the structure and function of the Club as a whole. Moreover the hostile attacks usually appear in newspapers whose influence is in inverse ratio to their vast circulation, while the authors seldom seem greatly concerned either with fairness of presentation or with accuracy of fire.

Roger Mortimer (1958)

It is over thirty years since Roger Mortimer wrote this appraisal. In the intervening years, much change and progress has taken place but the Jockey Club still rules racing and still sits very firmly in the saddle. The base has broadened considerably and leading figures in business and industry are no longer absent from membership; whether it is possible for many of them to devote the best years of their life to much Jockey Club business is, however, sometimes questioned.

The reference to the absence of racing during a spell of hard weather no longer applies, following the introduction of all-

*weather surfaces at Lingfield and Southwell in 1989; the benefits
to the sport have yet to be calculated.*

———

Caroline, Duchess of Montrose (1818–94)

Of the society hostesses who entertained at Newmarket during the
1880s, none made a greater impact than Caroline, Duchess of
Montrose. Defying the convention that restricted the ownership of
horses to men, she kept several in training, running them in the
assumed name of 'Mr Manton', her trainer being old Alec Taylor
at Manton.

Gifted with a vivid turn of phrase, and at times a very acid one,
she could be the terror of her jockeys, trainers and social circle
alike. About the only man who would not put up with her nonsense
was Alec Taylor. When she asked him what he regarded as the
danger to her runner, the gruff old man thought nothing of reply-
ing, 'Damned to hell if I know, your Grace.' The Duchess could
be an incredibly tiresome woman, but essentially she was good-
natured and there were not many people who disliked her. Behind
her ample back she was known as Carrie Red because of the colour
of her hair.

Born the Hon. Caroline Agnes Beresford, daughter of the second
Lord Decies, she married the fourth Duke of Montrose in 1836.
The Duke died in 1874 and two years later she remarried, her
second husband being William Stuart Stirling Crawfurd. He was
already a well-known owner. Three years after their marriage he
won the Derby with Sefton, who was trained at Manton.

Subsequently Stirling Crawfurd and his wife (who continued to
style herself Duchess, as widowed peeresses are entitled to do
irrespective of remarriage) had horses with Joe Dawson at Bedford
Lodge. Shortly after 'Buck' Sherrard had taken over the yard on
the death of Joe Dawson, they turned it into a private stable, the
other owners taking their horses elsewhere.

In 1881 Stirling Crawfurd won the One Thousand Guineas and
the Oaks with Thebaïs, who remained in training with Sherrard
as a four-year-old in 1882. That year Stirling Crawfurd landed the

Cesarewitch with Corrie Roy, and Thebaïs became a raging hot favourite to complete the double for him by taking the Cambridge-shire a fortnight later. To the consternation of a large section of the betting public, however, the Duchess insisted on Thebaïs being scratched the day before the race. As a result Martini was booed loudly when, on the day after the Cambridgeshire, he carried the all-scarlet Crawfurd colours successfully. After the ugly scene that ensued round the unsaddling enclosure, the Duchess herself was booed by disgruntled punters as she left the course.

Contrary to what was thought by those who spoke through their pockets, the Duchess had not scratched Thebaïs to spite the public. The Rowley Mile does not often ride soft but after all the rain that had fallen that autumn it was actually beginning to become hold-ing. In the circumstances, the heavily weighted Thebaïs would have stood no chance.

After Corrie Roy had won the Cesarewitch, one of the sporting papers came out with the following piece of doggerel about Stirling Crawfurd, who was generally known as 'Craw', and his spouse:

> Isn't Craw a lucky boy?
> With Carrie Red and Corrie Roy
> With Corrie Roy and Carrie Red,
> One for the course and one for his bed.

At the end of 1882 or early in 1883 the Duchess removed her horses and those of her husband from Bedford Lodge and took them across the Bury Road to Sefton Lodge. This establishment was built by a Frenchman called Lefèvre, in all probability the same C. J. Lefèvre who set up a record by winning 100 races with his horses in 1873. It was the Duchess who named the stable after her second husband's 1878 Derby winner, Sefton.

Hardly were the horses installed in Sefton Lodge than Stirling Crawfurd died in Cannes at the age of sixty-four in the spring of 1883. His death came as a severe blow to the Duchess, who was devoted to him. She had his body returned to Newmarket and it was eventually buried behind the church that she built as a mem-orial to him next door to Sefton Lodge. This church she dedicated to her own name-saint, St Agnes.

As a builder of the church the Duchess was its patron, with the right of nominating the rector, a matter of which she was not unmindful. Attending service in it one Sunday in late summer, she was horrified to hear the Revd Colville Wallis pray for fine weather in which the farmers could gather the harvest. Storming out there and then she afterwards informed the clergyman that he had better start looking for another living as he should have known that her St Leger candidate could only go on soft. The Revd Colville Wallis knew her ways. As he expected, the Duchess was soon back in a better humour and he stayed at St Agnes for many years.

After the death of Stirling Crawfurd, the Duchess took over his long string of horses, keeping it in training along with her own at Sefton Lodge, Gray, Golding and Day being her trainers at various periods. Another man with whom she had horses was the Lambourn trainer, Peace, whom she was accustomed to refer to as 'the Peace that passeth all understanding.'

A formidable figure generally dressed in a rather masculine manner with her outfit crowned by a Homburg hat, the Duchess had a deep knowledge and understanding of racing. All the same, she could exasperate her jockeys. She once remonstrated with Harry Huxtable, who rode her lightweights, saying, 'Why on earth did you not come when I told you to?'

'Beg your pardon, your Grace,' replied the little man, 'but I should have had to come without the horse.'

The royal trainer Dick Marsh was more than a match for the Duchess when it came to bandying words. One day when she asked him what he expected to win he mentioned a couple of horses, whose form suggested they would be hard to beat. 'Pooh,' she said, 'those are just newspaper tips,' and off she stalked. Both horses won, and next morning she went up to him, saying. 'Oh, Marsh, what will win today?'

'I regret, your Grace,' replied the suave Marsh, 'I have not yet read the newspapers today.'

The real bane of the Duchess's life was the handicappers. She hated them, being absolutely convinced that they went out of their way to give her horses far more weight than they deserved. Reginald Mainwaring, a tall saturnine man who could not help a slight resemblance to a stage villain, she used to call 'the man who murdered his mother'. To another handicapper, Major Egerton, she was heard to say, 'I see from the way you handicap my horses that you are desirous of riding them yourself. I only intend to say that on no account will your wish be gratified.'

In 1888, five years after she had been widowed for the second time, the unpredictable Duchess amazed everybody by marrying a young man of twenty-four called Henry Milner. For a time the horses ran in his name, but the marriage does not seem to have been a complete success, and soon they raced as the property of 'Mr Manton' again and carried the all-scarlet that she had taken over from her second husband. Rather more recently, the celebrated scarlet jacket has been carried by that fine chaser Cool Customer, who won the Great Yorkshire 'chase under the crushing weight of 12 st. 7 lb. in 1948. Trained by Captain Jack Fawcus at Middleham, Cool Customer was owned by Major R. Stirling Stuart, a nephew of Stirling Crawfurd.

The Duchess of Montrose died in 1894. On her death the stock at her Sefton Stud was put under the hammer and the land sold to become the site of Stanley House.

Richard Onslow (1983)

Caroline, Duchess of Montrose (1818–94)
The formidable Duchess was one of racing history's outstanding characters. As described by George Lambton in his memoirs, she appears to have had much in common with other members of her sex:

She was blessed with a soft and charming voice and when things were going right was the best company in the world; but she was hot-tempered and changeable and was easily put out if she did not get her own way. With all her peculiarities, the Duchess was a great lady and a good sportswoman. She loved her horses and was a good judge of racing and a great figure on the Turf.

Fred Archer

The first time I ever saw Archer (I did not know him till the following year) was on my first visit to Newmarket in 1879. Of course I had read in the papers of his marvellous feats, and I was naturally anxious to see the great jockey. At St Pancras Station I saw the Duke of Hamilton talking to a quiet, pale-looking young man, dressed in a dark suit with a black tie and a big pearl in it. I asked who it was. 'Why, that is Archer,' was the answer, much to my surprise, for he was quite unlike what I had pictured him to be.

About 5 ft 10 ins. in height, with a wonderfully slim and graceful figure, and remarkably small hands and feet, there was even at that time the shadow of melancholy in his face which indicated a side to his nature never far absent even in his brightest days, and which was partly responsible for his tragic death. No one seeing him for the first time would have put him down as a jockey, or suspected that such tremendous energy lurked in that frail body. It was that untiring energy which was the secret of his great success, leaving no stone unturned to achieve the one object of his life, the winning of races.

From the beginning of the racing season to the end, health, leisure and pleasure were sacrificed; walking nearer 11 st. than 10 st. in the winter he was always ready for Lincoln and Liverpool, riding 8 st. 10 lb. He had a Turkish bath in his own house, and he used some medicine which went by the name of Archer's Mixture, prepared by a clever doctor at Newmarket, called Wright. I tried it myself when I was riding races, and from my own experience I should say it was made of dynamite.

Archer ate practically nothing all day, but usually had a good dinner, which sometimes would send him up in weight 3 lb. to 4 lb., but the next morning with the Turkish bath and his mixture that would go. How his constitution stood such treatment for ten years was astonishing, but I have no doubt when he was taken ill with typhoid fever in 1886 his health must have been seriously undermined.

Taking him all round, Fred Archer was the greatest of all jockeys. Apprenticed to Mathew Dawson when he was eleven years old, it was not long before his master discovered that in this long-legged boy he had something out of the common. He was only seventeen when he won the Two Thousand Guineas for Lord Falmouth on Atlantic. From that time to the end of his life, at the age of twenty-nine, he was at the head of the winning jockeys. The number of races he won was astounding. In 1876, 209; 1877, 218; 1878, 229; 1879, 197; 1880, 120; 1881, 220; 1882, 210; 1883, 232; 1884, 241; 1885, 246; 1886 (the year of his death), 170. They included five victories in the Derby, four in the Oaks and six in the St Leger.

He had many great qualities. To begin with, marvellous hands and seat. I think it was Joe Cannon who once said, 'When you give Archer a leg-up he drops into the saddle, and in a moment he and the horse are as one; no pulling-up or lengthening of stirrups, but away they go, complete confidence between man and horse.' I have noticed the same thing myself about Stephen Donoghue.

Archer had a wonderful intuition regarding the character of any horse once he had been on his back, and knew how to get the most out of him. He had undaunted nerve and supreme confidence in himself without any atom of conceit. When he was beaten by a neck for a race, he generally thought that if he had just done this or not done that he would have won, and that is how a good jockey can make himself into a great one. Nothing escaped his notice during a race. Not only could he tell you all about his own horse, which is more than most jockeys are capable of, but he knew what the others had been doing. He had a great appreciation of other good riders, and he studied their methods. George Fordham he was always afraid of, saying, 'In one race George comes up and taps me in the last stride on the post. I am determined not to have this happen again, and then in the next race he just gets home and I beat him a stride past the post; with his clucking and fiddling you never know what the old chap is up to.'

Jim Snowden, when in form, he said, was a terribly hard man

to beat. 'You might have him, as you thought, well settled twice in a race, and then he would come at you again; you never knew when he was done with.' Tom Cannon he thought the most beautiful and finished of jockeys, Fred Webb the strongest. Charles Wood, he said, was a wonderful judge of pace and always in a good position in a race.

The Hon. George Lambton (1924)

It would be difficult to improve on George Lambton's word-picture of Fred Archer. Nobody knew him better or was more able to judge his immense talent. He became a legend in his lifetime and legend surrounds his memory. A strange story, linked with Archer, was told to John Hislop many years ago by Teddy Underdown, a well-remembered amateur rider. He relates it in Far from a Gentleman:

Teddy was bicycling home one evening, having been out to dinner near Exning. It was late and there was a full moon, the night clear, bright and silent, without a living thing in sight. As he approached the junction of the Exning and Snailwell Roads, he heard the sharp, metallic clip-clop of a horse trotting down the road at a fastish pace. At the corner he got off his bicycle, looked back the way he had come and then down the Snailwell Road, but there was no sign of a horse and the sound suddenly ceased. Completely puzzled, he rode home. When he told Tiny White* the story the next morning, expecting to be accused of having drunk too much, the latter said: "Oh, that would be Fred; he goes for a ride occasionally.'

* Tiny White, with whom Teddy Underdown lodged in Rous Road, Newmarket, was a retired jockey, who rode The Sailor Prince, beating Fred Archer on St Mirin in the Cambridgeshire, which was the final turn of the screw to Archer's suicide.

———

The Fifth Earl of Lonsdale

In addition to his sonorous titles, Hugh Lonsdale inherited a kingdom in Cumberland and Westmorland. Lowther Castle was one of the largest houses in the country. There was an agricultural estate upwards of 50,000 acres and another 50,000 of common land, over which he owned the sporting and mineral rights. There were the lakes of Windermere and Grasmere and the ruggedly beautiful Haweswater. In West Cumberland he owned the whole town of Whitehaven, the rich coalfields which stretched far out under the Irish Sea, and another family seat, Whitehaven Castle. In London two of the great mansions in Carlton House Terrace, knocked into one, provided him with a town house. There was another house at Newmarket and two steam yachts lying at anchor at Cowes. There were rich lands in the heart of the hunting country in Rutland and the magnificent hunting box and stables of Barley-thorpe.

Above all, from his own coalfields, iron mines and agricultural lands there flowed a prodigious tax-free income of almost £4,000 a *week*.

Hugh set about enjoying his good fortune with unsurpassed vigour. Trumpeting like a thirsty bull elephant who suddenly scents water, he cut a swathe through Society – which never quite forgave him for it. His boyhood had made him shy and uneasy with his social equals. His father's grooms, the tenant farmers and their workers he knew and understood. He covered up his shyness in Society with a flamboyance which, even in the ostentatious age of the Edwardians, people found hard to accept. At the same time his passionate devotion to sport, his sure instinct for fair play and his showman's love of the spectacular earned him the adulation of the crowds and a reputation as 'England's Greatest Sportsman' which spread far outside these islands.

His yellow carriages, his colourful entourage and his feudal style of living made him one of the best-known figures of his time. His big cigars, immaculate clothes and ever-fresh gardenia were the delight of cartoonists. His public appearances at sporting events were acclaimed with as much delight as if he had been royalty. As he drove down the course at Ascot behind the King, his yellow carriages and liveried postilions making the royal carriages almost drab by comparison, the cheers for 'Lordy' were at least as loud and prolonged as they were for the monarch.

He never grew out of the indiscretions of his early youth, but his involvement with beautiful women and unpopular causes added to rather than detracted from his popularity with the public. He never subscribed to the prudery of an age whose motto might have been 'It does not matter how you behave so long as you are not found out'. Instead he nailed his colours to the mast and kept them flying defiantly. In his own often-used phrase, life for him was 'lovely fun'.

But behind the glittering façade there was sadness. Even before he had inherited, the doctors decreed that his wife Grace could never have a child. Although, through his younger brother Lancelot, the line of succession was secure, Hugh would never admit to it. When taxed by his trustees about some new extravagance, he would hunch his shoulders and reply, 'What does it matter. I am the last of the Lowthers.' It was the same spirit as Lord Cardigan had shown as he prepared to gallop at the head of his Light Brigade into the teeth of the Russian batteries at Balaclava. 'Here goes the last of the Brudenells.' Perhaps in Hugh Lonsdale it reflected the same mood of do or die. As the safe world into which he had been born started to crumble about his ears and the noose fashioned by his own extravagance drew tighter and tighter, he did not let his public image suffer by one farthingsworth.

Before he inherited, in a desperate search for money, he had sold his reversion. It had been bought by the estate so that the settled land at Whitehaven and Lowther was managed by trustees who, in consequence, also controlled the purse-strings. For the whole of the sixty-two years he was the Earl, Hugh fought tooth and nail to extract every penny he could from the trustees in order to keep up his fantastic scale of living.

His lavish entertainment of the Kaiser and other European royalty, his vast stables of horses, his private orchestra, and even the money he poured into equipping the private battalions he raised to fight in the Boer War and the First World War was only paid for after bitter battles with the trustees, whom he came to regard as the Great Enemy.

By the time he died the outer defences had been breached. Step by step he had retreated as the lights of his personal empire were snuffed out one by one. Whitehaven Castle was sold, then Barleythorpe. Finally Carlton House Terrace and Lowther had to be closed. Like an old dog fox headed at every turn he went to earth at Stud House in Rutland, near the scenes of his carefree boyhood.

He had outlived all his contemporaries but to the end he preserved his own world of fantasy.

Never quite accepted by a Victorian Society, he became, with the public, a legend in his own lifetime. It was their cheers that he sought more than any other thing. Lord Ancaster once described him as 'almost an emperor and not quite a gentleman'; perhaps it was an epitaph to which he would not finally have objected.

Douglas Sutherland (1965)

Hugh Cecil Lowther, Fifth Earl of Lonsdale (1857–1944) When the second Earl died in 1872, in the arms of a well-known opera singer, he was succeeded by his nephew, Hugh Lowther's father. Within ten years both the third Earl and his eldest son had passed on and Hugh, in serious financial difficulties, inherited overnight a huge estate and a vast fortune. For the next fifty years no major race meeting or sporting event was without 'the Yellow Earl', elegantly and rather eccentrically attired, and conveyed in a convoy of yellow Daimlers.

Lord Lonsdale was a Steward of the Jockey Club in 1924 and Senior Steward in 1926. He did not race on a large scale and relied upon the National Stud to lease him a few horses every year. These included Royal Lancer (St Leger 1920), and the brilliant filly Myrobella, winner of eleven races and dam of Big Game.

——

The Hon. George Lambton

The 'Honourable George', although considered a confirmed bachelor, was thought to be one of the most handsome men in Newmarket and was never short of aristocratic female admirers, who included Edith, one of the four renowned Cadogan girls.* How-

* Edith married Lord Hillingdon; Sybil ('Portia') married Edward Stanley; Cynthia married Sir Humphrey de Trafford; Mary married the Duke of Marlborough. Their mother, Mildred, married Hedworth Lambton as her second husband. In 1911 Hedworth was persuaded by Lady Meux to change his surname to Meux by royal licence, his inheritance of her fortune being conditional upon this. Nothing would have induced George Lambton to do such a thing.

ever, he never succumbed to their plans to ensnare him into matrimony. His haughty good looks and charm of demeanour, together with his evident ability as a trainer and his prowess in the hunting field, set many hearts aflutter, yet he continued to retain his freedom. In the summer months he played tennis every Sunday. During the winter he spent every available moment hunting – usually with the Grafton or the Pytchley. He shared a hunting box near Market Harborough with Count Charles Kinsky, and when they rode to hounds it was claimed that 'Kinsky was brave to the point of recklessness and that Lambton had the Olympian calm and quiet judgement which showed the perfectly finished rider'.

During Ebor week 1908, when George Lambton was staying with Frederick Green at The Treasurer's House at York, he met Cicely Horner, who was also a house guest for the races. Cicely, whose younger sister had married the brilliant scholar Raymond Asquith, son of the Prime Minister, the previous August, made such an impression upon him that he decided to relinquish his bachelor status. He and Cicely became engaged in the autumn and were married on 7 December 1908. In the weeks before the wedding George's eldest brother, Jack, agreed to settle all his outstanding debts. At the meeting between the brothers to finalize the list of impatient creditors, the majority of whom were London tradesmen, Jack asked if the list was totally complete. 'Oh,' said George, 'I believe I also owe a few trifles to some locals in Newmarket.' These locals were requested to forward their bills for settlement to the Earl of Durham, who was disagreeably surprised to learn that his brother had run up a bill of £3,000 over the years with one grocer who had given him limitless credit in the sublime belief that the account would be settled eventually!

The Horner family, whose ancestral home at Mells had been described as a 'small gabled Somerset Manor House, a stone's throw from one of the finest churches of England', had been immortalized by the nursery rhyme 'Little Jack Horner', which was a political satire upon Sir John Horner, one of King Henry VIII's Commissioners for the Dissolution of the Monasteries, and a Steward of the Temporalities of the Abbey of Glastonbury. The 'pie'* in the nursery rhyme into which Sir John Horner 'put his thumb' was a reference to the Church lands which he took charge of and administered on behalf of the Crown. His prize 'plum' was the title deeds to the manor and estate of Mells. He was also mentioned in another mid-sixteenth-century Somerset jingle: 'Wyndham, Horner, Popham and Thynne; when the Abbot went out, they came in'.

Society approved of the Lambton-Horner match, although expressing surprise that 'Art' should be associated with 'the Sport of Kings', and described George Lambton's decision to become a professional racehorse trainer as bizarre. Nevertheless the fact that the bridegroom was the brother of the Earl of Durham, the Duchess of Leeds, the Countess of Pembroke, Lady Robert Cecil and Lady Anne Lambton, who acted as chatelaine for her eldest brother, endeared him to Society. At the same time the knowledge that he lived at Newmarket and earned his livelihood on the Turf was considered *infra dig.* by some social-gossip columnists who were at pains to point out that he was a 'gentleman trainer' often seen strolling across The Severals with his Pekinese at his heels, and who would go around his stables in the morning dressed in an impeccably cut suit from Savile Row, a flower in his buttonhole and wearing brown and white buckskin shoes.

George Lambton had never been perturbed by the comments of those members of Society who thought it extraordinary that a man of rank and title should demean himself by undertaking a professional career for which the original description had been 'training groom' and whose members had attended race meetings wearing the livery of their employers, as did footmen and coachmen. Nor did he give more than passing thought to the realization that he was largely responsible for changing the status of his chosen profession by proving that education, culture, and membership of exclusive London clubs did not preclude a man from fully

* Little Jack Horner sat in the corner
Eating a Christmas pie.
He put in his thumb
And pulled out a plum
And said, 'What a good boy am I!'

understanding how to manage thoroughbreds and train them to win races. Admittedly he was referred to as *Mister* Lambton in the training reports, whilst other trainers were assumed to be devoid of a prefix to their surnames, but this reference was thought to be justified due to his elegant figure, quizzical smile, his charm and his dandyism, allied to the fact that his brother was a peer of the realm.

Soon after their wedding and return from honeymoon the Lambtons moved into Stanley House. However Cicely did not relish living so close to 'George's work' and consequently Lord Derby loaned them Mesnil Warren, a large house on the opposite side of the Bury Road, which he had bought from Sir William Cochrane. Their life settled down to a routine which included the butler bringing George Lambton rainwater every morning at 6.45 a.m. The rainwater would be placed in a small copper pot by the side of his bed, and heated by means of a paraffin stove. Once shaved, George Lambton would go to Stanley House to supervise the horses.

Michael Seth-Smith (1983)

The Hon. George Lambton (1860–1945)

George Lambton's contribution to the literature of racing has already been referred to; his views on the training of racehorses are included elsewhere in this volume.

Newmarket still contains some of the Honourable George's old employees, who remember him with the deepest affection as a kind and thoughtful employer and an attractive and glamorous figure, even into old age.

The Sixth Earl of Rosebery

Lord Rosebery, who died on 21 May at the age of ninety-two, will be known chiefly as the outstanding figure on the English Turf for well over half a century. This should not be allowed to obscure the prominent part he played in other walks of life and thus give insufficient tribute to his remarkably versatile talents.

The sixth Earl, Lord Rosebery, was born on 8 January 1882, at
Dalmeny House, South Queensferry, Edinburgh, being the elder
son of the fifth Earl, famous not only as Prime Minister but also
as the owner of the Derby winners Ladas, Cicero and Sir Visto.
His mother was Hannah Rothschild, daughter of Baron Meyer de
Rothschild. Thus he inherited both prosperity and possessions,
including some fine pictures, furniture and art treasures. Despite
these material advantages, distinguished parentage, and his many
talents, Albert Edward Harry Meyer Archibald Primrose – 'names
enough in all conscience', his father observed – Harry, one of
whose godparents was the Prince of Wales (later King Edward
VII), had no easy path in life. One of more brittle fibre might well
have been crushed by the adversity which at various times overcame him.

To start with, his father was a hard, cold, cynical man, whose
fine scholarship tended to sharpen the edge of his caustic wit,
rather than warm his heart with affection and tolerance, except in
the case of his second son, Neil Primrose. While Harry in appearance inherited the somewhat heavy features of his mother, Neil
took after his father in looks and flair, becoming very much the
favourite son. Neil's death from a stray bullet in 1917, when he
entered the army after a bright, short political career, which seemed
to hold great promise, shattered his father. His sorrow at the loss
of his favourite son was such that, when walking with Harry and
a friend not long afterwards he turned to Harry and said, 'If only
it were you.'

As a boy and young man, before this shadow of his father's loss
fell across his path, Harry had proved himself in his own right.
He had a quick, clear brain, a strong, decisive character and a
natural bent for any sport to which he turned his hand. At Eton
he distinguished himself as a games-player, whether on the cricket
ground, in the football field or the racquets court; and later he
captained Surrey at cricket, in which capacity he awarded that
great batsman, Sir Jack Hobbs, his county cap. Leaving school, he
excelled as a polo-player, golfer and in the hunting field, becoming
Master of the Whaddon Chase, and acquired the reputation of

being the best heavyweight to hounds in the country; he was also
a fine shot.

After leaving Eton, he went to Sandhurst, from whence he joined
the Grenadier Guards. At that time he would have liked to have
made a career in the Army, but under pressure from his father
he resigned his commission and stood as Liberal candidate for
Midlothian, representing this constituency from 1906 to 1910.
Politics, with its intrigues and subterfuges, did not appeal to him
though his experiences in this sphere proved of great value when,
as an administrator of racing, he had to deal with governments
and ministries; and it was no sorrow to him when the outbreak
of the 1914–18 war enabled him to return to the Grenadier
Guards. Badly wounded, he won the DSO, the MC and the Legion
of Honour and was four times mentioned in dispatches. Later he
was appointed Assistant Military Secretary to General Allenby,
becoming this difficult commander's most trusted staff officer. The
fact that he went on Allenby's staff, instead of returning to duty
with the Grenadier Guards, and rose quickly to such eminence,
caused some ill feeling and jealousy in military circles of that age
of strict and hidebound principles, a prejudice which it required
considerable strength of character to overcome.

The death of Neil Primrose brought on a stroke in his father,
and though he lived until 1929, Harry had to manage his affairs
during this last phase of his father's life. The rift between father
and son, dating, it was said, from a racing indiscretion by Harry
in his youth and deepened by the warping of his father's mind as
a result of Neil's death, gradually healed and during the later stages
of his father's life he depended on Harry very much. In particular,
Harry helped to direct his racing interests and his stud farm, being
instrumental in persuading his father to send his horses to be
trained by Jack – later Sir Jack – Jarvis. This association was
continued by Harry after his father's death and became one of the
happiest and most successful in Turf history. In character and
outlook, Harry and Jarvis had much in common, understanding
each other perfectly. After Jack Jarvis died, the Rosebery horses
were trained by Doug Smith, Bill Watts and Bruce Hobbs.

Before considering Harry's great contribution to racing and his

Turf successes, it is necessary to dwell briefly upon the other aspects of his life. He was Regional Commissioner for Scotland and Secretary of State during the 1939–45 war and previously a Liberal MP, and leader of the National Liberals. He was chairman of the Fine Arts Commission for Scotland, President of Surrey Cricket Club from 1947 to 1949 and of the MCC from 1953 to 1954, member of the Royal Commission on Justices of the Peace and presided over the committee of inquiry into the export and slaughter of horses. He was also Justice of the Peace and Lord Lieutenant for Midlothian and, in 1955, was Chairman of the Scottish Tourist Board.

On the Turf, Harry Rosebery was outstanding as an owner, breeder and administrator. He succeeded Lord d'Abernon as President of the Thoroughbred Breeders' Association and in this capacity, aided by his intellect, strength of character and political experience, he succeeded in enabling racing and breeding to be carried on throughout the 1939–45 war. As a member and senior steward of the Jockey Club, Harry did good service. For this he was well equipped, both from his practical knowledge of racing and his experience in public life.

Though coming from an immensely wealthy family, Harry in his early youth was kept on a comparatively meagre allowance by his father, which he had to supplement by judicious betting and gambling. He once told me how, when sent to learn the language in France and down to his last few francs, he started with a successful run at the local casino, took his winnings over to England and played them up successfully at Goodwood and Alexandra Park, finishing up by emerging on top in a somewhat hazardous session at the card table at Tranby Croft during Doncaster Leger week. In his cricketing days, play would sometimes be interrupted by a telegraph boy running on to the field to hand him a telegram, whereupon the crowd would call out: 'Has it won?' Thus Harry got to know racing from every aspect and to develop a sympathy for and understanding of all concerned in it.

Despite his abrupt, downright manner, he had about him a great affection for the racing profession. He was never afraid to dispense stern justice, but his justice was always tempered with mercy. His outlook on racing was influenced by his understanding of men and of horses; from personal experience he knew that neither were infallible and that allowances must be made accordingly. That he was unpopular with more than a few of his own generation was probably due to jealousy at his success in whatever he touched, his disregard for cant, rank and pomposity, and to a certain natural arrogance.

In many ways, Harry was a contradiction to his generation. In ability and background he conformed, but in behaviour and outlook he was a rebel. Racecourse characters of the most bizarre types interested him and, in an age when it was unfashionable to be educated – the scholarship of his father was scorned by the young bloods of the Edwardian era – he was well read.

Having managed the racing affairs of his father during the last years of the fifth Earl's life, the latter's death did not disrupt the running of the Mentmore Stud or the racing stable. Thus the violent descent in status which studs can experience when their owners die did not occur, because continuity of direction was maintained. While his father had won the Derby with Ladas, Sir Visto and Cicero, as well as the One Thousand with Plack and the Two Thousand with Ellangowan, Harry in an era of far more severe competition won the Derby with Blue Peter and Ocean Swell, the former also winning the Two Thousand and the latter the Ascot Gold Cup; the Oaks with Sleeping Partner and the St Leger with Sandwich. All bar Sandwich, bought as a yearling, were bred by him. He may have been unlucky not to have won another Derby with Miracle, third to April the Fifth and Dastur. His other successes on the Turf are too numerous to list and include virtually all the chief races in the calendar. Though little concerned with National Hunt racing, Harry won the National Hunt 'chase at Cheltenham with Crown Prince ridden by his stepson, now Lord Belper.

As a breeder, Lord Rosebery worked on traditional lines. His aim was to produce classic winners and stayers of the highest calibre, as opposed to fast two-year-olds. He did not disregard speed, but viewed it as a means to an end, rather than as an aim in itself. He was not afraid to use unfashionable sires – one of his best racemares, Afterthought, was by the unconsidered Obliterate – and he laid great stress on the tail female line, one of his most masterly strokes in recent times being to reintroduce to his Mentmore Stud the line of Prue, through Bashful, whom he bought and whose close descendants include many good winners, including Gwen, who finished second in the One Thousand.

Though a traditionalist as regards bloodlines and principles of mating, Harry was always open to considering new approaches – he was the first to draw my attention to the value of liquid seaweed on pastures – and was never tired of discussing all aspects of breeding, being a patient and sympathetic listener, always showing especial kindness and tolerance to youth.

He had a natural way with animals, being particularly fond of his parrot, Inky, and was very loyal to his horses, so much so that he would seldom accept criticism of them. Understandably, he thought the world of his brilliant Two Thousand Guineas and Derby winner Blue Peter, who also won the Eclipse Stakes and was unbeaten as a three-year-old. Though Blue Peter proved a little disappointing at stud, he never lost first place in his owner's affections; and when a friend wrote asking if he could change his nomination to Blue Peter for one to Ocean Swell, whose first foals were deceptively promising, he received the reply: 'Dear—, I note you no longer require a nomination to Blue Peter.'

It was a great sadness to Harry when his son by his first marriage, Lord Dalmeny, a gifted and attractive young man who shared his father's interests, died when an undergraduate at Oxford. But Harry was born to face misfortune with courage and to make the most of life, whatever it might bring. In this respect his character was of more sterling quality than that of his father; and he found much happiness in his second marriage, to the Hon. Eva Bruce. In his later years, when I knew him best, I found Harry Rosebery a delightful and generous host, a fountain of knowledge and a most amusing and entertaining raconteur. He loved to talk on all sub-jects, but in the company of racing men he was perhaps happiest and at his wittiest, recounting the 'bad old days' of the Turf, its stars – among jockeys he rated Danny Maher and Sir Gordon Richards highest – and its eccentrics, such as Parson Parkes, the unfrocked priest who trained racehorses; but he always looked forward and never allowed nostalgia for the past to cloud his outlook.

Where he was, there was laughter, never gloom. To the last his mind was clear and sharp, his enthusiasm as keen as ever, but failing sight and lack of mobility had begun to impair his enjoyment of racing. That he should leave the scene so dear to him for so long, quickly and painlessly, was justly fitting to one who had contributed so much to its welfare. With him passes a great man and the end of an era. He is survived by his widow, by a daughter from his first marriage (to Lady Dorothy Grosvenor), Lady Helen Vivian-Smith, and his heir, Neil, from his second marriage.

                                                      John Hislop (1974)

Albert Edward Harry Meyer Archibald Primrose, Sixth Earl of Rosebery, KT, PC, DSO, MC (1882–1974)
Many years ago, a handicapper, newly joined and green as grass, was routed to the early part of the Scottish autumn circuit. He had been told in advance that his job wouldn't be worth very much if Lord Rosebery and Jack Jarvis didn't win at least three races in the first two days at Edinburgh; and he believed it. After all three of their runners had been well beaten in handicaps on the first day, the handicapper went to bed a worried man and, at this range of time, it would be hard to describe the acute nausea and shock that struck his heart, on his arrival on the racecourse the following day, to be told by Bill McHarg that Lord Rosebery wished to see him in his private room immediately.

Quivering with fear and foreboding, he reported to that then very formidable figure, who inquired of him gently what he would like to drink before lunch. Four races passed before that young official left the table after listening enraptured to stories of Edwardian life and racing in most of its aspects; the association continued for the rest of the week and on many occasions thereafter.

The handicapper, now vastly older and marginally less green, had had his leg properly pulled but came out on the right side; he never enjoyed a luncheon more and the remarkable range of wit and wisdom that accompanied it.

Mrs Vernet

Helen Monica Mabel Cunningham was born in 1877. She always maintained that one of the things she learnt at her mother's knee was that no woman should acknowledge the existence of a birthday once she had reached the age of fifty; she endeavoured to stick to this rule for the last thirty years of her life, during which few people had any idea of exactly how old she was.

Soon after her thirteenth birthday her father died, leaving her £8,000 – quite a princely sum in those days.

At sixteen she went on the stage, playing small parts under the managements of Tree, Alexander and Wyndham: this career lasted only for a year, terminating when she married her first husband, Spencer Thornton, a stockbroker. She later married Robert Vernet.

After a severe illness, which affected her lungs, she was advised by her doctor to spend as much time as possible in the open air. She always enjoyed gambling, and had already lost a considerable part of the money left to her by her father, so she now took to going several days a week to race meetings, where it did not take her long to part with most of the rest of it.

Having discovered, the hard way, that there are a few punters who make money, and a great many bookmakers who do, she adopted the principle of 'If you can't beat 'em – join 'em'.

At that time, although some women were heavy gamblers on the course, a great many of them liked to place small bets of five or ten shillings, often in cash, which bookmakers on Tattersalls' rails were reluctant to take. Mrs Vernet decided that here was a need for which she could provide a remedy, with likely profit to herself, so in 1918 she let it be known, amongst her friends, that she would accept small bets to be handed to her on scraps of paper, sometimes accompanied by cash, sometimes for credit. This was an illegal procedure which, as her clientele increased, came in for the attention of some of the professional bookmakers, who lodged objections to this poacher of their preserves, with the result that Helen Vernet suffered the indignity – at Ascot, of all places –

of being waylaid by ring officials and told, in effect, 'You can't do that there 'ere!'

Arthur Bendir, who had joined the bookmaking firm of Ladbrokes in 1902, and was by that time one of its principals, had noted Mrs Vernet's success with women punters. The idea occurred to him that a female representative of his firm on Tattersalls' rails might be a popular innovation, and here was one with the necessary experience and a ready-made clientele. He offered her the job, which she accepted, joining Jack Hampton, Jim Gantry and Lord ('Tommy') Graves, three colourful characters in the world of bookmaking.

The advent of an official woman racecourse bookmaker – especially one with weak lungs – caused a good deal of scepticism and ribald comment. Women had been ready enough to bet with her when she was circulating amongst them, but would they continue to do so now that they had to go to her?

It was not long before all such criticism was silenced: not only did the number of her women clients increase, but the men also flocked to bet with her, although women continued to outnumber men on her books. She maintained that many of them were more impulsive than methodical in their way of betting, often relying on superstition based on colours, numbers, coincidences or dreams, rather than common sense and the form book, when placing their bets.

Helen Vernet lived in London, in a succession of elegant houses, situated in such localities as Gray's Inn, Albany and Eaton Place, where she was able to indulge her taste for beautiful furnishings, set in beautifully decorated rooms. She was fond of dancing and always stipulated that her clerk should be good-looking and a good dancer. When she had to attend provincial race meetings staying for one or more nights, she selected an hotel with a first-class band and ballroom. There, after dinner, she spent the rest of the evening dancing with her clerk. For holidays she favoured the Riviera, where she could gamble in the casinos.

In May 1928 Mrs Vernet became a partner in Ladbrokes. Verbal speculation as to the amount paid to her in salary and commission was as varied as the size of wagers she struck, one notable one that year being at the Epsom Spring Meeting, when M. Pierre Wertheimer had a £500 bet with her on the French-trained Le Landy, which won the Banstead Selling Plate at 11–2. Mrs Vernet hedged the bet to such good purpose that the firm won £80 on the race. She carried the names and addresses of her many hundreds of clients in her head, and only once made an error of judgement in laying a big bet. This was at Ascot in 1946, when another Frenchman, Jean-Marc Gugenheim, approached her, saying that he had an account at Ladbrokes; she believed him and he placed bets which won him over £7,000 on the four days. When he took leave of her on the last day she congratulated him on his luck.

It was only when the accounts for the week were being worked out that Ladbrokes recognized M. Gugenheim as a disqualified person, who had been warned off the Turf in 1927, for failing to pay debts amounting to over £6,000 to four other English bookmakers. Following a court case, judgment with costs was given in favour of Ladbrokes.

Helen Vernet was small, slim, good-looking, charming and extremely chic, no easy task when you have to spend most of your afternoons leaning against unresilient iron railings, coping with the demands of individuals whose brains vary between the astute and the microscopic. She was extremely clever at pinching the odds with the latter variety, who were always made to feel that they had beaten the market, when in response to their inquiry as to the price of the favourite, she would say: 'Six to four,' and then, in lowered tones, 'Seven to four to *you*,' whilst other bookies, within earshot, were shouting: 'Two to one the field!'

She had an enormous following amongst punters who liked to place modest bets before the advent of the Totalisator. Her cards, handed in at important meetings, such as Ascot, were so numerous that Stock Exchange clerks used to be employed by Ladbrokes to work them out overnight. Often, when their starting-price or ante-post books showed considerable losses, Helen Vernet's cards got the firm out of trouble.

No sort of weather deterred her. One day at Epsom a vicious storm broke over the downs, with the rain descending as if flung out of buckets; everyone fled for cover except Mrs Vernet, who remained on her box by the rails, her huge umbrella covering her small form to such good purpose that it gave the impression of having nothing beneath it but a pair of very small feet.

She was equally heroic on hot summer days, with blazing sun turning Tattersalls into a gridiron; on such occasions she would send her runner, Alf Simmons, to the bar for a bowl of ice cubes which he slipped down the back of her neck. Towards the end of her life she became crippled with arthritis and also contracted Parkinson's disease, but she refused to give up working, even when she could no longer walk, and the faithful Alf had to push her to her pitch in a wheelchair. She died in March 1956, leaving estate valued at £7,573 6s. 8d.

Caroline Ramsden (1973)

Mrs Helen Vernet (1877–1956)

It is unlikely that all Mrs Vernet's clients were mugs but nearly all the mugs were her clients. She was totally disarming, intensely feminine and always beautifully dressed; it was a pleasure to bet with her and a privilege to be ripped off.

Unfortunately for the bookmaking profession and luckily for the mug punter, it is distinctly probable that Mrs Vernet was unique.

———

Fred Darling

I now started what was to be an uninterrupted period of sixteen years as Mr Fred Darling's first jockey at Beckhampton, and my story inevitably becomes very much the story of Beckhampton for the whole of that time. I was thrilled to be back on the downs which I loved and the great gallops which I knew so well. I was immensely looking forward to my association with the man whom I had always considered the greatest trainer in the world, and his wonderful horses. But it took just a little time to get accustomed to the new Guv'nor.

I think what I have to say about those happy years, and certain little tales which I propose to tell, will be more clear and have more spice if I first attempt to describe to you the character of Mr Fred Darling.

Not all that I have to say about him may appear charitable. Not all of his methods may appear to be very fair. But to understand his success, you must understand the man. I unhesitatingly describe him as a genius, confident that I am not misusing that too frequently used word. There has been no trainer like him, and there never will be another. And genius must be allowed its foibles.

Mr Fred Darling was absolutely ruthless. He was ruthless with horses and with men. If he thought a horse was not absolutely first-class, he had no use for that horse, and out it went. If he thought one of his men was not absolutely first-class, he had no use for him, and out he went. He had no friendships with his men, and he hated their becoming too friendly with each other. But strangely enough he inspired immense affection, even love, on the part of those he employed, as well as fear. His incredible ability and his immense craftsmanship were things which created a burning admiration. And, if you did your stuff, he looked after you. All his men knew that, although they knew also that one mistake might mean their instant dismissal.

He was extremely methodical and a wonderful organizer. His stable was run on a definite plan, which never altered. Unlike Foxhill, where the whole place was smartened up every weekend for Mr White's guests, there was no show at Beckhampton, but there were definite rules which could never be disobeyed. Every boy had to ride out wearing breeches, and with smartly polished leggings and boots. Everything else about them had to be smart and clean, and their hair properly brushed. Not for visitors: Mr Darling discouraged visitors, and he could discourage very well. Just for Mr Darling himself: that smartness was a part of normal Beckhampton. Every night there had to be a little sawdust down, and everything spick and span, before he came round. And the whole of the stables had to be right, including the boys' bedding in their rooms, which had to be neatly folded.

He himself was quite a small man, with rather a sharp nose and thin lips. He was always neat and tidy in his appearance, very dapper in his dress. He was very abrupt in his manner and in his speech, and he had a habit of jutting out his chin at you when he was telling you something important. When he did that, you never ventured to question what he said. And ninety-nine times out of a hundred, you would have been wrong if you had.

In the mornings, he would be at the stables before the horses came out, and everything would be reported to him by the head lad. He would be there to see the horses walk out, and he would be there to see them trot on. He knew then, in a flash, if anything was wrong with any of them. It was instinct, or second-sight, or anything you like to call it, and in all those years he was never wrong. He would say take that one out, take it back, and take its temperature. Whichever it was, it always had a temperature. If he had worked that horse, it would perhaps have been off for three weeks. As it was, it was probably back in work in three days, because he had seen the trouble in time.

I rode work for him every Wednesday and Saturday. We were always met to the minute with our hacks, and we rode out a short way up the hill, while he would tell me what he was going to do. Then we would walk back to what we used to call the Hollow, and we would swap and change and really educate all the horses. Then we walked back with them, and Mr Darling would go through the stables, and see that everything was all right before he went to get his breakfast. He did everything exactly the same with the second lot, and honestly I think that the horses could sense that their master was about when he was near them.

Naturally he had a wonderful staff. Templeton was the best head lad I have known, and a truly great one. Norman Bertie, who succeeded him, is now a most successful trainer, and trained Pinza to win the Derby. Wells and Sherry were two of his principal work riders, but there were others as good. The whole place was tremendously impressive.

One of the reasons why his staff liked him was because they knew that, no matter how good they were, Mr Darling could do everything just as well as they could, and so he was never asking anyone to do anything that he could not do himself.

There was only one Guv'nor at Beckhampton, and even the horses knew that. If he wanted to do something with a horse and the animal did not, Mr Darling made that horse do it. It did not matter one jot if the horse was a Derby winner or just something used to lead the others, he had to obey Mr Darling. It was wonderful how well that stern policy paid.

I shall never forget one morning, out on the gallops. A horse called Justification suddenly went savage. He got one of the boys down and went for him.

Mr Darling was out of his car in a flash, waving his whip. Everyone else was standing back, undecided and frankly frightened. I don't say that someone else would not have gone to the lad's help eventually, but it was a scaring spectacle and Mr Darling was thinking far quicker than anyone else. The Guv'nor belted Justification as hard as he could, and the horse got off the lad and bolted.

Some of us jumped into his car with Mr Darling. We chased the horse, and we cornered him in a field near the stable. Mr Darling never hesitated. He walked right up to that still savage horse, and hit him hard across the knees and brought him down. Then he got on to Justification's head, and gave the horse a tremendous beating. It was the only thing to do, although at that moment it seemed almost cruel; but that horse had savaged a lad, and he had to be taught. The Guv'nor got off him and led him into the stable, and Justification never put a foot wrong afterwards. It was a very brave thing to do, but Mr Darling was like that: he always knew what to do, and whatever the task he always did it at once without hesitation or any thought of possible consequence to himself.

His flair for planning was amazing. I always knew our runners and my rides three weeks ahead. He made up his programme for each horse, and that was that; bar accidents or sickness, the horse ran in its selected race with no thought of the opposition. Three weeks before the race, the horse started preparing for that race, and the Guv'nor was simply not interested in what else might be running from any other stable.

His plans for the two-year-olds were always cut and dried even before the season started. He would divide them into Ascot horses and then Goodwood horses, and then the rest, which he did not bother much about. He would usually bring out the Ascot horses at the early Salisbury meeting. If they did well enough, they would be prepared for Ascot, but as this preparation progressed, he would eliminate those which he did not think were good enough, until he was left with a final list of runners a full three weeks ahead. It simply did not matter what the owner said. If the owner did not like it . . . well, the owner could take the horse elsewhere.

It was the same for Goodwood, with the bigger and more backward two-year-olds. They also would probably be brought out at Salisbury, but at the later meeting. Then those which had not done well enough would be weeded out, until – three weeks ahead of the Goodwood meeting – he again had a final list. No owner ever objected to his plans. He was the Guv'nor to his owners as well as to all the rest of us, and just as much.

He hated his owners coming down to Beckhampton. It was all that he could do to suffer them if they came down at all often, although he admitted that it would not be fair to stop them altogether. If any of them stayed for more than one night, it annoyed him, and everyone knew it. There was one occasion when the late Duke of Portland came down for the night. His Grace had a small personal mannerism which no one else would probably have noticed, but Mr Darling spotted it at once. It got on his nerves straightaway, and he could not stand it. Mr Darling grumbled to me about it in the morning, and very shortly afterwards he arranged for the Duke to take his horses elsewhere.

And yet I dare to state that there was not one owner of importance who would not have sunk his self-importance and put up with everything if only he could have had his horses trained at Beckhampton by Mr Darling.

Sir Gordon Richards (1955)

Fred Darling (1884–1953)

Fred Darling is accepted as one of the greatest trainers of the century. He was a son of Sam Darling, trainer of the Derby winners Ard Patrick and Galtee More. Fred first trained in Germany, soon moving to England. He headed the list of winning trainers six times, first in 1926 and finally in 1947, preparing seven winners of the Derby. He died in 1953, shortly after the Derby victory of Pinza, whom he bred.

The ruthless perfectionism practised by Fred Darling is relic of another world, unimaginable today.

———

Cecil Boyd-Rochfort

Captain Boyd-Rochfort was without doubt one of the greatest trainers of his era and particularly excelled with three-year-old fillies because he had a special method of his own of training them. English Classic records and the fact that he won the Irish Oaks four times prove its value. Although Mr Persse was also a champion trainer and won Classic races he really specialized in two-year-old races, while the artistry of Jack Colling was often in the skill with which he placed his horses. A first-class example of the Captain's brilliance with fillies was the 1955 One Thousand Guineas, Oaks and St Leger triumph of Meld. Freemason Lodge was hit by a coughing epidemic before the Doncaster Classic. By dosing Meld with cod-liver oil and malt and also by disinfecting in the yard round her box, she was kept clear. However, the race came only just in time as she started to cough a few hours after her St Leger success and had a high temperature that night.

I remember that the Captain once had a horse called Longriggan running at Newmarket over the July course in 1937. He said to me, 'Give this horse a nice race but don't let Stephenson see.' Willie Stephenson was our work jockey. The plan was to land a quiet gamble at Goodwood in a few weeks' time. I over-egged the pudding because I carried out my instructions to the letter and kept *too* far behind. After church on Sundays I always saw the Captain about our runners for the following week. He said: 'Do you think Longriggan should run at Goodwood?' I replied, 'Oh yes, it will then be three weeks since he ran at Newmarket; he was on the wrong leg going down the Hill and flying at the finish.' Anyway we won the Foxhall Stakes over six furlongs for maiden two-year-olds, when I beat Doug Smith a neck with Steve Donoghue a neck away in third. I always loved to ride winners, especially 10–1 shots, but thought that I had better not appear too pleased about this one in the unsaddling enclosure. The Captain said: 'That was a surprise, Rufus!' 'Yes, Captain; he has improved,' I replied. Both of us kept completely straight faces.

I always took off my cap to Mr Persse at Chattis Hill when I arrived to ride work. As first jockey to the Captain I did not do this my first morning on duty and was reprimanded. The Captain said: 'Forget that you are Harry Beasley's youngest son and take your cap off when you meet me on the gallops.' I replied that I was sorry and would always do so in future. At Chattis Hill, my brother Harry and I always wore flannel trousers when we rode work because they are lighter than breeches and boots or jodhpurs and we had to fight against increasing weight. Mr Persse did not mind but the Captain objected strongly. I got another rocket. 'What next?' he asked. 'Will you appear in your pyjamas?' He ordered me to have breeches, boots and jodhpurs made. One day at a Midland meeting when the Captain was not there I won on the stable's runner. I telephoned him at about 7 p.m. to give him the good news and report that the horse had scored by a neck. I added that we would have been very unlucky to lose because the horse was hanging badly on the hard ground. After another scolding he said, 'It is the way that you sit on my horses', and banged the telephone down. Next day I told his nephew, Peter McCall, about this and he advised me 'never to ring the Captain after stables because some horse will "have a leg" or be coughing and he will be worried'. This was splendid advice and I never did so again. I now understand that evening stables worries are made a hundred times worse if the telephone rings constantly.

When Hypnotist was a strongly fancied runner in the Derby, the Captain retained Peter to share a double room with me at the Connaught Hotel, on the eve of the race, presumably to ensure that I got into no mischief! After an unsuccessful Derby I said to Peter on the Thursday, 'Now be human; we have no fancied filly in the Oaks, so loose me off!' He agreed and we both went our separate ways. On Friday morning Peter told me that he and his brother, David, had gone on to a night-club after dinner. As they entered they saw the Captain with his arms around a black woman.

But on Saturday morning after Epsom, as the Captain and I rode our hacks back to Freemason Lodge, he did not, as usual, ask me how the horses worked. Instead he said: 'Do you know, an extraordinary thing happened last night. Humphrey de Trafford and I dined at the Savoy and some young chap dragged us to a night-club. Who do you think came in but Peter and David McCall.' Already knowing the form I commented: 'Imagine running into *them* in London!'

For Royal Ascot week he often made me share a house with Peter, but we had to have dinner once or twice with him so that he could guarantee that I went to bed early. On another occasion he said: 'Would you like to shoot in Norfolk?' I thanked him and had great fun. When we got back to Freemason Lodge in the evening I again thanked the Captain, but he put the damper on it: 'I only asked you because I wanted you to drive me there.'

Taking the Captain all in all he was a good loser, except on one occasion. That was at Kempton in 1937. Two-year-olds did not have to be named in those days; I was up on the Nance colt in the seller and started a red-hot favourite. Frustratingly I was beaten a short head by Brownie Carslake on Tolarra, a 25–1 outsider trained by Mr Persse who had £200 on the Nance colt. Tolarra had blinkers on and Brownie, the greatest I have ever seen or ridden against, kidded him into winning. To make matters worse, the Nance colt was claimed after the race by Mr H. Cannon. The next Sunday, as always, I went to see the Captain. He greeted me with: 'I do not know what you were doing on the Nance colt yesterday. In the grandstand I said to Mr Persse, 'Why does Rufus not come on? Mr Persse had a good bet and I had the biggest bet of my life.' I replied: 'Sorry Captain, but the youngster did not get going until too late in the race.' He retorted: 'Oh, I see: you went to sleep on him.' He paced up and down the room like a lion in a cage, and every day for two weeks he harped on about this race. At the end of this time I lost my temper and said: 'I will tell *you* something, Captain. You do not know how to train selling-platers. Had the Nance colt been trained by Jack Colling or Victor Smyth, he would have won easily because they rocket them out of the

starting gate. You, with great horses, don't bother to do that.' He
took this in good part and never mentioned the matter again.

P. T. Beasley (1981)

Captain Sir Cecil Boyd-Rochfort, CVO (1887–1983)

*Boyd-Rochfort first took out a licence in 1923 and trained high-
class horses from Freemason Lodge, Newmarket, until his retirement in 1968. His thirteen Classic wins include the Derby of 1959
with Parthia. Alcide, one of his six St Leger winners, would almost
certainly have added another Derby the previous year had he not
been got at. The Captain was not averse to a gamble: when a
good horse of his was aimed at a big handicap, it was seldom
unsuccessful.*

*Rufus Beasley's association with Cecil Boyd-Rochfort was a
happy and successful one. After his retirement in 1945 Beasley
began training at Malton. Profiting from his experience with the
Captain and following his own dictum of 'never attempting a
robbery with a bad horse', he made a speciality of winning big
handicaps. As a character, he will never be forgotten by those who
knew him: 'A humorous, loyal and delightful Irish sportsman, who
set out to enjoy life and succeeded.'*

———

Jim Joel's Racing Reminiscences

1908 was the year when I first went to a race meeting – the Epsom
Spring meeting – to see our horse, Dean Swift, win his second City
and Suburban. He had previously won it in 1906 and had been
placed in the same race several times. He retired in 1911 and is
buried at the Childwick Stud. It was naturally a very exciting
introduction to racing for a young man!

Minoru, Neil Gow and Lemberg

In 1909 I was lucky enough to be at Epsom when Minoru won
the Derby for King Edward VII. This was a thrilling experience
for me. As a two-year-old Minoru won the Great Surrey Foal
Stakes first time out at Epsom. He did not do much as a two-year-

old but the following year, in addition to winning the Derby, he also won the Greenham Stakes, the Two Thousand Guineas and the St James's Palace Stakes. He then went on to win at Goodwood! He ran in the St Leger but was only placed fourth and wound up his three-year-old career by winning the Free Handicap at the Houghton meeting at Newmarket. As a four-year-old he ran only once when he carried 8 st. 11 lb. in the City and Suburban but he was unplaced. This gives the reader an idea of the class of horse that used to run in this race in the old days. It was very much an ante-post betting race until after the First World War when it was gradually downgraded in class. I think there were only two horses originally weighted at 9 stone that ever won this race and they were Bend Or and Black Jester.

1910 was a very good year for racing as two very fine horses – Neil Gow and Lemberg – appeared on the scene. As a two-year-old, Neil Gow won the National Breeders' Produce Stakes at Sandown and ran third in the Coventry Stakes. That same week Lemberg won the New Stakes. They then met in the Champagne Stakes at Doncaster and Neil Gow beat Lemberg very easily. I think Lemberg was third. That was their last meeting as two-year-olds but Lemberg finished up by winning the Middle Park Stakes and the Dewhurst Stakes. As a three-year-old Neil Gow won the Craven Stakes. When they met in the Two Thousand Guineas, Neil Gow beat Lemberg in a terrific finish, winning, as far as I can remember, by a short head. They then met in the Derby for which Lemberg started favourite and won, with Neil Gow finishing fourth. They did not meet again until the Eclipse Stakes and again there was a fantastic finish when they ran a dead heat! This was their last encounter as I expect they thought that Neil Gow did not get further than one and a quarter miles.

Then came the St Leger for which race Lemberg started a hot favourite. He was ridden by Danny Maher, whom a lot of people thought had been hampered in the race and could not get through his field thus having to snatch the horse up. He finished third but Maher later said that he would not have won even if he had not been hampered. The race was won by Lord Derby's Swynford who beat Jimmy Rothschild's horse Bronzino by a head, with Lemberg

1½ lengths away third. Swynford turned into a very good four-year-old and won many races, ending up at stud where he was an excellent sire.

Trial gallops for Sunstar

In 1911, my family had a wonderful year. We had a horse called Sunstar. He did not excel as a two-year-old but he did win. He improved enormously as a three-year-old. I remember going to Wantage with my family to see him tried out. It was Good Friday and the weather was like a hot summer's day – I remember lying on the downs without my jacket waiting for the horses to come up to Farringdon Road to be galloped. There were some very good horses (although I must confess I did not realize just how good they were until much later on). We had another three-year-old that year called Lycaon who also took part in the gallop. We actually galloped him with older horses including The Story, Spanish Prince, Dean Swift and, I think, a horse called Sunspot. As anyone who has ever been there knows, the Farringdon Road is a very tough gallop. It is all uphill and our horse Sunstar (who was ridden by the stable boy, a good work rider, the other horses being ridden by jockeys) was going so easily that he won the gallop by about three lengths from all the other horses I have mentioned, with Lycaon behind. After this we naturally were anxious to find out how good they really were: so we sent out a 'Willie the Searcher'. We ran The Story, who was second in the gallops, in a mile race at Epsom with 10 stone on his back. He was ridden by Danny Maher and won quite comfortably. So that rather opened our eyes to the fact that Sunstar might be a good horse since he could beat this horse at level weights at home. So we then thought he must have a marvellous chance of winning the Guineas. Well, he did win very comfortably, with his ears pricked, and we were third with our other horse Lycaon. The horse who ran second belonged to Lord Derby and was called Stedfast. He also was a pretty good horse.

As I have said earlier, the weather had been very hot and dry but we felt we had to give Sunstar a gallop before the Derby in spite of the going. Morton (our trainer) felt we might as well gallop him in a race as in a gallop because if he won he would pick up a prize. So we ran him in the Newmarket Stakes. The ground was very hard, but Sunstar duly won quite comfortably by about two to three lengths. Shortly afterwards he sadly developed leg trouble. Anyway Morton had to tell my father about this problem but, at the same time, he said that he must not give up hope because the horse was so fit in himself that Morton thought he might possibly be able to patch him up and keep him going (in those days cabbage leaves were wrapped around horses' legs to reduce swellings!). Sunstar's problems were a very well-kept secret; but, as always, the market seemed to know that something was wrong although they did not know what it was. I remember the bookmaker, Leo Harwood (who had his offices in Warnford Court, Austin Friars, next to our own offices). He used to come up to our office frequently to take bets for the family. I remember him saying to my father: 'Sunstar is very easy to back for the Derby,' to which 'the old man' replied: 'Well, I have got a lot of money on him and I can't keep backing him all the time. But to show my good faith in the animal you can go down and put a "monkey" on him.' Shortly afterwards Leo Harwood returned saying: 'He's still the same price.' 'I'm afraid I can't help that,' said my father. Anyway the horse did eventually go to Epsom. Morton warned us that he would be all right until he came round Tattenham Corner where he was pretty sure he would break down. And, sure enough, as he was just coming into the straight he faltered. George Stern, his jockey, gave him one tap with the whip and immediately the horse pulled himself together and won the race by two lengths! He never ran again. We tried to get him right but, sadly, without any success. However, he turned out to be a very good sire and bred a lot of very good horses.

Success at Doncaster

In the same year we were beaten a short head in the One Thousand Guineas with a filly called Radiancy. The race was won by Jimmy Rothschild's Atmah which was well backed at 6–1 – our filly being a 20–1 chance. But we were only beaten a head so we very nearly brought off the double.

On the Tuesday of the St Leger meeting, the stable was still in good form. The two brothers, Jack and Solly, won five of the six races – Jack winning three and Solly two. We ran Lycaon in the St Leger and he was second to Prince Palatine – a very good horse. We bought him later in the following year for £40,000. (We were told we would have to pay £45,000 if he won the Goodwood Cup but he didn't!) We took him to the stud at Childwick but he was a very poor foal-getter and was sold, I think, to France.

In 1912 we had an own-brother to Sunstar called White Star. He won the Woodcote Stakes as a two-year-old (the same year as Sunstar won the Derby), the July Stakes at Newmarket, the Mole-comb Stakes at Goodwood, the Champagne Stakes at Doncaster, was third in the Middle Park Plate and won the Dewhurst Stakes. He started a very hot favourite – about even money for the Two Thousand Guineas but he had had some very hard races as a two-year-old from which he did not recover and thus, I am afraid, did not come up to our expectations. He was mostly ridden by George Stern who was a very strong rider and the horse nearly always won his races by only a short head, head or a neck! He never really did much good afterwards although he may have won a couple of races.

1913 and 1914 were two more very good racing years for the family. We won the One Thousand Guineas in 1913 with Jest and then she went on to win the Oaks. In 1914 we again won the One Thousand Guineas with Princess Dorrie and she, too, went on to win the Oaks.

Lord Derby releases Donoghue

After this the war came and we sold all our yearlings in 1916 to America. We started up again in 1919 when our yearlings were sent to Morton again. The following year we had a very good horse called Humorist. He was always very delicate (nobody ever knew why). He won the Woodcote Stakes but I don't think he ran again until the Champagne Stakes, when he was third, beaten three-quarters of a length. He then went on to win a small race in one of the autumn meetings at Newmarket and was beaten a neck in the Middle Park when ridden by Brownie Carslake. We then aimed him at the Two Thousand Guineas which we thought he might win. He started at a very short price and coming down the hill it was odds on his winning the race; but then he suddenly stopped. He obviously felt something, and was beaten into third place, again by three-quarters of a length and three-quarters of a length. He next ran in the Derby because Morton told us that he seemed to be very fit and had worked very well on the gallops. For the big occasion he was ridden by Steve Donoghue and duly won. I think I must tell the story of how Steve came to ride for us. He was Lord Derby's first jockey at the time and my father asked Lord Derby if he would release Steve to ride our horse. He – quite rightly – said 'no', pointing out that he had a horse of his own running in the Derby and would therefore be using his first jockey himself. Well, in the end, my father asked the Hon. George Lambton if he would intervene on our behalf with Lord Derby to see if he would release his jockey to us. In the end he did, but Lord Derby later told Morton and my father: 'Never ask me again to release my jockey. I have never done it before and I will never do it again!' – what a different story from today! Perhaps I should mention that after Humorist won the Derby, Lord Derby was one of the first to congratulate my father.

Some years later Lord Derby told my father that he had a very nice mare called Tranquil who was naturally trained at Newmarket by George Lambton and who had won the One Thousand Guineas. That year at the Goodwood meeting Lambton asked my father if she could be taken over to Morton to be trained because if she stayed at Newmarket she would not win another race, the going on the gallops being so hard there. This was a great compliment as obviously George Lambton thought a lot of our own trainer. He was right because Tranquil was to win the St Leger.

'My father keen to buy Papyrus'

That same year my father was very keen to buy a horse called Papyrus who had won the Derby. He was running in the St Leger against Tranquil. My father had already backed Papyrus but as he knew I was going up to Doncaster to watch the race, he asked me to back Tranquil to save the bet he had laid out on Papyrus. He told me that first of all I should see Morton to find out if the filly was OK. This I duly did and Morton said: 'Don't do anything. I'll take the blame if the mare wins, the "Guv" will be only too delighted if she does since I was asked to take over her training.' Not half he was when I got back!

Well, after that the horses rather petered out. Morton retired and the stable got into a bad way because my father rather lost interest. Naturally he kept on until he died in 1940. When I took over, the stud was in a pretty bad way. I wanted to get back the line which had done so well in the past through the mare, Absurdity, which was by Melton out of Paradoxical. She bred us all those Classic horses like Jest and Humorist. I had a mare called Amuse, which was by Phalaris out of Gesture by Sunstar out of Absurdity, and by some miracle I sent her to Donatello and she produced Picture Play who won me the One Thousand Guineas during the war; she had been quite a good two-year-old and won twice or three times. She really started the stud up again.

Perhaps I might end with a note on Morton and Charlie Peck, who took over from Morton who retired in 1924–5. Charlie Peck was a fine trainer and stableman and used also to train for my Uncle Solly at Sefton Lodge. He trained Bachelor's Button who beat Pretty Polly in the Ascot Gold Cup in 1906 and Pommern who won the Two Thousand Guineas in 1915 and the Derby the same year – the Derby being run at Newmarket on the July Course during the war. Pommern went on to win the St Leger which was then known as the September Stakes. He also trained Polymelus who was by Cyllene. His descendants through Phalaris include such great horses as Nearco, Mill Reef, Nijinsky and many others. So the credit really must go to Cyllene who started this tremendously successful line.

Both Morton and Peck always fed their own horses. I doubt if any trainers do this today. But racing in the days of my father was so different from today. Up to 1921 there were no aeroplanes to transport the horses nor were there many motor horse-boxes, so horses had to do a lot of walking to and from railway stations as in those days they were transported by train.

H. J. Joel (1984)

H. J. ('Jim') Joel (b. 1894)

A leading owner-breeder after the 1939–45 war, winning every Classic race except the Oaks in which his West Side Story was beaten a short head, Jim Joel headed the list of owners and breeders in 1967 when his home-bred colt Royal Palace won the Two Thousand Guineas and the Derby. On the death of his father Jack Joel in 1940 he took over the latter's stud, which was at a low ebb through the use of indifferent sires and the retention of bad mares. This was remedied by weeding out the rubbish, building up the great family of Absurdity, through her granddaughter Amuse, with top-class stallions, and the judicious introduction of fresh lines of blood. In 1985 failing eyesight caused Jim Joel to wind up his stud and phase out his Flat racers, maintaining an interest in racing through his jumpers.

The Hon. Dorothy Paget

Miss Paget, a daughter of Lord Queenborough and an American mother, who was a member of the Whitney family, was wealthy enough to please herself as to what she did, and how and when she did it. Her chief interests in life were owning racehorses and gambling on their chances of winning, whether they belonged to her or someone else, her bets running into many thousands of pounds. When she went to a race meeting her whole attention was concentrated on the occasion outside, social contacts were not considered before the day's activities were over – and sometimes they were not over until well into the night. She was not easily approachable, and many of the apocryphal stories manufactured about her were based on envy and the malice that accompanies it. She knew the sort of life she wanted to live, and she *lived* it, sometimes sleeping for three successive days and nights, and then staying awake for the following three days and nights, during which, regardless of time, she would telephone her trainers, who usually took a poor view of being communicated with in the small hours of the morning.

In 1938 Miss Paget was looking for a racing secretary, and a friend, Daisy Walker, who rode showjumpers for her, re-commended a friend, Ruth Charlton, for the job.

Miss Charlton was not over-anxious, but agreed to an interview; she was told that Miss Paget would see her at Paddington station when she arrived there on the race train from Newbury.

When Ruth got to Paddington she was introduced to the station-master, who – frock-coated and top-hatted – was waiting to meet Miss Paget and escort her to her car. The train arrived, but, instead of the expected interview, the station-master reappeared and told Ruth that she would have to wait a bit longer; one of Miss Paget's cases had been left behind at Newbury and was being sent up on the next train; Miss Paget would see her after its arrival.

It was cold on the station. Ruth hung about shivering until, at last, the expected confrontation took place.

'Well – what do you have to say for yourself?' was Miss Paget's opening gambit, as she ran a perceptive eye over her prospective secretary. She was a very superstitious lady, and, having had a good day's racing, probably decided that this attractive young woman was part and parcel of the luck of the moment. She was right.

'What's your typing speed?'

'I don't know; I've not been trained as a secretary.'

After one and a half hours the interview neared its conclusion.

'What about languages? Do you speak German?' asked Miss Paget.

'No.'

'French?'

'A little.'

'Russian?'

Ruth said: 'Please don't bully me. I can see I'm not suitable, and anyway, I don't want to work for you. Let's say goodbye and call it a day.'

'I'll see you on Monday,' said Miss Paget. 'You'll find my bark is far worse than my bite.'

By this time Ruth was frozen to the marrow and feeling very unwell. She made her way to her sister's flat, where she was staying and retired to bed with influenza.

So that was that. No further question about taking a job she didn't fancy. No Monday meeting. She asked her sister to telephone her excuses.

She had reckoned without Miss Paget, who, with her mind made up, was just about as irresistible as a bulldozer.

Masses of flowers arrived at the flat: roses, carnations by the dozen, and a note saying: 'Get well – see you soon. Dorothy Paget.'

Having recovered from her bout of flu, Ruth found herself – much to her surprise – installed as racing secretary to the Paget empire, a task sometimes arduous, frequently amusing – which she faithfully performed for the next eighteen years.

Miss Paget's intuition served her well on that Paddington station platform: a confidential secretary can betray confidence, both verbally and materially – the number of spiteful biographies published after the deaths of long-served employers is one testimony of this – but Dorothy Paget never backed a more certain winner in all the colossal bets she made than she did on the day when she engaged Ruth Charlton (now Mrs Charlie Smirke) to work for her.

One point on which Ruth stood firm was her refusal to live in Miss Paget's house; she insisted on having a flat of her own, to which she could escape from her employer's irregular hours.

Anyone with a sense of humour, especially when the laugh is at their expense, can be forgiven many things. Dorothy Paget was one such. Stories in which she was ridiculed made her laugh till tears rolled down her cheeks; at parties she would call on Ruth to recount some of them.

Two adventures which they shared concerned Austin cars. Miss Paget was devoted to fast cars, which she usually drove herself. On one occasion, when the Paget entourage was visiting Manchester, she decided that she and Ruth would travel part of the way by train, finishing the journey in a twelve-cylinder Lagonda which she had just bought – her chauffeur, Harry Jackson, bringing the car to a prearranged rendezvous; the rest of the party would complete the journey by train.

Everything went according to plan until, soon after Miss Paget had taken the wheel, the car made a sudden dive towards the kerb.

'My God! The steering's gone,' said Miss Paget.

Ruth, who was experienced in driving second-hand cars, with worn tyres, suggested that it might be a puncture.

Miss Paget had a habit of addressing remarks to any third party who might be present through the medium of her companion of the moment.

'Ask Harry if he thinks we've got a puncture.'

'Harry, Miss Paget says, have we got a puncture?'

'No, miss.'

'Tell him to get out and see.'

'Miss Paget says, get out and see.'

So Harry and Ruth both got out, and, sure enough, one tyre was so flat that the metal rim was touching the ground.

'Tell Harry to change the wheel as quickly as he can.'

Easier said than done. The car was fitted with a hydraulic jack, which was supposed to respond to pressure on a button; this it refused to do.

There was no garage in sight, only a small village shop, with a young man of about nineteen or twenty in charge, who vouchsafed the gloomy information that, as it was bank holiday, all the local garages were closed.

Parked outside the shop was an Austin Seven.

'Whose car is that?'

'Mine.'

'I have to get to Manchester; I'll hire it from you; you can come with me and drive it back.'

'I'm sorry, I can't do that, I've promised to take Mum for a spin this afternoon.'

'Your mum can have a spin another time. Get into the back. Ruth, tell Harry to follow us to Manchester as soon as he can get that tyre changed.'

The young man, by now hypnotized, meekly climbed into the back of his car, Miss Paget – who was very generously proportioned – squeezed herself into the driving seat and Ruth, having given Harry his instructions, joined the party.

Miss Paget surveyed the dashboard, found the starter and pointed downwards.

'What's that pencil?'

'That', said Ruth patiently, 'is the gear lever.'

And so the journey began.

When they had gone a short distance, the young man ventured a remark.

'There isn't much petrol in the tank.'

'We'll fill it up as soon as we find a garage open.' When this was found, Miss Paget, with her mind on the tank capacity of her Lagonda, pulled in beside one of the pumps.

'Twenty gallons, please.'

The garage hand looked at her pityingly. 'It only holds four.'

They battled on, and Ruth, feeling sorry for the reluctant owner-passenger, said to him: 'I don't expect your car's ever been driven as fast as this before.'

'No, it hasn't.'

'Ruth, don't gossip,' said Miss Paget.

The young man navigated efficiently as far as the outskirts of Manchester, when he could give no further advice, as he had no idea where the racecourse was.

The car was fitted with a sunshine roof, which Miss Paget opened, rising up through it as she caught sight of a policeman.

'Racecourse?'

The policeman waved an imperious hand.

'If you'll pull over to the kerb, madam . . .' He prepared to give slow, precise instructions.

'You bloody fool!' snapped Miss Paget, and drove on.

Eventually they reached the racecourse, where the rest of the party was assembled on the steps of the Club Stand, keeping an anxious look-out for the enormous, unmistakable Lagonda; their sights were focused on a much higher level than the top of a tiny Austin, whose presence did not register itself on their comprehension till Ruth got out and drew their attention to it.

One thing on which Miss Paget always insisted was that Ruth should carry large sums of ready cash – sometimes as much as £5,000. As she edged herself out of the car, which by now had steam spurting from its radiator, she said: 'Give me seventy-five pounds.'

Ruth handed it over, and Miss Paget passed it on to the young man, saying: 'Thank you very much indeed. Go carefully on your way home, don't drive as fast as I did.'

The second adventure involving an Austin occurred during the war when Ruth was driving to Cheltenham with Miss Paget, from her house in Chalfont St Giles; the vehicle in which they were travelling was a Humber – not so heavy on petrol as the Lagonda. As they were climbing the hill out of High Wycombe, the engine seized up.

Ruth's handbag, in addition to carrying large sums of money, also contained an AA box key; she knew that there was such a box at the top of the hill, so she set out, making the best possible speed to summon the Lagonda to the rescue: as she returned, she saw Miss Paget waving down a small Austin, containing a driver and passenger. The driver recognized her, but before he could speak she said: 'I want to get to Cheltenham.'

'Oh, *we're* going there. Good morning, Miss Paget, how are you?'

'*Don't* ask me how I am! I want to borrow your car, mine's broken down, Miss Charlton's just telephoned for another one, it should be here in a short time.'

By now the Paget hypnotism was working; the owners of the Austin realized that they were not expected to give her a lift, but to surrender it to her. Meekly they helped her into it, before joining Ruth in the stricken Humber, to sit and wait for the arrival of the Lagonda.

On another Cheltenham occasion, May Snow, a cousin of Miss Paget's, lent her a Tudor cottage at Andoversford, in which she decided to stay, with a retinue of servants, installing the rest of her party, including Ruth, in an hotel at Cheltenham.

The morning after their arrival, Ruth drove over to the cottage, and was horrified, on approaching it, to see smoke issuing from between the bricks.

The housemaid rushed out to meet her. 'Oh, Miss Charlton, I'm so glad you've come; the place is on fire!'

'What about Miss Paget?'

'I didn't dare wake her; she said she was on no account to be disturbed before midday.'

Ruth soon discovered what had happened. The previous evening Miss Paget had built up a huge fire on the open hearth; a beam had caught alight, and, although not burning fiercely, it was smouldering, giving off a great deal of smoke.

She went to Miss Paget's bedroom and, in fear and trembling, knocked on the door.

'Come in. What's the matter?'

'The house is on fire.'

'I've no intention of getting up until the flames are licking my pyjama legs.'

She took her time over rising and dressing, whilst smoke seeped through the bricks at the back of her bedroom fireplace. When she was ready she descended the stairs unhurriedly, got into the car, and her parting words to the staff were: 'Now you can send for the fire brigade.'

When she went racing, Miss Paget always wore her own particular 'uniform', a long, blue-speckled coat, usually with a plain, dark blue collar. Needless to say, this was renewed from time to time, but the replacements were always identical, and she was fussy over all details of how the coats were made and cared for.

Her superstitions linked up with numbers, which included the date of her birthday – 21 February – around which everything had to be carefully calculated. Amongst other things which Ruth took to race meetings was a bundle of *nine* well-sharpened lead pencils: one Christmas she gave Miss Paget a gold one; next time they went racing, she took it along with the others, thereby increasing the number in the collection to *ten*. This practice continued for the next eighteen months, when, at the end of a disastrous day's betting, Miss Paget rounded on her and said: 'I've lost twenty thousand pounds today – and it's all because of your bloody pencil! You can keep the damn' thing!'

She returned the offending object to Ruth, who still has it.

Sometimes, when Miss Paget was driving to a race meeting, Ruth was sent out the previous day, to check the route and discover possible snags. If there were road-repair works anywhere along it, she would chat to the workmen, giving them £2 each, asking them to keep a look-out for Miss Paget's car and see that it had a clear run – which, of course, it did, frequently at the expense of other traffic, whereat Miss Paget would say: 'Wonderful organization, Ruth – simply wonderful.'

As she invariably left far too little time to get from one place to another, these near-royal progresses made a great deal of difference to her enjoyment of a day's racing. The best of them occurred at Stratford-upon-Avon, to which she had travelled by air, Ruth meeting her with a car at the aerodrome. She was anxious to get away as quickly as possible after racing, and left the arrangements to Ruth, who asked the officer in charge of the police if he could do anything about it; he arranged an escort which flashed them through the town as if they had been in open country. Miss Paget was delighted. 'Excellent, Ruth – in future you must always do this.'

Dorothy Paget was a very generous woman, but this was not widely known, because her many gifts to charities and individuals in need of help were usually anonymous. When she died, in 1962, her nearest relative was her sister, Lady Baillie, to whom she seldom spoke. For years her lawyer had been trying to persuade her to make a will, and she had got as far as naming people to whom she would like to leave bequests, but his last letter to her on the subject was found, unopened, after her death, so Lady Baillie was her sole beneficiary.

Caroline Ramsden (1973)

The Hon. Dorothy Paget (1905–62)

Although Dorothy Paget owned one great racehorse and a Derby winner, her success was not, on the whole, commensurate with her huge outlay. Perhaps Golden Miller more than made up for the highly priced failures and the cost of their upkeep.

Like many eccentrics, Miss Paget was an acquired taste. Her association with Sir Gordon Richards was a happy one and the respect was mutual, a situation not always applicable to her many other trainers.

Aly Khan

A friend once confided to me that he had irrefutable proof that Aly Khan had been to bed with his wife and his girlfriend in the same week, and that he was going to kill him. But when I met him a week or so later he told me that Aly had been so charming when he had run into him at Epsom that he couldn't bring himself to refer to the matter, especially after Aly had told him to back one of his horses which had won.

He went on, however, to tell me that he had spoken very sharply to his two erring women, who had admitted their guilt, and promised not to do it again. In point of fact it was most unlikely that either would have had the chance, at any rate for a long time. Aly never forgot a face or a body, and seldom a name, and if he had met either of them in a different environment in the years to come he would most likely have suggested a repeat performance. But for the time being they were on a par with yesterday's paper.

This story typifies much of Aly's love life, the one-night stands, the irate husbands who refrained from reprisals on account of Aly's charm, and the erring women who willingly confessed because it was Aly, though they would have strenuously denied the charge had it been anyone else.

It became a status symbol among the international set to have been to bed with Aly. It would be incorrect to describe most of these romps in the day as affairs, as an affair suggests that the couple have spent at least a week together, while in Aly's case the majority of his girlfriends considered themselves lucky if he was still with them when dawn broke the following morning.

For a period of three or four years, in the middle thirties, I suppose I knew Aly as well as any man could know this mercurial descendant of Mohammed; judging from the varying descriptions of him given after his death by his best-known mistresses, they too found him a complex character.

Aly had more charm than any man I have ever met, and this sums up his entire character. His desire to please and to extend hospitality was genuine, but he was selfish and self-indulgent, and like Steve Donoghue, he thought that rules and regulations were made for others. So long as it was only Aly Khan who was out of step, all was well in the best of all possible worlds.

Quintin Gilbey (1970)

Shah Aly Khan (1911–60)

Son of the late Aga Khan and father of the present Aga, Aly was bypassed for the title, possibly on account of his rather flamboyant life-style and his son's more serious character. He was an enthusiastic amateur rider and as a young man hunted and rode in point-to-points, latterly confining himself to the Flat, where he had considerable success. Aly owned some good horses in his time, the best being the outstanding Petite Étoile, who was still racing when her owner was killed in a motor accident.

———

The Maktoum Family Business, 1989

Nashwan, Old Vic, Zilzal, Polish Precedent and Shaadi . . . A few of the impressive list of Maktoum-owned horses in a year during which they have harvested the great races of Europe and hammered home the degree of their mounting superiority on the Turf.

The top end of the British owners' table reads more like a *Who's Who* of the Middle East than the *Almanach de Gotha*. The first five places are occupied by three of the four brothers from Dubai – Sheikh Mohammed, Maktoum Al-Maktoum and Hamdan – Prince Khaled Abdulla of Saudi Arabia and Karim, Prince Aga Khan. Only Ahmed Al-Maktoum has had a disappointing year but he has fond memories of last season when Mtoto's big-race victories were largely responsible for taking him into fifth place.

Although the Aga Khans have been westernized for three generations, they were originally Persian noblemen.

Abdulla and the Aga Khan, in common with the pre-eminent owners earlier this century, such as the diamond-enriched Joel family, and the traditional owner-breeders typified by the Earls of

Rosebery and Derby, are primarily commercial owners who like to make their racing pay.

But the Maktoums' frenetic spending in pursuit of their ambitious dreams is without precedent and at times difficult to comprehend. The Aga Khan hit the nail on the head when he said: 'It is difficult to compete with people who do not appear to be inspired by the profit motive.'

Their relentless quest for success has won them millions of pounds – although nothing like the millions they have spent – and it has been received with a mixture of envy and gratitude.

On the plus side, they have largely financed the restoration of British racing to the very top of the international league. Not since the 1930s has sport of such consistently high calibre been watched in Britain. The trend of the previous half-century, during which most of our priceless bloodlines, developed over 250 years, were exported to the United States, has been reversed.

The Arab-owned champions, such as Dancing Brave, Rainbow Quest, Nashwan, Mtoto, Oh So Sharp and Diminuendo, have helped make it a decade of excellence. Future generations of breeders will benefit.

On the down side, the Maktoums are attacked for seeking success at any price, frightening away would-be challengers who are merely wealthy rather than exceedingly rich.

The scope and size of the Maktoum operation is almost beyond understanding. Sheikh Mohammed alone owns around 1,000 head, including horses in training, stallions, broodmares, yearlings and foals. His group of studs include Dalham Hall, Newmarket, comprising 1,500 acres, and the Kildangan and Ragusa Studs in Ireland.

The Maktoum stranglehold on the great races has tightened in 1989 as more of their ambitions have been realized. Sheikh Hamdan's home-bred champion, Nashwan, is one of the outstanding horses of the decade – having this season won the Two Thousand Guineas, Derby, Eclipse Stakes and King George VI and Queen Elizabeth Diamond Stakes – and next year will stand at his palatial Shadwell Stud, near Thetford.

Sheikh Mohammed is about to become Britain's leading owner

for the fifth consecutive year. He also heads the French and Irish tables and has won seven Classic races in the three countries. Old Vic has given the Sheikh his first win in both the French and Irish Derbys; Polish Precedent is the champion miler of France.

The cash benefits are considerable. Nashwan is to stand at Shadwell with a capital value of £18 million on his head; Polish Precedent is to stand at Dalham Hall with a £7 million price-tag.

But, whatever the benefits now, the cost of the Maktoums' ten-year onslaught on the riches of the Turf has been mind-boggling. It is no exaggeration to say that the Maktoums must be the world's most extravagant family. They are estimated to have lavished $1 billion on their pleasure.

Consider their expenditure at the yearling sales. In 1988, they spent $30 million at the two-day July Select Sale at Keeneland, accounting for 30 per cent of the total. At last year's Newmarket Highflyer Sale, their official purchases amounted to more than $12 million, 34 per cent of the turnover. They bought thirty-five of the yearlings costing £100,000 or more at the Highflyer a year ago and again this week they have been dominant at Newmarket.

On Wednesday, the first Dancing Brave yearling to be sold at auction was bought by Sheikh Ahmed for 600,000 gns., the flag-ship of another concerted effort on the yearling market. A battery of six-figure purchases by their umbrella companies was to follow, including 510,000 gns. for a daughter of Sadler's Wells and 500,000 gns. for a half-brother to Old Vic.

At the North American sales in July this year, their expenditure was estimated by *Racing Update* at $50 to $60 million, 40 per cent of the take. And their unofficial purchases are always greater, as they bid through independent agents as well as through their own representatives.

Few signs have emerged that the early belief – that spending would decline once home-bred yearlings began to enter the operation – will prove to be correct. The Maktoums' firepower grows almost daily, and there is little evidence that their prodigious outlay will diminish. As recently as this week, it was revealed that Sheikh Mohammed is to buy two more Newmarket studs, White Lodge and Beech House.

The White Lodge Stud, developed by the Mollers, has produced the Derby winner Teenoso among a host of high-class horses, and with its thirty priceless broodmares and a similar number of horses in training represents a major and significant acquisition. The value of the deal for the studs has been estimated in tens of millions.

But is the game worth the candle?

The cost of maintaining Sheikh Mohammed's cavalry of about 440 horses with thirty-one trainers world-wide is in excess of £6 million a year. Yet, since Hatta gave Sheikh Mohammed his first winner in Britain in 1977, his total win prize-money earnings in this country to the end of 1988 amounted to £5,058,808. That is less than the $10.2 million he paid in 1983 for Snaafi Dancer, a horse that was never to race.

Just after making his record bid, the Sheikh gave an indication of the family's philosophy. Asked whether $10.2 million represented an exorbitant price for an immature, unraced yearling, he raised his head and said: 'Who can tell what a horse is worth?'

In attempting to impose European standards of thinking and behaviour on the Maktoums, the mounting wave of public disapproval from Britain beats against a barrier of incomprehension. The Maktoums' prodigal spending is the despair of their more commercially-minded rivals.

'Of course, we can't recoup what has been spent,' says Anthony Stroud, Sheikh Mohammed's racing manager. 'But there's a big emphasis on not losing money. We hope to break even. And in due course, the assets we have built up over the years will justify what we paid for them.'

After the family's heavy expenditure at the Keeneland July Sales this year, Stroud admitted: 'We certainly spent more than we meant to. But we've got a strong commitment to a lot of trainers. And if we support the breeding industry and the breeders make money, they can then support our stallions and buy our horses out of training.'

Those who fear that the Maktoums may suddenly disappear without trace, leaving the country's thoroughbred industry in a state of chaos, are blinding themselves to the ever-increasing value of the assets the Maktoums are accumulating, assets which cannot be easily realized and which they will wish to protect. Also, unlike in most normal businesses, which are created on a basis of bank borrowing and high gearing, these assets are totally unencumbered. There is always cash available.

Apart from this, they have no wish to leave. 'As long as we are welcome, we shall stay,' says Sheikh Mohammed simply.

Yet Sheikh Mohammed's total commitment also has its draw-backs. His policy of attempting to buy success at any price has been the target of severe criticism. He recently paid Ir£32,000 to enter two horses at a late stage for the Irish St Leger to give him a chance of becoming the first owner to make a clean sweep of the five Irish Classics. Both were beaten, but it was the Sheikh's wealth which bought them the opportunity to try.

The Sheikh's desire to succeed with no expense spared has been shown, too, by his aggressive purchases of horses in training. He bought Kerrera, one of the leading two-year-old fillies last season, on the strength of her home gallops before she won her first race.

But they do love the actual racing and it is their all-consuming passion. Zilzal, owned by Mana Al-Maktoum, a brother-in-law of Sheikh Maktoum, and Polish Precedent, owned by Sheikh Mohammed, raced against each other in the Queen Elizabeth II Stakes at Ascot; they have no wish to deprive the public of watching the best against the best. There is no reason to doubt that Nashwan and Old Vic would have been allowed to race each other in the Prix de l'Arc de Triomphe tomorrow had circum-stances permitted.

Charles St George, the owner of Michelozzo, winner of the St Leger and one of the people most likely to feel threatened by the Arabs, is in no doubt about the issue. 'It's brilliant,' he says. 'It's the best thing that's ever happened to racing. They're very generous in the way they race.'

Bob McCreery, a breeder who over the years has produced such high-class horses as High Top and Old Vic, says: 'It's marvellous the way they brought all these good horses back from America and are now standing them over here. The benefits for the industry as a whole are yet to come, when their not-so-good but superbly-bred stallions and horses out of training are available to everybody.

At the moment, it's only a few trainers, their staff, and breeders at the top end of the market who have been cashing in.'

The town of Newmarket has been transformed in the 1980s. Racing's headquarters was in the doldrums as the horse population declined to 1,300. Now the town is bursting at the seams and there are nearly 3,000 horses queuing up to work on the Heath.

The Arabs have created stud and stable facilities to the highest possible standard. Apart from trainers, all the auxiliary professions, such as builders, estate agents, saddlers, auctioneers, corn merchants, veterinary practices, are having the time of their lives.

Nor could the Maktoums' sense of honour be denied. Their loyalty to their own is legendary, as Sheikh Hamdan's recent purchase of Farncombe Down, to ensure that Dick Hern can continue training when he has to leave the Queen's stables at West Ilsley, gives striking evidence.

The drawbacks of such a top-heavy investment are a topic of continual and sometimes heated discussion throughout the industry. The tentacles of the Arab patronage, particularly that of the Maktoums, reach far and wide. And the inevitable two-tier level of prosperity and privation at times arouses widespread resentment in a traditionally jealous game.

Bob McCreery says, 'The trouble is that the grass roots are being threatened. Rich people – and there are some very rich people in this country – become turned off by the fact they can see no point in competing against the Arabs. That's why so many of them are switching to jumping.'

The effect on the distribution of prize-money is dramatic. In 1988, the four Maktoum brothers and Abdulla collected £3,274,750 out of a total of £23,506,552 prize-money in Britain; they won 348 of the 3,092 races run on the Flat. In other words, just five men collected 15 per cent of the prize-money and 11 per cent of the races.

The brothers' strike rate in the Classic and Group races is even higher. But it is their plundering of maiden and graduation races on the lesser tracks that continues to cause the most concern.

Racing at the highest level has always been the rich man's domain. The difference in the Maktoums' case is the fear that the sheer size of their equine army is depriving the small owner of the opportunity to make his racing pay.

Even so, the results of the Middle Park Stakes and Cheveley Park Stakes at Newmarket this week indicate that the smaller owner can still win against the odds. But they are increasingly the exception rather than the rule.

Whatever the drawbacks of the Arabs' presence, its considerable advantages are beyond dispute. Lord Ronaldshay, one of the straightest thinkers in the game (he is chairman of the Thorough-bred Breeders' Association, managing director of Redcar race-course, and owner of the Zetland Stud), says 'Of course, the Arabs now dominate the racing and breeding industries to an almost unhealthy extent. And it is worrying that Sheikh Mohammed should feel the need to continue to buy horses to such a degree and at all price-levels even now when his breeding operation is in full swing. But it is marvellous to see Nashwan and Old Vic racing over here rather than in the States. We should welcome their huge investment.'

That view is not shared by everyone. 'Where is it all going to end?' asks a Classic-winning trainer (whose stable houses no Arab-owned horses). 'If they go on like this, they must end up winning five races a day. Will they be content then? Or will they continue until they win all six?'

After Oh So Sharp had given Sheikh Mohammed his first home-bred Classic winner in the Oaks in 1985, he said, 'Money could never have bought the feeling that this has given me today.'

Of course, limitless wealth *did* buy the Sheikh his moment of supreme satisfaction. Perhaps part of the answer to the continued extravagance lies in the passionate but acquisitive nature of Sheikh Mohammed, whose boundless enthusiasm and love of animals is matched by his relish for the power game and the cut and thrust of competition at the highest level.

The game of Monopoly springs irresistibly to mind when seeking comparison. The acquirer of valuable sites is best advised to build houses and hotels rather than sitting on his cash If not, someone else comes along and relieves him of his wealth. The Maktoums are not making such an elementary mistake as they add relentlessly to their bloodstock empire.

Michael Seely, The Times, 7 October 1989

If not, as yet, entirely adopted by and absorbed into the racing community, the Maktoum family's involvement is both welcome and accepted for the many advantages it provides.

On their influence, Jeremy Tree, recently retired after thirty-eight seasons as a trainer, has this to say: 'I think it is quite alarming but I genuinely don't know what can be done about it. Presumably they came here because they enjoyed it and liked competing, but I think that if what is going on at the moment continues, they'll end up doing the business in because they'll simply be competing against each other.'

If any criticism of the Maktoums' racing operation is justifiable it must be centred on the early retirement of their Classic and Group 1 winning colts. This aspect of racing has been referred to elsewhere and, in particular, by Sir Noël Murless. His views are no less apposite today.

———

A Small-Scale Owner

My mother's uncle trained Hyperion. Some say that, when the foal was born, his owner and his future trainer looked into the box and one said to the other, 'He's too small – we'll have to sell him.'

Naturally opinions differ as to who it was who said it. Stanleys argue that Lord Derby would never have made a statement of that nature to his trainer; he was the perfect owner in that he refrained from interfering with the running of his stables. Lambtons say that great uncle George would never have made such a sweeping judgement at so early a stage in the little foal's career. In any case Hyperion was not sold. His statue stands today beside the road near Lord Derby's stud at Newmarket and, whether or not he looks small, his reputation as a Derby winner and a stallion remains intact.

I tell this tale to make clear that the sport of kings is in my blood. It was transmitted by my mother, who took little interest in it, though she did remark sometimes that uncle George had lost a lot of money betting – in his youth on horses that he rode himself and later in life on horses ridden by jockeys such as Archer, Sloan, Donoghue and Weston – and would I please heed the warning.

Like his wife, my father, though addicted to the hunting field, had little time for racing. Nor, apart from me, have his children – with the exception of his eldest son who reads the form-book avidly and sometimes gleans valuable information from it. At Ascot he once supplied me with five good-priced winners out of six, thus handsomely earning the ten per cent I give him from my winnings for the privilege of sharing the conclusions he reaches at the breakfast table and imparts to me by telephone soon afterwards.

My father made one of the two most memorable statements ever made on horse racing when, one night at dinner in the early thirties, he said, 'The only certainty in racing is that you can't win a race unless you enter your horse in it.' There was laughter all round because the proposition seemed so obvious, yet for nearly 50 years I have kept it in mind and used it.

On one notable occasion I did so to persuade my trainer of those days, Bill Wightman, to run the 3,000–guinea purchase he had made for me at Windsor in the Derby. Since its father was Sun Prince and Dante Gabriel Rossetti once wrote, 'I will make a goblin of the sun' (for reasons best known to himself), I called it Goblin. He won his last race as a two-year-old at Newmarket (L. Piggott up), breaking the seven-furlong record (which he still holds), and I decided his priority in the next year should be to win the Derby, never mind such hacks as Shirley Heights, one of his likely opponents.

Bill, perhaps, was not so sure about the soundness of this plan. However, with benignity and resignation he made the necessary entries. In those days one did not have to pay almost the purchase price of one's horse again to compete in the race. 'We'll run him if the going's firm,' Bill said. It was.

Goblin came out of the stalls some 10 or 15 lengths behind the field. My sister, Bridget, told me later that she noticed on the television that he had his tail caught in the rear gate of his stall.

In fact, he went to sleep, according to his jockey, as the loading of the French horses, who do not like our stalls, took 15 minutes. In spite of this initial set-back he came tenth in a field of 25 to Shirley Heights.

'I would have been much closer if he'd got off with the others,' said the jockey as he went off to the weighing-room. 'Horses sleep standing up,' said Bill, ever generous, as we went off to have a drink, 'and jockeys can't keep climbing up their necks to see whether their eyes are shut or not.'

So ended my first tilt at the Blue Riband of the Turf. Note the word 'first'. Should my son buy a colt some day with the laughable amount I allow him to lay out on my behalf (my last cost £1,500), the Derby will be in his owner's sights if there is any sign of promise.

I have owned a number of cheap horses; only two have won. Goblin won seven races under Bill Wightman and a hurdler, Bob and Peter, won two under my son, Jamie. The rest gave me great pleasure in their own non-winning ways. One, for example, trained by Sir John Astor on the flat (then by Nick Gaselee over the sticks), threw her jockey, Nicky Henderson, which landed him in John Thorne's house, where he was tended by John's daughter, whom he promptly married. Yet another, trained by Bill Wightman, ran in a hurdle race at Wincanton, John Oaksey up. 'How did you find him, John?' I asked, as he rode in. 'He ought to take up some other sport, like golf,' said his jockey.

It has all been fun, thanks to my father and the sound advice he gave all those years ago. Which reminds me of the second memorable statement about racing. It was uttered by the Iron Chancellor of Germany, Prince Bismarck, to Benjamin Disraeli: 'You will never have a revolution in your country, just so long as you keep up your racing.'

He meant, I imagine, that so long as Kings and Queens and you and me rub shoulders in the paddock on a racecourse, bet with the same odds available to all and race against each other, it is thumbs up for democracy. And so it is. *But was he also thinking that, because equality of opportunity is revolution's greatest enemy,*

*the powers in racing should make it their first priority that those
with slender purses can carry on?*

I am not suggesting that he knew how this could be achieved
but I like to think that he was aware of the need for practising
eternal vigilance in this respect. If not, doubtless wise old Dizzy,
with his phobia about two nations, put him right.

The Hon. William Douglas Home (1987)

WILLIAM DOUGLAS HOME *(b. 1912), noted playwright and enthusiastic owner, makes a vital point. With increasing domination
resting in such few hands it was never more important for the
authorities to ensure that 'those with slender purses' can carry on.*

TRAINING AND BREEDING

H. S. (Atty) Persse, trainer of the brilliant, unbeaten The Tetrarch and of the latter's son Tetratema and grandson Mr Jinks, both winners of the 2,000 Guineas.
(*National Horseracing Museum*)

The Choice of a Broodmare

I believe, if strictly adhered to, the following hints may be depended on as offering the greatest amount of safety in the choice of brood-mares:

1. To buy, without exception, mares from the best strains of blood only, more regard being had to the dam even than to the sire.

2. To bear in mind that a good pedigree alone is not sufficient, because the best-bred mare may be unsound; (I thought that by the acquisition of the own sisters to Gladiateur and Vermout, although neither had done anything remarkable on the turf, I had made sure of an enormous success; but both turned out unsound and worthless at the stud); to be, therefore, particular to buy from the best strains of blood such mares only as have

(a) themselves exhibited some form on the turf, and only on account of insufficient age not yet been tried at the stud, or have

(b) already bred winners, and thereby proved themselves sound dams and fit to propagate the excellent qualities of their respective families.

As a matter of course, of the mares coming within the limits of the foregoing conditions, the most powerful and truthfully made will be preferred; but no consideration of the exterior, however prepossessing it may be, if not accompanied by those requisite attributes, should be allowed to prevail, for there is no more bane-ful, no more certain hereditary evil than unsoundness – especially rheumatic or scrofulous disorders.

I am well aware that with regard to no. 2, and especially sub-division (a), I shall meet with vehement opposition, and that a number of instances to the contrary will be cited. They are not unknown to me, but I adhere to my own opinion, for the following reasons:

When I require in a young mare intended for stud purposes individual performances, I do not mean to say that I would not buy one that had not, on a given number of occasions, been first past the post.

Although I value racing form as such very highly, yet do I consider it of still greater importance that a mare should have proved, by repeated running, even if not attended by eminent success, that no unsoundness of limbs, no organic disease or defect of temper prevented her bearing the strain of training and racing.

I know perfectly well that in numerous instances, thoroughly sound animals with a good temper and all the necessary qualities for racing, through no fault of theirs, but in consequence of a mere accident, have been kept from appearing in public (absolute certainty in that respect can, however, only be acquired by personal superintendence of their training); but I know equally well that in nine cases in every ten, unsoundness, weakness or temper, have been the cause. It is advisable to rely on the Racing Calendar alone, and not believe a word of the fictitious marvels told of the innumerable mares without public form.

It will, no doubt, be argued, that there are many roarers to be found in France, although in that country two-year-olds do not run before 1 August, and the distances in races for horses above that age are twice as long as in England. It is true there are a good many roarers in France *now*, but the disease was imported from England, and has spread with the greatly enhanced prices of yearlings, caused by the vast increase in the demand for racing material.

Based on and caused by the rapid growth of racing in France, a great number of studs, principally breeding for the yearling market, have sprung into existence, carrying on wholesale production by means of unsound mares, imported from England by the dozen at £50 a piece and even less. Twenty years ago there was scarcely any roarers in France, but also no studs breeding for sale.

I am well aware that at present many public breeders may point to certain private studs, producing as many roarers as themselves or more. But I think this does not much shake my argument. No doubt a certain number of select studs breeding first-class yearlings for sale, as for instance the Blankney Stud and some others, contribute just as much to the improvement of the breed as the best private studs; but what I mean to say is, that the overgrowth of public studs, in comparison to home breeding, softens the thoroughbred race, through using too much weak, unsound, and altogether inferior material for the reproduction, and through forcing the foals too much with a view to the yearling market.

When the children or grandchildren of a stallion or a mare are mated, I call their produce *inbred*; but this term does not apply to the produce of great-grandchildren of the common ancestor. We must not forget that in the pedigrees of horses the word brother or sister often means half-brother or half-sister, and that here the definition borrowed from the human family connection is not applicable.

As breeding within *moderate relationship* I reckon the mating of stallion and mare that are removed from their common ancestor four, five, or six degrees. It is indifferent whether they are on both sides equidistant from, or one of them nearer to the male or female progenitor than the other.

The English breeder of the old school was of opinion that breeding from very closely related parents, even if possessed of the most excellent qualities, as a rule led to disappointing results; in isolated cases, however, to the production of individual animals of quite extraordinary capabilities; and on the whole I incline to that view myself.

Count Lehndorff (1883)

COUNT LEHNDORFF, *manager of the Imperial Stud in Germany, was one of the most famous names in horsebreeding in nineteenth-century Europe. His guiding precept for success in breeding was 'soundness'.*

The Training of Racehorses

When I first began training, horses went out to exercise smothered
in rugs and hoods, but in those days stables were kept very hot,
and were badly ventilated, and horses were much more liable to
colds and diseases than they are today. I can remember that when
Wishard, the American trainer, first came over to England we were
astonished to see his horses going out without a stitch of clothing
on them. We could not imagine how and why they looked so well.
I think there is a happy medium. Personally I am against much
clothing. If I have to take active exercise myself, I don't like to be
hampered with a greatcoat, either in cold weather or hot. Moreover, in hot weather I hate it, and it makes me irritable, but when
I have done my work then I do welcome a good warm coat, and
I do not see why horses should not have the same feelings. Anyhow,
it is on that principle that I train mine, and as soon as the weather
gets warm, about May, I have no clothing at all on my horses, but
a loose, comfortable, big sheet to put on after good work. You
sometimes get a big gross colt that it is impossible to get fit unless
you rug him up and make him sweat well every day. Hoods and
nightcaps, pretty as they look on a horse, I abominate, and it is as
bad as a man who always wears a muffler round his neck. It is an
old habit and custom which survives. It may have some advantages,
but I am hard put to it to think of them. It is certainly true that
few horses can be trained unless you get the pores of the skin well
open. If you cannot bring this about without clothing, then it must
be used. When training a horse for a long distance it is especially
necessary that he should sweat healthily after a long and fast
gallop. If there is a cold wind blowing, you should take particular
care to find a warm place out of the wind when you put the
clothing on after the gallop, otherwise the horse is liable to dry up
too quickly, and that may make him stiffen in his muscles. In the
early spring, when you get a nice warm day, a steady two-mile
gallop with sweaters on will often do a horse a lot of good. Another
thing to remember in long-distance training is not to let your horse

forget how to sprint. Occasionally give him a short sharp spin, but you must not send him with fast horses that cut him up, for that would probably upset him. After long work in hot weather it is very refreshing, and a good tonic for the legs, to play cold water on them through a hosepipe for ten minutes; the sand-bath also is of great value for horses in strong work, and once they take to this, they love it. I am a great believer in the sand-bath. I have a covered one, as well as two in the open, for in our climate the open one is often impossible to use. It always requires a considerable amount of trouble and patience in the early part of the season to get the two-year-olds to roll, sometimes even to get them on to the bed. Morning after morning you take them to it, and there is nothing doing, and you begin almost to despair, but in the end it nearly always comes off, and you will see them waiting their turn with the greatest impatience. At the same time I have had some horses, and some very good ones, who would never take to it. The sand-bath has another good point: if you are training a horse very hard, and he happens to be a good roller, and after a real good gallop he will not go down, or if he does he will not roll properly, you can be sure you have overdone it. In fact, at any time if a horse that likes his bath won't roll you will generally find there is something amiss.

The difficulty of training a horse for a long race lies in giving him the necessary work without getting him stale and bored with it. Two good gallops a week are enough for ninety-nine horses out of a hundred, and if you make Wednesday and Saturday your galloping days, on the Thursday and Sunday you can give the horse a quiet day on the road away from the training grounds. He will generally show you in the stable what effect the work is having. If he is eating up and shouting for more, you can as a rule go safely on, even increase the work, but the moment he fights shy of his manger, then you must ease off. Some horses when in strong work will not always eat up in the daytime; too much importance should not be attached to this, but if a horse leaves his corn at night it is a clear danger-signal; also, if a horse is restless in his stable before going out to work, it means that he is uneasy in his mind and thinking too much about it. To do well, man or beast must be happy and contented. On a day when you have some easy work to do try in every way possible to make it a pleasant day for the horses. Let them have a long steady canter, ten or twelve at a time, and when they pull up let them stand about and pick grass with the men off their backs, and then keep them away from the galloping grounds.

The first thing of all is to have a good head lad and good men. A rough, bad-tempered man can ruin a sensitive horse in a week. When your yearlings come up and you have had time to learn something about their characters, then make a careful selection from your boys before you settle who is to do each horse. With all the good will in the world some stablemen are far better than others, and nearly every stable will have four or five men who can do anything with their horses. I am not talking of the riding, but of how the horses are looked after in the stable, and no one but a trainer will believe the enormous difference there is between the good stableman and the moderate one. I am not a strict disciplinarian myself, and I am not fond of finding fault. I like to look over and forgive mistakes if a man means well, but there are certain things I will not tolerate. If I find a man ill-treating his horse he will never have the chance to do it again in my stable. I will not have any noise or roughness, and if I see a man 'jobbing' his horse in the mouth, or hitting him, unless he has been told to do so, there is trouble. Bad language, either in or out of the stable, I hate. Horses are very sensitive to sound, and a rough harsh voice upsets them far more than people think. I am fortunate in having many men in my stable who have been with me since they were small boys, and they set a good example to the younger ones. We are all good friends, and consequently things run smoothly. You must be on good terms with your men if you want them to work well for you, and when you have a good time see that they participate.

The feeding and management of horses in a stable is, of course, one of the most important parts of training, and this to a great extent can only be learnt by experience. The first thing you have to study in a horse is his stomach, and unless that is kept in good order nothing else will go right. With ordinary care and observation it is easy to find out when the stomach is wrong, but it is not so easy to put it right. The inside of a horse is a complex and delicate machine, and gets out of order very easily. Apply ordinary common sense to these troubles and you may very likely do the right thing, but experience in the curious constitution of the horse is the only real guide. A young man by keeping his eyes and ears open will learn it better than from books. When in doubt, let him go to his veterinary surgeon, if he has a good one. Don't be afraid of any amount of fresh air in the stable, but a draught is fatal. If you find your stable unclean and smelling, then is the time to have some words with your head man – there is no excuse for this. Give your horses the best oats, straw, and hay that can be bought, and if you are not an expert in these things yourself, employ someone who is, to buy them for you.

I hate the use of double rack chains. Horses certainly look well with these old-fashioned appliances, but I am sure they tend to make them irritable. Also I never allow my colts to stand tied up a moment longer than is absolutely necessary when alone, for it is at this time that they are inclined to show of what sex they are, and that is the beginning of a stable vice which is nearly always the complete ruin of the horse. When the owner comes round with his friends for evening stables it is often very late before the inspection is over, and the horses are kept waiting a long time for their evening feed. This they do not like, and become very impatient and irritable. I have found it a good plan to let my man go round and feed the horses, beginning with those that are to be looked at last. Then the owner and his friends can stand and look at their cracks as long as they like, and have an argument about politics or anything else. The horse with his head in the manger doesn't care a hang. But this cannot be done when a horse is tied up with double rack chains.

With regard to the hours of exercise, I think every horse should be out for at least two hours in the morning, except on the days after a very hard gallop, when one hour's walking about will be sufficient. I like my horses to get out as soon as it is light. In the summer I think it is a great advantage to be out as early as you can. For one thing, the turf has a spring and elasticity in the early morning which it loses later on when the sun has been on it. The dew, too, is very pleasant and refreshing to the horses' feet. Then also it makes it easy to have the horses out in the evening for about thirty-five minutes before evening stables. Those that are quiet enough should be led. Walk them about for fifteen minutes, and then let them stroll about, picking grass.

I have not attempted to enter into all the technical details of training – as I say, these must be learnt from experience and observation – but I have tried to show some simple and common-sense methods which I have myself found useful. And I will finish with the warning: let no trainer think that he knows all that is worth knowing. There is always something more to be learnt.

                                        The Hon. George Lambton (1928)

Lambton first made a name on the Turf as an amateur rider, his many victories including the National Hunt 'chase and the Grand Steeplechase de Paris. On giving up race riding he gained even greater repute as a trainer to the seventeenth Earl of Derby, for whom he sent out innumerable important winners, among them the Derby winners Sansovino and Hyperion. The connection was severed eventually, and in the last few years of his life, until he died aged eighty-five in 1945, Lambton operated as a public trainer.

This very brief extract from Lambton's extensive treatise on training contains all the wisdom of experience and a wonderful understanding of men and horses.

———

Training

Good trainers, like good wives, are born, not made.

Without natural flair it is far better to keep away from racing stables and to run a garage, for no amount of teaching will transform a horseman into a trainer of horses.

Moreover, there is more scope for the man who looks after cars than after horses nowadays; and, judging by the expenses attaching to training, there is likely to be still less opportunity for trainers in the future.

Though it may be many generations before the racehorse follows his almost vanished relative the cavalry horse into extinction, I do not think there is likelihood of a great increase in the number of Flat-race trainers, for there are already about 300 in the country.

But if anyone is determined to enter a calling which provides such limited scope I would say to him at the start that he must be a close observer of detail, able to understand thoroughly the subject of feeding, have a quick eye to notice a horse's progress and to spot instantly anything wrong.

I am not suggesting that a horse must be fussed over like a hen with one chick or a mother with one infant, though I have known trainers so to coddle their charges that they would even weigh them every week to see just how they were doing, just as a proud nurse might weigh a royal baby. This may be an excellent way of reassuring oneself if one has doubts; but, to my mind, if a trainer cannot tell how his charge is getting along by giving him the once-over he is not born to his job.

These are difficult times for racehorse trainers. It seems to be the general experience nowadays to find horses nothing like so robust as they were fifty years ago; and for this I blame the long-continued practice of inbreeding.

In the old days – how we love to talk about them – horses stood plenty of work and rarely went off their feed. But nowadays, alas! a trainer goes round stables in fear and trembling, because he expects to find that a number of his charges have failed to 'eat up'. Nevertheless it is during those regular watchful visits to the boxes at night that the best work in training is done. No man who relaxes his vigilance on the nightly round can ever make a trainer.

Very well then! Assuming that you have decided to enter our tiny corporation with hopes of the Derby, the other Classics and the cups in your mind, you will very soon find your way to the sales, expecting to pick up a few yearlings who, looking like the proverbial ugly duckling, will win you fame and fortune as they lead many a field past the winning-post. And here you will need a good eye if you have got one, and, what is still more useful, all the luck that you can command. Buying a yearling either privately or at a sale is very much of a gamble, for the element of luck takes such prominence in the picture, as it does in most things we do in

horse-racing. There is no guarantee of soundness given with a
yearling and so you have to take much on trust. It is not like
buying a car, which the manufacturer keeps in good condition free
of charge for six months. Twice at an auction have I picked a
good-looking yearling who, when he arrived home, proved to be
a 'roarer'.

It is fashionable to pay large sums nowadays for yearlings, but
I much prefer to buy three or four for £5,000, than to pay that
sum for one. Many good and quite fashionably bred yearlings can
be bought for 200 guineas or less with quite a good chance of
winning races. Yet such is the rage in these times for the ultra-
fashionable that I have seen what I considered misshapen animals,
unlikely ever to see a racecourse, quickly bought up for enormous
prices, usually to their new owners' sorrow.

In buying a yearling first of all look up the dam's pedigree. If
she has been a good winner herself or has produced winners, and
having satisfied yourself as to this, provided you like the appearance of her youngster, you are entitled to take a chance on him
(or her), even if not the progeny of a fashionable sire of the day.
I always prefer such a yearling than one by a fashionable sire out
of a mare who has no credentials herself or who has not come
from a good mare. It is a fact that really good mares nearly always
reproduce themselves, although they may miss a generation or so.
It is my experience that a good horse usually comes from a good
tap-root on the dam's side, the exception, of course, proving the
rule. The same remark also applies to sires. Personally I would
never use a stallion who came from a badly bred mare on the
dam's side, no matter how good a racehorse he may have been.
This dictum has been proved time and time again.

Take, for instance, the case of The White Knight. He was a
smashing good racehorse, but he derived his excellence from his
sire, Desmond. His dam Pella was a common-bred and very moderate steeplechaser, and she bred two moderate animals both of
which I rode, and on one of them I won a small 'chase. She was
put to Desmond, the result being The White Knight, who was a
dismal failure at the stud.

But to go back to the purchase of yearlings. The first thing one should look at is the head. I never like to buy one with a bad head and especially one with small prick ears. By a bad head I mean one with a small pig-eye or receding forehead, the kind of characteristics you dislike in a man. I prefer a wide forehead, a good large, bold, even bad, eye and good long ears; anyway they should not be short. Small ears may be all right on a Hollywood star but not on a racehorse. I have never yet trained a horse with short prick ears and a pig-eye that was not a rogue.

The next point I look at is the hind leg, which I like to see good and strong; and the straighter it is the better. I would never buy a yearling with a weak hind leg or a sickle hock.

If satisfied with the head and hind leg you can forgive a multitude of sins elsewhere. Yet I look for a horse with a good sloping shoulder and with forelegs that are not back of the knee, as such a one is generally difficult to train, the strain on his tendons being too severe. But a horse that stands over or one that is known as baker-kneed very seldom breaks down.

These, I think, are the main points to look at when buying a yearling. There is, however, a good old saying that they run in all makes and shapes, and so the man who buys blind sometimes gets value for his money, occasionally an astoundingly rich prize. For who has not heard stories of great horses that have been throwouts at the sales, or have been bought out of the shafts of a trap, and when put to the racing game have astonished the world? But if one is going to buy recklessly in the hope of picking up one of these rare birds one will squander as much money as some folks squander on crosswords before they win a gambler's prize.

Many yearlings come to the sales so overloaded with fat that their true nature is difficult to discover. In a couple of months when the fat has been worked off they are hardly recognizable as the sleek, fat animal of a few weeks ago.

Some people have an idea that if one has an old mare she should be put to a young stallion or that an old stallion will do better with a young mare. I do not think this to be correct, for statistics rather incline to show that yearlings bred from parents of about the same age are the most successful.

The man who buys yearlings must be on good terms with his

bank manager. Some years ago a friend of mine found himself overdrawn at his bank up to the limit. He was a good trainer, but nevertheless his bank manager was not inclined to give him a larger overdraft. The manager asked my friend to call on him and, when he did so, warned him to be very careful in future.

It did not seem to have made much impression on the trainer, who straightway proceeded to Ireland and began buying yearlings there at the sales, at prices ranging from £50 to £300 apiece. Having bought ten, he then realized that he had no money to pay for them. So he sent a diplomatic wire to his bank manager saying: 'I have bought you ten nice yearlings. Hope you will like them.'

The manager was a sport. He dared not allow my friend to overdraw any more, so he put up part of the purchase money from his own private account. Fortunately for the bank manager that little flutter in horseflesh was well rewarded, as nearly every one of those ten animals turned out a good horse, one of them a first-class winner worth at least £10,000.

The Day's Work

And now let us get on to more practical matters – the day's work and the actual training of horses, which are our real theme.

As to the daily routine of training, when the head lad has got the string ready they file out singly and walk round in a circle until the trainer takes over. As the trainer does so he receives from the head lad a list of the animals that have not fed and any other necessary information as to their well-being.

Having carefully scrutinized the horses as they circle round, the trainer then trots them to see if all are sound. When he is satisfied, which is usually about three-quarters of an hour after they have left the stables, he gives them their first canter. This is generally very slow for a distance of about three-quarters of a mile, and if possible up an incline. I like always to use the same cantering ground, as then the horses know they are not going to be jumped off for fast work, and so they do not get excited. I think it is never advisable to start off with fast work.

The canter over, then the real work of the day begins. The trainer picks out the first lot, which may vary from two to six horses, changes the riding boys, and then the animals. Then accompanied by the head lad, or someone reliable who knows just what to do, they go down to where they jump off. After the gallop they pull up and come straight back to the trainer, who runs his eye over them and notes their condition. Then the riding boys are put on another batch, and so the work continues until all is gone through.

Some horses require little, if any, training beyond sharp canters, and some excitable ones are better if worked by themselves. There is no hard-and-fast rule and the man who tries to make one will never become a successful trainer. When the work is done and the horses are safe back in their boxes they are dressed over, made comfortable and fed. Then the second lot, or, as they are called, 'the spares', are made ready, brought out, and the same routine gone through again. After 'the spares' are made comfortable and fed the boys go to their dinner and then rest or do whatever they like until four o'clock.

At this hour they go to their horses, tie them up, and report to the head man which of them has left, and the ones that have eaten up generally get what is known as a small 'standing' feed. Then the boys go to their tea and return to dress their horses over.

By 6.30 everything should be ready for the trainer's nightly inspection. Having ascertained which horses have 'left' he visits each in turn, notes how he looks, runs his hand over him and feels his legs carefully. This over, the horses are fed and shut up for the night.

Some trainers work differently from others – some work on Mondays, Wednesdays and Saturdays. As a rule my work-days are Tuesdays, Thursdays and Saturdays.

On Tuesdays I jump my two-year-olds off and come at a good three-parts speed for three or four furlongs. On Thursdays I let them come a bit steadier; but on Saturdays they come four furlongs fast. Yet these are not hard-and-fast rules, for, as I have said, some horses are better without so much work.

The great thing in training a two-year-old is to keep his speed, and if he loses it he must be rested at once. The trainer must always be watching to see that these youngsters do not get tired and that they keep their condition – always on their toes, full of fire, ready to jump off at any time and to come all the way required of them.

If they are going to get well away in their races horses must be carefully trained to jump off. To make them used to the gate, it is well to let them stand a good deal beside it. But I am not a believer in putting two-year-olds constantly under the gate; in fact I never put them under the tapes until about a fortnight before they run their first race. Then I let them stand still and watch it go up a number of times before asking them to jump through.

At this work I start them in company with one or, at the most, two two-year-olds, and a couple of older horses. Directly they have shown confidence in jumping away without pulling back, as the gate goes up, they are all right. Afterwards they need very little practice, and they need not be given it; for work at the gate excites the horses and sometimes spoils their temper. Yet, incredible though it may seem, I have actually seen batches of six or more yearlings being put to the gate as early as December, three months before Flat racing begins.

Secrecy as to a horses's chances in a race is incumbent upon a trainer if the owner is going to recoup his heavy outlay. But secrecy is not easily achieved. What with telephones, with tipsters hiding behind hedges, and in every fold of the ground, suborning one's employees, careless of the Corruption Act, it is almost impossible nowadays to keep the form of any horse quiet. I find that most of my boys know quite as much about the form of my two-year-olds as I do; some a great deal more; and that to their detriment. After he has spent a lot of money having his horse trained for a special event it is most exasperating for any owner to find that all the world knows everything about his form, and that he has to take a ridiculously short price for his money. However, nowadays it is practically impossible to keep anything quiet and so we must bow to the inevitable.

Yet sometimes I have contrived to veil the form of a good horse until the hour was ripe to reveal it to the world. I managed to do this with the first good horse I trained in England, who ran at Newmarket and won at 90–1. It beat the favourite, owned by the late Solly Joel, who rather lugubriously said to me afterwards: 'I suppose you didn't expect to win with that one?' To which I replied pacifically: 'I didn't expect to beat yours.'

A friend of mine managed, however, to get quite a respectable investment on the horse by starting-price wires, one of which went into the office of a certain well-known bookmaker in London. He too came to me afterwards saying that he supposed I had not got much money on that horse at 20–1 and so, to give him a pleasant journey home, I reassured him, knowing that when he got to his office he might have quite a shock. My fears for him were true. For he got such a shock that, so far as I am concerned, he has entirely lost his powers of speech. He has not spoken to me since! How sorely do some of us take the loss of a little matter of a few thousand pounds!

Every trainer knows it to be a great advantage to have a jockey ride a horse for a few times before he rides him in the race he is expected to win; for then the jockey knows the animal and is ready for any manifestation of eccentricity.

Given a jockey who knows the horse I have rarely had any difficulty in getting a two-year-old to run up to his true form the first time out.

Customs vary. Some trainers give their charges an easy race or two before asking them to come out and win. But to my mind, if a two-year-old is properly educated, there is no necessity for these easy preparatory races, as many of my two-year-olds have proved the first time out.

Trials

To the uninitiated, trials seem to be something easy of accomplishment; but to the experienced trainer they are difficult and often impracticable.

So often does one hear of the wonderful trials and of amazing results which, however, are never repeated in public. But I am now writing of the genuine trial, not of the mythical variety, spoken of with bated breath in the corner of the club smoking-room, or 'after dinner when we are all together', or 'of course it won't go any further'.

A trial never produces a certainty, though an approximation to the truth may be reached with a certain amount of accuracy. I have found two-year-old trials to be the most satisfactory, and the results come out more accurately in public than those with older horses. Two-year-olds are fresh to the game and so do all they can, whilst older animals need all the excitement of the racecourse to induce them to exert their utmost.

Furthermore, it is a far simpler job to try horses over five or six furlongs than over the longer distances. But in these short trials the great difficulty (unless one has experienced jockeys up) is to get stable lads to balance their horses before sitting down to send them along. If he is not properly balanced a horse can beat himself in a furlong. How often in a short race has one seen an experienced jockey sitting and suffering for as much as a couple of furlongs until one has given up all hope of his winning. Then the scene changes, for having got his horse nicely balanced at last he comes through to win.

The two greatest exponents of balancing whom I have seen were Carslake and the late Danny Maher. I have seen them win races by heads when some distance from home it has looked long odds against them. What a delightful jockey to watch was Danny Maher, and what a judge of pace. He always seemed to be part and parcel of a horse. But this is a divergence.

In trials I prefer all jockeys to be riding or else all stable lads. When I say stable lads I mean those who are constantly riding fast work and trials. But I am not keen to have a crack jockey riding against stable lads, for it means allowing for his greater experience.

In order to get a true result in short trials there must be no waiting about after the start. Once a horse is balanced he must come right through all the way.

In a short-distance trial if, as sometimes happens, they go no pace for the first 150 or 200 yards, then the course is appreciably shortened, and a non-stayer may get the journey, though he would have failed to do so had the race been run from end to end.

Many think that if a trainer has, say, twenty two-year-olds and wins a race with one of them he must know exactly how all the others stand with him. Nothing can be more fallacious.

Probably when your early two-year-old winner was fit to try

there were only two or three others fit to be tried with him. When the others have been made ready then those which were fit earlier on are now *hors de combat*.

It is wonderful how rumours get about. One has only to win with two or three two-year-olds off the reel when the next one produced must necessarily be at least ten pounds ahead of the last winner. The amount of nonsense that is talked and the ridiculous balderdash that is vouchsafed by professional tipsters to the unsuspecting public passes one's comprehension.

As I have said, a long-distance trial is a far harder proposition from which to get a result than a sprint. One must have at least four or five good horses all fit and well in the gallop, and they must come along fast from end to end. Then the various horses have to be ridden in the way that suits them best.

Giving orders to a bunch of jockeys in a trial is different from giving them just to one jockey in a race; there are so many more points for a harassed trainer to remember. Some horses have to be waited with; some go best when allowed to run along and not interfered with; and so on.

Again, many old horses will not do anything like their best at home – so, altogether, a home trial is not so easy as it looks in a newspaper. The best stayer I ever trained was Mr Raphael's Sanctum, who won the Cesarewitch in a canter. He was as great a horse at home as he was in public. I had in the stable another horse, called Aboukir, who was also very reliable at home. If I remember rightly, Aboukir, in the Cesarewitch, was set to give Sanctum 10 lb. I tried them together with some others and set Sanctum to give Aboukir 14 lb. over 2¼ miles.

This he did in a hack canter. As Aboukir, at the weights, would have had a good outside chance, it is obvious that Sanctum, as the saying goes, was a pretty good thing to job with. Had he not met with an accident which finished his racing career he would have been a certain Ascot Gold Cup winner. In the spring following his Cesarewitch win a two-year-old got loose and came at full speed towards the string, hitting Sanctum amidships and knocking him down. His back was hurt, and although every kind of remedy was tried he was never right again.

Some horses have to be dead fit or else they will not show anything like their real form at home. Apelle and Twelve Pointer were rather typical examples of this. Unless they were really fit they would soon begin to tire and refuse to do anything. When first I got Apelle to train I thought that, as the saying goes, I had caught a lobster. One day when I had him, as I thought, going fairly straight, I slipped him along a good mile, but without going top speed. Imagine my surprise when, a couple of furlongs from home, he began to drop out, with his head turned round and his ears back, as though to say: 'Thanks very much, but I do not want any more of that!'

He blew a lot and so, in a couple of days, I gave him another similar spin. He went much better, so I continued the treatment, and in a few weeks he was totally different. He finished his gallops with his ears pricked and no gamer horse ever looked through a bridle.

Another difficulty in trying a horse is to make the lads tell afterwards any little thing that may have escaped the trainer's notice. No matter how carefully one may watch a trial something is sure to happen, at the beginning or somewhere in the gallop, that the trainer has not seen, which may have militated against the horse's chance.

The riders do not like to admit that anything went wrong with their mount for fear they may be blamed, which is of course foolish, as no trainer would be so silly as to blame a boy for getting crossed at the start, for his horse stumbling, or getting shut in, which are some of the many episodes that occur in a trial.

Then there is the going – one may try a horse in good going, yet he may have to race on ground which is very heavy or very hard, and these things make all the difference. If all trials could be relied upon to produce the same result in public then the book-makers' profits would be considerably curtailed – although I am always being told that, as things now are, they very seldom make money. Nevertheless they seem to get on very well. Just as most other people do who say they never make anything.

H. S. Persse (1940)

H. S. (Atty) Persse (1869–1960)

A top amateur rider under N.H. Rules and a MFH in Ireland, Persse reached equal fame as a trainer, most notably through the unbeaten The Tetrarch, the latter's son Tetratema and Mr Jinks (by Tetratema). An expert in producing two-year-olds to win first time out, his skill was by no means confined to sprinters since he also trained a Cesarewitch winner, Sanctum, bringing off a spectacular gamble.

Although Atty Persse and George Lambton were contemporaries, in outlook, method and character they were markedly different. It was therefore thought relevant to include the views of both these great trainers.

———

Breeding to Win the Derby

Peter Burrell in a discussion with Kenneth Harris (1970)

KENNETH HARRIS: *If I were coming into racing completely from scratch – no horses, no commitments, but plenty of money – and I wanted to win the Derby, to which breeder should I go to buy the horse?*

PETER BURRELL: Well, you wouldn't have a great deal of choice, really, assuming that you wanted to buy a yearling in this country. Of the studs breeding for sale there are only half a dozen or so to which it would be worth your while going. Breeding a horse to win the Derby is such a frightfully difficult undertaking that only a few people are sufficiently wealthy and dedicated to risk the outlay necessary to do it.

KH: *But the Derby is such a world-famous and sought-after race, and the requirements for winning it have become so well known over a great many years, you would think that even though it may be difficult to breed the winner, there would be plenty of people chancing their arm at producing the kind of horse that might win.*

PB: No. On the contrary, years of breeding experience show that it is exceptionally difficult to produce a horse that might win the Derby, that would be up there in the last furlong with a real chance

of winning in an average year. It is not just difficult in the sense
of the money, and the technique, and all the other resources which
you have to invest; it is the degree to which luck is going to come
into it, the odds that are against you. I reckon that it takes at least
300 horses with the breeding to win the Derby to produce one
which is actually capable of winning it.

KH: *But why should it be so difficult to breed a Derby winner?*
PB: Because the Derby distance and course require a very special
kind of horse. It is the distance, really, I think, that is so crucial.
The nub of it is this: it is comparatively easy to produce horses
that can go really fast for distances up to a mile, even up to a mile
and a quarter. It is also comparatively easy to produce horses
which will stay distances of two miles or more at a good pace. But
what you are asking here in a Derby winner is a horse who can
go very fast for more than a mile and a quarter. A good Derby
winner can sprint and can stay a mile and a half. You are asking,
therefore, for a very special, a very peculiar type of animal.

Now this is where natural processes insist on coming into the
breeding process. With all animals nature is always trying to produce a norm. When the breeder mates a sire and a dam whose
combined qualities give him the peculiar progeny he requires to
win the Derby, nature, as usual, steps in and tries to arrange that
the progeny are not peculiar but revert to normal type. This is the
probable reason for the disappointing results from mating Derby
winners with Oaks winners. A possible method of breeding for the
Derby would be to put a sprinting mare, let us say, to a staying
stallion, hoping to produce a great intermediate. The records show
that overwhelmingly the chances are that those two animals will
produce stayers like the sire, sprinters like the mother, or something
not very conspicuous between.

I could give you the technical and scientific explanation of that,
if you like, but what it comes down to, as I have said, is that in
your quest for a Derby horse, which is in a sense a freak horse,
nature is working not with you, but against you. This is the process
known as 'retrogression to the mean'. Don't forget, I am talking
now of the difficulty in producing a horse that might win the

Derby. Given breeding promising enough for a yearling to be entered for the Derby, the odds against that, as I said, are in my view 300–1. Then you have to multiply those odds by the chances of the animal standing training, and then having the luck and good jockeyship to win the race. So there is nothing strange about how few breeders there are in this country who could provide you with a Derby yearling in the first place.

KH: *I would like to ask you in a minute why, if the Derby is so discouraging to breeders trying to produce the right horse for it, we make such a fuss about the race? But before that, can you tell me why one horse should be a sprinter and another so markedly a stayer? And why there seems this peculiar magic about a mile and a quarter as the distance which differentiates them?*

PB: Well, of course, the distances and the terms you use in relation to them, like sprinter and stayer, are all relative, and there are a large number that rank as middle-distance horses. But it is true that there is a difference in the physical make-up of a horse that sprints, and the horse that does not go fast, but stays. As a matter of fact, if it were possible for you to dissect a yearling and examine his cellular tissues, you could determine whether he was going to develop into a pure sprinter or a pure stayer, although many would fall into an intermediate class. The key to whether a horse sprints or stays is the point in the duration of his effort at which muscle fatigue develops.

A horse may produce enormous effort, but in a short space of time incur muscle fatigue. Another horse may not produce so great an effort – I mean output of energy, in terms of covering the ground – but can keep it up a much longer time without muscle fatigue developing. One horse develops fatigue relatively early, the other relatively late, because the formation of the muscle is different – the shape of the cells is different, even the colour of the cells is different. Once muscle fatigue develops, the horse slows up, feels discomfort, even pain – he has to stop. One of the most usual purposes of dope, incidentally, is to deaden the pain so that a horse will continue his effort beyond normal.

Any animal by nature will race at the rate of output of energy that his muscular formation, his cellular tissues, if you like, makes natural to him. Training, and riding tactics in the race itself, can obviously modify his natural tendencies, but no trainer or jockey can prevent muscular fatigue developing when the horse has been making his effort long enough for his particular type of physique to bring it about.

KH: *Now can I bring you back to the other question – if the Derby is in a sense a race requiring the breeding of a freak to win it, why extol it as the greatest race in the world?*

PB: We must be clear what we mean by this word freak. I agree a Derby winner is a freak in the sense that it is frightfully difficult to breed him, because of the peculiar requirements of the race, and because nature tries to thwart you when you try and get something out of the ordinary. But a Derby winner is not a freak in the sense of being inferior, eccentric or undesirable. On the contrary, the great majority of Derby winners are extremely remarkable horses. In human terms, great men, great athletes, are freaks in the sense that there aren't many of them; but not in the sense that they are undesirable.

But you have a point there. There is nothing sacrosanct, or definitive, or be-all-and-end-all about the Derby. It has been the most famous race for many, many years, and there it is because it is, so to speak, and everybody with a chance tries to win it. And, as I said earlier, the handful of dedicated and wealthy people try to breed to win it. There was certainly no point in the history of racing or breeding at which somebody said, 'Now let's think out the ideal race in terms of distance and course and call it this or that,' and came up with the idea of one and a half miles at Epsom.

KH: *What I am getting at is this: if your most famous race requires from its potential winners a continual contest between the breeder on the one hand and nature on the other, isn't there likely to be a considerable distortion of the country's breeding policy as a whole?*

PB: There is something in that. If you could wave a magic wand and somehow not have the Derby as your great race, the question would arise what race you would put in its stead. Taking things as they are today certainly it would make more sense if your great race were run at a mile and a quarter. You can breed horses to go a mile and a quarter at more or less top speed without feeling that the odds are prohibitively against you.

It is not just a matter of the odds being against you. The economics of racing today still very much favour the breeding and racing of sprinters. And because prize-money is much better abroad, the top-class horses we produce here, and the top-class middle-distance blood, is sought by foreign buyers, who come here, bid up the prices, and consequently make it much more difficult for people who live here to compete with them. So the vicious circle is perpetuated. More and more we go in for sprinters, and less and less can we afford to break out and breed from the top-class middle-distance horses.

There is not at the moment enough material to breed from in this country to produce enough potential Derby winners to fend off the challenge from abroad. I told you I thought you needed to produce at least 300 Derby-type horses to give you one potential winner. We aren't doing it. There are not enough horses of the right type to do it. The best stuff is going abroad. Look at the December sales at Newmarket last year. Ninety per cent of the best lots went overseas.

KH: *What is to be done about it?*
PB: Well, obtaining Derby-type horses would obviously be much less chancy if there were many more horses around in the desired category worth breeding from. This means more prize-money in this country for the kind of races those horses can win. This gets us back, I think, to the problem which affects racing in many other respects – how can more of the money that is being pumped into racing by the punter and the racegoer be diverted to benefit racing as a whole? There is a great deal of argument, as you know, about the desirability of a tax on betting, or of some scheme whereby bookmakers would have to put back a proportion of their profits, and there are the arguments for a Tote monopoly. I don't suppose you want to go into those, but in a way they are very much involved in your original question about how to set about buying a Derby winner, for the simple reason that unless more money is

available for raising the general level of prizes soon, there won't even be half a dozen studs you can go to buy your yearling.

KH: *One last question. Let us suppose you yourself had unlimited resources for starting a stud to breed a Derby winner. If you had to choose a single formula, how would you set to work?*

PB: My formula would be to collect a very large number of speedy mares, mares who had gone really fast up to a mile, and mate them with Classic winners which are proved stallions. You have got to have the two things, the speed and the stamina, so you have got to put them in, and experience shows that it is best to put in your speed through the dam and your staying qualities through the sire. It does not seem to work if you do it the other way around – sprinting blood then seems to be dominant. You might take me up on this and say that a number of recent Derby winners are out of mares which showed little or no form, but I think these were cases of ability lying dormant for one generation – that's nothing exceptional.

But talking of exceptions, let me remind you that if you want to you can always find exceptions to tear my formula, or anybody else's, to pieces, and even if I had the unlimited resources for breeding a Derby winner with which you invested me when you put this question, I would be mad if I guaranteed the results of my efforts. However, I don't think that alters the general point. And it certainly doesn't alter the fact that unless the economics of racing are very much improved, particularly in terms of the increase in the general level of prize-money, there may come a day when breeding Derby winners in Britain is no longer on for anybody.

In 1963 PETER BURRELL *as Director, was charged with the responsibility for setting up the National Stud on Jockey Club land outside Newmarket, following its move from Gillingham in Dorset. The stud that Burrell created is an example of vision, planning and layout at its best.*

After the Derby was run at Epsom on 7 June 1989, it had taken place on 210 occasions (including wartime substitutes), and a total of 148 individuals had owned a Derby winner. Statistically,

*it is probably a lot less difficult to accomplish a major pools win
– and far easier to get gored to death by a bull than to win a
Derby. It would be very hard to find a more lucid discussion on
a subject which has absorbed owners and breeders for more than
200 years; success has long been recognized as the pinnacle of
achievement in racing. Millions of pounds have been spent in
reaching that pinnacle – and in failing to reach it.*

*It is still, of course, possible to breed a Derby winner in England
but increasingly difficult for an English owner to do so.*

*In 1986, Faraway Dancer (USA), bred by Burrell, came within
three lengths of providing his owner-breeder with a Derby winner.
He finished fourth to Shahrastani and the unlucky Dancing Brave.*

———

Some Thoughts on Racing and Breeding

An Introduction by Sir Noël Murless to 'The Golden Post'
In 1946, when I had my first good year (thirty-four winners) as a
relatively young trainer in the north of England, Lord Derby's
stallion Hyperion had been at stud for eleven years, with eight
crops of three-year-olds at the racecourse.

He had just become England's leading stallion for the fifth time,
having also been second on the list twice, to Fairway in 1939 and
1944. He had sired the Classic-winning fillies Sun Stream, Sun Chariot,
Hypericum, Godiva and Hycilla; and the Classic-winning colts Sun
Castle and Owen Tudor. His son Hippius had won the Champion
Stakes twice, and Hyperion now had 185 winners to his credit.

He had also sired the top miler Khaled (sire of Swaps), Alibhai
(the grandsire of Kelso), and within a few months he would also
have sired Aristophanes, sire of Forli, grandsire of Forego. At this
time Hyperion's stud fee was 400 guineas, which is of course, at
the current rate of international exchange, about $500. A sum of
money which I well remember being considered on the high side.

In rather sharp contrast I noticed that it would cost Ir£125,000
(about $110,000) to breed to Sadler's Wells, the gallant and well-
bred son of Northern Dancer, and the winner of the 1984 Irish

Two Thousand Guineas, the Phoenix Stakes and the Eclipse Stakes (all Group 1 races).

And while I do realize that inflation has caused many commodities to go up by twenty or thirty times since 1946, it has caused nothing else to go up by over 200 times, except certain racehorses, usually untried yearlings and untested stallions. And I wonder how good an idea all of this is for the breed, or indeed whither it will all lead.

I mention Hyperion because he was not only an outstanding winner of the Derby, but because he was also the maternal grandsire of Nearctic, and according to that wisest of modern stallionmasters, the late Joe Thomas of Windfields Farm, Hyperion was the dominant influence in the pedigree of Northern Dancer, who was about the same diminutive size as himself, as are many of this most fashionable breed of feisty little runners.

Also Hyperion figured uncannily often in the pedigrees of many of the best horses I trained. Indeed he was a near ancestor of two of my three Derby winners, and four of my five Oaks winners. He was the grandsire of Abernant, the fastest horse I ever saw, never mind trained, and he was the great-grandsire of one of my Eclipse Stakes winners, Connaught, who chased home Sir Ivor in the 1968 Derby. He was also the great-grandsire of Hill Shade, the dam of the last champion I trained, J. O. Tobin, England's leading juvenile of 1976.

Curiously it was this latter sire line which led me to a long friendship with Richard Stone Reeves, the perfectly delightful American painter. My principal American owner, George Pope – he owned Hyperion's great-grandson Decidedly, winner of the 1962 Kentucky Derby – once showed me a lovely painting Dick had done for him of Hillary, sire of Hill Shade. And I resolved then that here was the artist who would paint for me the horses that seemed worthy of such exquisite attention. I thought then, as I think now, that his best work is the best there is.

The first painting Dick did for me was of my wife's filly Caergwrle, who won the One Thousand Guineas in 1968. He posed her down at the rubbing house on Newmarket Heath, in the place where George Stubbs had painted her faraway ancestor, Eclipse,

199 years previously. She was a lovely filly, Caergwrle, and we bred her dam, and her granddam, and soon she will visit Ardross, the superb staying horse who was beaten a head in the 1982 Arc de Triomphe. He was a hard-raced six year old at the time, and I am delighted to see that he figures prominently in this book.

Caergwrle won the fillies' one-mile Classic at Newmarket seventeen years ago now, and sometimes it seems to us like last month. And yet, in terms of change in the bloodstock industry, it was a lifetime ago. This new volume, written by Dick Reeves' long-time publisher and author, Patrick Robinson, is a timely reminder to all of us just how severely things have changed.

The recurring theme throughout the book is the startling values placed on young racehorses – $10 million here, $20 million there, $30 million somewhere else. My goodness, the first two home in the Derby this year, Secreto and El Gran Senor, are valued at something like $60 million, and neither one of them was sound enough to run one step in competition after the June of their three-year-old season.

Personally, my own policy, both as a trainer, a breeder and as manager of Sir Victor Sassoon's stud, was to ensure that *none* of our horses were given inflated values because I always tried to run them again at four. Never having had the slightest inclination to breed to unsound stallions myself, neither did I wish my clients to do so. To this day I seldom breed to a stallion who did not race beyond the age of three.

I am afraid that the modern policy of breeding for money, rather than for the quality of future runners, would probably prove beyond my comprehension now. My conversations used to revolve round breeding a mare to a certain stallion, and the myriad of reasons why this mating might throw a Classic horse. Today they breed because the ensuing yearling might fetch a million at the sales.

I suppose I may be considered by some people to be eccentric in my choice of Ardross, the long-distance Cup horse, for our Classic-winning miler. But I am not trying to earn a fortune at the sales, I am trying to acquire the toughness, the gallantry, the soundness and the quality of Ardross, and put it to the speed of Caergwrle.

It might however be worth noting that both Northern Dancer and Bold Ruler have Nearco as a grandsire, and he went almost two miles in the highest company, as did Ribot. Hyperion himself was prepared for, and ran in, the Ascot Gold Cup. Indeed Man O' War, Kelso, Princequillo, Citation, Nashua, Damascus and Buckpasser all won over two miles at the highest level. I should not have been surprised if any of those American horses had won the Ascot Gold Cup, as Ardross did, twice. I rather like staying horses.

In some ways the modern passion for lightly raced speed is taking the breed down a dangerous path, and I do not envy would-be breeders the millions they are currently spending. In fact I am scarcely able to think of the days when I used to buy yearlings. I once bought a couple of St Leger winners, Ridge Wood and Aurelius, for a total of 7,000 guineas. The latter won the Hardwicke Stakes at Royal Ascot at four. My first two-time Royal Ascot winner Oros – he beat the great stallion Petition in his second triumph at the meeting – cost me 250 guineas.

I could have bought England's 1967 Horse of the Year, Busted, for £5,000, at the end of his three-year-old season. And since I did train this grand racehorse at four, you may be amused to learn how this came to be. Well, it was 1966, on the day of the Irish Derby. I was at the little Surrey racecourse of Lingfield Park watching the big race at the Curragh on the television when I noticed a front-running bay colt going, to my eye, very fast indeed. He faded out of the picture in the end, but I made a note of him as a possible lead horse for my best two-year-old Royal Palace, for whom I had Classic hopes the following year.

The trouble was, the fast Irish horse, Busted, was owned by Mr Stanhope Joel, the cousin of Royal Palace's owner, Jim Joel, and I thought it prudent not to buy him, from one, for the other, just in case I managed to improve him a bit.

By the end of the season he had run unplaced in the Irish Cambridgeshire, and I did ask Stanhope what he planned to do with the colt. 'Well, I was considering cutting him and sending him jumping,' he replied.

'Christ!' I said. 'You'd better not do that.' And I suggested he send him to me for a year, which really worked out very well. Busted led Royal Palace in his early work, and in the Two Thousand Guineas Royal Palace got up to beat Taj Dewan by a neck. He then won the Derby. Busted himself won the Coronation Stakes, the Eclipse Stakes, the King George VI and Queen Elizabeth Stakes, and the Prix Foy at Longchamp. He was never beaten at four, and in 1968 you could have bred a mare to him for less than $5,000.

It was a very good year for me, 1967, because in addition to all of the aforementioned, Fleet won the One Thousand Guineas, my wife's home-bred St Chad won the Jersey Stakes at Royal Ascot and the Wills Mile at Goodwood; and Sucaryl also won at Ascot and Goodwood as well as going down by a half-length to Ribocco in the Irish Derby. This was all particularly gratifying since I had trained St Paddy, the sire of both Connaught and Sucaryl, to win the Derby and the St Leger, and indeed I had arranged the breeding of Sucaryl for Sir Victor Sassoon.

That was a wonderful year for me and my home-breds, and it did make me the leading trainer in England for the sixth time, an honour I was lucky enough to attain three times more before I retired. But, curiously, by then – I was fifty-seven years old – I had already been associated with, and seen the retirement of, the four 'great ones' I was privileged to work with.

The first was the flying grey sprinter Abernant by Hyperion's son Owen Tudor, out of Rustom Mahal, out of Mumtaz Mahal. He won four important two-year-old stakes races, and at three he was just beaten a short head by Nimbus in the Two Thousand Guineas. It was the first photo-finish ever, in an English Classic, and it showed Abernant not quite lasting out this testing Newmarket mile. But in the next eighteen months he won the Kings Stand Stakes, the July Cup (twice), the King George Stakes (twice), and the Nunthorpe Stakes (twice). I have never witnessed a better sprinter, and I do not expect ever to do so. I was thus very pleased to see that Patrick Robinson had devoted an entire chapter of this book to the breeding of the Aga Khan. In particular he points out the horses that descend from what I call 'The Tetrarch's grey mares' – Mumtaz Mahal and her descendants, which is still the most powerful bloodline for pure speed in the world.

My second 'great' was Sir Victor Sassoon's Crepello, a truly brilliant chestnut horse who won the Two Thousand Guineas, and then the Derby, from Ballymoss. Unfortunately he broke down on his off-fore later that year but I made him one of my rare exceptions, a stallion who had not run at four, and continually patronized him throughout his career. I was sure that Crepello was utterly outstanding, and a good friend he proved to be, siring both Busted and Caergwrle, and my dual Classic winner Mysterious, and Celina, with whom I won the Irish Oaks, and Bleu Azur, with whose daughter Altesse Royale I managed to win three Classics in 1971.

The third of my 'greats' was Prince Aly Khan's grey filly Petite Étoile, another temperamental lady from the wonderful grey mares of The Tetrarch. She was by Petition, from Star of Iran, from Mah Iran, from Mah Mahal, from Mumtaz Mahal. In a magnificent three-year-old season in 1959 she won the One Thousand Guineas, the Oaks, the Sussex Stakes, the Yorkshire Oaks, and the Champion Stakes. I have always been grateful that this all happened in the year *before* Prince Aly Khan was tragically killed in a car crash. He was a wonderful companion and a kind and considerate horseman. He deserved that glorious year, watching his home bred Petite Étoile, one of the greatest fillies ever to grace the turf.

The last of my quartette was another game, honest and thoroughly genuine friend, Sir Gordon Richards, my stable jockey until his retirement in 1954, champion jockey of England twenty-six times. We have not in my opinion seen a better rider, and to this lifelong pal, now aged eighty, I offer the highest praise any trainer can bestow upon a rider – he never lost a race he should have won.

When I was a very young trainer in 1944 I recall sitting in the home of the legendary Newmarket trainer Frank Butters – he sent out both Mahmoud and Bahram to win the Derby – when he received a phone call from Switzerland. It was in fact the Aga Khan calling, informing Frank that he was selling Nasrullah.

For almost half an hour I sat and listened to the great trainer begging and pleading with the old Aga not to sell him. 'Please don't sir,' he kept saying. 'Please don't. He's the best horse I've ever seen. I know he's a bit tricky, but please don't sell him.'

But it was no avail. Nasrullah was sold, for a song to Ireland, then for much more to Bull Hancock at Claiborne Farm, Kentucky. And now I am writing the foreword to a very lovely book, containing glorious pictures of his greatest descendants more than forty years on – Seattle Slew, Slew o 'Gold, Swale, Conquistador Cielo, Secretariat, Shirley Heights, Pleasant Colony, Bates Motel, Mr Prospector, Blushing Groom, etc.

Dear old Frank Butters, trainer of fourteen English Classic winners, was right. As usual.

Sir Noël Murless (1985)

SIR NOËL MURLESS (1910–87) *was one of the outstanding trainers of the Classic thoroughbred in the history of English racing. His record of nineteen Classic winners included three Derbys: Crepello (1957), St Paddy (1960), and Royal Palace (1967).*

If, from all the wisdom contained in this brief dissertation, one had to pick a salient point, it might be found in these words: 'To this day I seldom breed to a stallion which did not race beyond the age of three.' Were more breeders to conform to this tenet, how many more sound horses there would be in training; and, just possibly, a few more top-class three-year-olds would remain in training to run at four.

As things are, it has become increasingly difficult to find a Classic-winning stallion which has survived either unsoundness, defects of temperament or financial considerations and remained in training to run at four years old.

—

Messieurs Mathet and Pollet

To me one of the most intriguing aspects of touring the stables was the trainers' varied approach to the conditioning and nourishment of the horses in their care. 'Training', said Noël Murless, who believed in Australian oats and Canadian hay, 'is four-fifths experience, one-fifth intuition. And it's the last fifth that counts.' Noël would visit and feed a carrot to every one of his horses at evening stables. François Mathet never entered a box unless a horse was ill. 'They look much better inside,' insisted the first hundred-horse trainer in Europe. 'I prefer to see them out.' He regarded '*le coup de la carotte*,' as he termed it, with contempt, and cited a trainer's task as requiring 'the assessment of a horse's aptitude; the need to create a harmony of peak physical and mental fitness; not to overtax him at home; and not to exhaust him by setting tasks beyond his ability.'

Having started in 1945 with two horses whose aggregate cost was £375, he achieved a record 111 winners in 1958; was leading trainer of the Flat for the sixth successive time in 1962; and the first 200–horse trainer in the world by 1965. He had a horror of owners who wished to visit their horses, never received the local press, and was generally as gregarious as a Trappist monk. Further, although he patronized a London tailor and shoemaker, he was said to dislike the English.

The portents for a prospective interviewer were not wholly favourable when, during my 1952 tour, after leaving Geoff Watson who presided over the Rothschild collection, I spotted the hermit, as some referred to him, in a clearing alongside the main Chantilly work-grounds. I pulled off the road and, with the apprehension of a sacrificial offering hoping to find the lion in benign humour, introduced myself. Monsieur Mathet shook hands courteously enough. He had little to show me (I soon learnt that he seldom admitted to having any horse worth more than a passing interest in his care: when he confessed otherwise, it was worth heeding), but if I wanted to see his second lot they would be along in three minutes. They were, with military precision. In response to my request for a list of his horses – very few of the French stables featured in *Horses in Training* then, and Mathet's never – he invited me to his *bureau* for coffee and arranged for his secretary to send me details. We had an animated exchange (his 'I thought they only bred cattle in Ireland' kept the conversation going when I was extolling Irish bloodstock) and it became an annual date. By the late fifties the local specialist weekly was printing a translation (an excruciating one effected by a non-racing professor) of our March interviews which appeared in the *Express*. It was through François that readers were on Derby winners Phil Drake (1955) and Relko (1963), and on Bella Paola in the 1958 One Thousand Guineas and Oaks.

As unorthodox as he was brilliantly successful, François Mathet ridiculed the concept of horses being trained to stay or to sprint. 'They run,' he affirmed, 'according to their inherent capacity, which cannot be changed. Sometimes, of course, superior class enables them to win outside their distance. That has nothing whatever to do with a particular training method.' Although his patience with horses was in direct contrast to his intolerance of people, he was nevertheless responsible for the development of France's greatest jockey, Yves Saint-Martin. Reserved by nature, Mathet surprised me in September 1963 by sending an enthusiastic message following the success of Grey Lag, trained by Rae Johnstone, ridden by Roy Higgins and carrying the O'Sullevan colours in a Chantilly seller on a day I had to be working at Doncaster. Except during a short-lived rupture in June 1976, which is another story, we maintained regular friendly contact for thirty years.

Étienne Pollet's recipe was to restrict his stable complement to fifty; to pamper them with sweet-smelling hay from the deep south and get them up in the dark, if need be, to ensure working on fresh ground. Although he had a fine Classics record, his touch with the youngsters was uncanny – in a nine-year sequence he had six winners and four seconds in the Grand Criterium, France's richest two-year-old prize. Right Royal was a fair horse – winning the French Derby and King George VI and Queen Elizabeth Stakes in 1961 – but after visiting the stable for fourteen years, 1965, the year of Sea-Bird, was the first in which I'd known him confident of there being a proper three-year-old in the yard. Those of us who experienced the exhilaration of seeing Sea-Bird gliding to glory on the four spectacular public appearances of his second season – Prix Lupin, Derby, Grand Prix de Saint-Cloud and Arc de Triomphe – will be lucky indeed to see his equal.

Étienne Pollet did not enthuse readily over horses or jockeys. I always remember his reaction when he rang towards the end of April the following year saying, '*J'ai besoin d'un jockey pour dimanche*,' explaining that this was for a light-mouthed filly in the Thousand, and I proposed Scobie Breasley. 'Good heavens,' he exclaimed. 'He's older than you and I added together, isn't he?' Scobie was, in fact, a week off his fifty-second birthday when he rode Right Royal's daughter, Right Away, in the Poule d'Essai des Pouliches. But after winning his first French Classic on his first ride for the stable, Scobie earned the comment from the trainer, 'What a fabulous jockey that is!'

Étienne was always good for 'copy', but he reluctantly embargoed a good story in 1968. Vaguely Noble, object of intense competition at the Newmarket sales where he was part of his late owner Major Lionel Holliday's dispersal draft, had recently arrived at the exclusive Chantilly yard, having been bought by agent Albert Yank for a world auction record of 136,000 guineas on behalf of Hollywood plastic surgeon Robert Alan Franklyn. The immensely impressive seven-lengths winner of the Observer Gold Cup had no Classic engagements and was to be trained for the Arc de Triomphe. The spectacular bloodstock gamble made the son of Vienna the hottest horse news of the moment. After we'd looked him over, a powerful, commanding individual with a charming disposition, Étienne said that he would first carry the all-gold Franklyn colours in the Prix de Guiche (1¼ miles) on 7 April, 'Provided I still have him.'

Immediately after purchase Vaguely Noble had been sent to Paddy Prendergast. It was after Nelson Bunker Hunt had bought into him that, since the horse was to be campaigned in France, Nelson strongly counselled his transfer there. Now here was the three-year-old's new host saying, 'Provided I still have him.' In response to my look of surprise, he went to his desk and handed me a letter which had arrived from Dr Franklyn the previous day. The writer indicated that Vaguely Noble would be running in the name of his wife and, when he did so, he wished the animal's feet to be painted gold. He added that if this posed any difficulty he could arrange to have it done. Étienne Pollet stood back and awaited my reaction. Aware that the proposition would not hold great appeal for the perfectionist, who was already looking dangerously close to a stroke, but reluctant to kill a good story, I offered, lamely, 'C'est un peu bizarre.'

'Bizarre!' he almost screamed, hurling his arms in all directions (he was a little like Jacques Tati). 'It is utterly monstrous, totally inadmissible.' But what a story! I was already envisaging the caption, VAGUELY NOBLE TO BE GILDED. 'I am sure', I suggested diffidently, 'there is nothing in the rules of racing which stipulates that a horse's feet shall not be painted in a preferred colour or, for that matter, that his/her eyebrows might not be touched up.' (Would Mrs Franklyn think of that?) Étienne Pollet assumed his Queen Victoria mask. 'Irrespective of whether Vaguely Noble represents a gold mine,' he pronounced solemnly, 'the owner will be asked to remove him if he persists in his wish,' adding, 'Ici ce n'est pas un cirque!' Surely I could still write the story so far?

'Mon cher Peter,' regretted the trainer. 'I would love to te rendre service, but I don't want to lose the horse and my protest may be accepted, so I'd rather you said nothing.' He promised to ring me immediately if the Franklyns insisted. Wisely they didn't, and while the medium of the biggest gamble in bloodstock history to date turned himself into gold, another good story was mentally spiked.

Peter O'Sullevan (1989)

Since 1944 PETER O'SULLEVAN's contribution to racing's share of the media has been unique. As a race reader/commentator for BBC TV he is irreplaceable.

François Mathet (1908–83) was France's counterpart of Fred Darling: formidable, unapproachable and a brilliant trainer.

Sea-Bird was described by Étienne Pollet as 'très difficile', his

son Gyr (second to Nijinsky in the 1970 Derby) as 'très méchant'.
In different hands, neither might have reached a racecourse.

———

On Horses and Training

The observations which follow were addressed to those attending
the Hong Kong Racehorse Owners' Dinner and a subsequent sem-
inar, 1988.

The main drawback in racing today is the fading-out of the old
owner-breeders who knew and understood. They're being replaced
by many who do not understand and treat the animal as some
kind of object for a social step or commodity to make money. An
animal can be abused by those owners because the trainers aren't
strong enough to stand up to them. The horses are forced to run
to suit the owner, maybe because he has a box at Royal Ascot
and wants to entertain his girlfriends. So many top, successful
businessmen, shrewd and astute in their own fields, are gullible
when they go into racing; they think they know everything. A little
knowledge is always dangerous; and understandably they lack the
rapport between man and beast. There's a story about a backward
and ignorant two-year-old. The trainer approached the owner and
said, 'I'm afraid he's still green,' and the owner replied, 'He was
brown last time I saw him.' Ignorance provides an opening for the
sharks and conmen in racing, who unfortunately are more prominent in racing than most other industries.

Happy horses – I think you've got to have a very contented staff.
Happy horses – contented staff, it's very important. It doesn't
matter how much ability a horse has, if he's not happy and genuine
he's no good to anybody. To get the best out of a horse you've
got to give the best. Staff, feed, training and everything. Horses
must be relaxed in their work. I think horses that are too free –
you get a lot of morning glories – are not really any good. Distance-
wise, I feel that a horse either stays or it doesn't stay. You can't
make a horse stay. If he's bred to stay he'll stay. If he stays, then
I think the secret may be to work him the shortest possible distance
without souring him up. After all, it's the horse with a turn of foot

that wins the race. I think that is very important. I don't believe in trial gallops. I like working my horses on the bit. I think you can tell quite a lot by just working a horse on the bit – you don't have to try a horse.

I like an honest, broad head, and I like the eyes to be well apart, after all do we ever trust humans when their eyes are too close together? A wide muzzle – I've never found the horses I've been lucky enough to have, have ever been any good with small muzzles and narrow heads. I like a strong head. I think it's important, I really do. The next point is short necks. I don't like short necks and don't like swan necks. I feel that the windpipe is restricted. I think that a dipped back or swayed back leads to trouble with the muscles behind the saddle. Legs – over the knee sign of strength, back of the knee sign of weakness. Back of the knee leads to problems with the tendon. Tendons obviously are the trainer's nightmare. I know over jumps they seem to be able to patch up tendons and they can still run, but on the Flat, I've never, ever had a horse that's come right with a tendon. To me if I have a horse with a tendon, that is the end. The blood supply of the tendon is so minute, and the heart is so far away from the leg, the repair is very minimal. Short cannon bones – a horse with short pasterns, they don't seem to break down as much as horses with long pasterns although horses with long pasterns seem to have more spring and they're better movers, but on the other hand a really good mover doesn't have that extra gear. I like a deep girth in yearlings but unfortunately it's something that seems to develop between two and three, so when you're buying a yearling you're rather in trouble. When a horse walks away from you it wants to have that lovely swing, getting its hocks underneath it. I think if you're going to try to detect any error in a horse when you're buying – look through its back legs when it's walking away from you. You will see the things that are wrong much easier than if it's walking towards you.

The thing with a top-class horse, you've got to try and produce him six or seven times a year at his best, which is always very difficult because you know even with a human athlete it isn't easy. Some horses you can let them down in the middle of the season and give them a rest, but often they don't come back. They rarely come back to their best. So somehow you've got to keep them quietly ticking over. If you let a horse down too much, sometimes he just doesn't come back. Reference Point was very tough. He never did more than he had to do, he looked after himself. Probably when you asked him for 80 per cent, he always gave about 50 per cent at home. There's always a little bit in the tank. In every race really, once he got over his illness, he improved and improved and we thought he was probably as well, if not better, when he went for the Arc than he had been all year. But unfortunately he had an abscess brewing up in his foot. I'm not sure whether it was from a flint or what caused it. It may be because of the time of the year, you get a tiny bit run down, humans get boils on their necks, but when he was in the race, he hit the ground and it triggered it off. Even looking at the film afterwards he was definitely in trouble and very uncomfortable. I went home after the Arc thinking, 'Well, I've made a terrible mistake, he should never have run, he was over the top.' But in my own heart of hearts I couldn't believe it. Once I got home, I got a message saying the horse was so lame he couldn't put his foot on the ground and they thought he'd broken a bone in his leg. And then of course the abscess came out. Once that abscess had burst, about four days later we managed to get him home. Even when he went to stud, another one formed in his hind leg and he was lame. So it may have been something to do with just the time of the year and his condition. But I do think when he went for the Arc he was very well. I would never have dared run him, he'd done enough already, the Arc was going to be a bonus. He'd won the King George, the Leger and the Derby, and the two main trials, and as far as I was concerned that was enough. I had no intention of having him shot at if he wasn't right. So I think that was definitely the reason.

There were two horses walking round the paddock which to me were definitely over the top. They were worried, they were gone. Not only were they sweating between their back legs, which I always hate, but they were very nervous and tense and as they were walking round they were boring, pulling on the rope. It's always a sure sign, you know, when the head is nodding, nodding,

nodding, that he's gone. Those horses ran and I thought, considering that they'd gone, they ran very well. I think one was last, but one beat one. I don't think those horses could have benefited by that. And I'd expect that now they'd need to be left alone and rested, and have quite a lot of confidence put back into them. Working them with very, very bad horses to let them go past and win a gallop so they think they are the bee's knees, otherwise I can't see much future for them. I think a horse has also got to be reasonably fit. A lot of people think you can train a horse on the racecourse. 'Run him, he needs the race, doesn't matter, he'll win next time.' I don't think that works. The horse, if he's genuine, he's doing his best, he gets tired and he's got two furlongs still to go and his lungs are hurting him and he's beginning to hate it, although he wants to do it. I don't see how the next time he can be in the right frame of mind.

I think it's very important that when a horse is right, that's when you run him, not when it's wrong, just because the race is available. I mean that to me doesn't really seem to make sense. It would be rather nice if the programme could allow for a little more leeway. They're not machines. It's like people. It's like Sebastian Coe, he probably only really comes right once in every two years. It would be awful if he's at his best and he can't run, wouldn't it?

We had a problem a few years ago, and I think it probably still goes on. When you're buying sale yearlings in America they have used a certain amount of steroids in some of them. I wouldn't like to commit myself. But by the deterioration of the animal by the time I've got it back home I can tell they've definitely been used. The short-term steroids like Nanzolin on a very delicate, feminine horse or on a filly of not very strong constitution, during the winter can be very helpful. But you've got to be very, very careful because there are tremendous withdrawal symptoms. We found early on – we don't use anything at all now – we did have withdrawal symptoms. I personally don't believe in them really. I know they're meant to make the animal stronger, they produce more fluid, so the animal in some way probably does benefit from it, but I don't think it makes it go any faster. I think it probably may hold its condition better. If I'm two stone heavier it doesn't mean I'm going to be faster. I'll probably run much slower but I might be able to go on longer. I'm very anti any form of artificial help at all. I definitely think there are tremendous withdrawal symptoms for animals who've been on anabolic steroids and I have used them short-term in the winter in the past but I've never used them again.

In England we can't use any form of Lasix which stops bleeding. In America you can. If we're competing in a State where it's permitted, then we can use it too and we're not at so much of a disadvantage. They say bleeding all goes back in England to Hermit, and all that strain are all prone to bleeding. Vets don't agree with me at all but I think bleeding is through nervousness. Often you get a very good two-year-old wins six or seven races, and you train him on as a three-year-old and he's doing his best or her best, but basically the body won't go with them and I find it's a form of a nervous breakdown. I definitely think it's a nervous breakdown. If a horse bleeds it means he's had enough.

We do periodically take blood counts for horses. We don't blood-test just before a race. A lot of people weigh their horses, they do every sort of thing. But I like to think we can tell whether the horse is well or not right just by looking at him, really. If he's healthy, working very well, and he's bright, well, he's ready. A lot of people say he's lost weight, this that and the other, but I think if you know your horses you can tell just by watching them. I hate all these other things. I'm very old-fashioned really. I've been brought up in a very old-fashioned way. I use very, very few additives in feed, the old methods, and I just dread change. The old exercise saddle I find tremendous. But they're all changing now to the non-tree soft saddle. You have to change a bit. But I hate change. I'm very traditional. Apart from feeding some kind of supplement, probably because nowadays the hay or the oats are lacking in something, you might get it out of a supplement you use. Or if you've got a horse that's very nervous, it might help the nervous system. Apart from that I don't use anything at all. I do believe in dehydration. In England there are an awful lot of people who've never heard of electrolytes and dehydration. I do believe in that.

In England, as you know, our tracks have been going for years and years, and I think they've deteriorated a tremendous amount. First of all, taking England, what was a sport is now turning into a really high-powered industry. Bloodstock and racing is now the third largest industry in the country. And I think when you've got the value of the bloodstock and you see the conditions they're racing in, it's diabolical. So we have got to do something about it. Over here probably being very restricted with the amount of training ground and racing ground you've got, you have to think very seriously of the future especially as you're putting an awful lot of money into it. I mean racing in Hong Kong is now beginning to be acknowledged world-wide. From the training point of view, I don't care what anyone says, I'm absolutely certain that Equitrack, or whatever you like to call it, is a marvellous form of exercising gallop, very good for working on, there's no falseness, you can't compare it with the old bark all-weather tracks. Obviously, anything new, people will scratch their heads and say no. If you walk on it you think there's a hard surface underneath it, but there has to be a hard surface underneath it otherwise the animal may as well be working on quicksand. There's far more give in it than people realize. It doesn't affect a horse's action like sand, where I find they start to gallop higher. In England we've used Equitrack a tremendous amount in the last two years. I've had no trouble at all with it. I've had the odd horse break down, but they'd have probably broken down anywhere. I've managed to train horses on it and produce them at Ascot and win Group races without hardly getting on the grass at all. So in that way I think it's absolutely marvellous. So if you can use it as a training ground, at the moment I don't think you could find anything better.

Nowadays they don't seem to have the staff to mend the ground as they used to in the old days. They used to have hundreds of men walking round with wooden things filling in the holes. Nowadays everything seems to be tractors and they seem to fill the holes in with sand and it's quite dangerous. So this is a very interesting development. I think this new idea of sand-cum-plastic for the turf, if it holds, with a normal racing surface on top, it could make a tremendous difference. I think it could be quite exciting. I know some people who have already ridden on it are rather impressed with it. I only wished I'd invested in it myself.

Many stables in England are getting larger and larger. It's not uncommon to find a stable of 200 horses. I must say I'm one of the culprits. I always say it's easier to win a war with an army rather than a battalion. Every year gets harder and you're only as good as your last season or race. Some time ago at Newmarket an owner suggested to his trainer that it would be better to do this and that, and the trainer replied irritably that he didn't think so. The owner went on, 'Don't give me that, any old fool can train racehorses.' To which the trainer replied, 'Quite so, sir, but two wise men can't.' Jack Jarvis was Lord Rosebery's trainer. Once in the evening, when Lord Rosebery* was introducing him to the dukes and duchesses and aristocracy and royalty, he was heard saying, 'This is my trainer, Jack Jarvis; he's trained me hundreds of winners but none lately.' Training's rather like a game of bagatelle I find. You have twelve silver balls and you have a spring. You pull the spring and the balls go into holes, and at the end of the game you add them all up and you have a score. Then the balls all go down to the bottom again and you start all over again.

Henry Cecil (1988)

HENRY CECIL *(b. 1943) began training in Newmarket in 1968 and has, since then, been leading trainer eight times, trained eight Classic winners and in 1987 achieved a twentieth-century record of 180 winners on the Flat. He has trained two Derby winners, Slip Anchor (1985) and Reference Point (1987).*

* The prime minister (fifth Earl), not Harry Rosebery (sixth Earl).

Great Breeders and Their Methods

It will have been observed that breeders fall into two groups:

(a) 'Home breeders', mating their mares with their own stallions: the Alexanders, James R. Keene, and Calumet Farm belonged to this group, and each of them owned the best stallions of the period.

Lord Derby's operation could be classified as not more than 50 per cent in this group and Boussac was largely in this group.

(b) 'Outside breeders', who sent nearly all their mares to stallions not owned by themselves: Lord Falmouth and Tesio belonged to this group; and Lord Derby got more than 50 per cent of his best results (Hyperion, Phalaris, Swynford, Alycidon, Chaucer, etc.) from 'outside' sires.

It will also be observed that in both groups the breeders had access to the best sires of the time. It may be pure coincidence that most of the influential sires of modern times have been the result of 'outside' matings, such as Phalaris, Swynford, Hyperion, Nearco, Nasrullah, Blandford, and Tourbillon.

The repeated presence of speed and classic stoutness crossed in these key pedigrees is also obvious. Breeders such as Lord Astor in England and William Woodward in the US, whose model was to breed mares of Classic pedigree to sires of Classic pedigree and performance, achieved very little in the long run. In time, the speed dropped out of their strains, which then fell into obscurity.

Conversely, the breeders who advocated breeding 'speed to speed' have bred virtually nothing but sprinters and generally very cheap sprinters.

The presence of close inbreeding in a close-up ancestor of the key horse has occurred too often – Lexington, Domino, Commando, Phalaris, Pharos, Nearco, Blandford, Tourbillon, Djebel, St Simon, Stockwell – to be ignored as a favourable factor in the make-up of both stallions and mares.

The element of luck certainly seemed to play a very large part in most of these outstanding successes. Indeed it is obvious that overwhelming success in breeding cannot be attained without the ownership of a very few outstanding horses. They do not have to be many in number, but the champion breeder must have them or he will not be champion for long.

The great successes of this 'blue-ribbon list' of breeders were nearly all associated with the names of the greatest trainers of their respective countries and epochs. It is undeniable that there is an enormous advantage in having horses developed and trained by the greatest trainers of the time. However, the age-old dilemma has not yet been decisively answered: does the horse make the trainer, or does the trainer make the horse?

In all fairness, it has been hard to find the case of a breeder who was an outstanding success from the beginning, with the possible exceptions of the Alexanders (who had the luck of owning Lexington almost from the start), Lord Falmouth and HH the Aga Khan. This would indicate that even the most successful breeders have not begun their operations with a clear, well-thought-out program of breeding; rather, they have followed the channels of success when these became apparent after a considerable number of years.

Does this suggest that even the most successful breeders have been lacking to begin with in the knowledge of breeding programs needed to scale the highest peaks?

Perhaps HH the Aga Khan, using Lt-Col. J. J. Vuillier as his breeding consultant and the Hon. George Lambton as his 'physical consultant', had such a plan, and he was successful from the start. However, considering the very large size of his stud, and the limited success of his operation some years after the death of Col. Vuillier, there are some questions as to the relative long-term success of his operation. (His mares were about five times the number of the Lord Derby Stud.)

However much experimenting and unplanned 'mindless probing' most of these breeders had to do before striking a winning vein, this would seem to be no longer wholly necessary for new breeders entering the field today. New breeders are in a position to study the breeding operations of their predecessors and to screen out the important features which were the foundation of great successes in the past.

Abram S. Hewitt (1982)

ABRAM S. HEWITT *is a distinguished American owner-breeder and a writer on the thoroughbred.*

—

The Royal Studs, 1989

The Queen's quest for a winner of the Derby – the one Classic she has not won – has been virtually the *raison d'être* of the royal studs since her accession, yet the realization of the dream seems as far away now as ever. But the product of a mare she bred, from a family she inherited from her father, seems poised to attain that very goal.

It is hard to be definite on the matter of whether Nashwan should be considered as 'the one who got away'. Like every living creature, he has two parents, and only one of them was ever owned by the Queen. Had Height of Fashion been retained, she would certainly not have been the medium of $2.32 millions' worth of investment over the last seven years; that has been the aggregate cost of the nominations bought for her to Northern Dancer (twice), Blushing Groom, Danzig (twice), Lyphard and Mr Prospector.

There would unquestionably have been no Unfuwain, product of a $650,000 mating with Northern Dancer in 1984, and it is extremely unlikely that a year later there would have been a $275,000 date with Blushing Groom, the union which resulted in Nashwan. This year, when Blushing Groom is being used – on Nashwan's granddam Highclere – his fee is a more reasonable $160,000.

For all that, the fact remains that things have not gone well for the royal studs since the sale of Height of Fashion, for a sum reported to have been between £1.4 million and £1.8 million. Almost seven years have passed since Height of Fashion herself recorded the last Pattern victory in the Queen's colours, in the Group 2 Princess of Wales's Stakes. And although it is inconceivable that she would have been given the chances as a broodmare that her new owner has given her, it is also reasonable to assume that she would have proved a considerable asset to Sandringham.

So was the sale a mistake? With hindsight it is all too easy to say that of course it was, but, given the choice of owning West Ilsley Stables or a good three-year-old filly who might be anything or nothing as a broodmare (which is what the decision came down to) how many of us, hand on heart, could say we would have put our faith in the filly?

The chances of Height of Fashion actually proving to be worth the amount offered must have seemed remote, the chances of a similar or higher offer ever arriving from another party remoter still. Bear in mind, too, that Height of Fashion's parents – and an elder sister – were all still resident at Sandringham; the material was available to produce others as good, if not better. Seen in that light, it would have seemed folly to refuse the offer; other considerations might have made it seem almost a duty to accept it.

There are a number of striking paradoxes where the royal racing and breeding enterprises are concerned, and those who seize on the opportunity to criticize when success proves elusive are rarely conversant with the relevant facts.

All racing rejoices in the Queen's patronage of the sport, and wills the royal colours to succeed at the highest level. In lean times – from which no stud is immune – we tend to look for scapegoats among those charged with the management of either the studs or the stables, rather than consider natural, even economic, causes.

The £2 Tote punter would never credit the notion that an operation owned by one of such immense personal wealth could be failing for lack of finance. But the same fellow, even as a keen royalist, would probably take a dim view if his sovereign were to indulge in the massive expenditure which others have employed to enable them to achieve better results.

While the nation longs for Her Majesty to be competitive with the best, it also wants that to happen while expecting her to forgo the freedom available to all her rivals. There are constraints which apply uniquely to the royal bloodstock interests, constraints which the Queen herself readily accepts as proper, and there is no doubt that they have been major contributory factors to the declining fortunes of recent years.

The operation must be self-financing, and seen to be so; it has to be maintained and developed within strict budgets and without recourse to options both open and obvious to others. Some speculative ventures into the yearling filly and broodmare markets over the last few years might have seemed to represent a sound move, but the level of expenditure required to obtain the right quality stock would have meant forgetting that self-financing requirement, at least in the medium to long term.

Equally – probably even more – crucial is the fact that the Queen is not at liberty to use Irish stallions, which in an era when Ireland is home to most of the best in Europe constitutes a potentially serious setback to prospects of developing a stud to be competitive at the top level. None of Her Majesty's mares has been covered by an Irish-based horse since 1972.

Such constraints have inevitably proved inhibiting, and, as things appear to stand at present, only radical changes in policy can check their detrimental effects. In the immediate future change seems unlikely, so much may depend on external influences, most especially, perhaps, on the progress made by the many promising young stallions who have lately retired to stud in this country.

England has only two established proven Classic sires, Kris and Shirley Heights. The latter, of course, stands at Sandringham, but sadly – like his extensively-used sire Mill Reef before him – seems to be an ineffective match for the royal studs' most celebrated (Feola) family. In the early, highly successful, years of Her Majesty's reign, there were numerous prominent sires in England, the Irish option was available, and shrewd use was made of French horses; this year none of her mares has visited a French stallion, the last horse there of proven merit, Kenmare (whom she used in 1988), having since been sent to Australia.

The Queen and her advisers, racing manager Lord Carnarvon and stud manager Michael Oswald, were swift to appreciate the impact of American pedigrees on European breeding. A friendship forged with the late John Galbreath of Darby Dan Farm led to the acquisition of nominations to Graustark and Roberto in the early to mid-1970s, from which such as Gregarious and Duke of Normandy resulted. Since 1977 there has hardly been a year when none of the Queen's mares has been mated in Kentucky. In 1987 there were five, in 1988 there were six; this year the numbers are down again to four, probably on account of the substantial outlay expended on Highclere's mating with Blushing Groom.

Her Majesty has just returned from another of her now regular talent spotting trips to Kentucky, an area which offers a wide selection of proven stallions, many of whom are no longer prohibitively expensive to use. The search is all about finding value for money in horses of established merit; in the Bluegrass the problem is in identifying the most suitable among the many available, whereas at home the problem is a plain and simple dearth.

Of the seventeen mares mated in this country in 1989, seven have gone to stallions who have yet to be represented on the racecourse; that ratio is unsatisfactorily high, even though the commitment to the unknown is arguably expressed in a more promising group of young horses than in some recent years. Unless the numbers of proven stallions in England grow appreciably in the near future, the royal studs' Kentucky connection seems likely to become increasingly significant.

Tony Morris (1989)

Criticism of the management of the Queen's racing commitment surfaced in 1989 in all sections of the media, both in connection with the sale of Height of Fashion and the retirement from West Ilsley of Major W. R. Hern, the principal royal trainer. Both aspects received an overdose of conjectural comment.

For a fair and lucid explanation of the unique problems besetting the royal operation it would be difficult to improve upon Tony Morris's appraisal.

———

All in a Day's Work

Perhaps if I describe an average sort of day in a racing yard, the reader will better understand our peculiar life-style; but I won't guarantee it.

We stable lads start work while the rest of the world is still curled up blissfully in bed with another few hours to go – about six o'clock is average, and at this ungodly hour Newmarket is alive and stirring. Pedestrians wearing jodhpurs and boots, and carrying flasks and newspapers under their arms, walk briskly away from the town centre towards their places of employment; lads on ill-cared-for bicycles pass by, calling greetings, and perhaps pausing alongside the pavement, cockling about dangerously, for just long enough to beg a cigarette from their walking friends. Ancient jalopies, carrying six passengers, splutter along the streets and stop to cram in one more person who will otherwise be late; in the space of half an hour, the tide of stable lads will have ebbed and flowed, and the town is peaceful and empty once again.

The stable yards, though, are buzzing with activity. The horses are wide awake, finishing up their early-morning feeds, and banging against their doors with impatience. Buckets clatter, tractors roar into life, people shout and whistle and bustle about – another day is under way and, for the stable lad, the first daunting task is to muck out two or three dirty boxes. Usually, he will muck out the three horses he looks after. While they wait to be fed in the morning, the horses paw at the ground and pace about their boxes, churning up manure and straw into a steaming heap in the middle of the floor, so the lad will go to each of his horses in turn, tie it to a ring on the wall, and sort through the bedding, tossing clean straw into a corner, and forking the rest out of the box and on to a ridiculous square nylon mucksack laid out on the floor just beyond the door. The box is then swept out, the remaining clean straw laid back down tidily, and a fresh bale shaken up and laid around the walls of the box, making a cosy little nest for the horse to rest in. The lad will then have to fold up the four corners of the mucksack, hoist the smelly, wet parcel up on to his back, and totter off to dump it in the muck hill, hopefully before it begins to leak and drip down his neck. The procedure is then repeated with the next two horses, the whole operation taking about half an hour.

Somehow, we always seem to be in a rush. After mucking out, hide your fork and mucksack in your own favourite place, otherwise it won't be around next time you want it, then hurry round to the riding-out list to see which horse you are to take out first lot. There will be a crowd here, and there's bound to be someone complaining: 'Oh, not that bloody Kris filly, I always have that on a Monday when it's fresh. Pulls like a bloody train, it does.' No time to stop and sympathize, it's off to the tack-room to collect your tack, where a few early starters are having a break, sipping coffee and smoking. I never have time for this, preferring to spend every last second in bed.

Back to the stables, tie up your horse, groom it and put on your tack; the head lad begins to shout 'Jump up!', but if you are quick you can still clean out the water bowl and fetch the horse a piece of hay to save time when you get back in. By now, horses are emerging from doorways all over the yard. You pull out, jump up on to your horse's back, and walk away from the stables and into a paddock, circling in single file while the trainer issues instructions; 'Go to the all-weather, two canters. Two canters. You just do one. Take that for a walk, it runs this afternoon. Two canters. And you . . .'

The horses get impatient and, as we file off down the driveway and on to the horse-walks on our way to the Heath, they begin to dance and snatch at their bridles. From stables all over town, strings of horses come clattering out, and the lads call greetings across the road to one another. We stream across the road to get on to the Heath, and suddenly there are hundreds of horses, amazingly organized in single-file strings, heading for the canters.

This is the time when you are most likely to fall off – waiting to canter. Because the horses know, and begin to get excited. The lads have to ride very short, their stirrups pulled up almost into their pockets, in order to balance and control the horse while it canters. Unfortunately, it leaves you with very little grip, and if the horse makes any sudden move you have to rely on your own balance and split-second reactions to counter it. An experienced lad can feel a horse prepare to whip round, almost before the horse has decided to do it. Some mounts accept their work willingly; they enjoy it all, whatever you ask of them, and are always relaxed and happy. Some get very boisterous, launching themselves at the canters with squeals of delight, and kicking up their heels as they go. Others find it all – especially the waiting – rather intimidating, and look for escape routes, breaking out into nervous sweats, whipping round, and trying to scoot off home. And then there are just a few who will never do anything without a fight, who run backwards, rear up, spin round and kick out bad-temperedly, then suddenly give up and go willingly, as though they enjoy the fight as much as the exercise. The lads know the horses as a teacher knows her class, and adapt their riding accordingly.

As your turn comes, you gather up your reins and point the horse towards the canter; he looks, and underneath you a great surge of power rises up. You contain it in your hands, allowing the horse to move slowly forward on to the grass. His hindquarters sink away behind you as he prepares to spring into his stride; you soften your back and yield your hands forward, releasing the flow of energy. The horse reaches for his bit, and in a great bound he is away and cantering. Keeping the hands still, you push your heels forward and your rear up, balancing over his withers in the classic pose; everything is easy now. Between the horse's ears, the grass rushes up towards you in green stripes, like looking through a hole in the floor of a car. It feels incredibly smooth and rhythmical. His hooves beat a tattoo on the solid turf, he blows down his nose in even, rasping breaths, and he feels wild and strong. The lad is poised up there to balance the horse, to provide a fulcrum upon which it can swing in its stride. The horse leans his weight on to the rider's hands, his point of balance is forward over his withers; he trusts you, and his stride opens up with his confidence. This is what we nonchalantly call 'going well'. The end of the canter approaches. You brace yourself against the movement, relocating the horse's centre of gravity; close your fingers around the reins and squeeze, coming a little more upright. Message understood. The horse's head comes up, and the flowing surge of forward-moving energy slows to a trickle; his canter breaks into a trot. Pat his neck, feed him the rein. He lowers his head gratefully, blowing out of his nose, and a wisp of steam drifts up from under his belly.

We go for a long walk to give the horses time to recover, then do another canter before slackening off the horse's girths and wandering peacefully back to the stables. Once home, the horses have their legs washed down with cool water to clean off any mud which may chafe, and then their backs are rubbed dry before they are rugged up and left with hay and water to rest; their work is done. The lads take a break for breakfast, and then it is time to pull out the second lot.

This time you may not be so lucky. Not all horses give you a good ride. Some fidget and jiggle, shaking you about for the full hour and a half, which is very trying. Some pull very hard when cantering, forcing their heads down alarmingly, so that you feel as though the whole horse is somewhere behind you. Worse are those who pull with their heads up in the air, because you can't get a hold of them. They simply raise their heads higher and higher, beyond the level of control, and you end up with a mouthful of mane and a bloody nose. This sort of horse is frightened and lacking in confidence; it can only be righted with time and patience, steady canters on a long rein, until it learns that there is nothing to worry about, and begins to enjoy it.

Sadly, some horses are simply bloody-minded. They are horrific to ride and hugely entertaining to watch; easy to spot, they generally start by unseating the rider going on to the canter, which gives them the advantage of being already beyond control before the lad regains his balance. They thunder away, heads held at unusual angles, occasionally ducking from side to side or leaping through the air if they feel that the rider is not frightened enough. If a heathman is watching, they are sure to plough across some closed ground, too. If he is headed towards home, this type of horse will refuse to pull up and shoot off the end of the canter, intending to get back to his stable and have his breakfast eaten before anyone else; now and again, he will manage it. On the other hand, if he is cantering away from home, he will reach the end of the canter at breakneck speed, dig in his toes, and screech to a halt in two strides, flinging the lad up his neck, and sometimes, clean over his head.

Of the two tricks, the latter is preferable . . . every minute spent on the back of a bolting horse seems like an hour. Falls are over in the twinkling of an eye and are, for the most part, little more than a bump. The ones that really hurt, you don't expect and rarely see coming. Falls from bolting horses are the most dangerous of all, often resulting in broken bones and concussion – even brain

1 Oaks Day at Epsom, 1934. King George V and Queen Mary arrive on the course, met by Lord Rosebery (centre left), Lord Crewe (back to camera), and Lord Lonsdale (5th from left). (*National Horseracing Museum*)

2 Mr Jim Joel, followed by Jim White, travelling head man, leads in his Derby
winner, Royal Palace (George Moore), Epsom 1967, having already won the
2,000 Guineas. At four years old Royal Palace was unbeaten in his 5 races which
included the Eclipse Stakes and the King George VI and Queen Elizabeth Stakes.
(*by courtesy of H. J. Joel*)

3 The Hon. George Lambton, *c.* 1903, at Bedford Lodge, his first training establishment on his appointment as private trainer to the 6th Earl of Derby in 1893. He moved to the Stanley House yard on its completion in 1903, sending out 13 classic winners, including 2 Epsom Derbys: Sansovino in 1924 and Hyperion in 1933. (*Clarence Hailey*)

4 (left) Henry Cecil, an outstanding trainer of the eighties. (*Lesley I. Sampson*)

5 (below) Jack Jarvis, on his hack and two of his patrons, Lord Rosebery (centre) for whom he trained Blue Peter and Ocean Swell, each a winner of the Derby, and Sir Laurence Philipps (later Lord Milfc whose Flamingo won the 2,000 Guineas. (*National Horseracing Museum*)

6 (opposite) St Simon (1881), a mature stallion, at Welbeck. The marked slope of his shoulder and exceptional length from hip to hock are clearly shown. (*W. W. Rouch & Co*)

7 (opposite below) Hyperion (1930). Nine years old, at the peak of his stud career. Champion Sire 6 times. (*W. W. Rouch & Co*)

8 (top) Brigadier Gerard after winning his last race, the Champion Stakes, for the second time. With him are his owner-breeders, Jean and John Hislop. The year, 1972.

9 Sea Bird II (1962). At three years old. (*W. W. Rouch & Co*)

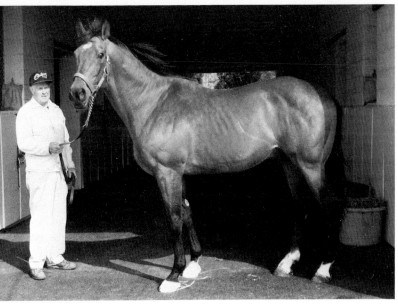

10 (top) Brigadier Gerard (1968). At three years old. J. Mercer up.
(*W. W. Rouch & Co*)

11 Nijinsky (1967). At seventeen, the magic is still there. (*Lesley I. Sampson*)

12 The 26-times Champion Jockey, Gordon (later Sir Gordon) Richards on Pasch after winning the 2,000 Guineas, 1938. This combination also took the Eclipse Stakes, finishing third in The Derby and St Leger. (*Alfiere Picture Service*)

damage. 'If a horse runs away with you, jump off,' is a bit of advice often quoted, but I have yet to see a stable lad fling himself from a horse doing half a ton downhill on hard ground. No. You always stay put and hope that the horse will stop of his own accord. It is pointless to engage yourself in a tug-of-war as the horse will always win, and the lad achieves nothing but rapid and total exhaustion. So much better if the horse simply drops you over his head before he sets off for home.

After second lot, there will be a third lot to go out, but if a yard is fully staffed, this should be quick and easy. Those horses who have just had a race, who are recovering from leg injuries, or who are soured off and in need of a few easy days, will go for a leisurely walk with perhaps one short canter. 'Go to the paper shop and back,' is a popular exercise for third lot, and if you are lucky there will be a kind bystander who will nip in for you and buy you a bar of chocolate and a can of pop. I like third lot.

Back at the stables, and we begin to rush again because it is nearly home time. We sweep the yards, tidy around the muckhill, clear away forks and pieces of baling string. The horses are given another feed and, at about noon, there is a mass exodus. Lads swarm out within seconds, and the horses rest until evening stables at four o'clock.

Evening stables are great fun in summer and utter misery in winter, although the duties are the same whatever the time of year. The lads go to each of their three horses in turn, muck out their boxes, fluff up their beds, then groom them thoroughly, and oil their hooves. The feed and water mangers are cleaned out, and the hay racks filled. In between horses, the lads gossip and joke with one another, and the head lad and trainer will walk round the yard, inspecting each horse for leg ailments, sore backs, significant weight loss, or any other potentially troublesome symptom. In winter the yard will be dark and it often rains, and the lads move about quietly, getting on with their work and hurrying to get back to the fireside and a hot dinner; but in summer, evening stables are wonderful, rowdy affairs. Four o'clock is frequently the warmest part of the day, and the lads get their horses out for bubble baths – washing them from head to toe with shampoo and warm water – then walk them into the paddocks to graze in the sun until they dry. Trainers are in good moods, especially if the yard is having a good season, and on odd occasions bring out cans of beer, and we all sit about chatting long after the work is done. There are the inevitable water fights, football games in the paddocks, fooling around on bicycles, and practical jokes; even the horses are happier. We round off evening stables with another session of tidying up and feeding, finishing the working day at around six o'clock. In all weathers, and all seasons, the routine goes on.

Summer is obviously the most enjoyable time of year, with the bright mornings, warm evenings, and the racing season under way; we are very much busier, and on Wednesday and Saturday mornings, in most of the Newmarket yards, first lot is devoted to testing the progress of the horses in training. These are the 'work mornings'.

The lads love to ride 'work', it is a privilege, a chance to play at jockeys and, because racing conditions have to be simulated, only the lads of racing weight are permitted to ride the trial gallops; the fat and feeble are left on the side of the Heath to spectate, as the work jockeys take over. This is frequently a delicate area; there are more upsets and notices given over being 'jocked off' than for any other reason. To be stood down by someone considered to be an inferior rider, or worse still, a girl, is an unpardonable affront.

On work mornings, the top jockeys come to the yards to ride work on those horses which they will be engaged to ride in future races; everyone likes to be in a gallop with a professional, but if you cannot ride your own horse work, then the next best thing is to stand beside the trainer and watch it stretched to the limits under the skilful touch of a jockey. The stable lads do all the hard work with the horses; it is us who deal with them when they first come into the yard as yearlings, who break them in, teach them to canter straight, to pick up the bridle, who give them the confidence to let themselves down to the ground and gallop; it is the lads who keep the horses sound and happy, who prepare them for their races. To stand aside and watch your protégé excel himself gives a glow of satisfaction.

The Newmarket gallops are consecrated ground, springy, ancient turf, smooth and green as a billiard table, and as lovingly cared for. Punters and professional tipsters come from far and wide, rising at heaven knows what time, seeking inside information, and their cars, along with those of the trainers and owners, crowd the verges alongside the Heath. Groups of people stand about with binoculars around their necks and notebooks and stop-watches in their hands, never missing a detail, and never parting with one either. Groups of horses come thundering up the gallops at intervals and, as they leave the Heath, the punters will study each horse carefully, perhaps asking its name, and watching to see how hard the animal is blowing; this is deadly serious! Sometimes they get their information wrong. The hard-core racing press will report that Dobbin did an encouraging half-speed up the Limekilns on Saturday, and the lads know that in fact Dobbin was in his box with a sore shin, and that it was merely Neddy doing a rather enthusiastic but ordinary canter. For the most part, though, the punters are accurate. You can sometimes ride a piece of work, and as you leave the gallops on your plain, bay horse, one of the professionals will remark: 'I should have thought he would have gone to France by now.' You play it cool, and reply casually, 'Just a blow-out. He leaves this afternoon,' and walk off, followed by the inquiring stares of those who are not so well informed.

The gallops, apart from being training-ground for the racehorses, are also where the apprentice jockeys learn how to ride, and I think this is one reason why we do not see many lady jockeys on the racecourses; many trainers don't think of their young girls as potential jockeys and won't let them ride work. Because they never ride work, they never learn to ride racehorses at all, and trainers say they are no good. A bit of Catch 22. In the last few years, there has been a flood of girls coming into racing, which can only be a good thing; now it is only a matter of time before the girls establish themselves and are given equal opportunities.

There must be hundreds of young men who get their apprentice licences every year, and yet only a tiny percentage ever make it as jockeys. Consider how few girls get rides in races, and it is hardly surprising that we have yet to see an outstanding lady jockey emerge from the ranks. But I'm sure it will happen, and I shall be the first to cheer when it does. I won't expect to hear much cheering from the lads, though. When it comes to girls in racing, they get very resentful. Racing is traditionally a man's job; although the lads have had to accept the arrival of women, they feel that their domain is being poached upon, and use scornful terms like 'I wouldn't work there, too many birds,' and 'That was a nice horse till the girls started riding it,' ignoring all the ham-fisted members of their own sex. As far as the lads are concerned, girls are only good for one thing and they get no respect if they are foolish enough to oblige in that direction, either.

Some trainers won't employ girls at all; others infinitely prefer them. Girls make better grooms. They are quieter, more reliable, less militant, and seldom abuse the horses. Lads complain that girls get preferential treatment, and I must admit that to a certain extent this is true. We are paid the same wages as men, and are expected to work just as hard for them, but if a rampant colt needs sorting out, or there is a drain needing to be unblocked, then it will almost always be a lad who gets picked to do the job.

Trainers who do like to employ girls are very gallant towards them. Rich men bring out the simpering fool in most women, and it is hard not to be a tiny bit flirtatious with even the most obnoxious of them. (I pride myself in being an exception to this rule. 'A tinker's dog', one of my employers called me, 'lean and mean'. I thought it a huge compliment at the time.) But trainers, I think, are much gratified by the admiration of the girls, and a young female, however plain, anxious to do your bidding, must be a damn sight more pleasant first thing in the morning than a foul-mouthed, complaining man. So girls are treated to little shows of consideration which the lads are denied . . .

Last summer I used to ride a hysterical filly out every day, and one morning she bolted with me up Long Hill, and continued down the other side at full tilt, heading towards the road. Her clattering hooves alerted everyone for miles around, and all eyes were on us as we charged away. Henry Cecil, looking outrageously handsome on his grey Arab steed, immediately abandoned his string and, like a true Sir Galahad, came thundering to my rescue.

This is the stuff of which Barbara Cartland novels are made. I don't know quite what he intended to do, but I had my plan mapped out in seconds – steer the filly alongside him, and fling myself into his arms. Alas, when I turned the horse, she pulled herself up and ruined everything. For which Mr Cecil will no doubt be very grateful, but talking to a friend from Cecil's yard later, he said: 'If that had been a lad on that horse, Henry would have just said "I wonder if they'll get over that road safely?" and left them to it.'

When one of the girls in our yard gave in her notice, the two good fillies which she cared for were promptly given to two remaining girls to look after, and the lads were most put out.

'Knew that would happen,' they said sourly, 'gave the good horses to the girls to do, straight away.' 'You know the old saying,' replied one of the girls, cheerfully, 'if you want to get ahead, get a twat.' Perhaps true, if somewhat crudely put. Maybe that is another reason why the lads resent the girls – because they can simper very prettily to the trainers, yet swear like sailors when addressing the lads.

This is a tough game. You have to give as good as you get, there is no room for the weak. All of us, lads and girls, complain endlessly about the endless, thankless slog, toiling in all weathers, lifting and carrying heavy mucksacks, water buckets, bales of hay and straw – everything around stable yards is invariably heavy, although we are, of course, about half the size of people who punch keyboards or push pens for a living. Yet I once read a letter to an agony aunt in a magazine from a distressed mother, whose precious little girl had gone working with racehorses; she had abandoned her pretty frocks, snapped off her pink fingernails, and started using the kind of language which her poor mum had never even heard of. The letter made me laugh a lot, and it also made me think . . . Hard labour, swearing, bruises, dirt and all – I wouldn't give up my job for a king's ransom.

Susan Gallier (1988)

Why, it may be asked, does anyone want to work with racehorses? Susan Gallier explains:

We do it seven days a week, from five in the morning, till six at night. We do it in the rain, in the blazing sun, in the frost and the snow and in the dark. We do it for a fraction of what we are worth and, if we should find a more lucrative job, we do it in our spare time, for fun. The truth must be that stable lads do it for love.

Once infected with this incurable addiction to thoroughbred race-horses, it is not possible to stay away from them. When stiffening joints discourage the riding of them they can be watched with unfading pleasure. What other sight is comparable to Newmarket Heath on a work morning in high summer?

HORSES

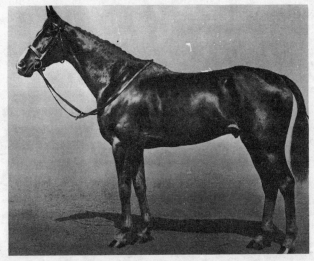

Easter Hero (1920), chestnut gelding by My Prince–Easter Week (Outbreak).
A truly great chaser.
(*W. W. Rouch & Co.*)

Origins of the Thoroughbred

The English racehorse boasts of a pure descent from the Arabian, and under whatever denomination the original stock of our thoroughbred horses have been imported – viz., as Turks, Barbs, or Royal Mares, there can be no doubt they were selected by the patrons of the Turf and by their agents during the reigns of James I, the two Charleses, James II, and the Commonwealth; and whether they were brought from Barbary, Turkey, or the continent of Europe, they were considered as the true sons and daughters of the desert. The first Arabian ever seen in England was imported by Mr Markham, in the reign of James I, and the first foreign mares of any note were brought over by the agents of Charles II, under the denomination of Royal Mares. The change of climate, the pasture, and extreme care and attention in breeding by the best stallions (and never forgetting the maxim that *fortes creantur fortibus et bonis*) have wonderfully increased their size, their strength, and their powers of endurance; and it is generally believed by the most learned men of the Turf that a first-class English racehorse would give 6 st. to the best Arabian which can be found, for any distance under ten miles. In 1828 a match was made at Calcutta between the English horse Recruit, 10 st. 8 lb., and the best Arab at that time in India, Pyramus, carrying 8 st. 3 lb., two miles. Recruit had been a very short time in India, and had tender feet, which disabled him from taking strong work; notwithstanding which he won in a trot.

The clearest proof of the improvement which has taken place in the English racehorse is the fact that no first or second cross from the imported Arab, with the exception of the produce of one mare by the Wellesley Arabian (Fair Ellen), is good enough to win a £50 plate in the present day; whereas in 1740 our best horses were the second and third crosses from the original stock; and we have no reason to assume that the Arabian horse of 1850 has degenerated from his ancestor of 1730. The most distinguished progenitors of the English racehorse are the Byerley Turk, the Darley Arabian,

Curwen's bay Barb, and the Godolphin Arabian; and no horse of any eminence has appeared in England in the last one hundred years which does not inherit their blood. Of the two former we know very little; they were the sires of Basto and of Flying Childers; but the blood of the Godolphin Arabian is in every great stable in England. He was a thick-necked, heavy-shouldered, over-topped horse, without apparently a single good point adapted to racing qualifications. Goldfinder and Eclipse, both foaled in 1764, were considered the most extraordinary horses in the last century – Sir C. Bunbury always asserted that Goldfinder was the best horse. The celebrity of Eclipse as a stallion has contributed to his fame far more than his public running, which only lasted two years. Horses of this era were rarely put into training before they were three years old; some never appeared until five years old; and all the great matches and sweepstakes were made for long distances, four, six, and eight miles. Many writers have therefore imagined that the horses in olden times were more adapted to stay a distance than our present breed; but it does not follow, because it was the fashion to run long distances in 1750, that the horses of that day had greater powers of endurance. Heavy weights and long courses were in vogue, because it was the custom for owners and amateurs to ride in the last half mile with the leading horses; a feat not very difficult of attainment, considering that the racehorses had run four miles before they joined the party. Our experience teaches us that the first cross from the Arab frequently shows speed; but there are very few instances of the first or second cross which can run beyond the distance of one mile in good company. I therefore suspect that the form of the best racehorse of 1750 is inferior to that of a common plater of the present day.

The Hon. Captain Rous, RN (1850)

Vice Admiral the Honourable Henry James Rous
(1795–1877)
The founder of racing administration and of the weight-for-age
scale. Appointed Official Handicapper to the Jockey Club in 1855.

The Darley Arabian

His Purchase and Shipment to England

This letter throws an interesting light on the Darley Arabian, the ancestor of the great Eclipse family. The document was found among old family papers by Miss Darley of Aldby, East Yorkshire. It reads as follows:

Aleppo
Ye 21st December, 1703.

Dear Brother,

Your obliging favour of the 7 Aprill came to my hands the 16th October, by our convoy, and by whom I assygne these, with hope will have better success in arriving safe than the many letters wrote you, besydes I have never been favoured with any letters from you but that I immediately answered ye first conveyance that succeeded after receipt thereof, being very desirous of maintaining a punctuall correspondence, for nothing is more gratefull to me than to hear the welfare of my Relations and friends, and more particularly your good Self. I take no notice what discourse you have had with my Father, and its very true he has ordered my returning, wch I should gladly obey would my affaires permit, therefore hope he will be pleased to excuse my delay untill a more propper season, for I assure I am not in Love with this place to stay an hour longer than is absolutely necessary.

Since my Father expects I should send him a stallion, I esteem myself happy in a colt I bought about a year and a half agoe, with a desygne indeed to send him ye first good opportunity. He comes four the latter end of March or the beginning of Aprill next; his colour is Bay, and his near foot before with both his hind feet have white upon them, he has a blaze downe his face, something of the largest. He is about 15 hands high, of the most esteemed race among the Arabs, both by Syre and Dam, and the name of the said race is called Mannicka.

The only fear I have about him at present is that I shall not be able to get him aboard this war time, though I have the promise of a very good and intimate friend, the Honble and Revnd Henry Bridges, son of Lord Chandoes, who embarks in the Ipswich. Captain William Waklin, who presume will not refuse taking in a horse for him since his brother is one of ye Lords of ye Admiralty; besides I desygne to go to Scandn to assist in getting him off. Wch, if I can accomplish, and he arrives in safety, I believe he will not be disliked, for he is esteemed here, where I could have sold him at considerable price if I had not desygned him for England.

I have desired Bridges to deliver him to my brother John or Cozen Charles, who he can find first, and they are to follow my Father's orders in sending him into ye country. For ye ffreight and all charges to his landing I will order payment of, though am not certain wht it may amount to. Am told by a friend, who sent home a horse last year, it cost him inclusive 100£ Stg. When you see Coz Peirson, pray tender him my humble salutes, and since his Daughter is ready, I shall endeavour, with all speed, to prepare myself. . . . I have given my friend, Mr Bridges, 2 chequuens to drink with you (in case you are in towne), and Brother John and Coz Charles, which I wd call to mind is a present worth yr notice.

I heartily wish you health and prosperity (and as the season invites) a merry Xmas with many succeeding.

I respectfully remain, dear brother,

Your most affec Brother,

THOMAS DARLEY.

In Vol. 1 of the Stud Book, it is stated that the Darley Arabian was brought over 'by a brother of Mr Darley, of Yorkshire, who, being an agent in merchandize abroad, became member of a hunting club, by which means he acquired interest to procure this horse'. From the foregoing letter it is obvious that the importer was Thomas Darley's father. That point is, however, of less consequence than the interesting particulars which the letter contains. Thomas Darley would appear to have been a very businesslike agent.

The Darley Arabian (1700) stood at Aldby Park throughout his

stud career and died at the age of about thirty. Through his sons,
the own brothers Flying Childers and Barlet's Childers, the Darley
Arabian is the ancestor, in direct male line, of most modern
thoroughbreds; his descendants widely outnumber those of the
Godolphin Arabian and the Byerley Turk, the other two founding
fathers.

—

Gimcrack (1760)

An extract from an address by Paul Mellon

On 11 October 1970, Paul Mellon, owner of the great Mill Reef,
was honoured by the Anciente Fraternitie of York Gimcracks at
their 200th Annual Dinner, in the presence of HRH the Prince of
Wales. He concluded an enchanting and scholarly speech with a
sonnet both appropriate and of quality. The occasion will long be
remembered by those who were fortunate enough to have been
there.

Before I close, and because I feel strongly that this momentous
occasion calls for it, I want to quote a brief history of Gimcrack
the horse, so that we may remember him and honour him on this
the 200th anniversary of his retirement to stud. It was written in
our American *Chronicle of the Horse* by your charming writer and
anthologist, Stella Walker:

The little grey, Gimcrack, by Cripple out of Miss Elliott, is one of the
most renowned horses of the British Turf. Foaled in 1760, and though
only a fraction over 14 hh., he proved a phenomenal stayer, winning
twenty-seven out of thirty-five races, and most of them over four-mile
heats. When in the ownership of Count Lauraguais he was taken to France
to win a wager that a horse could travel 22½ miles in an hour.

(I must interject here that I have read elsewhere that the Count was
severely criticized for this cruelty by his sporting contemporaries in
England and France, and by the Press of the day.)

Mrs Walker continues:

Gimcrack was later sold to Sir Charles Bunbury, whose beautiful wife referred to him as 'the sweetest little horse that ever was. He is delightful.' He continued winning races and became known in Yorkshire as 'The Wonder of the North'. He was bought by Lord Grosvenor for 1,200 guineas and in 1771 retired to stud ... Stubbs painted three different pictures of Gimcrack.

With this history in mind, I am going to ask your forbearance while I quote one other brief verse of my own: a sonnet to honour the Gimcrack Club and Gimcrack the horse. It is an acrostic. The Oxford Dictionary defines 'acrostic' as 'a short poem in which the initial, the last, or middle letters of the lines, or all of them, taken in order, spell a word, phrase, or sentence'. I leave it to anyone with a sharp pencil or a sharp memory, to discover the title of the poem from the *initial* letters of these lines.

> Grey was I, well-proportioned, but so small
> In stature that I scarce could shade a child,
> Many a master had I, from the mild
> Callow young lad who rubbed me in my stall
> Right on through Count Lauraguais, who asked all
> And more of me, for which he was reviled.
> Courage restrained me from becoming wild:
> Kindness and English grass soothed my deep gall.
>
> Swift as a bird I flew down many a course,
> Princes, Lords, Commoners all sang my praise.
> In victory or defeat I played my part.
> Remember me, all men who love the Horse,
> If hearts and spirits flag in after days;
> Though small, I gave my all. I gave my heart.

It was touch and go whether Mill Reef ran at York on 20 August 1971. An overnight deluge had turned the ground into a quagmire.

Mr Mellon, against the advice of Ian Balding, his trainer, and Geoff Lewis, Mill Reef's jockey, decided they should run. No decision was more justified; like all great horses, Mill Reef acted on any going, from firm to heavy – an example to all the 'one ground' specialists of contemporary racing.

———

St Simon

The names of many of the great horses who have helped to create the traditions of the British Turf are commemorated in race programmes, and it is right that this should be so. Races have been named after Eclipse, Ormonde, Voltigeur, Hyperion, Isonomy, Sceptre, Pretty Polly and many others so it seems both strange and lamentable that there should be no race in the calendar to keep alive the memory of the horse who was, perhaps, the greatest of them all – St Simon.

I use the word 'perhaps' advisedly, because the identity of the greatest thoroughbred of all time must always be a matter of opinion. On the other hand, I must declare myself straight away as an ardent supporter of St Simon's claim to that title, and it is my hope that I shall be able to give some substance to that claim in the course of this article.

It seems best to begin by quoting a paragraph from the memoirs of St Simon's owner, the Duke of Portland, published under the title *Memories of Hunting and Racing*. Portland wrote:

St Simon left an indelible mark on the Turf, and, I believe, all for its good. In my opinion, it is impossible to decide as to the comparative merits of great racehorses which lived in different periods, and which consequently never met in competition. For that reason I hesitate to say which was the better racehorse – St Simon or Ormonde. They were both of superlative excellence and I think they, with Isonomy, were the three best racehorses I have seen during my experience of the Turf, which began in 1878. But when they are considered as high-class specimens of the thoroughbred, and as stallions, there can, I think, be no doubt whatever of St Simon's superiority, for St Simon was an absolutely sound animal and sired sound stock, whereas Ormonde was unfortunately affected in his respiratory organs, and a similar infirmity marked more than one of the animals he begot in his first year.

To my mind this passage puts the problem in its correct perspective and sets up the threefold standard by which the greatness of any thoroughbred should be judged. This standard is derived from the quality of his best racing performance, his soundness and constitution, and his prowess at stud. St Simon was above criticism on all three counts.

In each of the three categories there have been horses on whose behalf parity at least with St Simon could be claimed. There was nothing unique about his soundness in all respects: Eclipse and Ormonde may have been equally invincible on the racecourse; Stockwell, the 'Emperor of Stallions', and Hyperion may have had comparable records at stud. But neither Eclipse nor Ormonde could compare with him as a sire; nor were Stockwell and Hyperion invincible on the racecourse. Ribot may be hailed as a twentieth-century St Simon, but he is still in his prime as a stallion, and we are still much too close to him in time to attempt a definitive evaluation of his greatness or his influence.

Portland may be regarded as a biased witness, but confirmatory testimony to St Simon's greatness is not lacking. That dour but lovable Scotsman, Mat Dawson, prepared six Derby winners – Thormanby, Kingcraft, Silvio, Melton, Ladas and Sir Visto – yet maintained to the end of his life that he had trained only one real smasher, and that was St Simon. Mat used to say that St Simon was fuller of electricity than any horse he had known, and stated roundly that St Simon was unbeatable at any distance from a furlong to three miles. Of the truly great horses of thoroughbred history, only Ormonde, foaled in 1884, three years after St Simon, was close enough in time to provide some valid means of comparison. In this respect it is significant that Fred Archer, who rode them both, never wavered in his opinion that St Simon was the better.

There is no doubt that Portland, as a young man of twenty-five near the outset of his career as an owner, had one of the greatest strokes of luck in Turf history when he bought St Simon as a two-year-old for 1,600 guineas. St Simon would never have come on the market if his breeder and owner, Prince Batthyany, had not died of a heart attack on the steps of the Jockey Club luncheon room at Newmarket on Two Thousand Guineas day in 1883. The Prince's dispersal sale was held during the July meeting and Portland, having been outbid for Fulmen, the horse he had really wanted to buy, acquired instead St Simon, the next lot to be led into the ring.

Mat Dawson had described St Simon as 'quite a likely-looking animal' when they had inspected the Prince's horses, but gloom reigned when St Simon was given his first canter on the morning after the sale, and appeared to have no action at all. He seemed to move more like a rabbit than a horse, giving the impression that he was quite incapable of striding out. However, his action began to improve as soon as he went into serious work, and once he was fit it was superb, as he laid himself out close to the ground, more like a greyhound.

In accordance with the rule which remained in force until the time of Call Boy, all St Simon's engagements became void on the death of his nominator. For this reason there could be no question of his running in any of the Classic races, which had closed when he was a yearling, although in fact he had been entered for the Two Thousand Guineas only. No one has ever been able to discover why Prince Batthyany did not enter him in the Derby or the St Leger, but the most probable explanation is that he simply did not think that the colt would prove good enough. It is true that St Simon was by Galopin, an outstanding racehorse and sire, and Prince Batthyany's favourite; but the colt's dam St Angela had only third-rate form and at the age of sixteen, when St Simon was foaled, had produced no offspring of note, although her daughter Angelica was destined to achieve fame later as the dam of Orme.

With opportunities thus restricted, St Simon had to gain his victories when and where he could, and the only two great races that feature on the roll of his successes are the Ascot Gold Cup and the Goodwood Cup. He went through the nine races in which he took part with an air of complete invincibility. His stakes earnings amounted to £4,676, a meagre enough sum even by the standards of the 1880s, and it is by the quality of his performances on the racecourse and on the training grounds, not by the importance or the value of the races he won, that his greatness must be judged.

St Simon's active racing career began with two easy victories at Goodwood and an equally easy victory in a nursery at Derby. His first real test came in the Prince of Wales's Nursery at Doncaster, in which he had top weight, being set to give many pounds to his rivals. He won in a canter by fifty yards, and it was at this point that his quality began to emerge clearly, for his opponents included St Medard, who finished second in the Two Thousand Guineas the next year. By this stage it was obvious that St Simon and Duke of Richmond were the best two-year-olds and, in the more adventurous spirit that prevailed among owners at that time, a match was arranged between the two colts at the Houghton meeting. In the meantime St Simon was galloped with his stable companions Busybody and Harvester, who respectively won the Oaks and dead-heated for the Derby the next year, and beat them out of sight. In the match St Simon led Duke of Richmond by fifty yards after the first two furlongs, whereupon Archer dropped his hands and allowed Duke of Richmond to come much closer. At the finish St Simon won pulling up by three-quarters of a length.

Archer could not do the weight in the Ascot Gold Cup, so the mount was given to Wood with the instructions to win by not more than two lengths. Wood did his best, but there was no holding St Simon once he was given his head, and he galloped right away from his field to win by twenty lengths from Tristan. Tristan was one of the best, toughest and most consistent horses of his day, and he scotched any idea that he might have deteriorated when he turned out again the next day to win the Hardwicke Stakes for the third year in succession.

St Simon spent nearly the whole of his stud career at Portland's stud at Welbeck. His success was immediate and sustained. He was champion sire nine times altogether and seven times in succession. Ten of his progeny won a total of seventeen Classic races. They included the Triple Crown winner Diamond Jubilee, the brilliant filly La Flèche, and Persimmon, a bright star in the galaxy of Derby winners. St Simon was high-couraged and impatient and, like so many equine characters, far from easy to manage in the stable. 'It's all very well to talk of the patience of Job, but Job never had to groom St Simon,' complained his lad. But John Huby, the Welbeck Stud groom, found out that the great horse had a weakness, which was a terror of an umbrella or a billycock hat held on the end of a stick, and by this means he could always be controlled.

Mat Dawson may be allowed the last word. Writing to a friend before the match with Duke of Richmond, he remarked: 'I know you love a real good horse, and I hope you come to the Houghton meeting to see St Simon. He is certainly the best two-year-old I have ever trained – he will possibly make the best racehorse who ran on the Turf.' St Simon richly fulfilled his trainer's prophecy.

                                                        Peter Willett (1966)

St Simon (1881–1908) b.c. Galopin–St Angela (King Tom). This absorbing article was written in 1966. Newbury took the hint and the St Simon Stakes (Group 3) has been run there ever since, over 1½ miles in the late autumn.

———

Scapa Flow, Fairway and Walter Alston

No story of Scapa Flow and her descendants would be complete without mention of the late Mr Walter Alston, who for many years so successfully managed the Stanley House Stud. During the latter years of his life he was a martyr to asthma and lived very quietly at Falmouth Cottage, Newmarket, surrounded by his Stud Books and other racing literature, but he was also a voracious reader; there was no good book or memoir that did not find its way into his library, and this enabled him to escape the one-track mind so often characteristic of a man living much alone. No one knew more about the Stud Book and pedigrees, and he was a man of strong opinions and often strong prejudices, but, like all clever men, he was never satisfied with what he knew and always wanted to know more. His life was with his mares, foals, and yearlings. His paddocks were beautifully kept, his stud men were devoted to him and well trained; no wonder that he made a success of the job to which he gave his life.

Perhaps his greatest flash of genius was when he bought the ex-selling-plater Gondolette, the dam of Sansovino, winner of the

Derby, and the grandam of Tranquil and Selene, the latter in her turn being the dam of the Derby winner Hyperion.

It was in the autumn of 1912 that Walter Alston told me that Lord Derby had suggested buying Anchora; he had looked up her pedigree and thought that she would be a suitable mate for Chaucer. Alston seldom went racing, and he had never seen her, so he asked me to have a look at her, and if I thought that in conformation and constitution she would make a broodmare, he would try to buy her. I was able to satisfy him on these points, and she was bought for the Stanley House Stud.

Anchora was a chestnut mare by Love Wisely out of Eryholme by Hazelhatch, seven years old, and the property of the late George Edwardes. She had run in no less than fifty races, of which she had won eight. She was just a good second-class stayer, game, sound, and with a grand constitution, which she no doubt inherited from Love Wisely, who Alec Taylor once told me was the stoutest horse he had ever trained. He said that it was very difficult to give Love Wisely enough work to get him fit, and that when he was training him for the Ascot Cup he used to have him out five hours a day, and even then he turned out for the race as big as a bull. Previous to winning the Ascot Cup, which he did as a three-year-old, he ran second to St Frusquin for the Two Thousand Guineas, and as a four-year-old he won the Jockey Club Stakes.

In 1913 Anchora was put to Chaucer, and Walter Alston awaited the result with more than ordinary interest. In due course she produced a small chestnut filly, Scapa Flow, as she was afterwards named, well made, with nice length and a particularly good head, but there was certainly nothing in her appearance to make one think that she would become one of the greatest broodmares of all time.

In 1924 Scapa Flow was barren, but returned to Phalaris, and in 1925 she dropped a brown colt foal to him named Fairway. This colt was leggy and light in frame, with good legs and feet, and as soon as he was at liberty in the paddock he showed his ability to gallop with that beautiful easy action which he retained all his life as a racehorse.

When he came into training as a yearling he was still a light-framed leggy customer, but from the very beginning of his active work neither I nor his trainer, Frank Butters, had the slightest doubt as to his being a colt of the very first class.

He had beautiful shoulders and the best set of legs and feet that I have ever seen on a racehorse – hard ground or soft came alike to him – and, added to other qualities, the bloodlike intelligent head of the high-class thoroughbred. He was not in any way like his sire Phalaris, and took after his grandsire Polymelus; but, like most of the stock of Phalaris, he was inclined to be nervous and fretful when first put into fast work, therefore Frank Butters wisely decided to let him learn the game of racing on the racecourse.

His first appearance was at York on 17 May. Although he had not been tried, his beautiful action had already caught the eyes of the touts, and he started favourite at 11–4 against. Getting away very badly and also running green, he was unplaced, but at the same time there was much to like about his performance. This race taught him what was wanted, and when he went to Ascot, although untried, he knew his business, and starting at 7–1 he won the Coventry Stakes in a canter by three lengths. Although he did not beat a very good lot of horses, his style of racing created an extremely good impression. His next race was for the July Stakes where he had to meet the very speedy colt Hakim. There was a long delay at the post and, getting away badly, his chance, two furlongs from home, looked hopeless; but he put in some great work in the last hundred yards and got up to beat Hakim a head. Weston, in this race, rode with the greatest patience, and although the verdict was only a head he did not give the horse a hard race.

Being still a backward and unfurnished colt Fairway was given every chance to develop, and he did not run again until the Champagne Stakes at Doncaster, where, with 9–4 laid on him, he beat a moderate field by a length and a half. There were divided opinions as to his merit after the race, some critics thinking that he could not have pulled out any more and that he would not stay, but that was not the opinion of either his trainer or his jockey. Like many other great racehorses, when he had won his race he knew he had done enough and there were no fireworks. After Doncaster coughing intervened and he was retired for the year.

During the winter and spring of 1926–7 he progressed the right way, and it was intended to run him in the Two Thousand Guineas, but he was troubled with boils a fortnight before the race and it was wisely decided to miss it, good as his chance of winning appeared to be. He was able to turn out for the Newmarket Stakes, which race he won in great style by three lengths, and he became a hot favourite for the Derby. The Two Thousand Guineas had been won by the game little Flamingo, who beat Royal Minstrel, a big backward colt, by a head. Fourth in the race, beaten about two lengths, was Fairway's stable companion, Pharamond, and, useful horse as Pharamond was, he was in quite a different class to Fairway, so there was every reason for the latter to be at a short price for the Derby; the small Flamingo was not likely to improve, and there was very little chance that Royal Minstrel would stay the mile and a half.

Frank Butters had no easy task to train this light-fleshed horse for a race like the Derby; there was a slight recurrence of boil trouble, but he contrived to send the horse to Epsom in good heart, and so well had he gone in his gallop that there was not the slightest doubt about his getting the distance. That year the arrangements at Epsom, or rather the want of arrangement, for the horses to get from the paddock ring on to the course were deplorable, and the moment Fairway got outside the paddock ring he was mobbed by an excited and enthusiastic crowd. He literally had to fight his way through it to get out on to the course. The same thing, in lesser degree, occurred after he returned from the canter, and being a very highly strung horse he was thoroughly and completely upset, and made no show in the race, being beaten before it started. Down he came from his pedestal: he was soft, temperamental, with no stamina! I was writing racing articles at the time, and I wrote that ninety-nine horses out of a hundred, if subjected to the same ordeal, would have failed, but I don't think anyone believed me. Three people, however, besides myself, still believed in the horse: Lord Derby, Frank Butters, and Weston.

It certainly took Fairway some time to recover, and he was sent to Ascot, not to run, but to forget the unpleasant memories of Epsom. The desired effect was achieved, and after the first day he settled down there and was full of confidence. He was then trained for the Eclipse Stakes, and everything went on most satisfactorily until a fortnight before the race, when he started a cough with a slight temperature, and there was a doubt, up to the very last moment, if he should run. On the morning of the race, Frank Butters took his courage in both hands and advised Lord Derby to run, saying he thought the horse would win.

There was the usual parade, in which, contrary to the expectations of his many detractors, he behaved perfectly, although for a moment on leaving the paddock he looked like getting upset, evidently remembering his Epsom experience. The field consisted of twelve runners, Booklaw, winner of the St Leger, being favourite at 9–4, Royal Minstrel second favourite at 5–2, and Fairway at 9–2.

The race is easily described. Fairway was always in a good place, and half way up the straight he went to the front, left his field standing still, and won easily by eight lengths from Royal Minstrel with Booklaw third beaten half a length. I have written previously about Fairway that when he was winning his races there were no fireworks, but on this occasion there certainly were, and I put that down to the excitement of his jockey Weston. Tommy Weston is a great jockey for a big race, he always rises to the occasion, but before the Eclipse Stakes I found him for the first time nervous and excitable, for he had been greatly upset by the Epsom fiasco. Some people think that Weston is severe on his horses, but in a long experience I have met no jockey who studies and loves his horses more, and, strong finisher as he is, when a horse has done its best and is beaten he is merciful.

After the Eclipse Stakes, Fairway was put by for the St Leger; there were no drawbacks to his preparation, and Frank Butters produced him for the race, a perfectly trained horse. There were thirteen starters, Fairway being favourite at 7–4, and Flamingo and Cyclonic at 100–15. The field was not a good one, and as far as the English horses were concerned it looked a certainty for Fairway, provided he could stay the course, which some people thought he would not do, believing that Phalaris would never sire a true stayer. The most dangerous rival, in my opinion, was the good French colt Palais Royal. The race was run at a nice pace, and for half the journey Weston was content to lie well behind, but half-way up the straight he put himself in a good position, and realizing that he had a lot in hand, took no risks, and going to the outside he drew out an easy winner by a length and a half from Palais Royal. Again there were people who declared Fairway had done all he could and that he did not stay, and it is curious how you will always find these critics of good horses that win their races in this easy way.

Fairway ran once again that year, when he won the Champion Stakes by a neck from Foliation.

The following year he had developed well, his somewhat spare frame having filled out, and he was a beautiful specimen of the English thoroughbred. He ran in six races, of which he won five. They included the Rous Memorial Stakes at Ascot, the Princess of Wales's Stakes, the Champion Stakes, and the Jockey Club Cup of two miles and a quarter. He won all these races with the greatest ease, and his only lapse was in the Eclipse Stakes at Sandown, where he was second to Royal Minstrel, beaten easily by four lengths. With all due respect to the grand Royal Minstrel, I think he was lucky in that he found Fairway not at his best that day, although there was no excuse that I know of except that he had been in hard training since the early spring.

Lord Derby, unlike many owners of these days, has always been ready to take on the best with his good horses, and after Fairway had won the Jockey Club Cup of two miles and a quarter he said that he would like him to be trained for the Ascot Cup the following year. The Jockey Club Cup had been run at a slow pace and was no test of stamina, so before he went into winter quarters he was given a gallop at Newmarket over two and a half miles, finishing at the Old Cambridgeshire winning-post. This two and a half miles is, I should say, the hardest gallop in the world, the last five furlongs being uphill much in the same way as at Ascot, but with only one slight turn in the whole distance. He was galloped with Bosworth who had only been beaten a short head for the St Leger and the Jockey Club Stakes, and to make certain of a good pace several other horses were in the gallop, two good handicappers for the first mile, and two more to jump in and take it up.

It was the best long-distance gallop that I have ever seen. Weston was told not to ride his usual waiting race, but to tackle Bosworth early and make it a real test of stamina, and after a great race Fairway beat him cleverly by half a length. They were running at weight for age, which at that time of year I believe to be greatly in favour of the younger horse. Bosworth had been a very backward three-year-old, but had now come to his very best; moreover, I am convinced that if Weston had been allowed to wait with his horse he would have won the gallop easily. In the evening Fairway had not left an oat in his manger, and came out the next morning as fresh as paint.

So this good horse remained in training, but the following spring he developed slight tendon trouble and was then retired. Lord Derby won the Ascot Cup that year with Bosworth, but I have no doubt that had he remained sound Fairway would have been the winner.

The Hon. George Lambton (1937)

Fairway (1925–48), b.c. Phalaris–Scapa Flow (Chaucer)
Fairway was undoubtedly one of the most brilliant horses to race betweeen the two World Wars. Bill Freeman, travelling head lad to Frank Butters during the years when Fairway and the unbeaten Bahram were in the stable, considered Fairway 'undoubtedly the better of the two'. Fairway headed the list of winning sires four times, his best offspring being Blue Peter, winner of the Derby and Two Thousand Guineas.

When Scapa Flow (1914) died in 1937, she had bred eight winners of sixty-three races worth £85,644, and founded a dynasty. Fairway's full brother, Pharos, was a high-class racehorse and sire of two of the outstanding European horses of the inter-war years: Nearco and Pharis II. The former's influence on the breed has been profound.

Death of a Derby Winner: Humorist

The list of [my] pictures shown at the Academy in 1923 is: *Humorist and Donoghue going out for the Derby*, *A May Morning at the Southcourt Stud*, *Thoroughbred Stallion – Radium*, *Brood Mares and Foals at the Southcourt Stud*, *Kilkenny Horse Fair*, and *My Horse is my Friend*.

It must be understood that pictures shown in a certain year would have been painted the year before. The titles of these six pictures convey more to me than I shall ever be able to describe, so I take only one – Donoghue and Humorist.

This was commissioned through a writer on the *Daily Telegraph* – the 'Hotspur' of that day – on behalf of friends and admirers who wanted to present a picture of the horse to the owner, Mr Jack Joel. It was an unsatisfactory picture; but, for all that, it awakens many memories. This, I believe, was the first of Donoghue's 'hat-trick' Derbys. To show how wrong it is to judge a horse: I was with Mr Donald Fraser, a breeder and owner of racehorses, when he took me with him into the holy of holies – the saddling paddock to see the Derby horses.

'I can't go in there,' said I.

'Come along,' said Donald, and began criticizing the horses. 'Has anyone seen such a lot? Look at that bay horse – common as dirt.' And so he went on about this horse and that, and then remarked with great scorn on a chestnut, 'Look at that brute over there! Look at his hocks! Could anybody ever see worse?' – this happened to be Humorist, who shortly afterwards was unsaddled as the winner of the Derby.

Some weeks later, after the Ascot meeting, staying with Charles Morton, the trainer of the horse, at Letcombe Basset, near Wantage, he told me about the horse bursting a blood-vessel in a gallop at Ascot before the race, and how they had decided not to run him. It was thus an easy matter to have the horse out in the afternoons to make studies of him. I had completed one of these on the Saturday and on the Sunday morning Charles Morton thought he would try a bottle of champagne out of one of the many cases presented to him by Humorist's owner – a slight addition to the generous cheque he had received. Why I use the word 'generous' is because that summer I had motored with Donoghue to Newbury race meeting and, calling for Donoghue at his rooms over the fishing-tackle shop in Pall Mall, I went upstairs, to find his housekeeper and his valet searching high and low for a cheque for £2,000 which Joel had given him for winning the Derby on Humorist – not that Donoghue thought this at all a large reward. Newbury races would not wait, and we left in a hurry in a large black Daimler.

How well I remember nearing Newbury on the main road! Occupants of charabancs – spotting Donoghue – shouted: 'Come on, Steve!' Near the weighing-room a telegram was handed to him, and he opened it. It was from his valet to say he had found the cheque in a waistcoat pocket.

To get back to the Sunday morning and Charles Morton and Joel's champagne. After sitting on a garden seat in the shade and drinking a bottle, Morton becoming friendly and talking of horses and racing, he went and opened another. Then came lunch, which left me in somewhat of a stupor. I sought the shade of the old yew tree on the lawn, and, resting my head on a cushion or two, fell asleep . . . After an interval of sheer oblivion, I heard a woman's tragic voice above me crying: 'Wake up, Mr Munnings, wake up! Humorist is dead!'

I opened my eyes. There stood Charles Morton's pretty little wife – far younger than he – looking like Ophelia in *Hamlet*, wringing her hands. 'Humorist is dead!' she cried again.

'No!!' said I.

Then the green door from the stable yard into the garden opened. Charles Morton came along the garden path with a bunch of keys in his hand. He hadn't turned a hair; neither the horse's death nor the champagne had affected him. He said in a quiet voice: 'You had better come along to the yard, and you'll see a sight you won't see again as long as you live.'

Out in the blazing glare of the chalk yard the light was dazzling. Becoming accustomed to the glare, I saw on the white chalk outside the door of the end box, a dark, dried-up trickle of blood. Morton then took the bunch of keys, unlocked the loose-box door and threw it open.

'There,' said he; 'did you ever see such a thing in your life?'

The horse lay dead on the straw, his head close to the door – the upper ear pricked, an eye still open. A large pool of blood was welling up to the threshold, churned into bright vermilion foam where the horse had breathed his last. Not only was there this pool of blood, he had thrown blood in great splashes upon the walls of the box, where he had turned round and round in his fright, and reared. Then Morton took me across to the iron manger in the corner. This was full of blood. Never should I have thought that the veins and arteries in any one horse could have contained such an amount.

It was a tragic sight. Looking down on this winner of the Derby, one almost expected to see him twitch his ear – so alive did he look.

'Well,' said Charles Morton, 'there lies fifty thousand pounds' worth!' . . .

And so we left the horse and he locked the door.

Morton had phoned at once to Joel, and soon owner, wife and veterinary arrived in a very large car from Joel's home at Childwickbury. The final discussion on this tragic event happened over a cold supper. Mrs Joel wanted the horse's head to be stuffed and mounted. Mr Joel said: 'No, we'll only mount his feet.'

Still the talk went on about the horse's tragic end, Mr Joel fortifying himself with brandy and cigars until Charles Morton at the head of the table exclaimed: 'Well, let's not talk about it any more; we're getting like people at an Irish wake.'

At that the company arose, the large car rolled away and we went back into the cigar-smoke.

Sir Alfred Munnings (1951)

Humorist (1918–21) ch.c. by Polymelus–Jest (Sundridge)

Triumph and tragedy characterized the victory of Humorist in the Derby of 1921. My memorable win with Sunstar ten years earlier was sufficiently dramatic to satisfy most people to whom the paramount appeal in racing is sensation. Well, they had their fill and more with poor Humorist. The spectacle of him lying dead that Sunday afternoon caused me a grief I shall never forget. Mr Munnings felt almost as upset as myself. He could not believe his eyes; only a few hours before he had stood beside the horse and remarked how well he looked.

These words were written by CHARLES MORTON (1855–1936), *Humorist's meticulous and dedicated trainer, soon after the tragic incident.*

Easter Hero

A cable from Mr J. H. Whitney told Jack Anthony that Easter Hero had died at Kentucky, USA, on 10 February 1948, at the ripe age of twenty-eight.

Generally regarded as one of the best horses never to win the Grand National, Easter Hero was one of the most popular jumpers the game has ever known. He won the Cheltenham Gold Cup twice, in 1929 and 1930, on both occasions by margins estimated at twenty lengths. He ran three times in the Grand National, in 1928, 1929 and 1931.

Easter Hero was the cause of a débâcle in the Grand National the first time he ran in the Aintree Classic. When leading his field as far as the Canal Turn in the first circuit he landed on the top of the fence and fell back into the ditch. Two or three horses close behind him had to be pulled up suddenly, and they in turn caused others to stop. As a result, nearly half the runners, which totalled forty-two, were out of the race, Tipperary Tim (the winner) and Billy Barton being the only two to complete the course.

Perhaps his best performance was in the National the following year. Top weight in a record field of sixty-six, he tried to give the winner, Gregalach, 17 lb., but finished second, beaten six lengths. It was discovered after the race that Easter Hero had spread a plate. Top of the handicap again, Easter Hero was knocked down in the Grand National of 1931, when Grakle beat Gregalach (12 st.) by a length and a half.

Rather less than a fortnight before the National of 1928, Mr

Frank Barbour, a Belfast merchant, sold Easter Hero to Mr A. Loewenstein, a wealthy Belgian, for £7,000, with a contingency of £3,000 if the horse won at Aintree. About three months later Easter Hero was sent to Paris to contest the Grand Steeplechase, in which he fell. Some few days later he won the Prix des Drags, giving a faultless display of jumping.

Three weeks after this success Mr Loewenstein was killed when he fell from an airplane into the sea when travelling from England to Belgium. Mr J. H. Whitney then bought Easter Hero, who was sent to Jack Anthony to be trained. He won twenty-two races, his last race being the Champion Steeplechase of 1931, when he dead-heated with Coup de Chapeau. On 31 August that year he was sent to America, to live the life of a pensioner on Mr Whitney's Kentucky farm.

Bred by Mr L. King of Crickstown, Ashbourne, Co. Meath, who also bred his dam, Easter Hero was a chestnut gelding by that great sire of jumpers, My Prince, out of Easter Week (who ran only once), by Outbreak out of a mare by Enthusiast, from a mare by Rob Roy. This is the half-bred family known as the Arab Maid Family.

B. J. O'Sullivan (1949)

Easter Hero (1920) was one of the many top-class chasers got by My Prince in the late twenties and thirties and a horse of exceptional quality and courage.

Since the introduction of the Cheltenham Gold Cup in 1924, every really great steeplechaser which has run in this country has won it, and it would be hard indeed to rank them against such as Easter Hero: Golden Miller (1932–6), Prince Regent (1946), Cottage Rake (1948–50), Arkle (1964–6), were all superlative performers.

The fact that so many of the brilliant successes of Prince Regent took place in the obscurity of wartime racing in Ireland has clouded a true appreciation of this great chaser; he was eleven years old when carrying 12 st. 5 lb. in the Grand National of 1948 and failing by seven lengths to give 2 stone to the winner, Lovely Cottage. But for the attention of a succession of loose horses he would probably have won.

During his retirement Easter Hero was hunted by his owner. Asked how he found him to ride, for Easter Hero was a hard puller, Mr Whitney replied that as he was the master he had no problems, being entitled always to be in front.

———

The End of a Long Life: Hyperion

Introduction by Lord Derby to 'Hyperion' by Clive Graham
I suppose one of the hardest decisions anyone has to take is when to put down an old dog or horse, or for that matter any other animal of which one is particularly fond. Frankly I could never give the order to have an old friend destroyed, but I equally appreciate that one should never allow any animal to suffer unnecessarily. For this reason I told Bunty Scrope, my stud manager, that he and the vets were to take the decision over Hyperion and only to let me know after it had happened.

On the morning of 9 December 1960, Bunty rang up to say that the old horse was in considerable pain with his feet and that the vets could not find any way of alleviating it; as a result they had decided to put Hyperion down.

It was sad news; after all I was only twelve years old when he was born and so Hyperion had always been very much a part of my life. The first time I saw him was with my father and George Lambton when he was a yearling at the Side Hill Stud. I remember Mr Lambton remarking that he was the most beautifully made little horse he had ever seen and would undoubtedly win the Pony Derby. It was, of course, said in jest, but it was quite obvious then that he was already getting a great affection for Hyperion. Owing to being at school I only ever saw him run once and that was in the Leger, which he won with the same effortless ease with which he had won the Derby. Small though he was, he never appeared small racing – he had a tremendous stride and as a three-year-old pulverized his opponents.

Hyperion retired to the stud when I was sixteen; so for the whole of my adult life, the little horse dominated the scene at the

Woodlands Stud. It would have been unthinkable for me to have gone to Newmarket without seeing Hyperion. He was part of the place as far as I was concerned.

I remember the day Hyperion died, the late Peter Hastings-Bass and some others were staying with me, and after dinner that night I got out the last bottle of Napoleon brandy at Knowsley and we drank to Hyperion's memory. Strangely enough that bottle had originally been opened for a visit by the late Sir Winston Churchill, who had thoroughly enjoyed this very old brandy. I still have the bottle in a glass case outside my estate office, along with some other family treasures. After all, it had been used to pay tribute to the two greatest G.O.M.'s of our time.

One felt when Hyperion died that Newmarket would never be quite the same. However, thanks to the wonderful statue of him by John Skeaping, he still dominates the scene at Woodlands.

Hyperion was a great racehorse, a great sire and a great sire of broodmares, but above all else he was a great character, and that is how I shall always remember him.

The Earl of Derby (1967)

Hyperion (1930) ch.c. Gainsborough–Selene (Chaucer)
A racehorse of great excellence, Hyperion was bred and owned by the 17th Earl of Derby and trained by the Hon. George Lambton. He was possibly the best small horse in the history of racing in this country: when in training he stood 15 hh. 1½. He had a high degree of intelligence and an individuality of his own; children could (and did) play with him in his box and all connected with him regarded him with deep affection.

He won the Derby and St Leger with the greatest ease and was champion sire six times (1940–2, 1945, 1946 and 1954), a record only beaten by St Simon, Hermit, Stockwell and Highflyer. He has been a profound and long-lasting influence on the thoroughbred. Between the years of 1975 and 1988 his name has appeared in the pedigrees of no less than 237 winners of Pattern and Graded races in England, France, Ireland, Italy and the USA.

———

Brigadier Gerard on Newbury Racecourse

Despite the downfall in the Champion Stakes of past heroes such as Colorado, Ballymoss, Royal Palace and Nijinsky, we were confident that a similar fate would not overcome the Brigadier. He was at the height of his powers, had no chinks in his armour apart from heavy going, in which case he would not be started, and on form had the beating of all his probable opponents. He could only be defeated by an act of fate, which is an integral hazard of racing and must be faced.

So, the die was cast and the Champion Stakes became the Brigadier's final exploit. This race came exactly three weeks after the Queen Elizabeth Stakes, on Saturday, 14 October.

As before the Ascot race, Dick Hern thought that the Brigadier would benefit from having his final gallop on Newbury racecourse, as opposed to completing his whole preparation at home.

When the morning of the Brigadier's gallop at Newbury dawned there was a fairly dense fog; so much so, that I wondered whether we should be able to work the horses at all. However, it cleared just sufficiently for the purpose, though it would have been too foggy to race.

The Brigadier and Almagest were going seven furlongs the reverse way of the course, that is to say right-handed, finishing at the Greenham end of the back straight. The going was beautiful, a real credit to Frank Osgood, who always has the Newbury course in such good order. While the Brigadier knew exactly where he was, he had always galloped and raced up the straight, as the races are run, so was interested to find himself undergoing a different routine. He also realized that he was working towards his horse-box and was alert and eager.

Fog sometimes has a disturbing effect on horses, perhaps because they can lose their sense of direction in it, causing them to want to go faster, possibly in the hope of getting out of the fog as soon as possible; and I remember the now successful trainer 'Fiddler' Goodwill, when he was working for the late Tom Leader, making about six circuits of the Links at Newmarket after the rest of us in the gallop had pulled up, before he succeeded in stopping the mare he was riding.

Happily no such misadventure befell the Brigadier, but he certainly worked with great zest.

There was a dramatic quality about the scene as we stood peering through the Cimmerian gauze, waiting for the horses to emerge. Nothing could be seen of the stands across the course, the silence was complete; we might have been in outer space. Then faintly at first and gradually increasing, came that unmistakable and thrilling sound, which in 2,000 years no writer has succeeded in describing better than Virgil with his '*quadripedante putrem sonitu quatit ungula campum*' – the hoofbeats of galloping horses – and out of the fog burst the Brigadier as he swept past Almagest. At a few yards' distance from him at which I was standing as he passed, he was a magnificent and awe-inspiring sight, ears pricked, nostrils distended, his great, powerful frame and limbs moving with the rhythm and force of an express train, his hooves tearing the turf from under him – my heart bled for Frank's groundsmen – the momentum of his progress leaving the swishing of its slipstream behind him. His sense of direction beamed on the end of the back straight, where his horse-box awaited him, and, determined to get there as fast as possible, he was really travelling. In a flash he had vanished into the fog, his hooves beating out in diminuendo until, once again, there was silence.

Never had I seen him work more impressively and in this form I was convinced that no horse in the world was capable of beating him.

With a good heart we faced the Brigadier's last battle, his second Champion Stakes. It was just a matter of all keeping well with him and the weather being kind to us. In both respects fortune favoured us: the Brigadier remained in perfect order and the fine weather held.

                                                        John Hislop (1973)

___

The Horse of the Decade

And so for the third time I have entangled myself with the Horse of the Decade. I am talking about Nashwan, of course, who won the King George VI and Queen Elizabeth Diamond Stakes on Saturday in such an effortful and gutsy fashion. He is the greatest racehorse of the eighties, without a shadow of a doubt.

But I am also talking about Shergar, who won the Derby with inconceivable brilliance in 1981. And I shall never forget Dancing Brave for that heart-stopping turn of foot he showed when he won the Arc in 1986.

So that is three times in the last ten years that we have seen the greatest horse of the decade. In fact, it is a rare year in which we do *not* have one; in 1987, the admirable but ultimately uninspiring Reference Point won the sort of praise that would turn men's heads (like the famous dubbing of Paul Jarvis as the fastest white bowler in the world) but which horses are able to take in their strides.

And I remember Gorytus who, for a brief moment in the autumn of 1982, was the greatest racehorse ever seen when he was still a two-year-old. I went to see him at Newmarket: he was butch, swaggering, superbly muscled – and beaten out of sight, widely believed to have been got at. At any rate, that was the end of him, more is the pity.

This is the nature of Flat racing. The jumps give us the same good ol' boys year after year, with their failures and their foibles and their triumphs. Desert Orchid is endearing; but no one has ever found these fleeting, transient kings of the Flat endearing. Nashwan, with his great strong head, and his long white sock in front, inspires admiration, but not affection.

There is no time, for a start, for affection to build up. Now you see them, now you don't. We see a great horse, we admire it, but at once it is whisked away to the mad pleasures of the stud.

There is no time for a horse to become a character, a Red Rum. A great champion of the Flat leaves behind a collection of memories: Shergar's white face; Dancing Brave's explosiveness;

Nashwan, at last finding himself under threat, blasting on defiantly and *refusing* to be passed on Saturday.

This is Flat racing – long legs and short memories. Every season has a different population of horses: different names to learn, different histories, different breeding. At a big racing yard, no one can remember the names of any of the two-year-olds, and of very few of what they call the 'older horses' – who are practically all just three, mere babies in normal equestrian terms.

It is too confusing to try and remember them all, especially those with Arabic names. And so most of the horses are referred to by the name of their sire – the Shirley Heights, the Blushing Groom, the nice Formidable filly.

And they flash by. They win, they lose, and move on, to their various fates, and meanwhile, a new and enormous consignment of two-year-olds comes into the yard every autumn, wonder horses and no-hopers all together. And no one can tell which is which.

In Flat racing, every season is different, and every one is the same. Every season brings victory and defeat, every season has its hero, and virtually every season has its Horse of the Decade.

We seek constant change as a stimulus, and at the same time, we want nothing to change, for our comfort. Both those things are provided by the seasonal patterns of these latitudes. Sport follows the seasons: cricket follows football which follows cricket, overlapping at the times of transition. And the Flat season follows the jumps, which follow the Flat.

The sporting creatures of the high summer are cricketers and three-year-old horses. The horse of the season – for a brief moment better than all that came before him – is soon gone.

Glorious Nashwan will be retired at the end of this season; but there'll be another wonder horse along soon enough. And I look forward to seeing every single one of the Horses of the Decade that the nineties will bring.

                                                      Simon Barnes (1989)

These admirably expressed views contrast starkly with the style of earlier but no less effective commentaries on the same theme.

The sight, on the Flat, of a top-class mature racehorse is one to be savoured. With so many classic horses in such few hands, it is a sight that is becoming increasingly rare. Set against the level of stallion fees demanded by Group 1 winners, the existing structure of prize-money available to top-class older horses does nothing to redress the situation. However, the imperfections of the Pattern system are due less to lack of incentives to race mature horses than to disregard by owners of the Pattern's original purpose of testing a racehorse at all stages of its career.

When the Horse was King

We live in a materialistic world. The philosophy of Mammon pervades every aspect of life, not least the Turf, which once was termed 'The Sport of Kings' and now is more often referred to as an industry, as if it were nuclear power, motor-car manufacture or electricity, which it is not. Though many earn a living out of racing, fundamentally it is still a sport.

The most important figure in the whole activity is the racehorse, who tends to be overlooked by administrators, entrepreneurs and bureaucrats, in whose hands his fate often lies. Much is heard about building new stands, prize-money, catering, betting, television and such like, but there is less consideration for the racehorse himself. Priorities seem to have gone awry.

Without horses, there would be no horse-racing; therefore the sport should be built round the horse, rather than the horse fitted to the sport. It must not be forgotten that racing could go on without stands, spectators, bookmakers, sponsors or any other appendages, human or material – not as we know it now but as it was in the beginning – because there will always be those dedicated to racehorses and the desire to pit one against another. The welfare of the horse and those who look after him demands more attention than it receives.

Prosperity can be double-edged. The unhealthy boom in top-grade bloodstock, now happily declining, resulted in racehorses becoming an international currency which attracted people with no knowledge of, or interest in, horses as such, and whose racing and breeding policy was entirely mercenary.

This attitude benefits neither the sport nor the breed, giving rise to avoidance of competition and such undesirable practices as treating yearlings with steroids to advance their development for the purpose of sale.

Racing has always been an expensive affair, but to say that it is solely a rich man's pastime is incorrect; people of slender means have occasionally prospered through it, though among all those involved few strike gold. The majority of owners are not in the game primarily to make money, even if they hope to do so; their participation is due to the enjoyment they derive from its many facets.

There was a time when a breeder, if asked why he was using a certain stallion, would quote reasons of conformation, temperament, inbreeding, outcrossing, blending of bloodlines and so on. Now, as often as not, the answer will be, 'Because he looked value for money' or 'His stock are selling well.'

Sale-ring profit is a popular aim, as opposed to racing merit, but it is not one calculated to improve the breed of the racehorse. Finance and fashion rule over racing ability and soundness. If a stallion is not an immediate success, he is soon out of favour; the fact that his failure might be due to matings with unsuitable mares is seldom taken into account.

Breeding to fashion may secure buyers, but it is no sinecure and it is an odd fact that the successful sires do not always appeal to buyers, in spite of their records.

As the chief actor in the show, the racehorse is entitled to good accommodation, but when plans for improvements on racecourses are drawn up the racehorse is usually bottom of the list, or not on it at all. Many of the buildings which house horses and lads are archaic, the amenities abysmal.

The intelligence and individuality of horses are not always appreciated. Many of the greatest racehorses have had their peculiarities. The bad-tempered Triple Crown winner, Diamond Jubilee, would only tolerate the stable lad Herbert Jones, who was thus promoted to jockey. Thereafter the pair formed a harmonious and successful partnership.

Sun Chariot, one of the best fillies of modern times, was unmanageable when in a bad mood – she once took Sir Gordon Richards off the gallops at Beckhampton into a field where she knelt down and roared like a lion. Yet the lad who looked after her could do anything with her.

When out at exercise, the Derby and St Leger winner Hyperion would sometimes stand stock-still for half an hour on end, looking into the distance.

Horses can be sensitive to circumstances which it is difficult to believe they can understand. One of the greatest hurdlers of all time, Trespasser, was a hard puller and invariably hit his hurdles. In one race his jockey, George Duller, who always rode him, was in considerable pain, having barely recovered from a broken collarbone. The horse sensed that there was something wrong with his rider, never pulled, jumped every hurdle cleanly and won.

A similar case was that of Joe Mercer and Brigadier Gerard in the Prince of Wales's Stakes at Royal Ascot. Two days before, Mercer had been severely shaken in a plane crash and was still feeling the effects – he collapsed after the race. Brigadier Gerard, then a powerful four-year-old who took a strong hold, realized that Mercer was unwell, took only a light hold of his bit, ran the race of his own accord, in the way he knew was expected of him, and triumphed.

More than anything, the public love a really good horse; such a horse fires their imagination and gathers admirers like any human star performer.

This is particularly evident in jumping, where top horses stay in training longer than their counterparts on the Flat, who so often leave the scene after a couple of seasons and half a dozen races. How favoured were our forebears with Flat racers of the calibre of Bayardo, whose twenty-two wins from twenty-five starts included the Middle Park, Dewhurst, Eclipse, St Leger and Ascot Gold Cup; Pretty Polly, who raced till she was five, winning the One Thousand Guineas, Oaks, St Leger, Coronation Cup (twice), Champion Stakes and nine two-year-old races; and Sceptre, who won every Classic except the Derby and was successful in fourteen out of twenty-four races.

Greed for money can lead to the defeat, even ruination, of horses, through racing them too often, when they are unfit, off colour or in conditions to which they are unsuited. While a racehorse must be thoroughly tested if he is to aspire and deserve to be entitled 'great', he can only be expected to race against top-class opposition a limited number of times in one season. If this precept is ignored, the penalty will have to be paid. Thus it is wise not to ask too much of him as a three-year-old, but to extend his racing career into another year, if the most is to be made of him.

On the Turf, there is only one rightful king – the racehorse; and if he is not served in the manner due to him, neither he nor his kingdom will prosper.

John Hislop (1988)

EIGHT OUTSTANDING
RACEHORSES

—

Mill Reef (1968). At three years old. Geoff Lewis up.
(*W. W. Rouch & Co*)

Alycidon (1945)

ch.c. Donatello II–Aurora (Hyperion)

Alycidon was the last of the many great racehorses to carry the colours of the seventeenth Earl of Derby, who died in 1948. Since then the fortunes of the Stanley House Stud have declined. Gone are the days when it was rare to see an important race without a runner in the familiar black jacket and white cap. The present Earl, also, seldom has a horse good enough to represent him in a Classic. Alycidon will be remembered not merely as one of the best stayers in English racing history, but as one who provided a much-needed boost to morale when French horses, particularly those owned by M. Boussac, were carrying all before them in the immediate post-war era.

Alycidon, a chestnut, was foaled in 1945, and was by the Italian-bred Donatello II out of Aurora. Donatello II was by the Derby winner Blenheim out of Delleana, a Clarissimus mare who went back to Pretty Polly. He was undoubtedly a high-class horse, and his only defeat – a most unlucky one, at that – was when Clairvoyant beat him by less than a length in the Grand Prix de Paris. Soon after that race Signor Tesio sold him for £47,500 to Mr E. Esmond, who sent him to the Brickfields Stud at Newmarket. As a sire, Donatello II was not consistently successful, but besides Alycidon he sired the Two Thousand Guineas and Derby winner Crepello; the One Thousand Guineas winner Picture Play; and Supertello, who won the Ascot Gold Cup. He also sired the dams of Pinza, winner of the Derby; Aureole, winner of the King George VI and Queen Elizabeth Stakes; and Wilwyn, winner of the Washington International at Laurel Park.

Aurora, bred by Lord Derby, came from the famous Marchetta family, and was by Hyperion out of Rose Red, by Swynford. She only won a single race, worth £363, but she was in fact a far better filly than the bare figures of her record indicate, and was runner-up in both the Richmond Stakes at Goodwood and the Cheveley Park Stakes at Newmarket. At the stud she proved an outstanding success, her seven winners including, besides Alycidon, Borealis, who was second in a wartime St Leger and won the Coronation Cup; Woodlark, grandam of the Derby winner Larkspur; Arousal, dam of Wake Up, winner of over £6,000; and Acropolis, who won seven races worth over £8,000 and was third in the Derby and second in the King George VI and Queen Elizabeth Stakes.

Lord Derby's trainer at this period was Walter Earl, who fully appreciated that Alycidon was a backward colt needing plenty of time, and accordingly made no attempt to hurry him. In fact Alycidon only ran twice in 1947, finishing down the course in a couple of seven-furlong events at Newmarket in the autumn. During the winter, Alycidon made more than normal progress, and it soon became clear that he was going to prove an extremely useful colt. Before going into the details of what he actually accomplished as a three-year-old, it is important to bear in mind that Walter Earl, who died in 1950, was in failing health, while the stable jockey, Doug Smith, had been ill, too, and was not available to ride Alycidon in his early races. But for these factors, Alycidon's record might have been even better than it was.

Alycidon's first race in the spring was in the ten-furlong Christopher Wren Stakes at Hurst Park. Quietly backed at 8–1 and ridden by Eph Smith, he whipped round at the start and took no part. From then on he invariably wore blinkers. A fortnight later he was sent up to Thirsk. Ridden by R. Shaw, a lad attached to Earl's stable, he showed admirable acceleration in the last two furlongs to win the one-mile Classic Trial Stakes by three parts of a length. His victory in this event, achieved on good going against ten opponents, disposes of any notion that he merely possessed boundless stamina and singularly little in the way of speed. At this stage of the season he ran in the name of Brigadier T. Fairfax-Ross, the Stanley family being in mourning for the seventeenth Earl, who had died in February.

Alycidon next ran in the Chester Vase. Again ridden by Shaw, he finished a creditable third. Thirteen days later Alycidon won the Royal Standard Stakes, run over ten furlongs at Manchester, by a neck from Nathoo, a useful colt belonging to the Aga Khan. At that point it seemed that Alycidon possessed at least an outsider's chance in the Derby, but Walter Earl had both Usher and Ottoman engaged in that race, and as he considered Alycidon was still rather backward he decided to reserve him for the King Edward VII Stakes at Ascot. If Lowrey had adopted more enterprising tactics, Alycidon would very likely have won. As it was, Lowrey held him up until well into the straight, and though Alycidon battled on courageously he had been left with too much to do and insufficient use had been made of his stamina.

The racing public were surprisingly slow to recognize Alycidon's merit, and in the mile-and-a-half Princess of Wales's Stakes, run at Newmarket on 1 July, he started at 100–8 in a field of five. From the start Alycidon, again ridden by Lowrey, was in close touch with the leaders, and taking the lead in the Dip he ran on up the hill like the true stayer he was to win by two lengths from Sayajirao. At the end of the month, ridden for the first time that season by Doug Smith, who was to partner him for the remainder of his career, he won the thirteen-furlong St George Stakes at Liverpool.

Starting at 20–1, Alycidon ran second in the St Leger to Mr W. Woodward's American-bred Black Tarquin, beaten a length and a half. Solar Slipper was third and the Derby winner My Love unplaced. It was a fine performance on Alycidon's part, as, owing to the moderate pace early on, Doug Smith felt obliged to take him to the front after a couple of furlongs. He was compelled, therefore, to make his own running for the greater part of the race, and not surprisingly was beaten for speed when the handsome Black Tarquin tackled him well inside the distance. A number of shrewd judges took the view that if Alycidon had had a pacemaker to help him it might well have been a very close thing between him and the winner.

It was now apparent that Alycidon was indeed a high-class stayer, and at Newmarket on 30 September he was an odds-on favourite for the mile-and-three-quarters Jockey Club Stakes, in which he made every yard of the running and won with ease. By now he had had a strenuous season, but he showed not the slightest trace of staleness, so it was decided to allow him to take his chance in the King George VI Stakes, a two-mile race for three-year-olds then run at the Ascot October meeting. This race had been instituted in 1946, in which year the Derby and St Leger winner Airborne was well and truly slammed by the French horse Souverain. Another French horse, Arbar, had won in 1947. There was powerful opposition from France on this occasion, too, Flush Royal, who actually started favourite, Rigolo and Djeddah being among the runners.

For the first time Alycidon had his stable companion Benny Lynch as pacemaker. Benny Lynch did his job well, and set a true gallop right from the start. Alycidon was second for a mile and a half, at which point he swept past Benny Lynch, drawing right away from his rivals in the straight to win unchallenged by five lengths from Djeddah, with Flush Royal third. His victory, achieved at a time when the French stayers seemed to be invincible, was received with tremendous enthusiasm and a successful Derby favourite could hardly have been given a warmer reception. The cheering began from the moment he took the lead, increasing in volume as he strode away from his opponents in the last three furlongs. '*Si licet exemplis in parvo grandibus uti*,' Alycidon's win was the El Alamein of the immediate post-war era in racing.

The Ascot Gold Cup was the target in 1949 for both Alycidon and Black Tarquin, and intense rivalry developed between the supporters of these two fine horses. Partisans of Black Tarquin were inclined to regard Alycidon somewhat scornfully as no more than a very good one-pacer who would always be beaten by a high-class horse with real acceleration. They expected the Gold Cup to prove a repetition of the St Leger. On the other hand, admirers of Lord Derby's colt reckoned that with one, or perhaps two, pacemakers to help him, such a strong gallop would be set that Black Tarquin would be off the bit before he was in a position to deliver his challenge. Furthermore, they felt inclined to doubt whether Black Tarquin, a son of the Eclipse winner Rhodes Scholar, was really a genuine stayer.

Alycidon had preliminary races at Chester and Doncaster, both of which he won.

The going at Ascot was perfect. The betting on the Gold Cup was fierce and close, with Black Tarquin ending up favourite at

.11–10, a fractionally shorter price than the 5–4 available about Alycidon at the off.

Stockbridge went off in front at a good gallop and held his place for a mile and three furlongs, after which Benny Lynch took over. Alycidon was always in close touch, and a terrific cheer went up from every part of the course when, with five furlongs to go, he strode past Benny Lynch.

Approaching the final bend Black Tarquin, moving very easily indeed, drew up to tackle Alycidon and the excitement mounted. 'Now watch the real racehorse come away and win,' observed a sanguine racing correspondent who had 'napped' Black Tarquin. There was no question, though, of Black Tarquin 'coming away'.

The pair raced together for about a hundred yards and then Britt had to feel for his whip. It was to no avail, though, as the gallant Black Tarquin had given everything he had. Alycidon, on the other hand, showed not the slightest sign of weakening, and, hand-ridden by Doug Smith, he galloped right away from his rival from the distance to win by the decisive margin of five lengths. Not since Persimmon's victory in the royal colours had there been such a popular Gold Cup win. Alycidon's time was only a second outside the record set up by Flares in 1938.

The weather was hot and dry for much of that summer and going at Goodwood was hard, which did not suit Alycidon at all. In the Goodwood Cup Doug Smith was hard at work on him throughout the last three furlongs, and there was a dreadful moment, as Riding Mill came up to him just below the distance, when it looked as if he was going to be beaten. Inside the final furlong, though, Riding Mill began to roll from sheer exhaustion and Alycidon, responding to the whip, rallied courageously and pulled out a bit extra to win by a couple of lengths. It was not one of Alycidon's more spectacular performances, but the conditions underfoot were abhorrent to him and he certainly displayed no lack of fighting spirit when the issue of the race was in the balance. At Doncaster in September the ground was more to Alycidon's liking, and he completed the stayers' 'Triple Crown' by winning the Doncaster Cup by eight lengths from Aldborough. That was his final race, so never again was he defeated after Black Tarquin beat him in the St Leger.

There was a sad side to Alycidon's story in 1949. That very able and much-liked trainer Walter Earl, who had brought Alycidon on so skilfully and patiently, collapsed during racing at Newmarket in April. Three months later he underwent a brain operation, and he remained a desperately sick man until his death the following autumn. During his absence the stable was taken over by Willie Pratt, who, as a boy of fourteen, had dead-heated for the 1893 Cesarewitch on Cypria. Later he went over to France and rode the winner of the Grand Prix on four occasions. He trained with success in France and in England, and he won the Cesarewitch with Whiteway fifty-four years after he himself had ridden the winner of that race. He died at the age of eighty in 1957.

A long, low chestnut with a tremendous stride, Alycidon retired to his owner's Woodpark Stud, having been syndicated for £140,000. Unfortunately, like his sire Donatello II and other stallions from the Blandford line, he proved a shy breeder. There were no complaints about his fertility during his first five years at the stud, but from then on a decline set in. By 1962 his fertility had dropped below 30 per cent and the following year he was retired from stud duties. He was painlessly destroyed in the autumn, being then in his nineteenth year. Altogether he sired 235 foals; that is a far better record than that of The Tetrarch who only sired 130, but it compares poorly with the record of Hyperion, for example, who sired well over 500.

However, there was plenty of quality among Alycidon's stock. The best of his colts was Alcide, who would almost certainly have won the Derby had he not gone wrong shortly before that race. He recovered to win the St Leger handsomely and the following year he won the King George VI and Queen Elizabeth Stakes.

Of Alycidon's fillies, Meld, winner of the One Thousand Guineas, the Oaks and the St Leger, was of course the best.

Trainer: W. Earl   Roger Mortimer (1967)

―

Abernant (1946)

gr.c. Owen Tudor–Rustom Mahal (Rustom Pasha)

Only in Great Britain do sprinters enjoy a status amounting to an estate of the thoroughbred realm. Even in the United States, where precocious speed is cultivated to a degree unknown elsewhere and six-furlong races for horses of all ages abound, older horses are expected to run a mile or a furlong or so more in order to force their way into the big leagues, and are consigned to an inferior grade if they cannot do so. In Great Britain the sprinter, the horse who excels at five and six furlongs and is unable to race effectively at longer distances, is accepted and honoured in his own right, and the category of sprinter embraces some of the famous names in Turf history.

Among sprinters few horses have ever achieved a supremacy to compare with that of Abernant, or have conveyed a stronger sense of greatness in the context of the thoroughbred population as a whole. His trainer Noël Murless once described Abernant as one of the best horses he had ever trained, and this was high praise indeed from the man who developed the brilliance of Petite Étoile and prepared the Derby winners Crepello, St Paddy and Royal Palace. He was beaten in only three of the seventeen races he contested, and there were extenuating circumstances in each case. In the vast majority of his races his superior speed and class settled the issue within the first few hundred yards.

Bred by Major (later Sir Reginald) Macdonald-Buchanan of Cottesbrooke Hall in Northamptonshire, Abernant was sent into training at the celebrated Wiltshire stable, Beckhampton, as a yearling in the autumn of 1947. A big change was impending at Beckhampton at that time. The choleric Fred Darling, who had trained seven Derby winners there, was about to retire on grounds of ill health and to be succeeded by Noël Murless, a man in his middle thirties who had made a name for himself by his skill in sending out horses from his small stable at Hambleton, near Thirsk, to take on and often beat the representatives of the powerful stables in the south. That year he had won the Stewards' Cup, the most coveted sprint handicap of the season, at Goodwood with Close-burn.

It is no easy transition for a trainer to adjust his methods from the second-class animals that made up the strength of the Hamble-ton stable to the animals of Classic breeding and aspirations that gave the Beckhampton stable its distinctive character. Murless showed his professional genius by carrying on precisely where Darling had left off, and was leading trainer in his very first season at Beckhampton. Although his most resounding triumphs came after his subsequent move to Warren Place, Newmarket, his ability to extract the best from horses of the highest class was apparent from his earliest days at Beckhampton.

Abernant made his first public appearance in the Spring Stakes over five furlongs at Lingfield on 16 April. Some horses seem to know instinctively what is required of them from the moment they set foot on a racecourse; others take a little time to familiarize themselves with the strange surroundings. Abernant was one of the latter. At the start he screwed round when the tapes went up, and then wandered along completely off balance for most of the race. It was not until they were approaching the last furlong that Gordon Richards was able to get him on an even keel and racing in earnest. Then Abernant began to eat up the ground in spectacular fashion, but the winning post came one stride too soon for him and he failed to catch The Potentate, who had made all the running, by a short head.

The extent to which the form of a two-year-old first time out may be false is stressed by the fact that, whereas Abernant was given top weight of 9 st. 5 lb. when the Free Handicap was com-piled seven months later, The Potentate was not good enough to be included at all. It is true to say that The Potentate would not have been able to live with Abernant in any of his races after the Spring Stakes.

The Lingfield race had taught Abernant all he needed to know. When he appeared next in the Bedford Stakes at Newmarket a month later he cantered away from his two opponents, and in the Chesham Stakes at Royal Ascot he shot from the gate like a bullet and made all the running to beat El Barq by five lengths. His first searching test was in the National Breeders' Produce Stakes at Sandown Park in July, when he met Star King, who had won the three races in which he had run in scintillating fashion and by margins of at least five lengths. Odds of 2–1 were laid on Abernant, with Star King at 9–4 and the other three runners virtually ignored. Sam Wragg took Star King off in front from the start. After three furlongs Gordon Richards called on Abernant for his effort and the colt responded immediately with a burst of acceleration which took him to the front in a few strides. The race looked over, but Star King began to run on with determination under the whip and suddenly the struggle became really tense. Abernant edged to the right under pressure, and Star King got closer with every stride. Only the judge could tell which had won as they flashed past the post together, as the five-furlong winning post is set at an awkward angle to the stands, and he awarded the verdict to Abernant by a short head.

The waiting tactics adopted at Sandown Park had not seemed to suit Abernant. Like many horses endowed with brilliant speed, he preferred to get on with the job and race in front from start to finish. From that time on he was allowed to run his races his own way and on only one other occasion, in heavy going at Royal Ascot as a four-year-old, was he waited with – and then he was beaten.

Abernant was running over six furlongs for the first time when he reappeared in the Champagne Stakes at Doncaster in September. Only two horses opposed him, but one of them was Nimbus, who had run Royal Forest to a head in the Coventry Stakes at Royal Ascot. The race showed just what a horse of Abernant's brilliance can do to a reputable opponent. Abernant set off at such a blistering pace that Nimbus was taken off his legs and was soon sprawling, and Abernant raced home practically alone to win by six lengths.

Two weeks later Royal Forest gave his first sign of fallibility by suffering a sensational defeat by Burpham in the Clarence House Stakes at Ascot, for which he had been considered such a certainty that he started at 25–1 on. The plan had been for Royal Forest to wind up the season by running in the Middle Park Stakes, but the

Ascot fiasco led to a revision and Abernant was substituted. Again Abernant had no more than two rivals, Decorum and the French colt Targui, owned by Marcel Boussac, and Abernant strode right away from Targui up the final hill to win by five lengths.

In the Free Handicap Abernant was given 1 lb. more than Star King, who won the Gimcrack Stakes after his Sandown defeat, and 4 lb. more than Royal Forest, who had repaired his damaged reputation by winning the seven-furlong Dewhurst Stakes at the Newmarket Houghton meeting. Star King, incidentally, won three of his five races as a three-year-old and afterwards became one of the most successful stallions of all times in Australia, where he was leading sire of winners five times. In Australia he was renamed Star Kingdom.

Abernant had proved that he could stay six furlongs as well as a two-year-old, but his ability to stay much further as a three-year-old was in doubt. His favourite style of running precluded long-distance running, and his pedigree did not generate confidence in his stamina. It is true that he was by Owen Tudor, who had won a wartime Derby for Mrs Macdonald-Buchanan in 1941, but the pedigree of his dam Rustom Mahal was strongly biased towards speed. Rustom Mahal was by Rustom Pasha out of the flying Mumtaz Mahal, whose parents, The Tetrarch and Lady Josephine, have been two of the most potent influences for pure speed in the modern thoroughbred. Students of breeding did not fail to note that the other brilliant but non-staying son of Owen Tudor, Tudor Minstrel, also traced his pedigree on his dam's side back to Lady Josephine. Abernant inherited his grey coat from The Tetrarch via Mumtaz Mahal and Rustom Mahal.

His ability to stay a mile was put to the test in the Two Thousand Guineas. He had an easy reintroduction to racing in the seven-furlong Somerset Stakes at Bath on 6 April, when one of the other two runners was his stable companion Kinlochewe. Despite the all-round strength of the three-year-old team at Beckhampton, Abernant was so superior to the others in short-distance work at home that Murless was able to make an early announcement that the grey colt would be the stable's only runner in the first of the Classic races. Star King, who had won the Greenham Stakes at

Newbury, was considered his most dangerous rival at Newmarket, but Abernant started a hot favourite at 5-4. Gordon Richards adopted the tactics that suited him best, allowing him to bowl along in front from the start. The pace was too hot for most of his opponents and, as he began the descent into the Dip with Star King already beaten, it seemed that he was going to come home alone. But then Nimbus, ridden with nice judgement and grim determination by Charlie Elliott, started to whittle down his lead. Abernant was still clear in the Dip, but his stamina began to ebb away as he met the rising ground and in the last hundred yards Nimbus got to grips and finally inched in front to win a thrilling race by a short head. The third horse, Barnes Park, finished four lengths away.

A storm of criticism broke about the ears of Gordon Richards immediately afterwards. The critics asked two questions: why had he tried to make all the running on a doubtful stayer? and why had he been content to sit and suffer without drawing his whip when Nimbus was challenging? Gordon himself gave the answer in his autobiography *My Story*. Having recalled that some people had said that he should have won the Guineas on both The Cobbler in 1948 and Abernant the next year, he explained: 'I think The Cobbler was unlucky not to win, but only because he could not have the advantage of the tuning-up which a preliminary race provides. But there is no excuse for Abernant, who would never have got so near to Nimbus again over a mile. They would both have petered out just the same if I had waited on them. They were just sprinters; wonderful sprinters, but with no real staying power, as was afterwards proved in each case. I stick to my contention that in straight races at Newmarket you must let your horse run at his own speed and not pull him about, providing of course that he is running well within himself and that you have the confidence to ride such a race.'

The jockey's apologia received the whole-hearted endorsement of Noël Murless, indeed the trainer went much further and claimed that Gordon rode one of his greatest races on Abernant in the Two Thousand Guineas. 'If Gordon had moved a muscle on him in the last furlong Abernant would have fallen to pieces,' said Murless years later. Gordon Richards excelled in the difficult art of riding on the Rowley Mile at Newmarket. He won one Classic there, the One Thousand Guineas on Queenpot, which he was not entitled to win, and he very nearly did the trick again on Abernant.

The ways of Nimbus and Abernant parted after the Guineas. Nimbus went on to win the Derby, but Abernant's capabilities were realistically assessed and he found his vocation in sprinting. He was not beaten again that season as he swept aside the opposition in the King's Stand Stakes, the July Cup, the King George Stakes and the Nunthorpe Stakes. The only cause for regret was that he did not meet Solonaway who, after winning the Irish Two Thousand Guineas, raided England to win the Cork and Orrery Stakes and the Diadem Stakes, both run over six furlongs at Ascot. There is no doubt that he was the best sprinter to run in England that year apart from Abernant, and an encounter between them would have produced fireworks.

Abernant ran through a similar programme as a four-year-old. He was hardly extended as he won the Lubbock Sprint at Sandown Park on his first appearance and after that the July Cup, the King George Stakes and the Nunthorpe Stakes. The only check to his progress occurred in the King's Stand Stakes at Royal Ascot. The going was soft at the end of a wet Ascot meeting and Abernant had to give 23 lb (14 lb. more than the weight-for-age allowance) to the three-year-old Tangle, who had won his previous two races easily. Gordon Richards argued that it would be courting disaster in the conditions to adopt his usual tactics and that he must hold him up. In the event, however, the champion jockey fell between two stools, neither permitting Abernant to stride along in the hope of taking his two opponents off their legs nor saving his speed for a late run. Though in front at half-way, he failed to shake off Tangle, who challenged strongly in the last two furlongs and exploited his weight advantage to win by half a length. There is no doubt that Abernant was a better horse on firm than on soft ground, but faulty tactics certainly contributed to his downfall in the King's Stand Stakes.

Murless's opinion of Abernant has been given already. Gordon Richards, too, thought the world of him. Independent confirmation of their views was offered by that most experienced and pro-fessional of journalists and watch-holders James Park in the auth-oritative *Bloodstock Breeders' Review*: 'I am a believer in the watch when it comes to sprint races. Usually they go out of the gate and hop along as merrily as they can. I know what to expect on the various courses and I want to put it on record that my watch revealed Abernant as the fastest horse in post-war years. Even as a two-year-old he kept coming up in times that frankly astonished me.'

Apart from his hocks, which were rather away from him, Aber-nant was a lovely specimen of a thoroughbred sprinter. He had a lean head of great quality, tremendous power in his quarters and shoulders, and excellent depth through the body. And if he was an aristocrat in looks, he was also a true gentleman in character. No kinder horse has ever lived. One afternoon Murless's daughter Julie, in later years well known in the racing community as the successful trainer's wife Mrs Henry Cecil but then a mischievous little girl, was found in Abernant's box. She had managed to scramble up onto the horse's back, and he was entering happily into the spirit of the game. Gordon Richards recorded that on one occasion at York Abernant's attention became riveted by a group of children playing on the ground near the starting gate, and he made it perfectly plain that he wanted to join in.

Abernant was always quiet as an old hack until he began to line up at the start. Then his whole demeanour changed in an instant, and he was all eagerness to be off.

Abernant spent his stud career at Mrs (afterwards Lady) Mac-donald-Buchanan's Egerton Stud at Newmarket, where he had to be put down at the age of twenty-four in July 1970. He transmitted a lot of his own speed to many of his progeny and sired animals like Zarco, Liberal Lady, Abelia, Favorita and Gwen. His daughters have bred the One Thousand Guineas winners Caergwrle and Humble Duty. If speed is the primary and essential asset of the thoroughbred, then Abernant served both to exemplify and to propagate it.

Trainer: C. F. N. Murless   Roger Mortimer and Peter Willett (1972)

—

Ribot (1952)

b.c. Tenerani–Romanella (El Greco)

The horses who have taken their names from celebrated painters are many, though by some quirk of ironic compensation, fate has in general decreed that the more obscure the artist, the greater the fame achieved by his namesake on the Turf. The Titians, Rembrandts, Manets and Velasquez have made little stir in the world of racing. Veronese is better known as an artist than either Donatello or Daumier, but the converse is true of the horses who bore those names, while the chief claim of Solario and Sansovino to the memory of posterity is that they had Classic winners named after them. And the nineteenth-century French painter Théodule-Augustin Ribot has earned posthumous renown only through the exploits of the unbeaten winner of sixteen races.

After Ribot's victory in the King George VI and Queen Elizabeth Stakes at Ascot, critics were found to cavil on the grounds that the field was not of the highest class, that the horses who had finished nearest to the winner were stopping in the last two furlongs, and that Ribot had had to be scrubbed along for quite a bit of the way. It is true that discretion resides in the avoidance of superlatives, but the fact remained that at weight for age, without making any excuses for him, Ribot was at least five lengths better than High Veldt, and before the Ascot race regret had been expressed in some quarters that High Veldt had been denied the opportunity of contesting the Derby. The subsequent defeats to which Todrai was subjected in Belgium and High Veldt's failure in the St Leger were adduced in confirmation of the carping. Ribot silenced his critics very effectively by his performance at Longchamp. It is, however, only fair to add that the racing journalists of Italy, who, after all, had had the immense advantage of having seen the horse in the vast majority of his races, were agreed that Ribot was the best horse ever to have been bred in Italy. Though Italian Classic form does not as a rule bear comparison with that of England or France, no one would deny that in Nearco, Donatello, Ortello, Apelle,

Niccolo dell'Arca and Daumier, to mention only half a dozen of recent years, Italy has produced horses who would have been worthy winners of a Classic race in either England or France, and the conviction in Italy that Ribot was the superior of all these was a tribute that might have been heeded, especially as it was expressed with some force by Mr Desmond McGowan in his penetrating articles in the *Sporting Life*.

There have been many more imposing horses than Ribot, but it is difficult to fault his conformation. It is, however, in action that he is seen to the best advantage. Comparison with previous generations, whether in racing or in any other sphere, is always invidious, and seldom other than lost labour, since subjective judgements are incapable of proof. What can be said without fear of contradiction is that after his triumph in the Prix de l'Arc de Triomphe, Ribot is entitled to a place among the great horses of history. There have no doubt been horses as good, and some of them have kept their records unblemished by defeat, but perhaps Ribot's outstanding achievement was to gain his victories in three different countries under vastly different conditions, and all distances and going came alike to him. In spite of all the warnings that he received about breeding from Romanella, Signor Tesio's foresight was triumphantly vindicated, and the only pity is that he did not live to see his faith justified. Although Ribot's pedigree is not a fashionable one from the English Classic point of view, it is studded with the names of Italian Classic winners. Tenerani won the Italian Derby and St Leger, Bellini the Italian Derby, El Greco the Italian St Leger, and Apelle the Italian Derby. Cavaliere d'Arpino was unbeaten, and Pharos and Papyrus, of course, fought out the finish of the Epsom Derby of 1923. After his victory in the Prix de l'Arc de Triomphe of 1955, it was reported that Ribot's owners had refused an open cheque for him. After his second victory in the race it is said that an American buyer made an offer of £575,000 for him. Despite the rumours that Ribot might stand at stud in England, it is understood that Italian Ministry of Agriculture regulations forbid his standing abroad until he has had a least two covering seasons in Italy. Perhaps the most striking tribute to Ribot was that of the French jockey Palmer, who said, after the

Prix de l'Arc de Triomphe, that it had been a privilege to ride against him.

Trainer: U. V. Penco   From *A Selection of Timeform Essays* (1982)

———

Petite Étoile (1956)

gr.f. Petition–Star of Iran (Bois Roussel)

Petite Étoile's all-conquering progress came to an end at the Ascot July meeting, where she was beaten by Aggressor in the King George VI and Queen Elizabeth Stakes. Significantly that defeat stilled the constant claim that Petite Étoile is the best filly since Pretty Polly. Why, incidentally, are Sun Chariot and Coronation V invariably omitted from these comparisons? At one time or another during her career several commentators have expressed the wish that Petite Étoile might be let down off the bit, and allowed to stride away and show how far she could win. The realization of that hope at Ascot was not, however, received with much appreciation. As readers of *Racehorses of 1959* will remember, we ourselves were always somewhat sceptical about the amount that Petite Étoile had in hand at the finish of her races, and it seemed to us that if ever she was really put to it, she might surprise her more ardent supporters by failing to find as much as they expected. And so it proved at Ascot.

Among the top-class sprinters who always gave the impression that they were winning with a lot more in reserve than in fact they had, we can recall in recent years Princely Gift and Right Boy, and among horses who stayed a mile and a half Primera and Petite Étoile. Besides their exceptional speed there is another factor common to these four horses. All were ridden regularly by Piggott. So it is reasonable to assume that Piggott's style of riding has at least something to do with this impression. Piggott rides shorter than most jockeys nowadays, though on the other hand his hold on the reins is not as short as that of some Australian riders. Riding short has the disadvantage of making it much more difficult to keep a big, long-striding horse properly balanced, or drive along those horses that need a lot of riding. But this style is extremely effective on all horses who are in any degree free runners, and who have learned to take a good hold when ridden in this way. It is worth notice in passing that all the four horses mentioned were in their element on a sound surface, as indeed their action would have led one to suppose, and all of them were handy horses. Of course the seat favoured by Piggott is not the only important factor in his style. There is much more to jockeyship than that, and the sum total of Piggott's attributes seems to us to have contributed in no small measure to Petite Étoile's reputation for invincibility.

Our first duty is to put in its proper perspective this question of Petite Étoile's ranking in the hierarchy of the thoroughbred. Let us not hesitate to assert dogmatically that there have been several better horses in the history of the Turf, but there have not been many better fillies, at least in this century. Taking a period that covers the last twenty seasons, we submit that there have been three outstanding fillies racing in Europe, Sun Chariot, Coronation V and Petite Étoile. In this contention we omit from our calculations those horses who have revealed exceptional ability only at two years. These three fillies were of approximately equal merit, but in one respect, that of temperament, Petite Étoile is superior to both the others.

Trainer: C. F. N. Murless From *A Selection of Timeform Essays* (1982)

———

Sea-Bird II (1962)

ch.c. Dan Cupid–Sicalade (Sicambre)

1965 will go down in racing history as Sea-Bird II's year. For the record he won the Prix Greffulhe by three lengths, the Prix Lupin by six lengths, the Epsom Derby by two lengths, the Grand Prix de Saint-Cloud by two and a half lengths, the Prix de l'Arc de Triomphe by six lengths, and the first-ever Racehorse Association's 'Horse of the Year' Award by a very wide margin. Five races he had, and five races he won. So much for the record – what of the horse behind the record, and what impression did he leave in the minds of those privileged to witness his superb performances?

Writing in the *Sporting Chronicle*, Quintin Gilbey – one of our most experienced and respected racing journalists – described Sea-Bird as 'unique among Derby winners of my experience', and referred to his victory in the Arc de Triomphe as 'the greatest performance by any horse in my time'. Gilbey's colleague Tom Nickalls of the *Sporting Life* wrote in similar vein. 'The sight of Sea-Bird outclassing his nineteen opponents in the Prix de l'Arc de Triomphe was', he said, '*something quite out of this world*. In a fairly long career I have never seen a spreadeagling performance like this in a weight-for-age Classic.' John Lawrence, under his pen-name of Audax in the *Horse and Hound*, described Sea-Bird as 'one hell of a horse', and doubted whether anyone who saw the Prix de l'Arc de Triomphe could say with any certainty that there 'had ever been a greater three-year-old'. To Scobie Breasley, who rode Oncidium in the Arc de Triomphe, Sea-Bird was 'fantastic', and Pat Glennon, Sea-Bird's jockey, summed up his mount by saying he was 'by far the best horse I have ever seen – let alone ridden'. These were the views of men of considerable experience, of men at the top of their profession. And they were echoed the racing world over. Whenever Sea-Bird, the Derby or the Arc de Triomphe was discussed, the verdict was unanimous – Sea-Bird was magnificent!

So much for opinions – what of the facts upon which these opinions were based? The Derby and the Arc de Triomphe were, of course, the highlights of Sea-Bird's career. His other races, important as they were, impressive as he was in them, must of necessity suffer by comparison. Sea-Bird's performance in the Derby was *on paper* not so good as the one he gave in the Arc de Triomphe, but for all that it was no less impressive, and as the Derby was run before the Arc de Triomphe, for that reason, if for no other, it might as well be given pride of place retrospectively.

Sea-Bird's performance at Epsom had to be seen to be believed. He beat his twenty-one opponents *without coming off the bit*. It is true that in the last furlong Glennon started to push Sea-Bird, but the horse, having taken the lead on the bit, had the race won, but was threatening to idle and look about him, so Glennon found it necessary to rouse him to *keep his mind on the job*. Sea-Bird responded by going into a four-length lead, and after about a hundred yards was back on the bit. Glennon was pulling him up over the last twenty yards, and Meadow Court, finishing very strongly, was rapidly reducing the gap between himself and Sea-Bird at the post. Had he not been eased, Sea-Bird would have had four or five lengths to spare. Bearing in mind that Sea-Bird had, without any great effort, opened up a four-length gap in the space of a hundred yards, by how far would he have won had he been sent about his business for all he was worth from Tattenham Corner, and kept up to his work the rest of the way home? Of course there was no point in giving the horse a hard race, when he could just as easily have an easy one. There was his future to consider. But has there ever been an easier or a more impressive Derby winner?

Trainer: E. Pollet   From *A Selection of Timeform Essays* (1982)

———

Nijinsky (1967)

b.c. Northern Dancer–Flaming Page (Bull Page)

'Never use a superlative,' the late Joe Estes, long-time editor of *The Blood Horse*, once said to one of his junior reporters. 'Nothing you run into on this kind of beat ever justifies a superlative.' Estes had a scholar's dislike of superlatives, for undoubtedly in many instances a sounder, more rational appreciation of events is to be arrived at by avoiding them, and certainly discretion resides in limiting their use, but the very essence of horse-racing is to discover the best horse and when an animal such as Nijinsky appears on the scene, superlatives can hardly be cold-shouldered altogether. Nijinsky made the racing year: such were his feats that he dominated it from start to finish, and for the best part of the season he towered over the opposition. Had he been retired after the St Leger he would have gone to stud unbeaten, the winner of eleven races, including the Two Thousand Guineas, the Derby and the St Leger;

the first winner of the Triple Crown since Bahram, who was retired unbeaten after nine races. Although, in our opinion, Nijinsky never earned the title of the horse of the century, still less that of the greatest horse ever, when judged primarily not on the importance and the quantity of the races he won but on the quality of his performances in them, he was, without much doubt, one of the best Derby winners since the war.

History records that Nijinsky lost the Prix de l'Arc de Triomphe, beaten by Sassafras, who only got the French St Leger in the stewards' room, and history sets us an insoluble problem. Did Sassafras win the race or did Nijinsky lose it? Did Nijinsky run below form or was Sassafras as good as Nijinsky? If Nijinsky did not show his best form was this because Piggott gave him too much to do or because he was physically not at his peak? Vincent O'Brien, we know, is convinced that the severe attack of ringworm Nijinsky suffered at the beginning of August, plus the fact that he was prepared for and ran in the Leger, affected his performance in the Arc. Although the horse appeared to be at the peak of condition and in excellent form before the Leger he weighed 29 lb. less when he arrived home, and to O'Brien this showed that he wasn't as hard and fit at Doncaster as he should have been. Nijinsky recovered the lost weight in quick time but his trainer, in retrospect, thinks the Arc came too soon after the Leger. Piggott, himself, is recorded as saying that the old fire was missing from Nijinsky in Paris. Piggott's handling of Nijinsky brought criticism after the race, and to say that the run he asked Nijinsky to make was an exceedingly long one, probably too long, is fair comment. Half a mile from home Nijinsky was in the last four and Sassafras in the leading four, with the gap between them such that we think even Piggott, if given the knowledge that Sassafras was the one he had to beat, would admit that Nijinsky had a tremendous lot to do even for Nijinsky, a horse with easily the best pace in the race. Nevertheless, when set alight Nijinsky found a tremendous burst of speed, and passing our point of vantage about a furlong from home he looked for all the world as though he was going to swamp Miss Dan and Sassafras. But right at that moment he began to run out of gas, and what seemed likely to be a convincing win became a battle for the line. We still thought he'd get there, but in the last half-furlong he began to drift out to the left and that cost him the race. Sassafras came back at him extremely gamely to win by a head. As the difference between winning and losing was only a head, there is some justification for believing that if Lester had ensured only a slightly better place approaching the final turn he wouldn't have needed to set the horse really alight so far from home, would have been able to deliver a challenge in the last furlong with some reserves in hand and would have won the race. It is evident, however, that ridden differently Nijinsky would not have been much in front of the field at the end, unless one is to believe the unlikely proposition that both Gyr and Blakeney ran below form. Nijinsky beat the fourth-placed Gyr by a longer distance than he beat him in the Derby and he more than doubled the margin by which he beat the fifth-placed Blakeney at Ascot.

If Nijinsky as a stallion is only half as good as he was a racehorse he will still be a success at stud. Good racehorses don't always make good stallions but they have most things in their favour, and a really high-class one like Nijinsky all the more so. As a racehorse Nijinsky had almost everything. He never showed his ability to act on soft ground but that was because he never had to run on it; and he acted well on firm ground. He was soundness itself, which for a horse of his ample proportions is not all that common. For a horse that stayed as well as he, Nijinsky had an astonishing turn of foot, and his ability to quicken in an instant was his main asset. That and his fine looks were the two things that made everyone who saw him agree that here, indeed, was a horse that stood out in the crowd.

Trainer: M. V. O'Brien   From *A Selection of Timeform Essays* (1982)

—

Mill Reef (1968)

b.c. Never Bend–Milan Mill (Princequillo)

Mill Reef's career as a three-year-old fulfilled all that had been presaged by the best of his performances of the previous season.

In winning the 1970 Gimcrack, Mill Reef had returned by far the most impressive display by a two-year-old all that year: he was never off the bridle, pulled his way to the front inside the last two furlongs and strode home ten lengths clear in a manner that had to be seen to be believed. This, on top of an eight-length win on the bit in the Coventry Stakes, suggested that an exceptional horse had arrived on the scene, though in between he had lost his unbeaten record by a short head to My Swallow in the Prix Robert Papin. Except for losing the Two Thousand Guineas to Brigadier Gerard, Mill Reef went through his second season unbeaten. He picked himself up off the canvas after the Guineas, and in a series of races over middle distances that culminated in the Prix de l'Arc de Triomphe, he outpointed most of the best horses in Europe (with the notable exception of Brigadier Gerard), and proved himself a brilliant animal. We use the epithet with the full knowledge of its implications. In four races after the Guineas, Mill Reef never appeared in any great danger of defeat. Three of those races were three of the toughest in the English calendar, the Derby, the Eclipse Stakes and the King George VI and Queen Elizabeth Stakes. At no time did any of his opponents finish closer than two lengths, the distance Linden Tree was defeated in the Derby. Mill Reef beat Caro, one of the most improved older horses in Europe as well as the best four-year-old outside the United States to our mind, by four lengths in the Eclipse; he finished six lengths clear of the field in the King George, and in the Prix de l'Arc de Triomphe he came home three lengths clear of the strongest field assembled in Europe all year. Without a doubt the record not merely of a good horse, but a brilliant one.

If Mill Reef is such an exceptional horse how did he ever come to be beaten as a three-year-old? Our answer would be that 1971 was a very unusual year in England: there were two brilliant horses trained in the country in the same season. Mill Reef was defeated in the Two Thousand Guineas on merit by a horse even better than he when it came to racing over a distance of a mile. Later he undoubtedly improved over longer trips. Whether his best performance equalled the best of Brigadier Gerard's is a moot point, for it is extremely difficult to set a true value on Brigadier Gerard's wide-margin wins from top-class horses like Gold Rod and Dictus, and we would not be so rash as the official handicapper and place Mill Reef 4 lb. above Brigadier Gerard, particularly as the latter is unbeaten and inflicted the only defeat of the season on Mill Reef. If the pair ever meet again the deciding factor may well be the distance of the race. On our figures no horse's performance at a mile in 1971 compare with Brigadier Gerard's while no horse got within 7 lb. of Mill Reef's at longer distances. If Brigadier Gerard cannot improve on his form in the Champion Stakes, his only attempt at a longer distance than a mile, he will not beat Mill Reef at a mile and a quarter, all other things being equal.

Mill Reef is not a big horse, but he is strongly made and compact; he reminds us greatly of Hyperion or Exbury, and he is, in performance, a giant. He is just as brilliant at a mile and a half as at a mile and a quarter, and is just as effective in the mud as on firm going. He has an exceptionally fine action. With such a paragon remaining in training as a four-year-old, 1972 should be a season to remember. We would like to see Mill Reef meet Brigadier Gerard at a mile as well as a mile and a quarter, but in view of the cramped appearance of the fixture list would settle for one meeting at any distance. Our fear is that the pair will never meet against unless Mill Reef is put back to a mile or unless Brigadier Gerard is given the opportunity he deserves of tackling a mile and a half. A meeting is widely anticipated in the Eclipse, but there is only a fortnight between the Eclipse and the King George VI and Queen Elizabeth Stakes, and Mill Reef is not likely to be risked in both. If a choice has to be made between engagements he must surely go for the more valuable King George VI, boosted to approximately £70,000 by sponsorship from De Beers. Similarly there seems no compelling reason why Mill Reef should be turned out in the Champion Stakes so soon after running in the Prix de l'Arc, if indeed, he is still in training by that time. If Brigadier Gerard does not oppose Mill Reef it is difficult to see Mill Reef being beaten as a four-year-old, barring accidents or a loss of form: he rates among the best horses of our experience. For the very next crop of three-year-olds to produce a horse as good as he would be truly remarkable, would it not?

Trainer: I. A. Balding   From *A Selection of Timeform Essays* (1982)

Mill Reef remained in training as a four-year-old. After winning the Prix Ganay at Longchamp in a canter by ten lengths, he next appeared in the Coronation Cup at Epsom where he struggled home from three inferior opponents; this poor showing was almost certainly due to a hold-up in Mill Reef's work as a result of foul weather.

A virus infection precluded the long-awaited second meeting with Brigadier Gerard both in the Eclipse and the King George VI and Queen Elizabeth Stakes (both of which Brigadier Gerard won). During a strong canter at the end of August, Mill Reef fractured his near foreleg. He recovered fully to become champion sire in 1978 and 1987 and the sire of many high-class winners.

———

Brigadier Gerard (1968)

b.c. Queen's Hussar–La Paiva (Prince Chevalier)

It is hard to write anything about Brigadier Gerard without producing a cliché. The English language is in such a bad way that it can no longer cope adequately with the exceptional. This is as much the fault of the journalist as anyone. Words have become twisted out of their original meanings by over-use and by the lack of precision with which they are employed in newspaper copy. Contemporary writers on racing cannot altogether escape criticism in this respect. Whenever an exceptional horse arrives on the scene the ready-made words and phrases are called up like cavalry horses answering the bugle. A Nijinsky, a Mill Reef or a Brigadier Gerard is written up as 'the horse of the century' and the adjective *great* has been so over-used that it has virtually lost its meaning.

It is important for the reader to realize that when we use the word *great* we do not do so thoughtlessly. In the past thirty years fewer than a dozen horses have merited the description *great* in these pages. Brigadier Gerard is one of them. In fact, we rate him one of the three best horses in our experience, equal in merit to Tudor Minstrel, and inferior only to the mighty Sea-Bird II. Of course, when a horse as outstanding as Brigadier Gerard comes along there is always the danger that one's enthusiasm may get the better of one's judgement. However, the more we reflect on the best of Brigadier Gerard's performances, the more satisfied we are with our valuation of them. The task of assessing Brigadier Gerard's worth was relatively straightforward because in most of his races he was made to show the full measure of his superiority over those he ran against. Impressions created by the manner of a horse's victories can be questioned in that to a large extent they lie in the mind of the person expressing the viewpoint. When a horse wins seemingly without coming out of a strong canter as, for example, Nijinsky did in the 1970 King George VI and Queen Elizabeth Stakes, nobody can be certain how much he would have produced had he been made to race through to the end. It is a matter of opinion, not of fact. With Brigadier Gerard the performances are there in black and white for all to see.

Brigadier Gerard won seventeen races from eighteen starts. His earnings of £243,924 (disregarding his second-place money in the Benson and Hedges) are a record for stakes won in this country. The races that he won included the Two Thousand Guineas, the King George VI and Queen Elizabeth Stakes, the Eclipse Stakes, the Champion Stakes (twice), the Sussex Stakes, the St James's Palace Stakes, the Queen Elizabeth II Stakes (twice), and, as a two-year-old, the Middle Park Stakes. However, if we were asked to select his best performances, we would unhesitatingly look among the victories that he gained at a mile. Four races stand out. His victory in the Two Thousand Guineas is one of them, of course, but his runaway wins in the Goodwood Mile (by ten lengths from, Gold Rod) and the Sussex Stakes (by five lengths from Faraway Son) as a three-year-old were also gained in brilliant style. Yet, even those performances, magnificent as they were, did not impress us more than his win in the 1972 Queen Elizabeth II Stakes. The memory of Brigadier Gerard storming up the Ascot straight and brushing aside Sparkler as if he were a selling-plater will remain with us for a long time. With the exception of Tudor Minstrel, no horse in our experience has matched Brigadier Gerard's performances at a mile.

Some of the best broodmares in the stud book will visit Brigadier Gerard in 1973 and he is assured of a fine selection of mares for years to come. We expect him to sire many high-class performers, though for him to produce one as good as himself would be remarkable. Racehorses of Brigadier Gerard's brilliance are seen rarely.

Trainer: W. R. Hern   From *A Selection of Timeform Essays* (1982)

JOCKEYS

Danny Maher, the 'Steve Cauthen' of his day, headed the list of flat race
jockeys in 1908 and 1913. This gentlemanly American and superbly
artistic rider was generally considered by those who saw him in the saddle to be
the finest jockey of the era.
(Sherborn, Newmarket)

Genius Genuine

The first fine part in riding a race is to command your horse to run light in his mouth; it keeps him the better together, his legs are the more under him, his sinews less extended, less exertion, his wind less locked; the horse running thus to order, feeling light for his rider's wants; his parts are more at ease and ready, and can run considerably faster when called upon, to what he can when that he has been running in the fretting, sprawling attitudes, with part of his rider's weight in his mouth.

And as the horse comes to his last extremity, finishing his race, he is the better forced and kept straight with *manner*,* and fine touching to his mouth. In this situation the horse's mouth should be eased of the weight of his rein, if not, it stops him little or much. If a horse is a slug, he should be forced with a *manner* up to this order of running, and particularly so if he has to make play, or he will run the slower, and jade the sooner for the want of it.

The phrase at Newmarket is, that you should pull your horse to ease him in his running. When horses are in their great distress in running they cannot bear that visible manner of pulling as looked for by many of the sportsmen; he should be enticed to ease himself an inch a time as his situation will allow.

This should be done as if you had a silken rein as fine as a hair, and that you was afraid of breaking it.

This is the true way a horse should be *held fast* in his *running*.

N.B. If the Jockey Club will be pleased to give me two hundred guineas, I will make them a bridle as I believe never was, and I believe can never be excelled for their light weights to hold their horses from running away, and to run to order in, as above mentioned, as near as I thus can teach; and it is much best for all horses to run in such; and ladies in particular should have such to ride and drive in, as they not only excel in holding horses from

---

* The word 'manner' is knowing, putting, keeping self and horse in the best of attitudes. This gives readiness, force, and quickness.

running away, but make horses step safer, ride pleasanter, and carriage handsomer.

Samuel Chifney (1792)

Sam Chifney (1753–1807)

The outstanding jockey of his day, with an unusual understanding of horses. His career disintegrated in 1791 when he was beaten on the Prince of Wales's horse Escape, the favourite and won on it the following day at a long price, as a result of which Chifney was warned off and the Prince retired from racing. The justice of this decision was much debated. Chifney died in prison, penniless. Chifney's verbal instructions on jockeyship may have been an improvement on his written ones but at least he was under no illusion where his own ability was concerned. The bit that bears his name has kept his memory alive.

'Jocked Off' a Derby Winner, 1860

Mr Merry, the owner, had telegraphed to John Sharp, who was trainer to Count Henschel at some obscure place in Russian Poland, to come over and ride Thormanby in the Derby. Sharp obeyed, and when the slow continental trains of that time stopped for an hour or two at a wayside station, Sharp would get out and do something towards reducing his weight. Travelling was weary work; Sharp started at four o'clock on the Sunday afternoon before the Derby – he arrived at Berlin at five Monday morning, and reached Ostend at eleven a.m. Tuesday. He had to wait till six in the evening for the Dover boat, but spent the time in sweating. Reaching London at four, on Wednesday morning, he at once proceeded to Epsom, and continued the sweating process till it was time to scale, when he was only three-quarters of a pound above the stipulated weight. Sharp's name was on the card as rider of Thormanby, but before mounting, Mr Merry said to him – 'Custance knows the horse so well that he had better ride Thormanby.' This must have been a great disappointment to Sharp, after travelling nearly 2,000 miles and wasting about 9 lbs. on the journey.

Thormanby (1898)

After travelling non-stop across mid-nineteenth-century Europe for over eighty hours in extreme discomfort, with limited sleep and a restricted diet, Sharp, on being 'jocked off', was entitled to his 'great disappointment' but Mr Merry, the owner, was by all accounts an unattractive, mean, hard man, obsessed with money.

Though markedly less prevalent since 1985, the replacement of an engaged jockey by a fellow professional tends nowadays to stir emotions well beyond disappointment.

Fred Archer (1857–86)

When Fred Archer's death was announced on the afternoon of 8 November 1886, the sporting world grieved. After his funeral, The Times reported: 'A town in mourning was Newmarket yesterday. Not a house was there that was not darkened, not a shop that was not closed, from end to end of the long main street.' Set in the turgid prose of the time, Archer's death attracted more column feet than would the obsequies of a modern prime minister. Contemporary poets were stirred into verse of varying merit.

IN MEMORIAM

> Fred Archer's dead! The words ring out
>   O'er verdant plain and valley wide
> And ears distended hear with doubt
>   The news that he no more will ride.
> His last race done, he sleeps in peace,
>   And what may now his requiem be,
> When all his efforts sadly cease?
>   'He rode right well and gallantly!'
>
> His heart was stout, his hand was light,
>   And riding swiftly through the day,

He rode into the shades of night,
    By one dark, straight, and awful way.
So there is pity for him here,
    Since envy dare not touch him now,
And stooping o'er his open bier,
    We drop a laurel on his brow.

(*From a pamphlet published by Messrs Palmer and Co. on the day following Archer's death.*)

FRED ARCHER

The shoppy slang of turf is hushed today;
    No cry of 'Tinman! won, sir, by a head!'
The dull November seems all mere grey –
        For Archer's dead!

The punter mourns the man who brought him luck
    Who, heedless of the 'Ring's' resounding din,
Would bursting come from out the hopeless ruck,
        And land a win!

And though he kept the penciller *en garde*,
    They beamed on Fred, nor owed him any grudge,
Save, sometimes, when his skill had hit too hard –
        The keenest judge!

The glories of the Downs are shadowed o'er;
    'Twill seem a link has snapped in memory's chain,
When Epsom comes without the deafening roar –
        Archer again!

Farewell, best jockey ever seen on course;
    Thy backers weep to think, by fate's decree,
The rider pale, upon his great white horse,
        Has beaten thee!

November 1886   From *St Stephen's Review*

Tod Sloan

It was Sloan's misfortune to be always surrounded by a crowd of the worst class of people that go racing. Once a man gets into that set, I have hardly ever known him get out of it, even if he wants to. This was the ruin of Sloan, and eventually brought about his downfall.

He was a genius on a horse; off one, erratic and foolish. He threw away a career that was full of the greatest promise. As a jockey, in many ways he reminded me of Fred Archer. He had the same wonderful hands, and was as quick as lightning to take advantage of any opportunity that occurred in a race. Like Archer, once he had been on the back of any horse, he had an almost uncanny intuition into its peculiarities and nature.

A race I remember well was when he rode Knight of the Thistle in the Jubilee. The Knight was a great big good-looking horse, but a loose-made sort of customer, and easily unbalanced, in addition to which he was not too generous. He was owned by Lord William Beresford, who had backed him very heavily for the race, and he started favourite.

In the parade, Sloan seemed like a pea on a drum on this big horse, and, knowing that other good jockeys had found him more than a handful, I would not back him. The horse was as obstinate as a mule at the post. During that long delay it looked very much as if he would be left. In the end he got off fairly well, but all Sloan's usual quiet persuasive efforts to induce him to race properly were unavailing. He had to fall back on the whip, and in the end slammed him home by a length. When he rode back to the unsaddling enclosure, Sloan looked quite exhausted.

I had engaged him to ride a two-year-old filly of Horace Farquhar's in the next race. Bill Beresford came to me and said, 'Sloan has asked me to tell you he can't ride for you, as he is so tired.' I tried to get another jockey, but as there was a big field I found every one was engaged. So I went to Sloan and told him he must ride. With his funny American twang he replied, 'That was the meanest horse I've ever ridden. I'm tired to death, and I can't ride any more.' But I insisted and weighed him out. When he came into the paddock he lay on his back in the grass, repeating, 'It's no use: I can't ride.'

Bobette, who was a beautiful little filly, was walking about close by. Sloan, still lying on his back, asked, 'Is that my horse?' When I said, 'Yes,' he was on his feet in a moment, and all his depression and lassitude disappeared. He won the race easily. Sloan was like that: when he was full of life and confidence he could do anything, but when he was down he could do nothing, and would get beaten on the best thing in the world.

                                             The Hon. George Lambton (1924)

James Forman Sloan (1874–1933)

'Tod' Sloan, on arrival from America, was the first jockey to popularize the modern style of riding in England, the effectiveness of which he discovered by accident: on one occasion he had pulled up his knees to control more easily a bolting horse. He later perfected the seat which distributed his weight more evenly over a horse's withers and dramatically reduced wind resistance: the English jockeys were slow at first to appreciate the advantage. In the two full seasons that Sloan rode in this country he achieved 254 winners from 801 rides.

Sloan's character did not match his great ability as a jockey; by 1901 he had so seriously flouted the Rules of Racing that he was refused a licence and his career came to a premature end. He died in the charity ward of Los Angeles City Hospital.

———

The Night before the Grand Prix, 1938

The visit to Paris of which I have the most vivid memory was for the Grand Prix de Paris of 1938 in which Gordon Richards was to ride the Epsom Derby winner, Bois Roussel. After Bois Roussel had won his first race by a narrow margin Aly Khan bought him from Leon Volterra, who was always prepared to buy or sell if he thought the price was right. By this time Aly had earned himself the reputation for being a pretty astute 'coper', and though it was not suggested that he had taken his friend Peter Beatty for a ride when he passed Bois Roussel on to him for £7,000, those who knew the form thought that Peter had paid plenty for a colt who had won a race, for horses that had never raced before, only by a short head. Peter sent him to be trained by Fred Darling, who had won the Two Thousand Guineas with the brilliant Pasch, ridden by Gordon, who of course rode him in the Derby, in which Bois Roussel was ridden by Charlie Elliott. Jimmy Rank's Scottish Union, about whom Pat Rank had laid me 100–7 to a tenner each way a few nights earlier at the Four Hundred, having got the better of the non-staying Pasch, looked home and dry, when Bois Roussel came out of the clouds to beat him by four lengths.

In the field for the Grand Prix was the Italian colt Nearco, the unbeaten winner of thirteen races, who was regarded by his owner trainer, Signor Tesio, as the best horse he had ever had in his stable.

There were long faces when we arrived at Northolt Airport, and we were told that Le Bourget could give us no idea when we would be allowed to land. It seemed that we might be grounded indefinitely, when our pilot had a brainwave. We would land at Villacoublay, but as there were no Customs on this airfield we should have to land first at Le Touquet to declare Customs. This we did, and as we were waiting while the formalities were being gone through, Steve Donoghue ordered two bottles of what he always called 'the Rosie' – pink champagne. After we had checked in at the Chatham Hotel, an Edwardian establishment, all gold and red plush, which for generations had been patronized by racing men from all over the world, Gordon asked me to ring up Maxim's and reserve a table for twelve. I knew that our only hope was for me to go round and plead with my old friend Albert.

One of France's most famous maîtres d'hôtel (he was also the guiding light at Ciro's in Deauville), Albert shook me warmly by the hand, but when I said I wanted a table for twelve in an hour's time, he gave me the sort of pitying look one gives to the very old when they can no longer be treated like other people. In his kindest voice, and with tears in his eyes, he remonstrated with me for my folly. Did I, with my experience of Paris, not know that on the eve of the Grand Prix every table at Maxim's had been reserved a month ago. 'It isn't for me, Albert,' I explained, 'it's for Gordon Richards.'

'Gordon Richards,' he echoed, with the reverence normally reserved for a reigning monarch, 'I will see what I can do.' When we arrived, the small space on which dancing would have taken place was occupied by a table for twelve, bearing the name 'Gordon Richards'.

On our way to dinner we had stopped for a drink at Frank O'Neill's bar. The great American jockey looked much as he had done when he won the Derby on Spion Kop eighteen years earlier. After dinner, John Bisgood, a successful trainer for many years, and I went to the Sphinx, and as far as I know Gordon went to bed. Soon after our arrival I saw a very attractive girl saying goodnight to a man, and I asked her to join us, which she did, and that was how I met Arlette. As the crowd began to thin out, we invited more girls to our table, and having supplied them with all the champagne they could drink, we organized a sing-song and very well they sang. Their favourite song was the still popular 'J'attendrai', and they sang it a dozen times, John and I joining in after we had been taught the words.

At around twelve o'clock on Sunday morning, my telephone rang, and it was a very irate Gordon at the other end. What the hell was I doing? We were going to lunch before we left for the racecourse, and would I come down at once. So I packed Arlette off home, with the promise that I would contact her when I next came to Paris, which I did. The promise was not hard to keep. Although Gordon had ridden Bois Roussel a canter on Longchamps racecourse at some ungodly hour, he said he still had a hangover, and of course it was my fault, though I hadn't seen him from the moment the party broke up at Maxim's. For once Gordon rode a bad race, though it made no difference to the result. Nearco was a horse and a half, and he won like one. Had Gordon steered clear of trouble, Bois Roussel might have finished second instead of third, but in no circumstances would he have won. If Bois Roussel had won, we were to have stayed in Paris for another night, but after the race Gordon couldn't get home quick enough. When the Customs official, on landing, asked us if we had contracted any-thing while we were abroad, Gordon replied 'I haven't, but Steve Donoghue, Commander Bisgood, and Mr Gilbey won't know till next Wednesday – at the earliest.'

Quintin Gilbey (1970)

Quintin Gilbey (1900–79)

A prolific and highly entertaining journalist of the thirties and the post-war period, 'Quinny' Gilbey was a bon vivant and sophisti-cated observer of the racecourse, the theatre and those who inhabited both scenes.

One night when Quinny was dining with a female companion at the Savoy Grill, a friend stopped to say hello and Quinny introduced him to the lady. After he'd gone, Quinny told her that they'd been at Eton, Sandhurst and in the Grenadiers together, to which she replied, 'For someone who has suffered and endured all those ghastly handicaps, you're surprisingly human.' He was certainly that, and wonderful company.

———

Piggott and Sir Gordon

A letter from John Hislop to the Sporting Life, *13 November 1985, is reproduced below. It provoked some interesting comment in later editions from authoritative sources.*

After the adulation evoked by Lester Piggott's recent retirement, a reminder of his great predecessor Sir Gordon Richards does not seem out of place, since many critics and racegoers of today never saw him ride.

His was a tough era, with no camera patrol, laxer safety rules, starting-gate instead of stalls, less racing and travel more arduous.

Above all it was an age of exceptionally good jockeys, the general standard of riding being higher than it is today. Immediately coming to mind are such as Steve Donoghue, Charlie Smirke, Charlie Elliott, Brownie Carslake, Frank Bullock, Harry Wragg, Joe Childs, Bob Jones, Michael Beary and of the younger division

Eph and Doug Smith. These were backed up by a wealth of talent only marginally behind those mentioned, such as Billy Nevett, Fred Fox, Sam and Arthur Wragg, Tommy Weston, Rufus and Harry Beasley.

Such was the competition of those times that, to succeed, a jockey had to be master of all facets of his profession: secure in the saddle, quick at the starting-gate, able to use the whip fluently and correctly in either hand, especially the left, capable of keeping horses straight and balanced and able to hold his own in the rough riding and gamesmanship to which conditions then sometimes gave rise.

Trainers could afford to be more choosy and demanding than nowadays, and mistakes were seldom forgiven. Had a jockey fallen off for no other reason than overbalancing through riding excessively short, let alone with the race at his mercy, a fate which once overtook the great Lester Piggott himself, he would never have been put up by the trainer again.

Lapses such as using the whip in the wrong hand, failing to pull it through deftly and swiftly when occasion demanded, or holding it upside down were looked upon as the mark of an amateur.

In this competitive, demanding period Gordon Richards attained his astonishing record of 4,870 winners and 26 years of being champion jockey. If he had not missed part of the 1941 season through injury he would have been champion 27 times, 23 consecutively. Had his philosophy been that of Lester Piggott, that of getting on winning rides at all costs, Gordon Richards' tally would have been higher still: but once he had committed himself to a retainer or a ride he would never beg off, however attractive the alternative.

Piggott's Classic record entitles him to be held supreme in this category in modern racing history, but he would not have found it so easy had he been riding in Richard's day. With so many other top riders available, owners and trainers would not have tolerated Piggott's chopping and changing of his riding agreements.

And though Richards' Classic victories fall short of those of Piggott, he never lost a Classic he should have won; either the horses he rode were not good enough or they failed to stay.

As much as Piggott, if not more so, Gordon Richards possessed supreme strength and determination in a finish and inspired horses to achieve the apparently impossible. No jockey has ever lost fewer races that he ought to have won.

Above all, Gordon Richards' integrity, loyalty and his warm, cheerful, generous nature drew the affection and respect of the public and profession alike. This, together with his magnificent riding record, brought him his well-deserved knighthood, an honour which no jockey before or since has ever received.

From Brigadier C. B. Harvey, DSO:

It gave me great pleasure to read John Hislop's letter of 13 November comparing the relative merits of Lester Piggott and Sir Gordon Richards.

I agree with every word he wrote. Sir Gordon Richards' record is extremely unlikely ever to be equalled, let alone surpassed.

But quite apart from his achievements, it is the man himself that I admire. His integrity and loyalty were unquestioned and he commanded the affection and respect of all his fellow jockeys. What he said in the jockeys' changing-room was always listened to and obeyed.

I was a stewards' secretary for over twenty years and, while there may be great jockeys to come, there will never be another who can command the respect and admiration of both the public and his fellow jockeys for a period of twenty-six years as champion jockey.

From Mr Lionel Cureton:

I would like to endorse every word of John Hislop's letter which you published last Wednesday.

It is extremely unlikely that the overall record of Sir Gordon Richards will ever be surpassed. In his riding days there was far less racing – most Mondays were blank – and travel was far more demanding.

In addition it was said of Sir Gordon that he could ride a finish for two furlongs. This was never more apparent than at defunct Hurst Park where the Press Stand looked straight *down* the course.

Many thanks, John, for putting in print words which I have been constantly using over the past few weeks.

From Mr George Vergette:

I was interested to read John Hislop's letter, 'Piggott and Sir Gordon'. I agree with what he said and would like to add another tribute to Sir Gordon.

He was always very helpful to young riders. I remember, when I was an apprentice, him coming to me in the weighing-room after a race and explaining to me what I had done wrong in the race; he also shouted advice to me during another race when I was too close to another horse's heels.

I also remember the time that I was 'jocked off' Chumleigh by the owner in favour of Sir Gordon two days before the St Leger, which the horse duly won. He came up to me straight after the race and offered me either a cash present or a suit of clothes. Riches indeed! In those days my wages were ten shillings a week.

I think the above remarks show the character of the man.

From Mr Darrell M. Wicks:

John Hislop's letter was most interesting and I must admit that I did not witness the likes of Richards, Wragg and Donoghue. Mind you, none of us remember the talents of Archer, Buckle or Robinson either.

To say one era is better than another is always tricky, as all eras have their outstanding jockeys and trainers.

Riding styles change dramatically over the years although today we have the help of television in analysing them. The jockey of today is therefore under greater scrutiny than ever before.

Sir Gordon Richards was a fine jockey and horseman and holds a phenomenal record of winners ridden. But it is the big races we all remember – the Classics – and, while Sir Gordon won his share, Lester Piggott has completely dominated the Classic scene this century.

He has managed to do this despite riding at some two stone below his natural weight and while I agree his 'jocking off' of other riders was his least attractive side, he himself has lost a fair few rides to others over the years.

Perhaps if Fred Archer had not died at an early age, he would have broken all records and with more luck Sir Gordon might have ridden more Derby winners.

But in my era at least, Piggott is the greatest jockey, the big race king, the greatest of his era and, most will agree, the greatest of all time.

The comparative figures are these:

	Seasons	Winners in Gt. Britain	No. of rides	%	200 or more winners in season	Times champion	Classic wins
RICHARDS	34 (1920–54)	4,870	21,843	22.29	12 times	26	14
PIGGOTT	37 (1948–85)	4,349	19,806	21.95	–	11	29
ARCHER	16 (1870–86)	2,748	8,084	33.99	13 times	13	21

Between Richards' first championship in 1925 and Piggott's last in 1982, only eight other jockeys have held the title over those fifty-seven years: T. Weston (1926), F. Fox (1930), H. Wragg (1941), D. Smith (1954–56, 58, 59), A. Breasley (1957, 61–63), W. Carson (1972, 73, 78, 80), P. Eddery (1974–77), J. Mercer (1979)

In the season of 1933 Sir Gordon Richards rode 259 winners, thus breaking a record which had stood since 1885 when Archer had 246 winning rides.

———

The Strength of an Acrobat

Lester Piggott explains in an interview with Kenneth Harris the many facets of race-riding (Observer Review, June 1970).

KENNETH HARRIS: *Has any jockey influenced your riding?*

LESTER PIGGOTT: No. If you're as tall as I am – 5ft 7½ ins. – you've got to work out your own method. Most jockeys are small men. There weren't any models for tall jockeys like me in my time. Gordon Richards was small even as jockeys go: he could do eight stone without effort.

There's an advantage in being tall, big: I think it's my main one. A horse responds to a good weight on its back – live weight – no dead weight – lead, under the saddle – to make up the right scale. When a biggish jockey gets up, the chances are that the horse feels – well, the authority. Not always. There is a great American jockey, Shoemaker, and he's only seven stone. And Gordon Richards again – eight stone. If you've got a good length of leg, you can communicate more with the horse, squeeze him with your knees, control him generally – show him you are there.

There's the other side, the disadvantages; I've got to earn my living in a pretty strenuous game working at about one and a half stone below my natural weight. Some people exaggerate how I live; I don't starve, and I don't live on cigars and the *Financial Times*, and I don't drive to every race meeting in a rubber suit. But you can't eat and drink what might come naturally to you.

If I'm riding at eight stone six, I have a boiled egg and a bit of toast for breakfast. If I have to do eight stone five that day, I'll give up the egg. I have a sandwich in the jockey's room after I've finished riding, and I'll always have a meal at night. You lose the habit of eating, really – the less you have, up to a point, the less you want.

You were asking me about influences. Susan's a great influence on me. She's almost like my manager. She's a trainer's daughter, and she rides well, and if I can't hear somebody on a long-distance telephone call, Susan talks. Sometimes she persuades me to do things I don't want to. Like this interview, because she says it'll do me good to do something I don't normally do. And the two girls influence me – you know, Maureen and Tracy. If I'm getting a bit serious about something they come in and one of them's bound to say something that makes me laugh.

You ask about being influenced by other jockeys. Race-riding changes with the years. Not all that much: you've always got a leg each side of the horse, but things do change. For instance we go much faster in the first two furlongs than they did fifteen years ago. It doesn't do to model yourself on your predecessors.

Another disadvantage about being big is style. Style is how you look. If you're small, it doesn't matter so much how you look, there isn't so much of you to be seen. And your legs don't take up so much room. If you're big, you can be seen better, and there's less horse showing.

It's difficult for me to look stylish because I like to ride short. People ask me why I ride with my bottom in the air. Well, I've got to put it somewhere.

KH: *One of the things often said of you is that you're a tremendously 'strong' jockey. What does 'strength' mean? Is it the kind of strength that bends iron bars?*

LP: Well, you need muscular strength to hold a horse that's pulling for his head, a big horse and a real puller, on his way down to the post. And if a horse is big and broad, and he's lazy, and he needs to be squeezed and kicked along to keep him exerting himself, a small, light jockey can't do it so well. But when you talk about a jockey being 'strong' or being able to ride a strong finish, it's a bit different.

It's like this: a lot depends on the horse's balance. If he loses balance, he loses speed and direction, and that might cost him the race – he'll lose his position, or just get passed in the last fifty yards. Part of a jockey's job is to get his horse running balanced, and keep him balanced, and this means you've got to be balanced yourself all the time to fit in with the horse.

The horse has his own centre of gravity just behind his shoulders. The jockey has a centre of gravity. But the jockey can shift his, and the horse can't. At every stride the horse's centre of gravity is shifting in relation to the jockey's. Getting a horse balanced means keeping your balance, every stride, every second, to suit his.

Where strength comes in is that to keep doing this all the time without throwing yourself about in the saddle needs a lot of muscle control – you've got to be holding yourself as still as you can while you're making the right movements. The more control you have of your body, the fewer movements you have to make – but the more muscular effort you need: you need more strength to stand still on one leg than to walk down the street.

No, I don't say its the strength that bends iron bars. It's the strength of an acrobat on a tightrope. Or of a juggler.

In the finish of the race as well as keeping your horse balanced you've got to be doing things with him. You've got to be encouraging the horse – moving your hands forward when his head goes forward, squeezing him with your knees, urging him on with your heels, flourishing your whip, maybe giving him a crack, and all this without throwing him off balance, which means doing all these things and not letting yourself be thrown around in the saddle.

In a tight finish a strong jockey may seem to be doing nothing in the saddle except throwing his hands forward – that's all you'll see, but the horse is going flat out, and still going straight. In the same finish a 'weaker' jockey will be throwing himself about in the saddle, and his horse will be rolling about off balance. Keeping the horse balanced in that last hundred yards, and making him put it all in, can take a lot out of a jockey. It's got to be there to start with.

Weight and length come into it again. If a jockey is strong, and he's good, I reckon live weight is better than dead weight. If all of the weight the horse is carrying is live, and the jockey can put it in the right place at every stride, the horse runs freer than he would if part of the weight is in a fixed place, in a bag on his back.

KH: *What other attributes must a jockey have?*
LP: A jockey has got to make horses want to run for him. Sometimes a horse and a jockey won't hit it off.

Then, you've got to have judgement – can you get through that gap or not? Is the pace too slow? Is it so slow that if I poach a lead of four lengths here, three furlongs out, I can hang on and win by a neck? And you've got to do your homework – find out as much as you can about the other horses, so that when you see one in front of you, you can guess what he can do.

Sometimes you can work out tactics in advance, but sometimes you've got to change them. You've got to keep thinking about racing all the time – it's no good starting to think about a race just before you get up on the horse's back. That's one thing about not wanting to talk very much – I get time to read about racing, and to listen, and to think.

KH: *How far do you think the discipline of having to keep your weight down to this unnatural level changes, perhaps detrimentally, your natural personality?*

LP: I don't think it does very much. I don't think I'd be very different from what I am now if I didn't have to keep thin. But it's hard to say. As soon as I grew up I had to watch my weight hard and I've done it ever since. So I don't really know if I'd be different if I started living normally.

Wasting depresses a lot of people – it's the way you're made. They say Fred Archer committed suicide because having to keep his weight down got his mind down as well – got him so depressed he couldn't go on living.

I'm lucky because, well, you might say I'm pretty quiet and restrained by nature. I've never been one for living it up. Some people work to earn enough money to have fun. I enjoy the work best of all. If you like racing more than anything else, it's easier to give up things. It's easier to keep up your regime, without breaking out, and the steadier you keep it up the easier it is to live with it.

I told you when you asked about motor-car racing that I liked to compete, that I liked to try and win – the winning isn't all that important, it's the *wanting* to win that matters. The competition. It's competing more than winning, if you see what I mean.

In keeping your weight down you're competing. You're competing with yourself. After a time it becomes a habit and you're in one long competition with yourself. And you only keep winning if you're trying to win all the time.

If I got on the scales one morning intending to be 8 st. 4 lb. and I was 8 st. 6 lb., and I hadn't meant to be, even if I wasn't being asked to ride at 8 st. 4 lb., I'd want to get those two pounds off. You've got to get what you started out to do. Otherwise you start getting beat. The others start to beat you when you start being beat by yourself.

KH: *You don't develop a feeling of resentment at having to subject yourself to the regime, a feeling that might erupt occasionally into ill temper?*

LP: No. I don't resent it because I want it. And the life I lead is very good to me. I don't think I am ill-tempered. I think I'm very patient. Sometimes you read that I've told people to, well, to push off, but that's never because I'm hungry; it's because I'm angry.

Now and again I'm criticized unfairly, misreported; people say I did something which I didn't. I put up with as much of that as most people, and sometimes I say 'No'. For instance, I rode Sir Ivor in a race in Washington DC, two years ago, and I won. But some newspapermen – only some, I mean – criticized my riding. Unfairly, and they didn't really know the facts. Well, when I rode Karabas, last year, and won, they wanted to talk to me about it. But I didn't want to talk to them. I said so, too. And they didn't like me for it. I understood that. I didn't like them the year before.

I live and work in a tough world. I can be a decent human at 8 st. 4 lb., but I can't be a saint even at 9 st. 7 lb.

LESTER PIGGOTT (b. 1935) rode his first winner for his father on the Chase at Haydock on 18 August 1948; he was twelve years old. At the time of his retirement on 29 October 1985 he had ridden 4,349 winners from a total of 19,806 rides (21.95 per cent) in this country, which included a record twenty-nine Classic victories, two more than the figure achieved by Frank Buckle between 1792 and 1827. Piggott's Classic wins in France and Ireland brought the tally up to fifty.

———

The Jockeys' Championship, 1987

For only the fourth time this century the final day of the Flat season dawned at Doncaster last week with the jockeys' championship still undecided.

Since April there have never been more than thirteen winners between Steve Cauthen and Pat Eddery and, in the end, there were only two.

But the reigning champion ran out of time in the last-but-one race of the season, and with 197 winners to his 195, Steve Cauthen took over the title. Their sporting battle, fought throughout with real friendship and good humour, has been the most enthralling and attractive feature of a splendid season.

Charlie Maidment tied for the title in 1870 and 1871 – with William Grey and George Fordham – and there has been just one dead heat since, in 1923, when Charlie Elliott, then still an apprentice, finished level with Steve Donoghue.

Elliott was champion in his own right the following year and it was in 1925 that Gordon Richards' long and glorious reign began. In twenty-nine years he was only deprived of the title three times: by tuberculosis in 1926, by injury in 1941 – and by Freddy Fox in 1930.

What a last week it must have been that year! I have just been reading Sir Gordon's own account of it in *My Story*.

In those pre-war years, the last six days of the season consisted of three at Warwick and three at Manchester. Freddy Fox arrived at Warwick with a lead of six, but Gordon rode four winners there and Freddy rode none.

On the first day at Manchester Gordon drew level but on the next Freddy Fox went one ahead. He came to the last day with just that slender lead, so imagine the scenes when Gordon not only won the first race by ten lengths (on Rivalry) but then went on to win the Manchester November Handicap on Glorious Devon – at 25–1.

'It was the first time I had been in the lead for weeks,' Sir Gordon wrote years later. 'But I only had one more ride while he had two.'

When Freddy Fox went out for the second and last of those two rides, having duly drawn level on the first, Gordon could not bear to watch. He sat all alone in the jockeys' tea-room until 'as great a roar as I have heard before or since' told him that the worst had happened.

'But then I remembered how Steve Donoghue had been the first to congratulate me when I took the championship from him – and rushed down to congratulate Freddy.' It was in exactly that spirit that the title was won and lost last week and I only wish Sir Gordon could have been there to enjoy the sportsmanship of his successors.

Thanks once again to Henry Cecil, who sent Proud Crest up to win for the fifth time on Friday, Steve went into the last day two ahead. He lost no time in improving that position – winning the EBF Nursery on Vague Discretion. Though apparently held on form by Pat Eddery's mount Portvasco, Vague Discretion rose to the occasion splendidly, partly no doubt on account of the drier ground.

Neither jockey could follow Sir Gordon's example in the November Handicap (of which more later) but Pat Eddery was not done for yet. Three behind with only three races left, he sailed home on Night Pass in the EBF Armistice Stakes, one of the easiest winners he has ridden all year.

But there was no room for manoeuvre now. The light was fading and, when the Irish-trained filly Vilusi came out of the mist only fourth to Sharp Reminder in the EBF Remembrance Stakes, it really was the end of the road.

Ironically, Sharp Reminder's trainer Ray Laing had offered Pat the ride on Monday – but so had his countryman Liam Browne who trains Vilusi. The filly had won her last two races – while Sharp Reminder had no very obvious recent form. It is, of course, on decisions like that, made daily throughout the season, that championships depend.

Thanks to his brother-in-law Terry Ellis, Pat has got it right much more often than not this year – and so, thanks to John Hanmer of *Raceform* and the BBC, has Steve.

The sagacity of the two great rivals' form advisers is pretty clearly demonstrated by the fact that they have, together, ridden 392 winners in 1987. In all the famous 'close finishes' I have referred to, the previous best 'combined' total was 351 for Scobie Breasley and Lester Piggott in 1963.

Of the new champion's winners, 113 have been trained by Henry Cecil. It goes without saying that the support from the most successful stable there has ever been was a vital factor in Steve Cauthen's third championship. But Pat Eddery had ammunition of comparable quality from Prince Khalid Abdulla and his lighter weight has allowed him the best part of 200 more rides than the young American.

But who cares about such empty 'ifs' and 'buts'. These are two superb jockeys whose rivalry has given us all tremendous pleasure and done nothing but good to the game.

They flew off to Rome on Saturday night (for Steve to win the Premio Roma on Orban) with the heartfelt gratitude of the whole racing world and I only hope that both of them, but particularly Steve Cauthen, for whom the last three months have been an especially arduous ordeal, will be able to take a real holiday, eating meals and, preferably, without a horse in sight.

John Oaksey (1987)

The dying embers of the Flat season have often been stirred and even inflamed by a 'close-run thing'. The duel between Steve Cauthen and Pat Eddery in 1987 was a particularly memorable one, in which these two outstanding jockeys showed sportsmanship and skill of the highest quality.

In an era of less racing, far worse road communications, no helicopters and evening meetings, and against much stronger opposition than today's, Gordon Richards was able, on twelve occasions, to ride over 200 winners. It has never been satisfactorily explained how this was achieved and why the magic 200 has eluded every champion jockey since Sir Gordon rode his last double century (231) in 1953.

How Fred Archer achieved 200 winners eight times, between 1876 and 1885, defies comprehension; he habitually galloped a hack from Newmarket to catch 'the race train' at Cambridge, returning at night by the same means.

———

Peter Scudamore's Record, 1989

Three hours on from the ride which made racing history, and 100 miles north of the clamour and glamour of Ascot, Peter Scudamore stood in the deserted wooden shack which passes for a racecourse bar at Warwick. He was pale, sore and exhausted.

A bottle of champagne was on ice but virtually untouched. The champion drank lime juice after a day which, in the traditions of a sport which shows no favouritism, had put him on a platform and then whipped it from under him before he could begin to enjoy it.

Scudamore had set himself an unforgiving schedule: a breakfast television appearance, schooling for Charlie Brooks at Lambourn, drive to Ascot for one ride and a dash five miles to a helicopter pad where he had personally hired a flight to Warwick for two more rides.

There was scope for chaos, but, at first, all went well. The record which had taunted him for three days fell at last as he drove Brooks's hurdler Arden to a neck victory. His spontaneous smile was of relief as much as triumph – and then there were dozens of hands held out for him to shake and a moving reception from the big crowd.

His wife, Marilyn, drove him to his helicopter and he landed at Warwick like a home-coming hero. Spectators rushed to form a tunnel across the course and into the weighing-room. He was applauded every step of the way, his six-year-old son Michael trotting proudly by his side.

Scudamore was shrewd enough to guess he might now be dealt the equalizing card. He had gone to Warwick only because he remains obsessed by winning. 'Success is my one driving force,' he admits. 'I could have stayed at Ascot but I don't like anyone else getting on Martin Pipe's horses!'

Predictably, the Pipe pair were both short-priced favourites but Walnut Way was beaten in the novice 'chase and Galwex Lady gave his rider a shocking fall when looking poised to win the novice hurdle.

He was shaken, though nothing worse, by his third fall in six rides. 'It can happen at any time and I am always happy to get up,' he said, a view which will be appreciated by the man whose career record of 1,138 winners he had just broken.

It was a freak fall at Cheltenham which persuaded John Francome to give up riding but as he recalls: 'I was tired out. I know Stan Mellor, whose record I broke, felt the same. Yet here is Peter passing my total with three or four more years still in him.

'I must say I am more surprised than anything,' said Francome, adding memorably: 'When I packed up I thought there was more chance of the Berlin Wall coming down than of anyone beating my record.'

Francome still remembers the first time he saw Scudamore ride. 'It was at Fakenham in a full field of amateurs. He stood out from the rest and I turned to someone in the stand and said: "Bloody hell, who's that?" '

Mutual respect grew between them but their life-styles were very different. 'I was probably happier in John's company than he was in mine because I looked up to him,' says Scudamore. 'He was forever telling me I was too serious.'

It is an accusation he has never denied and it explains why the greats of the past tend to hold him in high regard rather than deep affection. They simply cannot identify with him. 'Old-time jockeys left their job behind when racing was over for the day. I have always tended to take it home with me,' he admits.

While he is never likely to follow the exuberant Francome into the media, Scudamore is not the shrinking introvert of old. He has taken speech lessons to improve his public image and his business interests now extend to a company formed with Steve Smith Eccles to promote the increasing marketability of jump jockeys.

Riding, however, still consumes him. He is two winners ahead of his figure this time last year and has until 20 December to break his own record for the fastest 100 winners. There will always be new goals but the one achieved on Saturday means more to his self-esteem than he was immediately able to take in.

'There were times when I felt an inferiority complex about John Francome,' he explains. 'I once went to a function as joint champion jockey and was introduced to a business man who said: "Oh, yes, you're the jockey. I always thought you had curly hair." ' The days of such an identity crisis must now be long gone.

Alan Lee (1989)

National Hunt racing has been richly served in the post-war period by some outstanding champion jockeys: Bryan Marshall, Tim Molony, Fred Winter, Tim Brookshaw, Stan Mellor, Terry Biddle-combe, Josh Gifford, Ron Barry, Bob Davies, Jonjo O'Neill and

John Francome. Martin Molony's brilliance in the late forties and fifties is still a memory treasured by many.

At approximately 1.40 p.m. at Ascot on Saturday 18 November 1989, Peter Scudamore surpassed them all, riding his 1,139th winner on Lord Howard de Walden's Arden.

The instinctive flair of so many of the great National Hunt riders has always reduced the incidence of damaging falls but jockeys chasing records cannot afford to pick their rides.

———

Wasting to Ride

No man ever employed more heroic measures to keep down his weight than did the late Frederick Archer. I once accompanied him from a race-meeting to a well-known training establishment in Berkshire, where the jockey was due to ride in a trial on the following morning. Our host had a reputation, like most trainers, for doing his guests well in the way of creature comforts; and the dining-table was already spread with snowy napery and solid, old-fashioned silver, with in the centre a race-cup filled with choice hothouse blooms. From the kitchen in the distance was wafted the perfume of savoury meats, and we had no sooner changed our clothes and descended than a sturdy rosy-cheeked man-servant (who looked like a stableman who had put on flesh) made his appearance, his back bending under the weight of a great Tay salmon on a lordly dish.

Poor Archer's face, as he surveyed the initial preparations for the evening meal, was quite piteous to watch. Then, with a shrug of the shoulders and a sigh, but ill concealed by a cynical remark, he left us, and shortly afterwards we saw him pass the window on a hack, galloping towards the training-grounds. Later on he partook of a tiny glass of champagne and a water-biscuit, played one game of billiards, and retired to his couch.

Edward Spenser (1900)

It is unnecessarily charitable to sympathize with a jockey because he has to waste, particularly a successful one. Fred Archer, Lester

Piggott (and many others) wasted for the very good reason that they wanted to ride winners in the life in which they had chosen to excel. The stimulus of competition obliterates the pangs of hunger.

The Whip: Use and Misuse

'He took up his whip and stopped his horse' is a summary which has very often described races which ought to have ended otherwise than they did, and it is beyond reasonable doubt that a Grand National has been won because the experienced guide, philosopher, and friend of the successful rider took his whip away before the start.

It may be necessary to hit a sluggish horse during a race if he jumps carelessly or shows a disposition to lie out of his ground; but when the whip is wanted to drive a game and willing horse to make the supreme effort in a race, it is worse than useless to begin to flog him half a mile from the post. He cannot maintain the pressure, and will shrink from continued punishment, the effect of which will be to make him shorten his stride. The being in too great a hurry to reach home prevents many riders from ever reaching home successfully. If when the little-experienced jockey feels the temptation to use his whip he would refrain and, instead, take a pull at his horse for some half-dozen strides to steady and prepare it for the run home, his prospects of victory would, in nineteen cases out of twenty, be largely enhanced. There are generous horses that make their effort, falter, and come again; but these are rare, and when this is seen it is probably the case that they have been badly ridden, the first run having been made too soon.

Two or three well-applied strokes of the whip in the last hundred yards or so, always supposing that the rider does not let go of his horse's head for the purpose of administering them, with perhaps a prick of the spurs a hand's breadth behind the girths, means probably the gaining of a length. If the jockey of the horse that is leading has his whip up this distance from home, and the horse that is lying at his quarters has not been touched, the chances are very greatly in favour of the man whose effort has yet to be made. As long as the horse can keep his place, or avoid losing it, without the whip, that dangerous implement should on no account be raised. If it be anything of a race the rider should not leave too much ground to make up at the end, or the final rush may just fail. In case the rider have the good fortune to be winning easily, he may be warned against making too sure of victory. It is pretty, no doubt, to see a race won easily by a short head with no unnecessary exertion on the part of horse or man; but it is, nevertheless, dangerous. The best jockeys sometimes make mistakes of this sort, and a vigorous struggle on the part of one of the competitors whom the should-be victor has regarded as hopelessly beaten may completely change – has often, beyond doubt, completely changed – the result of a race. Here, as elsewhere in the contest, 'Chance nothing'. The man is in a very false position who has had the race safely in hand and has permitted a rival to snatch it from him. On wide courses it is particularly difficult for the man who has not ridden many races to know precisely where the winning-post is. The inexperienced rider will often believe that he has reached the post when the judge entertains a contrary opinion.

Anon. (1885)

It is unlikely that a twentieth-century jockey would have parted with his whip before a Grand National; had he done so it is arguable that at least one rider in recent times would have finished first instead of second in the great steeplechase.

This extract, which contains much useful counsel for modern times, was first published in 1885 in the Badminton Library volume on racing.

———

Advice to Amateur Riders

If you have a really hard puller who stays it is best to let him stride along in front, but the best 'chaser I ever rode, Dudley, was a tremendously hard puller and would beat nothing if you let him do this. He was also a very quick jumper and if he jumped his way to the front nobody could hold him then, so I used to get him well tucked in behind at the start, and keep him there. You could hold him comfortably then, and if you challenged from the last fence he would produce a turn of speed that was enough to beat all the best two-milers of his day, and the same tactics applied to National Hunt flat races, though he didn't stay anything like two miles on the flat. I won forty-two races on him, so naturally have a very soft spot for him though he was not exactly an armchair ride.

Jack Anthony found with Troytown, who was another very hard puller, that if he dropped his hands on him Troytown would settle down all right. It was a tragedy he was killed at Auteuil after winning the National. I am sure he would have won it again with 12 st. 7 lb.

The ideal 'chaser for a beginner is a good plater or, if you can afford it, a good point-to-point horse. It is no good an inexperienced amateur buying a young horse to start on who is equally inexperienced, but a good selling-'chase plater can be bought without a very big outlay. He can run about once a week, will take care of his owner and himself, and unless he is a very lazy horse, will win him races and give him the confidence he needs, but it is extraordinary how few budding amateurs do this. Instead of this they prefer to start on some wild maiden that would take a good jockey all his time to get round, get run away with, have a crashing fall and, unless they are very tough, soon decide the game isn't worth the candle.

When you have a fall the golden rule is to lie absolutely still till the remainder of the field has passed on. As most of my riding was done before the days of skull-caps, I used to put out a hand to save my head, and then cover up with both arms. You may break a collar-bone or arm doing it, but all through a pretty long career I only had concussion once. One of the worst accidents I had was through getting on to my hands and knees too quickly after a fall, thinking every horse had gone by and getting a broadside from a tailed-off horse I never reckoned with. A horse will always avoid you if you lie still.

I detest seeing a whip used at the finish of a race on a tired horse who is doing his best, and amateurs would be well advised not to do so. If he is a 'dog' it will only make him sourer still. You will never see Gordon Richards hit a horse though he will often flourish a whip at him, or Martin Molony, who is the strongest and best finisher I have ever seen for his size on a 'chaser, but I have seen scores of races lost through the use of the whip.

Only recently at Liverpool a jockey lost a 'chase he would have won comfortably if he had not picked up his whip and hit his horse close to home, with the result that the horse stopped to kick at it and was beaten a short head on the post.

I would never allow jockeys to hit the horses I trained except to liven up a lazy horse at the start, and during a pretty long career I only remember one horse I used to have to liven up all through a race as he was so incorrigibly lazy he would tail himself off otherwise. He was a stallion called Wingman. I sold a friend of mine a bull calf for £100, and as he was hard-up I took Wingman in exchange, who had been in a loose-box for two years without ever going out of it. He proved a wonderful bargain and won the last Flat race that amateurs were allowed to ride in against jockeys, another long-distance amateurs' race at Newbury, and several long-distance hurdle races, the last one at Cheltenham where he was apparently hopelessly beaten three hurdles from home, but I never stopped smacking him and shouting at him and he got up close home and won it. Poor little Billy Speck, who was killed at Cheltenham afterwards, asked me on the way to the paddock what had won, and when I said I had he wouldn't believe me and thought I was pulling his leg!

A whip is very useful for keeping off a loose horse who is interfering with you, one tap on the side of the head will soon drive him away. It is also essential for fishing for and catching the reins if they break at the buckle. This once happened to me in the National Hunt Steeplechase.

If Lord Mildmay had done this quickly enough on Davy Jones, when his reins broke close home when he had the National in the bag, he would have realized his life's ambition, and nobody in this world has ever deserved it more.

Lots of amateurs think hunting alone will keep them fit for

riding 'chasing but that is a great mistake. There is nothing like riding work regularly. If you cannot spare the time or get the opportunities to do this the two best alternatives are boxing, even with a shadow ball, and riding a bicycle really fast, including some uphill work on it. You will soon realize how unfit and short of breath you are.

If you are really fit and fine-drawn it is very difficult to even get 3 lb. off, though a friend of mine who had been seeing the New Year in got off 3 lb. in an hour in a Turkish bath. The last time I tried it I spent the whole night in the Savoy Baths, fainted in the hot room, but got off the required 3 lb. to ride a good thing and then found racing was abandoned through frost! A good long steady jog-trot with plenty of sweaters on is far better. Most of the Flat-race jockeys who have to ride about a stone below their normal winter weight die young.

I had to ride in Troytown's National with a 3-lb. saddle, and nothing on but a silk jacket, very thin breeches and boots, with tropical rain all through the parade and the race itself when even spectators on the stand afterwards died of pneumonia, but I do not recommend that for pleasure!

Harry Brown (1954)

Harry Brown (1889–1961)
The finest N.H. amateur of his day and the last to head the list.
After falling at the penultimate fence in the Grand National (1921)
on The Bore he remounted to finish second, with a broken collar-
bone. He trained with a fair measure of success after retiring from
riding.

He was a brilliant shot, a hard man to hounds and a talented
fisherman but failed mentally in his later years and died in a home.

The Amateur Rider

Him going to ride for us! *Him* – with the pants and the eyeglass
  and all.
Amateur! don't he just look it – it's twenty to one on a fall.

Boss must be gone off his head to be sending our steeplechase crack
Out over fences like these with an object like that on his back.

Ride! Don't tell *me* he can ride. With his pants just as loose as balloons,
How can he sit on a horse? and his spurs like a pair of harpoons;
Ought to be under the Dog Act, he ought, and be kept off the course.
Fall! why, he'd fall off a cart, let alone off a steeplechase horse.

Yessir! the 'orse is all ready – I wish you'd have rode him before;
Nothing like knowing your 'orse, sir, and this chap's a terror to bore;
Battleaxe always could pull, and he rushes his fences like fun –
Stands off his jump twenty feet, and then springs like a shot from a gun.

Well, he's down safe as far as the start, and he seems to sit on pretty neat,
Only his baggified breeches would ruinate anyone's seat –
They're away – here they come – the first fence, and he's head over heels for a crown!
Good for the new chum, he's over, and two of the others are down!

Second time round, and, by Jingo! he's holding his lead of 'em well;
Hark to him clouting the timber! It don't seem to trouble the swell.
Now for the wall – let him rush it. A thirty-foot leap, I declare –
Never a shift in his seat, and he's racing for home like a hare.

Battleaxe, Battleaxe, yet – and it's Battleaxe wins for a crown;
Look at him rushing the fences, he wants to bring t'other chap down.
Rataplan never will catch him if only he keeps on his pins;

Now! the last fence, and he's over it, Battleaxe, Battleaxe wins!

Well, sir, you rode him just perfect — I knew from the fust you
    could ride.
Some of the chaps said you couldn't, an' I says just like this a'
    one side:
Mark me, I says, that's a tradesman — the saddle is where he was
    bred.
Weight! you're all right, sir, and thank you; and them was the
    words that I said.

                                                    A. B. Paterson (1910)

Andrew Barton ('Banjo') Paterson (1864–1941)
The bush ballads, as founded by Adam Lindsay Gordon and per-
fected by Paterson, are one of the most characteristic features of
literature in Australia and have had a success without parallel in
that country. They are a delight to read and retain a freshness and
vigour unchanged by fashion.
  'Waltzing Matilda' is probably Paterson's best-known memorial
but 'The Man from Snowy River' is unsurpassed in its genre.

VICTORY AND DEFEAT

The Cheltenham Gold Cup, 1964. Arkle (P. Taafe) jumps the last fence ahead of Mill House (W. Robinson) on his way to his first Gold Cup victory.
(*W. W. Rouch & Co*)

An Unusual Double, Ascot 1881

I had coveted Peter, 5 yrs, by Hermit out of Lady Masham for
some months, and old Gee, who had bought him at General Peel's
sale, had given me the refusal of him for 6,000 guineas, for being
an old friend of Dawson's he was very wishful that the horse
should stop in the stable. I wired off to Gee that I would buy Peter,
asking him to meet me at Newmarket on the Saturday. He duly
turned up and the bargain was concluded; though not without the
assistance of an old friend, who lent me £2,500 out of the £6,300
I paid for the best horse of his day – if not of any other. On that
Saturday morning I caught Archer on the Bury Hills, and he opened
his eyes wide when I told him I had bought Peter, as he imagined
that one or two men whose income was more per week, than mine
was per year, would buy the horse. I chided him for thinking they
would be so rash, and told him I hoped he would ride Peter for
me in the Hunt Cup at Ascot, which he was sure to win no matter
what weight he was handicapped at, and he at once agreed.

One morning, about a week after, Peter went so well one mile
and a half, that I asked Sherrard, who had now taken the management of the horses at Bedford Lodge (poor Joe Dawson being very
ill), to let Peter go round the Lime Kilns with Foxhall, 3 yrs, who
was then being trained for the Grand Prize, and I never saw a
horse cut down another easier than Peter did the Yankee; and
when we weighed their riders after the morning's work, we found
that Peter was giving Foxhall two stone and a half, and it looked
as if he could give him another stone, anyhow. So I made up my
mind to have a cut in with him for the Manchester Cup, one mile
and three-quarters.

Now comes (to my mind) the most extraordinary bit of bad luck
I ever heard of. Of all the unwritten laws of racing the one most
generally observed is, that an owner ought never to take off the
jockey of the stable, if he is a good rider, and has served him well
and faithfully; so I had told C. Wood he was to ride Peter in the
Manchester Cup. The week before the race, as Archer was riding

out of the gate at Kempton he gave me a note, saying: 'This will interest you, Sir John. I will ride Peter if you wish,' and away he cantered down to the post. I read the note he had handed me, it was from Captain Machell to Archer: 'Dear Sir, if you will ride Valour in the Manchester Cup I will run him; if not, I shall not send him to Manchester.' When Archer came back he asked, 'What answer shall I send the Captain?' I told him on no account would I take the stable jockey (Wood) off my horse. I had asked him (Archer) to ride Peter in the Hunt Cup, because I knew two of Wood's masters – who had prior claims on his services – were certain to want him; and added – with a slight dash of scorn – he might ride Valour by all means, but what chance had he to beat Peter at four pounds? Well! it came to pass that my doing the proper thing was the cause of great disaster to me, for in the race, Valour beat Peter a neck, which made a difference to me of over £12,000; beside which, had Peter won, I should have then and there bought Barcaldine of his Irish owner.

It was aggravating, very! Archer never rode a better race than that Manchester Cup, and I verily believe Peter could have given Valour twenty-one pounds. I should have made a match with Machell, but Peter was not to be relied upon; he might not start, or he might stop in the race. That was not my only bad luck that day. I had brought two useful selling-platers to get my money back in case Peter did not win, and the very next race after the Cup, I started Costa in a selling-race and backed him freely. He won cleverly; but, as I was talking to someone, I did not go to see the horse weigh in, when, suddenly, up ran somebody and told me Wood could not draw the weight. I scuttled into the weighing-room, and whilst the horse's bridle was being taken off, I told the clerk of the scales to put four pounds in; as that hardly turned the scale, of course the bridle was useless and Costa was disqualified; therefore my losses were considerably increased, instead of lightened. A four-pound cloth must have been abstracted by some interested individual; for it is any odds that Wood weighed out right.

I never recollect to have heard of any harder luck than those two consecutive fiascos. In the first place, had I taken Wood off and put Archer up, Valour would not have run and Peter would

have won lengths; in the second, had the weights not been tam-
pered with I should have been handy 'home, sweet home'. No, it
was hot – very hot. However, I pulled out Zanoni next day, and
he not only won, but weighed in all right; so I had a smirk, and
a smile left; for I had bought Zanoni at Epsom last year under
somewhat peculiar circumstances, fancying that he would bring
me some chips, and he *did*, at a most useful juncture, and no error.
Well! the sometimes naughty Peter was none the worse for his
Manchester race, and he and I duly arrived at Ascot, and as there
were only some rips in the Queen's Vase on the Tuesday, I thought
Peter might canter with them, and place that piece of plate on my
sideboard. But there must be two to any bargain, and Peter didn't
fall in with my views, for when he got to the stable turn he pulled
up and began kicking, and eventually returned to the paddock.
That looked bad for the Hunt Cup on the morrow; but, notwithstanding his foolish pranks on Wednesday morning, I found he
was first favourite, and I had to take 5–1.

I warned Archer, when about to mount, to treat him kindly,
and, if he felt like stopping, to pat his neck and coax him. I also
sent the jockey Giles on my cob down to the post with a hunting-
whip, being afraid that Peter might run back and try what the iron
gates were made of, at the start for the new mile. All who were
there, know what a wonderful animal Peter proved himself that
day. Soon after he started he began to scotch, and was on the
point of stopping to kick, as he had done the day before; but
Archer patted him (according to my orders) and though at the
half-mile he was a long way last, he suddenly took hold of his bit,
and, coming up hand over hand, he won quite cleverly, and that
with 9 st. 3 lb. on his back. When Giles returned on my cob he
could not believe it possible that the horse had won; for he declared
he was so far behind at the half-mile post when he went over the
hill, that he felt certain he would be last at the finish. However,
he realized the fact when I gave him a 'pony' for his trouble; and
he bought a black pony with it, which he afterwards rode constantly at Newmarket.

On the Friday, Peter looked good (if in the humour) for the
Hardwicke Stakes, worth over three thousand, and here Archer's

wonderful forethought came in useful. Before the races began he said to me: 'I have been thinking over this race, Sir John. You know the start for the mile and a half we run today is just below the spot where Peter stopped to kick on Tuesday, and it is very likely, if I canter up past it with the other horses, he may take it into his head to repeat his Tuesday's performance. If you will get leave from the stewards, I will hack-canter him round the reverse way of the course, and arrive at the starting-post just as the other horses fall in; by so doing, he may jump off and go kindly.' 'A brilliant idea, my lad,' said I, and Peter was seen to emerge from the paddock some minutes before the other horses. Luckily, they were off at the first attempt, and he literally *walked in*, eight lengths ahead. I didn't bet till I saw Peter was fairly off, but was fortunate to have two good bookies, hungry to get back some of the Hunt Cup money I had won of them, and so I landed some £1,500 at evens.

I wonder where Valour would have been that day? Why, sprawling like a drunken gypsy under the Spagnoletti board, whilst Peter was pulling double past the post.

Sir John Astley, Bt (1894)

Lieutenant-Colonel Sir John Dugdale Astley, Third Baronet (1828–94)

Sir John Astley, known widely as 'The Mate', was one of the most popular figures of the mid-nineteenth-century sporting scene.

Victorian standards of loyalty to jockeys clearly transcend those of today. Sir John relied upon betting to sustain an expensive way of life, thus Archer's assistance at Manchester would have meant much. Despite running in his three engagements at Ascot – and winning two of them – the unreliable Peter failed by a wide margin to rectify the already serious damage to his owner's unstable finances.

In an age of rigid social distinction, indifference to the lot of those on a lower stratum of society was widespread: Sir John's attitude and kindliness to his employees was in sharp contrast. The Astley Institute was built from money raised entirely by himself, within the racing community, to improve the arid existence of stablemen in Newmarket. It still flourishes, as the New Astley Club, as a fitting memorial to its founder.

Astley's memoirs, Fifty Years of My Life, *were published in 1894 and, unlike most reminiscences of the period, are a lively mirror of Victorian sporting, social and military life.*

———

The Two Thousand Guineas, 1910

There was a good field for the Two Thousand Guineas and no horses ever started for it in more beautiful condition than Lemberg and Neil Gow. Another lovely horse in the race was the American Whisk Broom, owned by Mr H. Whitney and trained by Andrew Joyner.

I went some way down the course to see the race, and it was indeed one worth seeing. Coming into the Dip, Lemberg, who was ridden by Dillon, and Neil Gow were close together on the Stand side, and after Whisk Broom had made a bold show they singled themselves out from the rest of the field, Lemberg with a trifling advantage. Then Danny sat down to ride with that confidence and determination that will not be beaten. Leaning over the rails close to the struggling pair I could see the jockeys' desperate faces, the horses with their ears flat back on their heads, both running as true as steel: it was a great sight. The last two hundred yards I looked at them from behind. Although being close together, neither horse swerved or flinched. Dillon hit his horse oftener than Maher, but the latter, when he did use his whip, did so exactly at the right moment, and Neil Gow won by a short head. It was the riding that did it, though I must say that Dillon rode the race of his life that day, and it was hard lines for him and Lemberg to have Maher to beat. So fierce was the struggle that I remember wondering if either of the horses would ever forget the race.

I have lately heard and read that racing is no real test of the value of the thoroughbred horse, but where could you find any animal except a horse of the best English blood that could show the gameness and pluck of these two beautiful and high-strung horses, for later in the year they met again in the Eclipse Stakes, at the same weights, and with the same jockeys. I did not see the race, but after a magnificent struggle it ended in a dead heat. There is a case of consistency for you!

The Hon. George Lambton (1924)

As a description of a horse race this account has not been equalled. It brings the race so vividly alive that it can be re-enacted in the mind on every visit to the Rowley Mile.

Danny Maher (1881–1916), an outstanding rider of the Edwardian era, was one of several American jockeys to arrive in England at the turn of the century. He rode three Derby winners, Rock Sand (1903), Cicero (1905) and Spearmint (1906) and was champion jockey in 1908 and 1913. He returned to the United States at the outbreak of war in 1914 and died from tuberculosis, brought on by excessive wasting, at the age of thirty-five.

————

The 1913 Derby

The Derby in 1913 was one of the most dramatic in the history of the race. The King's Anmer, named after a village on the Sandringham Estate, was a 50–1 outsider with little chance of success. Nevertheless as the fifteen runners started to round Tattenham Corner, Miss Emily Davison, a leader of the suffragette movement who had previously been imprisoned for her views, dashed on to the course and brought Anmer and his jockey Herbert Jones crashing to the ground. It was an act of utter foolhardiness which did nothing for the suffragette cause. Luckily neither Anmer nor Jones was badly hurt. When Herbert Jones was brought back in the ambulance, the stretcher on which he was lying was found to be too wide to allow it to pass through either the jockeys' room door or the passage leading to the back of the stand, so the royal jockey was unceremoniously dumped on the ground outside the weighing room in full view of all whilst it was decided how to get him to the local hospital.

Miss Davison received a fractured skull and died in Epsom Hospital the following Sunday. The most remarkable fact of the incident is that Miss Davison managed to single out the horse whose jockey was wearing the royal colours. In the opinion of many, including Steve Donoghue who was riding in the race, it was purely coincidental that Miss Davison brought down the King's horse, who happened to be nearer last than first at the time. If the misguided woman had elected to rush forward a few seconds earlier a far greater catastrophe would have occurred.

As Anmer was struggling to his feet, a desperately close finish to the Derby was in progress, with the favourite Craganour beating the 100–1 outsider Aboyeur by a head with Louvois (a full brother to Louviers) a neck away third. Whilst Craganour and his owner, Mr Ismay, stood in the winners' unsaddling enclosure receiving the congratulations of their friends, it was learned that the Stewards had objected to the winner on the ground that he interfered with the runner-up. After a considerable time, with opinions and tempers, inflamed by the warmth of the day and the tension of the moment, causing many altercations amongst the crowds assembled outside the weighing room, the Stewards announced that Craganour was disqualified and placed last. In his private diary King George V, who on Derby Day wore a Brigade of Guards tie and a white carnation with his grey morning dress, wrote:

We all left for Epsom at 12.40 to see the Derby. The police say it was the largest crowd that has ever been seen there, the road was blocked and it took us some time to get on the course. It was a most disastrous Derby. Craganour, the favourite, won by a head, from Aboyeur (who had made all the running) and was led in by his owner Mr Ismay, but was afterwards disqualified for bumping and boring by the Stewards, and the race given to Aboyeur (100–1) with Louvois 2nd and Great Sport 3rd. I ran Anmer, just as the horses were coming round Tattenham Corner, a Suffragette (Miss Davison) dashed out and tried to catch Anmer's bridle. Of course she was knocked down and seriously injured, and poor Herbert Jones and Anmer were sent flying. Jones unconscious, badly cut, broken rib and slight concussion; a most regrettable scandalous proceeding. In the next race Leo Rothschild's horse Felizande fell and broke his leg and had to be destroyed. His jockey was not hurt. It was a most disappointing day . . . I gave my usual dinner to the Members of the Jockey Club, at 8.30 and we sat down 61. I talked to a great many of them afterwards.

It was a very eventful Derby Day, and although Whalley, the

Anglo-Indian jockey who rode Felizande, was only bruised, it should be mentioned *en passant* that the father of W. Saxby, who rode Louvois, fell out of bed and broke his neck that evening.

Jones, battered and angry with women in general, and suffragettes in particular, was discharged from hospital two days later. He found on his return to Newmarket that many letters on the subject of Anmer's fall had been sent to him. One, from an influential member of the Church of England, suggested that if Miss Davison died it would be a Christian act if Jones attended her funeral. Jones, usually the kindest of men, was not amused at this proposal, and his reply made this abundantly clear.

One of the first to enlist in 1914, Jones was stationed at Norwich. One Sunday a visiting brigadier told him to look after his charger whilst he went to lunch and warned Jones that the horse was strong-willed. Jones could not resist the opportunity of mounting the animal – with the result that after lunch the brigadier came out of the mess to see the disobedient Lance-Corporal Jones hacking around the parade-ground. His shouts of 'Look out, the bloody fool will be killed!' were hushed when it was explained that the horseman had already ridden two Derby winners.

Michael Seth-Smith (1983)

In the far-reaching scope of its drama, the 1913 Derby has fortunately remained unrivalled. The controversial decision to disqualify the favourite, Craganour, totally overshadowed the tragedy at Tattenham Corner. The prevailing outlook on this aspect was later reflected in robust and direct terms in a telegram of condolence to Herbert Jones:

Queen Alexandra was very sorry to hear of your sad accident caused through the abominable conduct of a brutal and lunatic woman. I telegraph now by Her Majesty's Command to inquire how you are getting on and to express Her Majesty's sincere hope that you may soon be all right again.

DIGHTON PROBYN*

* General Sir Dighton Probyn, VC (1833–1924), served King Edward VII and later the widowed Queen Alexandra as Comptroller and Treasurer for nearly fifty years.

With the benefit of hindsight in a case conducted with notable disregard for accepted procedure, and not without bias, Craganour and his connections were, almost certainly, very unlucky losers.

As a finale to 4 June 1913, the news of Saxby's father's unusual end came close to light relief.

———

The Derby, 1934

It all started, as so many things did in the racing world in that era, with Steve Donoghue. Charming, feckless, arguably the best horseman who ever sat in a racing saddle, irresponsible beyond the point of foolishness where obligations to owners and trainers were concerned, in 1934 he had reached the age of fifty leaving behind him a whole history of broken contracts, retainers thrown aside and engagements evaded, together with an assortment of wrathful and disappointed owners, some of them the greatest in the land.

As early as 1920 he had been a party to the 'jocking off', to use the modern expression, of Jelliss from the well-fancied Abbott's Trace in order to get himself the ride in the Derby of that year. In 1921 he displeased Lord Derby and his trainer, George Lambton, by wheedling and charming his way out of Lord Derby's retainer in order to take the mount on the fancied Humorist for Mr J. B. Joel. On Humorist he rode possibly the best of his many great races to win the Derby, but the following year he lost Lord Derby's retainer and with it the possibility of riding two future Derby winners in Sansovino and Hyperion. Once more in 1922 he was concerned in yet another 'jocking off', to enable him to take the ride on Captain Cuttle, this time for Lord Woolavington. But again the Woolavington connection did not last, for he let down the enormously rich and powerful whisky baron the following season by deserting his Derby runners – and breaking his retainer – in order to ride the well-backed Papyrus on which he won, giving him three Derby winners in a row. Although the formidable Fred Darling, having observed these manoeuvres, refused him a retainer, he did not object to one of his owners, Mr Morriss, making an independent arrangement with Steve to ride Manna in 1925. Manna won, and thus gave Steve four Derby victories in five years. He was a public figure and a public favourite. The cry 'Come on Steve' echoed round every racetrack in England. The story that he told King George V's racing manager: 'I should like to ride for His Majesty, my Lord, but I'm afraid his horses aren't good enough,' may be apocryphal but certainly then the whole world seemed to be at his feet.

All these things had a bearing on what was to happen in 1934. By then Steve had reached fifty, was nearing retirement and was desperately anxious to rehabilitate himself by riding another Derby winner before he hung up his boots. And during 1933 he had made up his mind that he had a very good chance of doing so.

Lord Glanely had been born William James Tatem in a small town in Devon. As a young man he went to sea and worked in a shipping office. Clever, industrious and ambitious, he fought his way to the top, accumulated wealth and founded his own shipping line. In 1909 he entered racing and enjoyed some small success. In 1918, in reward for services during the war, he was created a peer, and in the following year won the Derby with Grand Parade. His outlay on yearlings during the 1920s was prodigious and mostly ill-advised, rivalling that of Miss Dorothy Paget a decade later. But Grand Parade only cost him 470 guineas and in 1932 he secured another bargain when he paid 510 guineas for a colt by Manna out of Lady Nairne whom he called Colombo.

When Colombo started his racing career as a two-year-old Lord Glanely had no jockey retained. Colombo had a difficult temperament and had been troublesome to break, and when Captain Hogg, who had now become Lord Glanely's private trainer, started to work him he proved a far from easy ride. Knowing that Steve was down on his luck and knowing also what a beautiful horseman he was, Hogg asked him to ride Colombo in one of his early gallops. The colt went beautifully for Donoghue and made a great impression on him.

Richards, however, had the mount on Colombo in five of the colt's two-year-old races. Because he was claimed elsewhere Donoghue was given the ride on him when he won the Richmond

Stakes at Goodwood and, his last race of the season, the Imperial Produce Stakes at Kempton. Colombo wound up the season unbeaten and headed the Free Handicap with 9 st. 7 lb.

Donoghue, probably better than any other jockey in history except Archer or Piggott, could 'sense' a Derby winner when he sat on its back and he was convinced that Colombo would win not only next year's Derby but the Triple Crown as well. He was sure that Richards would be claimed by Beckhampton and so he persuaded himself that he would be offered the Derby ride. So certain was he of this that he did not indulge in any of his usual wheeling and dealing about the ride nor did he make any direct approach to Lord Glanely, but in his happy-go-lucky way went off at the end of the season on a holiday to South America without leaving a forwarding address.

Despite his doubts, Glanely did make an attempt to get in touch with Steve with a view to discussing plans for the next season, only to find that no one knew just where he was, no letters were being forwarded and nothing had been heard from him since he left England. Glanely cannot therefore have been exactly mollified to learn via the Press that the jockey had apparently pre-empted his decision, when answering a question from a South American reporter as to what would win next year's Derby, by saying: 'Colombo with myself in the saddle.'

Whether it was this rash answer that finally swung the scales against Steve no one now can say, but unquestionably around this time Lord Glanely decided that he must look elsewhere for a jockey. And at this point another actor comes on to the scene. William Raphael (Rae) Johnstone was an Australian from New South Wales riding in France.

Johnstone, who admits himself that at this period of his life success was a wine he could not carry, had come to England certain that he had the racing world at his feet. It was therefore a considerable blow to him when the Jockey Club stewards refused him a licence to ride. The stewards were not obliged to give any reasons for their refusal, nor did they, save the singularly unconvincing one that they were not granting any new licences at that time. Johnstone, however, was convinced and indeed was told on the grapevine that it was because of his unruly record in Australia. In the meantime he was stranded in England, passing his days mostly in Steve's company, travelling about with him, learning something of the idiosyncrasies of the various tracks and watching him ride. More and more he fell under the spell of the famous charm and was entranced with Steve's skills in the saddle. When Steve went to Paris to ride in the Grand Prix Johnstone accompanied him and while there, out of the blue, he received an offer to ride the Wertheimer horses.

As the records show, Johnstone was a really great jockey. He loved to ride a waiting race, which earned him the nickname from the French public of 'Le Crocodil' because, they said, he came on the scene late and ate up the other horses. Long ago, in Australia, he had had another nickname, 'Togo', which he hated and which sprang from his oriental cast of features. He certainly had something of the oriental impassivity for his face remained unchanging and inscrutable through triumph and disaster. This, coupled with an original sense of humour drily and tersely expressed, did not serve him well in the Derby sensation which was soon to erupt.

In the winter of 1933 feelers were put out to ascertain if he would accept Lord Glanely's retainer to ride his horses during the coming season in England. These horses included, of course, Colombo, who was regarded as a certainty for both the Guineas and the Derby and being backed accordingly. In his memoirs Johnstone says Colombo 'had all the appearance of being the racing machine of the era'. He accepted without hesitation.

When the news broke and Steve heard of it on his return to England he was furious. He had confidently expected that he would be given the ride on Colombo, and now here was Lord Glanely offering the ride behind his back – so he thought and said – to an outsider, an Australian, one who had made his name Down Under, in India and France, and had little or no experience of English racetracks and above all of Epsom.

Steve had no possible justification for his anger and resentment, for he had no claim whatsoever on Lord Glanely's bounty or his retainer. But all his life, regrettably, where fancied rides were concerned he was a spoilt child and like a spoilt child he convinced himself that what he wanted was his by right.

So far as racing was concerned, although Lord Glanely's two-year-olds did not come up to Johnstone's expectations he and Colombo got off to a great start. At his first outing of the season Colombo won the Craven Stakes in a manner that seemed to stamp him all over a champion. Once again, however, there were some murmurs among the *cognoscenti* that he had beaten nothing. Not all of these doubters had their fears put at rest by the result of the Two Thousand Guineas. Colombo, starting at 7–2 on, the shortest-price Guineas favourite since St Frusquin in 1896, won it all right but he seemed to some people to have been extended in doing so. For the first time since his very early days he showed signs of temperament and sweated up in the parade-ring. He had settled down at the start and jumped immediately into his stride. At the bushes, though, he had faltered and Johnstone had had to show him the whip before he ran on to beat the French horse, Easton, by a neck. Johnstone's comment afterwards, a strange one in view of what was to happen on Derby Day and the views expressed by experts on that race, was, 'The impression I got was that he had won *by staying*' (Johnstone's own italics).

At all events, that, for the moment, was that. Colombo's next race was to be the Derby. Public confidence in him, only momentarily shaken, was restored by the news that he was working well at home. He continued to be backed like a certainty for the big one.

In the meantime at Lambourn a young trainer called Marcus Marsh was quietly bringing on another colt to peak fitness before the Derby. Marsh, who until recently had been assistant trainer to Fred Darling, had bought Windsor Lad as a yearling in 1932 for 1,300 guineas on behalf of the Maharajah of Rajpipla. As a Classic prospect no fault could be found in his breeding, for he was by Blandford out of Resplendent who had won the Irish One Thousand Guineas and Oaks and run second in the Oaks at Epsom.

There was no ballyhoo at all about Windsor Lad or his preparation, but he won the Chester Vase and the Newmarket Stakes, his only two outings before the Derby. In the latter race he was ridden by Charlie Smirke who had only recently 'come in from the cold' after a five-year suspension for his riding of a horse called Welcome Gift, a sentence almost universally considered to have been unjustified.

By a coincidence Johnstone had himself later ridden Welcome Gift in India. He had very nearly got into trouble with the Calcutta stewards over the horse's crazy antics. He called him a 'heartbreak horse' and refused to ride him again.

Smirke was never one to hide his or his horse's chances under a bushel. He had formed a high opinion of Windsor Lad from the moment he first rode him. Full of confidence as he always was about his mount in a big race, and not slow to express it, he warned Johnstone when they met at Chester and Johnstone replied laughingly that Windsor Lad might give him a nice lead into the straight at Epsom: 'He'll lead you all right, Rae. All the way.'

Things were happening, too, at Beckhampton. Fred Darling had come to the conclusion that his one-time Derby prospect, Mediaeval Knight, was not of Classic quality, and he purchased Easton, whom Colombo had so narrowly defeated in the Guineas, for Lord Woolavington at, it was said, £15,000. Gordon Richards as first jockey would have the mount on Easton. Darling, however, was determined to run Mediaeval Knight as well so as to ensure that the gallop, to suit Easton, would be a good one. He had no jockey for Mediaeval Knight, and he looked around for one.

Just what Steve was up to in the few weeks before the Derby no one knows. Outwardly he and Johnstone were still on the friendliest of terms, with Johnstone constantly in and out of Steve's luxurious chambers in Albany. Inwardly we do know – for he has said so himself – that he was seething with disappointment and resentment. He approached Lord Glanely and tried all the famous wheedling charm to persuade him to stand down Johnstone and to give him the ride on Colombo. It had worked before but his escapades at the expense of owners, his comings and goings, his history of contracts torn up and retainers set aside had at long last earned its recompense. 'Old Guts and Gaiters' was adamant. Johnstone had the retainer and he would have the ride.

Hearing that Steve was free, Darling offered him the mount on

Mediaeval Knight. Disgusted, Donoghue nevertheless accepted. So, for the second successive year, the great Epsom jockey was reduced to playing the humble role of pacemaker.

It has been suggested that Steve played on his friendship with Johnstone and on Johnstone's hero-worship and his confidence in Steve's knowledge of the best way to ride the tricky Derby course. 'Track me and you will be all right' is what it is believed in some quarters Donoghue said to him – and this with malice afore-thought, for Donoghue knew Mediaeval Knight had stamina limi-tations.

If Steve did all this he acted quite out of character, for he was not a man to bear grudges and to hatch a plot of this kind would be utterly foreign to his nature. But he was ageing, he was in financial difficulties, he had been in the wilderness or something approaching it for too long, and his one last chance of crowning his career had been unfairly, or so he had persuaded himself, swept away from him.

On the great day confidence in Colombo was undiminished. He was backed steadily down to 11–8 against, the hottest Derby favourite for years. Lord Glanely had already stated that he believed Colombo to be a great horse and the only thing which could beat him was bad luck. To underline his belief, before he left for the races he ordered his favourite restaurateur to prepare a celebration dinner in anticipation of his triumphant return. To say the least of it, this smacked of the kind of hubris racing rarely forgives.

In the parade ring Colombo looked lean and hard and trained to the minute, but once again he showed signs of temperament. He began to sweat up and some observers noted a tell-tale bump between the eyes which could denote a lack of generosity if things did not go all his own way. Windsor Lad, on the other hand, a tougher, bulkier sort than the favourite, was as calm as could be and the testing Derby preliminaries bothered him not at all. There was considerable stable confidence behind him too, and he was well backed at 15–2.

In a very high-class field both Johnstone and Smirke had summed up the dangers – apart from each other – as Easton, ridden by

Gordon Richards, Umidwar with Harry Wragg in the saddle, and Mediaeval Knight, representing the incalculable and unpredictable since he was ridden by Steve, who might well produce a touch of pure magic from somewhere. Mediaeval Knight had won the Lingfield Derby Trial which had persuaded Johnstone he would stay, but Smirke had marked him down as 'a quitter'.

The pressures on Johnstone that day were immense. He was riding the favourite, a horse who had been built up as all but unbeatable, stories were going round which he must have heard that the English jockeys resented his presence on Colombo and would not let him win, and the precedent of Reiff being brought over from France to ride Craganour and what had happened to him cannot have been reassuring. To cap it all he had, he says, some days before, been offered £10,000 to stop Colombo.

As in the Guineas, Colombo had settled by the time they reached the starting-gate. There was no delay and the moment the tapes went up Steve pushed Mediaeval Knight into the lead on the rails with Johnstone tracking him. Behind Johnstone but more out towards the centre of the course were Smirke on Windsor Lad and Richards on Easton.

At Tattenham Corner the order was much the same. Then, as so often happens just there in the Derby, things began to happen very quickly indeed. Mediaeval Knight began to hang out distress signals. Smirke, whose reactions were more nearly instantaneous than those of any other jockey then riding, and who had in any event anticipated something of the sort, saw his opportunity and took it. He slipped past Mediaeval Knight, followed by Richards on Easton.

Johnstone, who realized what was happening to Mediaeval Knight a fraction of a second too late, was by then boxed in by a wall of horses. There was nothing he could do but sit and suffer until he could pull out and make his run on the outside. The instant the opportunity arose, he did so.

Colombo answered him with tremendous courage. He got to Easton's girths, held him and then started to wear him down. But Windsor Lad had got first run and was gone beyond recall. He passed the post a length ahead of Easton who, in turn, only held off Colombo by a neck. And then, of course, the inquests and the recriminations began.

One of the first things widely said was that the English jockeys had ganged up on Johnstone and stopped him. Johnstone himself disposed of that with one laconic word – 'bunk'. But it was accepted then, as it has been ever since, by most critics that Johnstone, by following Steve and allowing himself to be shut in, rode an atrociously bad race. Steve himself wrote afterwards: 'Mark you, had he called out to me to let him through when I realized I was whacked, I would, of course, have let him through . . .' Quinny Gilbey, the well-known racing writer who knew all the actors in this drama personally, made the aptest comment on this statement when he wrote: 'Like hell he would!' Nor, indeed, was there any obligation whatever on Steve to pull out and let the favourite up. But Gilbey goes on to voice the surely controversial opinion that the check did Colombo good, not harm, since as a non-stayer it 'gave him the breather he so badly needed'.

Perhaps Gilbey was right, but what evidence was there or is there that Colombo was a non-stayer? Johnstone himself says he won the Guineas like a stayer and puts the statement in italics in his book. And he was catching Easton hand over fist at the line despite coming round a wall of horses. It should, however, be added that after the Derby Johnstone, arguing from events, says he became convinced that Colombo did not stay. The kindest and probably truest comment on Johnstone's riding came from a fellow jockey, Freddy Fox: 'He stayed on the rails just too long,' he said.

The fact that he did not ride Colombo must have indeed rankled with Steve, for in his reminiscences, written four years later when one might have expected someone of his resilient and ebullient character to have mellowed, he wrote: 'Had I ridden him [Colombo] he would have won, on the bit, by lengths. He would have had an easy race and a decisive victory.' He may have been right, for the 'non-staying' theories were never put to the test. In any event the Derby has been won before and since by non-stayers through brilliance of jockeyship.

Lord Glanely appears to have vacillated between the view that Steve had 'done' Colombo and stopped him from winning and that

Johnstone had thrown the race away. Relations between Johnstone and 'Old Guts and Gaiters' were never the same after the race. In mid-season, by mutual agreement, the contract giving Johnstone the retainer was rescinded and the jockey returned to France. Before he left the English flat-race scene his fellow jockeys clubbed together to give him a dinner at the Piccadilly Hotel. It looked like a sporting gesture to one whose race-riding career, so far as England was concerned, was over for ever. At the airport a reporter asked him: 'Any final word on Colombo?'

'Yes,' Johnstone answered: 'if he'd been ridden in the Derby by a jockey, he'd have won ten minutes.' Though he spoke sardonically and in jest, that opinion was echoed by most of the pundits. It was said that he would never make a Derby jockey.

Yet after the war he was triumphantly to prove them all wrong for he rode three winners of the Derby (and was perhaps unlucky not to have ridden a fourth) and the same number of the Oaks. It was noticeable, all the same, that in all these victories he did not hug the rails, preferring to preserve his freedom of action by keeping to the centre of the course. The lesson of 1934 had been learnt the hard way.

                                                        John Welcome (1980)

Windsor Lad's Derby was a racing cause célèbre of the 1930s, but as the laconic Johnstone remarked to a muck-raking journalist of the time: 'At least no lives were lost.' Johnstone's reputation was later to be regained, in full measure. Between 1947 and 1956 he rode the winners of ten Classic races in this country, including the Derby three times: My Love (1948), Galcador (1950) and Lavandin (1956).

As a word-portrait of Steve Donoghue, this extract says it all. It is also remarkable that history did not repeat itself in a Derby, to quite the same extent, for over fifty years. The contentious defeat of Greville Starkey and Dancing Brave in 1986 gave elderly pundits and journalists an opportunity to recall Rae Johnstone and Colombo and ride another faultless race from the stands.

The Queen Alexandra Stakes, 1934

The bell rang and Brown Jack and Solatium entered the straight well clear of any other runner. It was certain then that one of the two would win. Solatium, on the rails, hung on most gallantly to Brown Jack. Indeed, he hung on so long that the suspense to me became almost unbearable.

Solatium belongs to a great friend of mine, but how I hoped his horse would fall away beaten so that Brown Jack could win! And then slowly but surely Brown Jack and Donoghue began to draw away; at first by inches and then by feet, and then, quite close to the winning-post, they were clear and the race was over. Brown Jack and his friend won by two lengths from Solatium, who had run a most gallant race and had been ridden as ably as a horse could be ridden by Caldwell. Some of the runners were struggling past the winning-post after Brown Jack had been pulled up and was returning to the paddock, and Mail Fist received a special cheer as he went by long after his friend.

I have never seen such a sight anywhere, and especially never at Ascot, as I was privileged to see when Brown Jack went past the winning-post. Eminently respectable old ladies in the Royal Enclosure gathered up their skirts and began, with such dignity as they could command in their excitement, to make the best of their way as quickly as they could towards the place where Brown Jack and Donoghue would return after the race. Hats were raised in the air in every enclosure and there were cheers from all parts of the course. Such a scene could be witnessed only in this country, and it has never in my time been witnessed here in such intensity. The unsaddling enclosure to which Brown Jack was returning for the sixth time after winning this race was surrounded many times deep. Crowds were waiting round the gateway leading from the course to the enclosure. Police made a lane for the triumphant pair, Brown Jack and Donoghue. The trainer, Ivor Anthony, as shy and bashful as ever, had already gone into the unsaddling enclosure where he was standing stroking his chin and trying to look unconcerned; he had been too nervous to watch the race, and had sat alone under the trees in the paddock until the great roar of cheering told him all was well.

And then at last Brown Jack came in. He looked to the right and to the left as he walked through the lane from the course to his own enclosure. His ears were pricked and he knew full well what was happening and what had happened. He was being patted on both sides from head to tail as he made his progress. 'Half his tail was pulled out,' Sir Harold Wernher told me afterwards. And then when he got to the gateway to his own enclosure he stood still. Donoghue tried to persuade him to go in, but he would not move. His ears were pricked and he was most certainly watching the people still pouring into the paddock to see his return. He would not disappoint them. When he thought that all had arrived he walked in quietly and received the congratulations of his owner, his owner's wife, and his trainer. Donoghue, in some wonderful way, wormed his way through the people to the weighing-room, and after that came the end.

R. C. Lyle (1934)

Brown Jack (1924), br. g. by Jackdaw-Querquidella (Kroonstad)
In his final race under N.H. rules, Brown Jack, ridden by Bilby Rees, won the Champion Hurdle 1928, having run ten times, won seven races and was only once unplaced. He ran in fifty-five races on the Flat, won eighteen and was ridden by only five different jockeys in six seasons.

——

'20–1 and Not a Pal On'

It must seem absurd to owners and trainers of big strings of horses to say how occupied I was with my small stable and what enjoyment I found in it, but nevertheless I spent all my leisure time either on the training-track or in our yard, and many hours in the evenings studying form, filling in a diary of the horses' training, and keeping an account of what each horse cost. Roscoe [Harvey] was a polo-player and I was not, so I did all the offices of trainer. Besides our own, we had two other Arabs in the yard, one of Captain Alex Schrieber's, who was visiting Egypt that winter, and one of the late 'Charlie' Church of my regiment. Neither were any good and never won for their owners, but at least they did not cost them very much in training bills.

All morning up to parade time, and sometimes after, we spent on the racecourse riding our own horses and other people's at work. I was desperately keen to learn all I could about training – especially Arabs, and very anxious to learn about riding on the flat. I made many friends among the trainers, and one and all were kindness itself in answering the scores of questions which were put to them. Though in a way my amateur training establishment was robbing them of a small piece of their rightful bread and butter, they could not have been more helpful or more ready with their congratulations when any successes came our way. Fergusson, who trained for Mrs Chester Beatty, Marsden, who trained for the King of Egypt, and Hadden, who combined a saddler's business in Cairo with a very successful private racing establishment at Heliopolis, were always ready with advice and helpful suggestions, and would always lend me one of their horses for a gallop. The jockeys, too, were willing to ride work for us for nothing, knowing that they would get the rides on our horses in the non-amateur events. Barnes, Gibson and Charlie Lister would often come over to our 'ring' in the middle of the sand track to ask after their old friends, Goha and Bareed. They gave Roscoe and myself many useful tips on the art of race-riding.

By this time I had pulled my stirrups up from average steeple-chasing length to that adopted by the modern flat-race jockey. I was very uncomfortable – especially on Arabs who are so short-coupled – but I was determined to do the thing properly, and get the right 'perch' somehow. It requires far more nicety of balance to achieve this when one is longish in the thigh than when one is short and thickset, but in the end I found the right length of stirrup and the right length of rein – more or less. When one achieves this, the feeling of balanced suspension is a real delight. I know that I still bumped a bit when I tried to sit down to ride one out, but no one had told me to bend the *bottom* joints of my spine, and tuck my seat right under me. I only learned that years afterwards, right at the end of my riding career. How I wish someone had mentioned this important detail years before! Then I might perhaps have reached a little nearer to my goal somewhere near the orbits of 'Tuppy' Bennet and Paddy Doyle.

One thing I did learn in Egypt, and that was to use my whip in my left hand. Both Heliopolis and Gesireh were right-handed courses, and it was essential on many occasions at least to show the whip in the left hand so that the horse ran on straight between whip and rails. On parade I rode the most sluggish animal in my squadron – one on whom I could wave my whip by the hour without him flinching or even noticing it. He had no more nerves than a wooden rocking-horse, and occasionally I could crack him one for practice, and then he would only open his left eye! Every trainer ought to have a horse of such insensibility and sloth for the benefit of their apprentices.

The only place where one could gallop a horse was on the sand track on the inside of Heliopolis racecourse. Roscoe and I had not worked out horses very long before we came to the conclusion that the average Arab's so-called ungenerousness was entirely due to his being utterly sick of being galloped on the same place every day. We also suspected that galloping in the sand, which except directly after being watered was very heavy going, spoiled their action. We took Marty Hartigan, who was on a busman's holiday away from Ogbourne, into consultation, and asked his advice. He said at once, 'I should gallop them on the sand as seldom as possible. Let them do their slow work trotting and hack-cantering on the desert. After all, since it only costs a pound to run, you can give your horses their fast work *in races* every weekend on grass. In addition you'll have the fun and experience of riding them yourselves.'

This proved excellent advice and suited us very well, for we were both anxious to ride as often as possible in races. Although neither Bareed nor Deban were anything like fit to win, and Goha was having a rest in order to try to get some flesh on his ribs, we entered them for each amateur race that was advertised. When there was not an amateur race suitable we put them in a professional race, and gave our good friends Barnes, Gibson or Lister the ride. In this way our horses were given one fast gallop a week, on grass and in colours.

By Christmas, Bareed had run three times in races of a mile and over, and though he was not fit enough to win over that distance, I thought he was about ready to win a small race over six or seven furlongs. There was a selling race over seven furlongs at Gesireh just before Christmas, and after a long and secret conference with Roscoe we decided that in that there was a chance of him providing a Christmas present for us. We engaged Barnes to ride for us, but did not tell him that we were contemplating a mild coup.

Fortunately the touts and the racing reporters treated our joint racing stable as a mild sort of joke, and because they seldom saw our horses worked on the course in the morning, wrote us off as a pair of crazy theorists who, because they refused to follow the stereotyped training methods, could be disregarded. Not a single paper tipped Bareed, and not a soul bothered to ask us whether we fancied his chances. That was just as well both for our pockets and for our reputations for truthfulness.

Roscoe and I watched the race from the top of the press stand. Bareed got badly away from the gate, seemed in a sulky mood, and took up a position right in the ruck. Coming to the turn for home he was still last, and we both put down our glasses and regarded each other with long faces. Then we saw that Barnes had picked up his whip and had pulled him out to the outside of the field. Our colours became quite definitely more visible. He was at least there with a fighting chance. It was a fighting chance and only that, but every time Barnes hit him he seemed to pull out a little bit more. As the crowd shouting the favourite home became less and less cheerfully vociferous, and began to ask, 'What's this on the outside?', Roscoe and I were bawling Bareed home as if our shouts could make him go faster. Something did. Right on the winning-post he pulled out a little bit more, and got home by a head.

We fell over each other running down the stairs to lead him in and be photographed with our first winner.

On Christmas Day we received a copy of the photograph from our friend Fergusson, the trainer. Across it was written, 'One of the old sort. Twenty-to-one, and not a pal on!'

Colin Davy (1939)

Whilst serving in Egypt between the wars with their regiment, the 10th Royal Hussars, MAJOR COLIN DAVY *and Captain C. B. Harvey exploited their small string of Arab racehorses with skill and profit. Returning home before the Second World War, both rode many winners in England*

Back in Egypt during the Middle East campaign in 1942, Roscoe Harvey was to become one of the outstanding tactical commanders of the Desert War, earning three DSOs. Those who served under him in the Army or as a racecourse official, during his time as Senior Stewards' Secretary, remember him with admiration and affection.

In 1938 Roscoe won the Cavalry Open Cup at Tweseldown, outside Aldershot. He tells this story: 'The Cup was presented to me by Mr Hore-Belisha, who was Minister of War at the time. After handing it to me he turned to Colonel Willoughby Norrie, who was Senior Steward, and said, "Not a bad type for a professional jockey." I don't know if he was a good minister but he didn't know as much about the Army as he did about beacons.'

———

The Grand National, 1935

A colossal crowd had come to cheer their champion home, firmly believing that he would win his second Grand National; he had been backed all over the world by all and sundry; the crowds arrived at Aintree hours before the race. The queues of cars were miles long; aeroplanes droned over the course. The liners from the States were full of American Sportsmen. Ninety-five per cent of this colossal crowd had come to witness The Miller. The vast crowds surged round him, whilst I and my head man saddled him up, and the detectives and the stable lads made a cordon to protect him. There had been a rumour that the favourite might be 'got at',

13 Harry Brown, the last amateur to head the list of National Hunt riders, including professionals, in 1919. Here seen at Aintree with Lady Warrender in 1935. (*National Horseracing Museum*)

14 (top) Pat Eddery (b. 1952). Champion Jockey for the first time in 1974, when 2 years out of his apprenticeship which he served with 'Frenchie' Nicholson. At the top of his profession and Champion Jockey for the 7th time in 1989. (*Lesley I. Sampson*)

15 Lester Piggott. A fine study of the 10 times Champion Jockey and rider of 29 Classic winners. (*Colorlabs International*)

16 (top) Steve Cauthen (b. 1960). After a brilliant early career in the US Cauthen won on his first ride in England at Salisbury, 7 April 1979. Adapting his style to English race courses he became in 1984 the first American since Danny Maher to be Champion Jockey. From that year he has shared the title with Pat Eddery, winning it again in 1985 and 1987. (*Lesley I. Sampson*)

17 Peter Scudamore, 5 times top National Hunt rider to date, who broke the record of 1,138 winning rides set up by John Francome. His father Michael, on Oxo, won the Grand National, which as yet (1989) eludes his son. (*Gerry Cranham*)

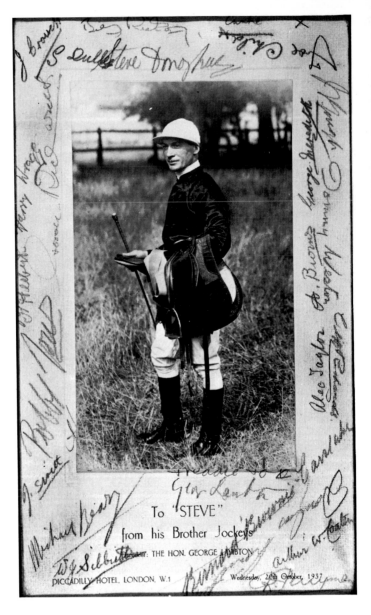

To 'STEVE'
from his Brother Jockeys
President: THE HON. GEORGE LAMBTON
PICCADILLY HOTEL, LONDON, W.1   Wednesday, 20th October, 1937

18 Stephen Donoghue (1884–1945) photographed in the twenties, in the colours of Lord Derby. 'Steve' rode winners of 14 Classic races, including The Derby 4 times between 1921 and 1925, at a time when his dash, nerve and the delicacy of his riding was a feature of English racing. (*National Horseracing Museum*)

19 Charles Smirke (b. 1906) and Palestine, an outstanding two-year-old and a brilliant miler at three years old, winning the 2,000 Guineas, St James's Palace Stakes and The Sussex Stakes. Smirke was one of the greatest jockeys in the history of racing, winning 11 Classic races, including 4 Derbys. His brilliant ride on Windsor Lad brought about the defeat of Colombo at Epsom, 1934.
(*National Horseracing Museum*)

20 (top) Golden Miller (1927), bay gelding by Goldcourt – Miller's Pride
(Wavelet's Pride). (*W. W. Rouch & Co*)

21 Becher's Brook first time round in the Grand National of 1934 won by Golden
Miller (right) ridden by G. Wilson and trained by A. B. Briscoe, the owner being
the redoubtable Miss Dorothy Paget. One of the greatest chasers of all time,
Golden Miller also won the Cheltenham Gold Cup 5 years in succession.
(*National Horseracing Museum*)

22 Piggott in the classic position in the field at Tattenham Corner in The Derby,
1957. The winner, Sir Victor Sassoon's Crepello (L. Piggott), with the large
triangular star is 6th, one off the rails. Ballymoss, 2nd, is 5th on the rails. Pipe
of Peace, who was 3rd, is obscured by the horse in blinkers and is on the rails.
Crepello was trained by Noel (later Sir Noel) Murless.
(*London Bureau, National Horseracing Museum*)

23 (top) Prince Khalid Abdulla's Dancing Brave going down to the start for The Coral Eclipse Stakes. Winner of the 2,000 Guineas. The Coral Eclipse Stakes, Le Prix de l'Arc de Triomphe, 1986. An outstanding racehorse. (*Lesley I. Sampson*)

24 Desert Orchid (Simon Sherwood) at Sandown, 1988. A national hero of the eighties. Winner of the Cheltenham Gold Cup (1989), King George VI Chase, Kempton (1986, 1988, 1989). (*Lesley I. Sampson*)

and so we were leaving nothing to chance. His guard saw him into the parade-ring, and the detectives followed him round inside the rails. He walked round the parade-ring with the greatest composure, paying little heed to the shouting of the bookmakers and the terrific noise of the vast crowd. His old opponent, Thomond II, was on his toes and sweating a bit. It was a good-looking field that was to face the starting-gate, and all the horses looked trained to the minute. A few minutes later the jockeys came into the parade-ring. I told Wilson to mount The Miller as late as possible, for he had a big weight to carry; we then took his paddock clothing off him and, followed by his detectives, he walked out of the parade-ring. The stable lads gathered round him, and we guarded him out of the paddock on to the racecourse. Our job was then finished. I walked nervously back, smoking many cigarettes. I watched the race from the trainer's stand.

When The Miller turned round to gallop back to the starting-gate he strode out like a lion. He stood at the starting-gate quite unperturbed, and there was a terrific roar as the gate went up and he set off to a good start. The first to break was Theras, who made the running from Thomond II, Emancipator, Golden Miller, and a batch of others. Huic Holloa and Brave Cry were the first to fall, both of them coming down at the first fence. Slater came down at the next and Fouquet refused at the fourth fence. At this fence Southern Hero fell. Really True came down at Becher's the first time round; Thomond II made a bad mistake at this jump and blundered. Castle Irwell then went to the front and made the running from Golden Miller and Blue Prince. At Valentine's, Castle Irwell held a clear lead. *At the next fence Golden Miller unseated Gerry Wilson. There was a roar from the crowd such as never had been heard on a racecourse before. The hopes of all The Miller's tens of thousands of admirers had been dashed to the ground.*

I walked off the stands at Liverpool a heart-broken man, and on to the course, where I met Gerry Wilson. Wilson considered that the horse should not have run and that something was amiss with him. I felt that, although he had been watched by all this number of people, and although a Newmarket veterinary surgeon had watched him constantly since he had arrived at Liverpool, we should take further consultations, so I asked Miss Paget to agree to two Liverpool racecourse veterinary surgeons examining him. These two veterinary surgeons, in company with Miss Paget and myself and Wilson, examined The Miller. They asked Wilson to ride him a canter. They watched him in all his paces and could find nothing wrong with him. His owner asked the Liverpool veterinary surgeons whether it would be wise to run him in the Champion 'Chase the following day, a race in which he was engaged, and worth £1,480 to the owner of the winner. The surgeons said there was nothing wrong with the horse and there was no reason why he should not run.

That night he fed up again and he showed no ill-effects from his experience the previous day. Miss Paget engaged Wilson to ride him. He went down to the post as fresh as paint, but unseated Wilson again – this time at the first fence. Miss Paget unfortunately blamed me for the incidents and considered her horse had not been properly trained. I felt that, under the circumstances, if those were her views I could not possibly continue to train my old pal. I had hunted him as a three-year-old and had watched him ever since the days he had his breaking tackle first put on him, but as his owner had taken that strong view I asked Miss Paget to find other quarters for her 'chasers, giving her a week's time to make her arrangements. Roughly a week after that, The Miller left his old home. Mick, the stable lad who had looked after his old favourite for so many seasons, also said goodbye to his old friend, for, as big as the wrench was, he preferred to stay on at Beechwood House rather than move to another trainer's quarters. The old horse went to Donald Snow for a short time and then on to the late Owen Anthony to be trained. Owen did well with him considering that he was not likely to improve. He trained him a winner of a further Gold Cup, bringing his record to five Cheltenham Gold Cups off the reel – a record which is unlikely to be equalled and one which is almost certain not to be surpassed in the annals of racing history. He unfortunately did get beaten when trained by Anthony in the Gold Cup the following year, after his fifth win. This was the only time he was ever beaten at Cheltenham, and it was, indeed, a sad day for all those people who had known The Miller in his prime.

Gerry Wilson's explanation of The Miller's lapse was that he found him going short on his off foreleg in the canter and in the race; Wilson said, 'When going to the fence after Valentine's, he propped and seemed to fall lame before reaching the fence. He did not actually fall, but shot me out of the saddle.' This statement naturally mystified both Harry Beasley and myself, for Harry had ridden him in most of his home gallops, in his final winding-up gallop at Newmarket, and had also ridden him in his canter on the course at Liverpool the previous day.

When The Miller arrived at Newmarket from Liverpool I asked one of the leading Newmarket veterinary surgeons to meet him at the station and examine him there, but he could find nothing wrong with him. Miss Paget, unfortunately for me, accepted Wilson's explanation, and the sequel ended in the conclusion of a long and successful association between owner and trainer. There was a general hope in the racing world that the matter would be amicably settled. Miss Paget was silent for some time and did not reply to my letter, but eventually she made a public statement to the Press. It was clear that she had sponsored Wilson's point of view. A few days later she telephoned me to say that she had made arrangements for her horses to go to Donald Snow's training establishment at Eastbury in Berkshire, and at the same time Miss Paget's secretary telephoned a *Sporting Life* representative and made the following statement: 'Golden Miller and his stable companions leave Beechwood House tomorrow. Twenty-four hours before, Mr Briscoe requested Miss Paget, by the Press and by letter, to have them removed from his yard.' And so ended my long association with both The Miller and his owner. The old favourite left the stables the following morning, and I said goodbye to him for ever. He was seen out of the gate by his faithful friend Grouse, my huge Great Dane. When The Miller left the stable gate Grouse sadly trotted back, and lay in the straw in the empty box.

Basil Briscoe (1939)

Golden Miller (1927) won five consecutive Gold Cups at Chelten-ham between 1932 and 1936 and is the only horse to have won the Gold Cup and the Grand National (1934) in the same year.

Fifteen days after an exhausting struggle with Thomond II at Cheltenham, Golden Miller ran in the Grand National of 1935. The fact that he blundered and unseated Gerry Wilson at the fence after Valentine's was almost certainly due to the effect of a very hard race from which he had not recovered fully.

Unlike Arkle, Golden Miller suffered from the eccentricities of his owner, the comparative inexperience of his trainer, Basil Briscoe, and the fact that he was ridden by a total of seventeen different jockeys. In spite of these handicaps he was possibly the greatest 'chaser ever to have run in this country.

———

Anthony Mildmay and Davy Jones

Grand National Day 1936 was favoured with perfect weather. The sun shone, the atmosphere was crystal clear. The going was perfect after overnight rain. The setting was ideal for a race that was to provide sensation after sensation from the first fence to the last.

Thirty-five runners went to the post, and the field was acknowledged to be well above average standard. A hot favourite was Mrs Mundy's brilliant seven-year-old Avenger, ridden by young Fred Rimell. There were two former winners in Golden Miller, ridden by E. Williams, and Reynoldstown, ridden by Mr F. Walwyn, of the 9th Lancers. Castle Irwell, owned and ridden by the American amateur Mr G. Bostwick, was a firm 8–1 chance, and others fancied included Lord Rosebery's Keen Blade, ridden by Elder, and Emancipator, a great big brown gelding owned and ridden by Peter Cazalet, trainer of Davy Jones. No one appeared to have the slightest fancy for Davy Jones and his amateur rider, and the combination was quoted among the '100–1 others'.

Now Davy Jones took a very strong hold, and it was Anthony's custom to tie a knot in his reins when riding him. As he was leaving the paddock, Peter noticed that Anthony had not tied his usual knot. He was about to advise him to do so when he changed his mind and decided it was best to allow Anthony to do as he thought fit. Anthony had in fact decided not to tie a knot in order to make it easier to slip the reins when landing over the drop fences. This perfectly reasonable decision was ultimately to cost him the race.

There was very little delay at the start, and as the field thundered over the Melling Road to the first fence, Davy Jones, taking a good hold as usual, could be seen well up with the leaders. In fact, he jumped the first fence, where the famous Golden Miller came to grief, just in front.

The big chestnut soon settled down well to his task, measuring fence after fence with wonderful accuracy and taking little out of himself with his effortless jumping. Anthony wisely made little attempt to restrain him, and allowed him to stride along boldly in front. Jumping Becher's, he was just ahead of Kiltoi, Delaneige, second in 1934 to Golden Miller, and Avenger. Delaneige, however, came down at the Canal Turn, and Blue Prince, second the previous year, at Valentine's. Continuing to jump without a semblance of a mistake, Davy Jones still led coming on to the racecourse, followed by Kiltoi, Keen Blade, Double Crossed, Avenger, Emancipator and Reynoldstown. By the time they reached the water, Avenger had moved up to second place and Reynoldstown was gradually improving his position as well.

There were still eighteen horses left standing as they streamed away for the second circuit, the favourite just behind the 100–1 outsider. At the very next fence, however, Avenger hit the top, fell heavily and broke his neck, a tragic end to a brilliant young horse that had jumped superbly up till then. Happily his owner, who was devoted to him, was not there to see him die.

With Avenger gone, Davy Jones was left with a clear lead and by then it must have occurred to Anthony that he was probably going to win the Grand National and achieve the great ambition of his life. However, Reynoldstown continued to make up ground and by Becher's had drawn almost level. On they went together, Davy Jones barely a length in front, both horses jumping boldly and full of running, the two amateur riders going perfectly with their horses. It was a magnificent race to watch, and in the clear light of that spring day, every incident could be seen from the stands.

At Valentine's it was obvious that one of the two must surely win, while Keen Blade, running on stoutly ten lengths behind, seemed certain to be third. With three fences to go they approached that fence with a pronounced drop on the landing side which some riders say is the worst fence on the course for a tiring horse. Keen Blade did not jump it well and his rider became unbalanced and disappeared backwards over the horse's tail. More important still, Reynoldstown made his first real mistake. He hit the top of the fence and blundered badly. Fulke Walwyn recovered in the way that only a first-class horseman can but he lost an iron, and Reynoldstown, with some of the stuffing knocked out of him, now had a dozen lengths to make up. At that point Davy Jones looked as certain to win the Grand National as any horse can look when there are still two Aintree fences in front of him.

Tired as Reynoldstown was, with magnificent courage he set out to make up the lost ground. By the second-last fence, Walwyn had almost driven him up to the leader, but Davy Jones was still on the bit, and Anthony, as cool as any man can be in such circumstances, had not moved on him.

Davy Jones did not take the second-last fence quite cleanly and pecked a little on landing. To give him every chance to recover Anthony let slip his reins to the very buckle, and then in one nightmare moment, disaster descended. The prong of the buckle in some way managed to slip through the hasp and in a trice, there were the reins flapping loose round Davy Jones's neck. Desperately Anthony tried to guide him with his whip to the final fence. It was of no avail. Davy Jones ran out to the left, and the gallant Reynoldstown was left to win as he pleased from Ego, ridden by Mr Harry Llewellyn, a far less famous figure then than he is today. In a few terrible, unforgettable seconds, the vision that must have seemed to Anthony too good to be true had been cruelly erased.

For a little time after the race, Anthony was simply numbed by the whole affair. Peter, too, not only shared the bitterness of disappointment, but felt acutely that as he was responsible for the tack, such blame as there was must fall on his shoulders.

Anthony's grief, however, did not last long. Never, in his wildest dreams, had he expected to win, and at least he had had an unforgettable ride on a horse that had given one of the most flawless exhibitions of jumping in the history of the race. More-over, Anthony had enjoyed the sensations that most winning riders of that race experience, even if the cup had been snatched away at the very last moment. By the evening his spirits had revived and he was ready for the traditional rigours of Grand National night at the Adelphi.

Peter himself had had a splendid ride on Emancipator. It was only after Becher's second time round that he began to drop out of the leading group and he eventually came down at the big open ditch four fences from home. He had been able to see Anthony sailing along in front and assumed that he had won the race. He remounted Emancipator, trotted back towards the paddock, and could hardly believe his ears when a policeman told him that Reynoldstown had won and Davy Jones was unplaced.

Lord Mildmay was in hospital at the time. He listened in to the race, and any sense of disappointment was swamped for the time being by the pride and delight that he felt at the wonderful show Davy Jones and Anthony had put up. For the rest of his life he loved to watch the film of the race. The conclusion, however, would be too much for him to bear. After the last fence but one it was his invariable custom to emit a dreadful groan and to leave the room.

Roger Mortimer (1956)

Anthony Bingham Mildmay (1909–50)

An outstanding and much-liked supporter of N.H. racing, Lord Mildmay, who succeeded to the title in 1947, was leading amateur in five seasons, 1945–50. Twice unlucky not to win the Grand National, in 1936 when Davy Jones ran out after the second last fence, and again in 1948 when a neck injury reasserted itself during the race, despite which he finished third, on Cromwell. Tragically, Anthony Mildmay was drowned bathing off the Devonshire coast on 12 May 1950. As an owner and administrator he was a great loss to N.H. racing.

A Wartime Interlude

That winter of 1941, because of the restriction to racing, Tom Masson moved his string to Cheltenham for the N.H. season. Among his horses was one called Overseas, on whom I had won a number of hurdle races before the war and whose owner, Mollie Gregson, gave him to me. He was a neat, well-made little bay gelding by an obscure sire, Mitchells, but a brilliant jumper over hurdles; and since he was high in the handicap I thought that his best chance of success in the future lay in novice steeplechases, in which he would be set to carry appreciably lower weights than over hurdles.

I was not able to get away to ride him schooling, but Tom reported that he jumped fences well, if rather carefully; and he was entered in a novice 'chase at Cheltenham, where I arranged to ride him. A few days before the race I rang up Tom to confirm that all was well with Overseas and that he was going to run.

Rather to my surprise, Tom seemed a little doubtful about the whole project.

'Why don't you let Matt (Matt Feakes, who was riding for Tom that season and after the war trained King's Bench, winner of the Middle Park Stakes and St James's Palace Stakes) give him a run round and ride him yourself next time out, when he'll have had a good school and learnt what it's all about?'

But with the uncertainty of the war and of getting leave when it was required, I did not want to risk the chance of missing a ride. It might be a sound enough plan in peacetime, but now it's too long-term a policy, I thought.

'Why, Tom, he jumps all right doesn't he?'

'Yes, he's safe enough, but he doesn't really loose himself at a fence like a 'chaser should. He's a bit too cautious about the whole business.'

'Oh, he'll be all right – it's the ones that pay no regard to the obstacles that I don't like. Anyway, goodness knows when I'll be able to have a ride next, and I don't want to miss this one.'

So we agreed to let the arrangement stand.

My squadron was stationed at Richmond at the time and Jakie Astor, who was riding in a hurdle race, and I drove down to Cheltenham together.

It was a beautiful, calm, winter's morning, and as we headed west thoughts of the war and the army fell behind with the miles, and our hearts were light with joy and excitement at the prospect of a return to an aspect of pre-war life and environment, which at times seemed irrevocably far away.

We were a little on edge from nervous anticipation and I expect that we talked volubly and flippantly. But what did it matter? We were still young, life was good and, for all we knew, the course of the war might suddenly put us out of the running for ever.

As one grows older, at times a faint shadow of weariness tends to fall on even the most favourite diversions: the last day of an important meeting can become the prelude to a welcome respite from the hustle and noise of the racecourse; a few days' frost to disrupt the fox-hunting season can bring a sense of ease in place of irritation. But youth feels the urgency of not losing one second of any play or entertainment: the desire to be at a race meeting long before the first horse appears in the paddock, leaving only when the 'weighed-in' has been signalled after the last race; mortification at missing a hunt through going home too soon.

In keeping with our age and inclinations, we were at Cheltenham in good time. The racing scene had changed greatly with war. Cars were fewer, crowds smaller, and uniforms of the three services were prominent among both spectators and participants. In some ways the atmosphere was gayer. For many it was a reunion of peacetime friends and acquaintances separated by war, to be celebrated as freely as the exigencies of the times allowed. People betted more heavily and recklessly than before, either to establish a reason for possessing money acquired by less reputable transactions, to give legitimate profits a chance to earn tax-free gains, or through the unconscious impulse to make the most of the present in case there should be no future. In the 1914–18 war, if anyone was spoken of as having 'done well' it was presumed he had been decorated for valour; in the last war it was taken for granted as an indication that he had made a killing in the black market or a fortune from Government contracts. Jockeys rode, if no more courageously, with fewer cares; I never felt less nervous or fearful during the whole of my riding career than at that period.

Thus the zest which the environment of the Turf had always induced in me in peacetime was redoubled during the war. On this particular day these sensations were strangely intensified, blending that feeling of being in a different dimension, which is sometimes brought on by fever, with unusual tranquillity and clearness of mind. At the same time I was filled with great excitement, as if on the brink of some momentous occasion in my life – and with a peculiar foreboding which, oddly, was accompanied neither by fear nor gloom. It was as if the path of my immediate future had been immutably fixed; and while I was powerless to influence or change it in any way, the strength and fortitude necessary to following it had been born suddenly within me.

When I met Tom Masson the reluctance at my deciding to ride Overseas, which he had expressed to me on the telephone, had not abated: 'I wish you weren't riding him; Matt's here and would be only too pleased to climb up, and there's still time to change the declaration.' But he could not persuade me to alter my mind, and I believe that even if I had wanted to do so the words expressing the wish would not have formed on my tongue or emerged from my mouth.

When the time came, I changed in the same dark, gloomy, ill-appointed jockeys' room which I had got to know so well before the war and which, though I have not entered it for some years, is probably exactly the same today.

As ever, Charlie Stalker, my racecourse valet since I began riding, was there to look after me. I had always been fond of Charlie, and his presence was pleasing and comforting. He had taken an interest in my career since he valeted me on the occasion of my first ride – it nearly proved my last – and I liked him to be there if I won; and if disaster overcame me I knew he would not fail to see that I was being looked after, before he left the racecourse.

'Well, guv'nor; it's good to see you back – perhaps you'll be able to get away for another ride or two this winter. Anyway, I hope this one goes in for you.'

As I walked from the weighing-room to the parade-ring I was even more conscious of the atmosphere which had prevailed since the start of the day – the feeling of remoteness from my surroundings and all that was going on, of an unusual clarity of perception, as if the scene was being viewed through exceptionally powerful field-glasses from a great distance, but without any loss of sound. The sun still shone, but the air had become keener and the sky above Cleeve Hill, standing out sharp and clear on the horizon, showed an ice-blue tint which presaged cold weather.

Just as well I've managed to get this ride in; we might be due for a spell of frost that would stop racing for weeks, I thought.

On the way I ran into Billy Maiden, an owner for whom I had ridden several times in the past. 'How'll you go here?' he asked.

'Pretty well, I hope: he jumps all right at home and with reasonable luck might win,' I replied.

'All the best,' he called to me as I walked away.

I moved on and entered the ring. There were twelve runners in the race, none looking anything out of the ordinary, or better than Overseas. Though smaller than most of his opponents, he was muscular, strong, in perfect condition and full of life, his copper-tinted coat shining in the sun. To see him gave me confidence. The favourite at 11–8 was a horse called Rest Assured from Victor Tabor's stable and ridden by Ron Smyth, who now trains at Epsom.

'You'll find that he looks at his fences and jumps carefully, so you can afford to kick him into them – he won't take one on. But watch him at the water; he doesn't jump out like a 'chaser should, and if you don't make certain he's going on at it he might land short – be sure and give him a couple going into it, but nip hold of his head and don't loose him till he's in the air or he might take off too soon.'

With these instructions, Tom gave me a leg up, wished me luck, and I rode out on to the course.

At times the refrain of a song or some lines of verse, for no reason, will suddenly come to mind, milling round in the head for hours on end, in a state of what begins to seem like perpetual motion until, as suddenly as it began, the haunting repetition will vanish. And that afternoon I found snatches of one of Adam Lindsay Gordon's poems recurring incessantly within my brain. I had long outgrown my youthful ardour for his verse, much of which I had learnt on my own account as a boy, but perhaps environment reawakened this poem in my mind. Anyway, as we cantered to the post, to the rhythm of Overseas' hoof-beats came back those long-forgotten lines:

> I remember some words my father said,
> When I was an urchin vain; –
> God rest his soul, in his narrow bed
> These ten long years he hath lain.

I used to know the remainder of the verse, and the next two – the poem, subtitled 'A Treatise on Trees – Vine Tree v. Saddle Tree', is out of Ye Wearie Wayfarer – but only odd lines came to mind.

> But the stimulant which the horseman feels,
> When he gallops fast and straight,
> To his better nature most appeals
> And charity conquers hate . . .
>
> So the coward will dare on the gallant horse
> What he never would dare alone,
> Because he exults in a borrowed force,
> And a hardihood not his own.

While this continued as a ceaseless form of mental background music – like a Greek chorus who wouldn't stop – it did not withdraw my attention from the task on hand, or change my feeling of unusual calmness, suppressed excitement and premonition.

Overseas was an experienced racehorse and no trouble at the gate; and though not a drone he was neither nervous nor excitable by disposition.

We took up a position about two places from the inside and, when the gate went up, broke to a good start. Approaching the first obstacle in a steeplechase on a horse who has never run over fences, and on whom you have never ridden schooling, can give justifiable grounds for apprehension; but Overseas was such a brilliant jumper over hurdles, which he always cleared cleanly and quickly, that I had little to worry about on this account. Still, it gave me a sense both of joy and relief when he sailed over the first without touching a twig. Approaching it, he checked ever so slightly, to enable him to measure his take-off exactly, as Tom warned me he would; but he jumped fast and boldly, landing and getting away in the leading group. We crossed the next two fences in the same fluent and agreeable manner, taking the lead as we made the turn passing the stands. Overseas liked being in front, perhaps because this position gave him a clear view of the obstacles and kept him from being crowded by other horses – since he was rather small and light he was liable to come off the worst in any mêlée involving bigger and heavier opponents.

He cocked his ears in appreciation of having gained his favourite place, taking a slightly stronger hold, his smooth, measured gallop continuing to beat out in my mind: 'I remember some words my father said,' and so on.

My confidence increased. We were going so well that I was sure that we had only to stand up to win, and since Overseas had jumped the first three fences as accurately and consistently as an experienced and skilled 'chaser, there seemed little reason to believe that misfortune would overtake us. In those days there was no fence between the last one in the straight and the one before the water, which was the next to be met. Overseas sailed over it as he had the preceding three, and we headed for the water. Approaching it, I remembered Tom's advice to give him one or two quick taps as we entered the wings, to make sure that he extended himself sufficiently. Perhaps through over-confidence, because he had jumped so well up to this point, and through fear of hitting him at the wrong moment and making him take off too soon, which once had put me into the water at Wolverhampton, I refrained from doing so. Instead, I kicked him into it with my heels and hoped for the best.

He seemed to take off all right. There was that unpleasant

fraction of a second as he described the parabola of his leap and I could not tell whether we were safely over or not. And then he landed – but short, coming to his knees on the far bank and shooting me on to the ground. Out of the corner of my eye I saw Rest Assured flash past on his way to eventual victory. With the instinct developed by innumerable past falls I hunched myself up into a ball and lay as still as possible – the surest way to get hurt steeplechasing is to get up before the horses following have passed by. I caught a glimpse of Overseas cantering awkwardly away, one of his hind legs moving in an ominously disjointed manner: bitterly, I realized it was broken.

I was about to get up, when to my considerable surprise a couple of St John's Ambulance men pounced on me and gently but firmly held me down.

'Take it easy, son; you'll be all right.' Saying this, they began to put my leg into a splint. At first I wondered whether they wanted to get some practice and therefore had seized upon me before I had time to thwart them by rising to my feet; but the serious concentration with which they worked made me believe that, perhaps, after all, some damage had been done, though I felt no pain. They signalled for the ambulance and in due course I was driven to the racecourse hospital, taken in on a stretcher and laid on the floor. The nurse on duty began to remove the splints while the two racecourse doctors looked on.

'You'll have to cut away the rest of the boot,' I heard one of them say, and the nurse began to do so.

At this moment Charlie came in to find out what had happened to me, as he always did when one of his jockeys was hurt. 'Hallo, guv'nor, what are you doing here? How d'you feel?'

'I don't know what's up, Charlie. Anyway it doesn't hurt.'

By this time the nurse had ploughed through the remainder of my boot and began to remove it. As I was lying flat on my back I could see nothing of the operation, but for the first time felt something of the injury which I appeared to have suffered; but it was only a slight, stinging pain – as if I had béen touched by a nettle. As the remnants of my boot came off my leg, which the nurse had raised a little to enable her to remove it, I saw from

Charlie's face that all was not well: his jaw dropped and an expression of horror spread over his countenance. He told me afterwards: 'I never saw anything like it: a strip of flesh about a foot long hung down off your leg and from your calf to your heel there didn't seem much left except the bones and what there was was in an awful mess.'

Tom Masson had also come along to see me, and while I was being examined I remember catching his eye and his making a slight movement of his hand, as if he was giving a horse two or three quick taps of the whip, indicating that if I had followed his instructions exactly I might not be in this predicament.

John Hislop (1965)

———

The Derby, 1949

Nimbus was bred by Mr William Hill and was a big bay colt by Nearco out of Kong, by the grey Irish Derby winner Baytown. Kong had won the Wokingham Stakes with 6 st. 12 lb. Mr Henry A. Glenister bought Nimbus as a yearling for 5,000 guineas and gave him as a present to his wife. Glenister, who possessed a remarkable knowledge of the Stud Book, was always something of a man of mystery to his trainer, George Colling. He liked to describe himself as a farmer and indeed he did farm 700 acres at Sible Hedingham in Essex. He did not invariably choose to inform people that he was in fact a salaried bank official, employed as assistant manager of the London branch of the Midland Bank Executor and Trustee Company in the City. Bank officials closely identified with racing are rare; ones that can fork out 5,000 guineas for a yearling rarer still. On 16 August 1952, Mr Glenister committed suicide in his car in Sussex. At the inquest, it was revealed that he was in default of 'a considerable sum' entrusted to his department at the bank. The full story of that episode has yet to be told; nor has the Midland Bank ever revealed the exact amount that their employee got away with.

As a two-year-old, Nimbus won the Coventry Stakes at Royal

Ascot but in the Champagne Stakes he was outpaced by Abernant who finished six lengths in front of him. Before the Guineas (which he won by a short head from Abernant), he won the Thirsk Classic Trial ridden by Elliott, who was to partner him in the Newmarket Classic.

Nimbus did not run again before the Derby but his final gallop was thoroughly satisfactory. His preparation had not been helped by the fact that Colling was ill and much responsibility devolved on his head lad, Dick Jones, and on Elliott. Colling was too unwell to go to Epsom and asked Jack Jarvis to saddle Nimbus. In his book of reminiscences entitled *They're Off*, Jarvis gave the following account.

When I went down to the paddock I found Nimbus standing still in the centre of it with a distinctly apprehensive small boy on his back. Nimbus was obviously very much on edge, kicking, sweating and refusing to move. George's head lad was there, too, and so were Mr and Mrs Glenister and George's wife. I told the boy to dismount and I then got Nimbus to walk quietly down to the saddling stalls that used to stand up against the fence dividing the paddock from the Durdans. Then we dried Nimbus off and settled him down.

Colling had given orders that Nimbus was to be ridden by the boy in the parade-ring but Jarvis was sure that Nimbus was happier without the boy on his back. Jarvis, therefore, took the responsibility of ordering the boy to walk along in readiness in case he was needed but not to get mounted. It was not an easy decision for Jarvis to make as it was contrary to Colling's orders and if Nimbus, a high-mettled colt, had played up and got loose, Jarvis would undoubtedly have had to carry the can. It would not have been possible for the head lad to make a similar decision. Luckily, though, everything went well. Jarvis never received a word of thanks from Mr and Mrs Glenister.

It proved to be one of the most exciting and controversial Derbys of this century. With typical boldness, Elliott elected to make the running on Nimbus whom many reckoned unlikely to stay the distance on account of the stamina limitations of his dam. At Tattenham Corner Nimbus still led but Lord Derby's Bois Roussel colt Swallow Tail was close up and apparently going every bit as well. At this stage Amour Drake was lying eighth.

Just below the distance, Swallow Tail managed to get his head in front but Nimbus fought back and regained the lead. In the meantime Amour Drake was making up ground fast towards the centre of the course. In the final furlong Nimbus, obviously tiring, began to veer to the right and went very close indeed to Swallow Tail. If he did not actually touch Swallow Tail, he certainly unbalanced him and Swallow Tail, too, edged to the right. It looked as if Amour Drake's powerful challenge might well be impeded by Swallow Tail. Rae Johnstone, Amour Drake's rider, had to make a split-second decision. At this late and critical juncture, he switched Amour Drake over to the inside to the left of Nimbus. That manoeuvre looked sure to have put paid to Amour Drake's chance but he finished so fast that he only failed by a head to catch Nimbus – it was the first photo-finish Derby – and he was in front two strides beyond the post. The blinkered Swallow Tail was a head away third.

With ordinary luck Amour Drake would probably have won by a length. If Swallow Tail had been second, his rider, Doug Smith, might well have objected to Nimbus. If Swallow Tail had won and Amour Drake been second, then there might have been an objection by Johnstone. Nimbus, though, had not interfered with Amour Drake. There was no camera patrol in those days and no inquiry was held by the Stewards.

There was drama off the course as well. M. Volterra, whose health had suffered during wartime internment by the Germans, was dying in Paris. He was too ill to listen to the broadcast of the race but his wife let him think that Amour Drake had won, thereby giving him a little happiness before he expired the following day.

Roger Mortimer (1979)

With the assistance of the patrol camera, and under the existing rule, it is improbable that Nimbus would have kept the race, having leant on Swallow Tail, unbalancing him and causing him to balk Amour Drake. Johnstone's switch to the left within a hundred yards of the winning-post was widely criticized but with Swallow

*Tail hanging across the path of his run he had little alternative.
Amour Drake was, without question, unlucky.*

———

Mandarin and Fred Winter, Auteuil 1962

*This spontaneous tribute appeared under Marlborough's byline
in the* Daily Telegraph and Morning Post *the day following the
memorable feat of courage and endurance at Auteuil on Sunday,
17 June 1962.*

Grand Steeplechase de Paris

HEROIC MANDARIN GAINS HIS GREATEST TRIUMPH

Bit breaks: Winter rides three miles without reins

From MARLBOROUGH

PARIS, Sunday.

Without a bridle – with only his own great heart and Fred Winter's
matchless strength to keep him going – Madame K. Hennessy's
Mandarin this afternoon became the first English-trained horse to
win the Grand Steeplechase de Paris at Auteuil since Silvo in 1925.

The bit broke in Mandarin's mouth after only three fences, and
for three twisting, hazardous miles Fred Winter had neither brakes
nor steering. So when in the end, unbelievably, Mandarin thrust
his head across the line in front, we who were here knew beyond
doubt we had seen a feat of courage, skill and horsemanship never
excelled on this or any other racecourse.

For a few dreadful moments, however – staggering, dazed and
hoarse from the stands – we did *not* know if this was victory or
just a bitter-heroic defeat. A photo had been called for.

Then the right number was in the frame and, as Winter and
Mandarin pushed their way back through the wondering crowd,
a cheer went up – from French throats as well as English – that
would have made the Irish yell at Cheltenham sound like a feeble
whimper.

Forty minutes later the incredible Winter was back in the same enclosure, having won the Grande Course de Haies for four-year-olds on Beaver II. For a French jockey I imagine this would be a formidable double. For an Englishman, in these circumstances, it simply proved what we already knew – that Fred Winter has no equal in the world.

But once more this was Mandarin's day and, as he bounded past the stands, a gay, determined bundle of fire and muscle, already up in front and pulling Winter's arms out, there was no hint of the disaster to come.

The little horse was wearing his usual bridle, the one with a rubber-covered bit in which he won both the Hennessy and Cheltenham Gold Cups last season. But going to the fourth, (a privet fence nearly 6 ft high) some hidden fault appeared; the bit parted, and Winter found the reins loose and useless in his hands.

'What could I do?' he said afterwards to Bryan Marshall. 'I couldn't steer him; I couldn't stop – and I was much too frightened to jump off!'

In fact, of course, the thought of giving up occurred neither to horse nor jockey. On they went, pitching dangerously over the big water, and it was not till the second circuit that we in the stands realized the desperate situation they were in.

Desperate indeed it was! Quite apart from the near impossibility of steering without reins round this tortuous figure of eight, Mandarin, a horse who always leans hard on his bridle, must have felt horribly ill at ease and out of balance. As for Winter, his task defies description.

'I could give him no help at all,' was how the jockey put it, and no doubt by his own high standards that was true. But, if ever I saw a horse given all possible assistance it was Mandarin today and I do not believe any other man could have got him there.

Round most of the bends Winter managed to keep a horse or two outside him, and the French champion Daumas, upsides on Taillefer when the bit broke, did his best to help.

Close up fourth down the far side for the last time, Mandarin flicked cleanly over the post and rails that undid him three years ago – and then, at the junction of the courses, the worst all but happened.

For three strides coming to the turn it seemed Mandarin was going to run out the wrong side of the marker flag. His own good sense and some magic of Winter's kept him on the course, but the hesitation had cost precious lengths and round the last bend he was only fifth, six lengths behind the leader.

'Just wait till Fred gets him straightened out.' Dave Dick's voice beside me was much more hopeful than confident. But, a moment later, going to the bullfinch two from home, the impossible began to come true.

With all the stops pulled fully out, Mandarin's head appeared like a bullet through the dark brown barrier – and by the last, answering, as he has always done, Winter's every demand, the little hero was actually in front.

He made no mistake and landed perhaps a length clear, but up the long run-in, hard and brilliantly though Winter rode like a man sculling without oars, Mandarin was tiring. Inch by inch Lumino crept up and at the line not one of us could really be sure.

But all was well, and as Mandarin walked, dead tired, back to his stable, led by his faithful attendant, Mush Foster, speechless with delight, all the dreams of his owner, Madame Hennessy, must have been realized.

Fulke Walwyn has done so many miracles with the little horse that this might seem like just one more. But it was different – something that no English trainer has been able to do for nearly forty years.

'Marlborough' (Lord Oaksey)

Fred Winter (b. 1926)

One of the greatest N.H. riders in the history of the sport, he was champion in three successive seasons, won the Grand National twice, the Cheltenham Gold Cup twice and three Champion Hurdles.

As a trainer he achieved comparable success, heading the list eight times, five in succession. He sent out three Champion Hurdle winners, two Grand National winners and a winner of the Cheltenham Gold Cup before retiring through ill health in 1988.

History relates, perhaps apocryphally, that the following telegram awaited Fulke Walwyn's return to Lambourn:

WHY DON'T YOU BUY YOURSELF SOME DECENT TACK. (SGD) CRUMP.

———

The Cheltenham Gold Cup, 1964

The weather was bitterly cold, and Icy Wonder, a topical bet for the County Hurdle which preceded the Gold Cup, duly won. But already huddled hordes of racegoers had their backs to the track and were pressing against the rails of the preliminary parade ring to enjoy a close look at Goliath and David before they were saddled. Ten minutes before the Gold Cup the snow came whirling over the Cotswolds and the air spun sparkling white. Then the wind whipped the snow aside like tissue paper off a present, and the sun suddenly, madly, blazed down through the fresh-frozen, azure sky and the race was run in visibility so brilliant that the course seemed lit. A great crowd, including vociferous bands of bubbling, babbling Irishmen jigged in the stands and craned their necks and talked in the quick impatient jerks which pass for conversation in the seconds which stretch out, like a nervous yawn, before the start of any epic steeplechase.

Peter O'Sullevan takes over by permission of BBC TV.

'They're under orders and they're off. And Mill House jumps straight into the lead from Pas Seul, Arkle and King's Nephew, and as they come up to the first of the twenty-one fences it's Mill House the leader from Pas Seul, Arkle and King's Nephew. Now this is the first open ditch: Mill House setting a steady pace from Pas Seul and Arkle and King's Nephew. All immaculate there! A downhill run to the next with King's Nephew the back marker and Mill House making it by a good four lengths from Arkle who's taking a fairly strong hold. Then Pas Seul and King's Nephew.

'This is the water, number 4: Mill House from Arkle.

'Coming up towards the fifth, Mill House from Arkle towards the outside.

'This is an open ditch now, number 7: Mill House by two lengths from Arkle, Pas Seul and King's Nephew.

'Now the fence at the top of the hill. And a long run down to the next fence.

'Arkle still taking a *very* strong hold. Pat Taaffe trying to restrain him on the outside, not having a very happy ride on him at the moment. Mill House bowling along in front, from Pas Seul now second, and King's Nephew.

'Coming up to number 11 now of the twenty-one fences. Mill House, the big horse, ears pricked, the leader – measures it *beautifully*! This is number 12, another open ditch. Mill House a good two lengths from Arkle – oh! he just had to put in a little short one there, Mill House, but he did it so cleverly that he didn't lose any ground, just patted the ground with that spring-like stride of his, hopped over it.

'And a *beautiful* jump there by Mill House! Arkle goes into second place, Pas Seul third, King's Nephew fourth, coming down to the water.

'Mill House by four lengths now. Mill House from Arkle – lovely jump by Arkle as well there! This is number 17 and it's the last open ditch, twenty-one fences in all, and Arkle is beginning to close now on Mill House.

'Mill House and Arkle – *both* beautiful jumps! Mill House just slightly the better of the two. And now there's a long gap between Pas Seul and King's Nephew. And it's the big two now as they run down the hill to the third-last fence. The big horse, Mill House, with Arkle closing on him. And it's Mill House and Willie Robinson, Arkle and Pat Taaffe and Pat being shouted for from the stands now. Irish voices *really* beginning to call for him now as he starts to make up ground on Arkle. It's Mill House, the leader, from Arkle. Arkle making ground on the far side at the third-last fence. Mill House is over, the leader from Arkle second. They've got two fences left to jump now in the Gold Cup, with Mill House the leader from Arkle and a long way back is Pas Seul then King's Nephew. This is the second-last fence and they're still both full of running, still going great guns – both of them! It's Mill House on the inside, jumps it only *just* ahead of Arkle.

'Now they're rounding the home turn and this is *it*! And Willie Robinson's got his whip out and Pat Taaffe is shaking up Arkle and this is the race now to the last fence! It's Arkle on the stands side for Ireland and Mill House for England on the far side. And this is it with Arkle just taking the lead as they come to the last fence. It's gonna be Arkle if he jumps it! Arkle coming to the last *now* and Arkle a length over Mill House. *He's* over. Mill House is trying to challenge him again but it's Arkle on the stands side. Mill House over on the far side coming up towards the line and Arkle is holding him. Arkle going *away* now from Mill House. This is the champion!

'Mill House is second . . . And then a *long* gap before the 1960 winner Pas Seul comes up into third place and finally King's Nephew.

'I've *never* heard such cheers from the stands at Cheltenham as Arkle proves himself the champion 'chaser in the British Isles.

'So the result of the thirty-ninth Cheltenham Gold Cup: first Arkle, owned by the Duchess of Westminster, trained by Tom Dreaper and ridden by Pat Taaffe. Second was Mill House owned by Mr Bill Gollings, trained by Fulke Walwyn and ridden by Willie Robinson, and third was Pas Seul owned by Mr John Rogerson, trained by Bob Turnell and ridden by Dave Dick. The distances: five lengths and twenty-five lengths.

'Well, there's no doubt about it now. There was no conceivable excuse. It was a fine, clean, perfectly run race, a clear-cut victory with Arkle producing a fine burst of speed. Well, I'll let the crowd take over as you'll hear the reception this great horse is receiving here at Cheltenham from the crowd, English joining Irish in giving him an immensely well-deserved ovation.' (*Sustained deafening cheering.*)

'Pat Taaffe's first Gold Cup triumph.

'Bill Gollings in the bowler hat, just going over to shake hands with Tom Dreaper, the trainer of the winner: there goes the owner of Mill House just being dismounted by Willie Robinson. Surely undisgraced in defeat, the English champion just beaten by an even greater horse.

'The two riders agreed last night that whoever won, as a consolation to the loser, he would pay for an airline ticket for a holiday for him, so Pat's got to foot the bill for a holiday ticket for Willie Robinson. As he so firmly predicted he would have to do.

And so the result of probably the greatest Gold Cup run at Cheltenham: first Arkle, second Mill House, and third Pas Seul.'

Ivor Herbert (1966)

On 30 November 1963, Arkle, the hero of Ireland, came to New-bury to take on England's champion, Mill House, in the Hennessy Gold Cup. Mill House upheld his reputation and won. Arkle fin-ished in third place for reasons that were not immediately appar-ent; he slipped and lost ground landing over the last fence.

The prospect of a return match at Cheltenham in March became a subject for prolonged discussion in both countries. The prelimi-naries and the outcome of that memorable clash will never be better described than they were by Ivor Herbert and Peter O'Sullevan.

Mill House was an outstandingly good horse that day at Chelten-

ham but he was probably never quite as good again. Arkle was a
great horse with magnetic appeal, but was he a better horse than
Easter Hero, Golden Miller or Prince Regent? As good, maybe,
but probably not better.

———

The Derby, 1986

Plans for Dancing Brave after the Two Thousand Guineas were at
first unclear. 'He's got such speed that we've always thought of
today as his race,' said his trainer afterwards. Bakharoff, who
topped the International Classification after winning the William
Hill Futurity, and Armada, very impressive on his début in the
Wood Ditton Stakes at the Craven meeting, were other Ever Ready
Derby entries trained by Harwood for Dancing Brave's owner.
However, after Bakharoff's narrow defeat by Mashkour in the
Highland Spring Derby Trial at Lingfield on his reappearance,
Dancing Brave was announced a Derby runner. He started 2–1
favourite at Epsom after being deposed for a short time the week
before the race by the Mecca-Dante winner Shahrastani following
reports that he had suffered a slight leg injury and had disappointed
in a gallop. Dancing Brave lost the Derby, beaten half a length by
Shahrastani after almost snatching victory from the jaws of defeat
with a prodigious late run. Dancing Brave should have won. His
rider the vastly experienced Starkey, usually a sound tactician,
contributed to Dancing Brave's downfall by giving away too much
ground early on with the result that Dancing Brave was set with
too much to do in the home straight. It is more desirable in the
Derby than in any other major race of the same distance to be well
placed throughout and usually of paramount importance to hold
a good position on the steep descent to Tattenham Corner; the
three-and-a-half-furlong run-in at Epsom continues on a gradually
decreasing downhill gradient until approaching the final furlong
and very few horses win the Derby after being among the
backmarkers at Tattenham Corner. Although Starkey expressed
complete confidence beforehand in Dancing Brave's stamina, the
horse hadn't been tested beyond a mile, either in a race or on the

home gallops, and it was expected that waiting tactics would be adopted with him at Epsom; but to see him a dozen lengths behind the leaders, third from the back, coming down Tattenham Hill – he had been purposely dropped towards the rear of the field from the start – was perplexing. Starkey rode hard from the entrance to the straight but Dancing Brave, unbalanced for a few strides after being switched sharply for a clear run on the wide outside, made only gradual progress at first. But in the last two furlongs he ate up the ground and was making up the leeway hand over fist on Shahrastani, who got the textbook ride for a Derby, as the post was reached. The 1986 Derby seems destined to be remembered as the one Dancing Brave lost, rather than the one Shahrastani won.

From *A Selection of Timeform Essays* (1982)

Dancing Brave's defeat in the Derby has produced as much argument as that of Colombo in the race of 1934.

Undoubtedly the best horse, Dancing Brave failed chiefly because he could not act downhill. He lost ground through interference about the top of the hill but, as the Arc de Triomphe showed, he would not have had the slightest difficulty in making this up, with time to spare, on a flat course. However, though hard ridden he made no progress till the ground levelled out and then it was just too late.

Notwithstanding a brilliant three-year-old career in which he dominated his generation in Europe, Dancing Brave cannot be rated in the same category as such acknowledged champions as Seabird II, Brigadier Gerard, Ribot, Mill Reef and Nijinsky. He may not have been as good as Shergar but he was unlucky not to have stayed unbeaten in Europe.

Dancing Brave's defeat in the Breeders' Cup Turf at Santa Anita in November came at the end of a strenuous European campaign. Even at his best it is pure conjecture to say that he would have beaten Manila on that horse's home ground; it is equally open to doubt whether Manila would have beaten Dancing Brave in Europe in midsummer. He was moved briskly to stud in 1986 and the racing public was denied a further sight of this good horse on a racecourse.

———

Desert Orchid

It was when my father began talking about him that I realized it had all got out of hand, for my father is, by upbringing and choice, an unmitigated townee. He regards horses with a mixture of indifference and suspicion, and finds my own horsiness a matter of complete bewilderment.

It is clearly something for which there is no genetic basis whatsoever. It is also one of the few things we are unable to have a conversation about.

'I've seen a horse I think I'm going to buy next week.'

'Oh good.'

Similarly, love of hazard and gambling plays no part in his life. He has been to the races once, and that was not for pleasure but duty. He said it was quite nice being out of doors.

Imagine, then, my amazement, when we spoke on the telephone earlier this year. 'Did you see it?' he asked immediately. 'Isn't he wonderful? One of the most beautiful things I have seen in my life. I was sure he was going to get caught in the end, weren't you? But he wasn't going to let them past him, was he?'

He had turned on the television to watch the rugby league, which he regards as the GREAT winter game, but had been too early and had found himself caught up in the making of a legend.

Of course, I am talking about Desert Orchid: Dessie, as the world knows him, Dessie who runs for the Cheltenham Gold Cup, the greatest prize in the steeplechasing game, this afternoon.

Of course my father knew nothing about Desert Orchid's reputation, prodigious though it already was. I don't suppose he has ever read a line on the racing pages, save from out of loyalty when I have written something there.

But there was something about the horse that captured his imagination. And if my father can get excited by a horse, there must be something extraordinary about the animal.

Everyone who has ever owned a horse will try and make you believe that there is something special, beautiful, unique and generally wonderful about his or her animal. It is equally true that no one can ever explain what that thing is.

'Oh, he's such a character,' people say, hopelessly. Naturally, the non-horsy world think this is all a load of rubbish.

Horse people know it is not – but the special quality of any individual horse is simply non-translatable. Horsiness is a language for which no subtitles exist.

But now we have Desert Orchid: the acceptable face of horsiness; the horse that makes horsiness comprehensible. The first test of horsiness is to be able to recognize one's own horse in a crowd: something that many racehorse owners are unable to do.

But any one can recognize Dessie, with his *Hi-oh Silver* looks, and from the fact that he is always the one at the front. Hates other horses going past him: won't let them do it. His bullishness, boldness and bloody-mindedness are obvious to people who had never given equine nature a moment's consideration. He is the world's most obvious horse: unsubtly beautiful, courageous and lovely.

But I have a secret. That is what they are all like. Any horse you get to know, better still get to own, is beautiful and lovely, full of character, unique, and you could pick him out in a herd of a thousand.

One of the pleasures of betting on a horse is the brief sharing in the animal: my horse ran well, didn't he? But Dessie takes the thing much further. Half the nation has an emotional stake in Desert Orchid now. He makes horsiness universally understood: he is the Esperanto horse, the distilled essence of all the lovely things a horse can give a human.

I hope he murders the lot of them, and so would my father, if he knew that the Gold Cup was being run this afternoon and that Dessie was running in it.

Simon Barnes (1989)

This remarkably apposite piece appeared in The Times *on 16*

March 1989, the morning of the Cheltenham Gold Cup, in which Desert Orchid was to take part later in the day.

Simon Barnes's hope was more than fulfilled. Desert Orchid, under a wonderfully understanding ride by Simon Sherwood, ran on to win with great courage and tenacity, earning a high place in steeplechasing history.

———

The Melbourne Cup

There's a lull in the tumult on yonder hill,
    And the clamour has grown less loud,
Though the Babel of tongues is never still,
    With the presence of such a crowd.
The bell has rung. With their riders up
    At the starting point they muster,
The racers strip't for the Melbourne Cup,
    All gloss and polish and lustre;

And the course is seen, with its emerald sheen,
    By the bright springtide renew'd,
Like a ribbon of green, stretched out between
    The ranks of the multitude.

The flag is lowered. 'They're off!' 'They come!'
    The squadron is sweeping on;
A sway in the crowd – a murmuring hum!
    'They're here!' 'They're past!' 'They're gone!'
They came with the rush of the southern surf,
    On the bar of the storm-girt bay;
And like muffled drums on the sounding turf
    Their hoof-strokes echo away.

The rose and black draws clear of the ruck,
    And the murmur swells to a roar,
As the brave old colours that never were struck
    Are seen with the lead once more.

Though the feathery ferns and grasses wave
  O'er the sod, where Lantern sleeps,
Though the turf is green on Fisherman's grave,
  The stable its prestige keeps.

Six lengths in front she scours along,
  She's bringing the field to trouble,
She's tailing them off, she's running strong,
  She shakes her head and pulls double.
Now Minstrel falters, and Exile flags,
  The Barb finds the pace too hot,
And Toryboy loiters, and Playboy lags
  And the *bolt* of Ben Bolt is shot.

That she never may be caught this day,
  Is the worst that the public wish her.
She won't be caught; she comes right away;
  Hurrah for Seagull and Fisher!
See, Strop falls back, though his reins are slack,
  Sultana begins to tire,
And the top weight tells on the Sydney crack,
  And the pace on 'the Gippsland flyer'.

The rowels, as round the turn they sweep,
  Just graze Tim Whiffler's flanks,
Like the hunted deer that flies through the sheep,
  He strides through the beaten ranks.
Daughter of Omen, prove your birth,
  The colt will take lots of choking;
The hot breath steams at your saddle girth,
  From his scarlet nostril smoking.

The shouts of the Ring for a space subside,
  And slackens the bookmaker's roar;
Now, Davis, rally; now, Carter, ride,
  As man never rode before.

When Sparrowhawk's backers cease to cheer,
   When Yattendon's friends are dumb,
When hushed is the clamour of Volunteer –
   Alone in the race they come!

They're neck and neck; they're head and head;
   They're stroke for stroke in the running;
The whalebone whistles, the steel is red,
   Nor shirking as yet nor shunning.
One effort, Seagull, the blood you boast
   Should struggle when nerves are strained; –
With a rush on the post by a neck at the most,
   The verdict for Tim is gained.

Tim Whiffler wins. Is blood alone
   The *sine qua non* for a flyer?
The breed of his dam is a myth unknown
   And we've doubts respecting his sire.

Aye, Shorthouse, laugh – laugh loud and long,
   For pedigree you're a sticker;
You may be right, I may be wrong,
   Wiseacres both! Let's liquor.
Our common descent we may each recall
   To a lady of old caught tripping,
The fair one in fig-leaves, who d—d us all
   For a bite at a golden pippin.

Adam Lindsay Gordon (1865)

Adam Lindsay Gordon (1833–70)

*Born in Fayal in the Azores, Gordon was taken to England in
1840 and sent to Cheltenham College. Wild and eccentric as a
young man, fonder of steeplechasing and boxing than learning, he
was nevertheless a keen reader of Latin classics. After failing for
the Army he emigrated to Australia in 1853. There he served in
the Mounted Police, later earning fame as a steeplechase rider as*

well as a poet and writer. He married the daughter of an innkeeper, with whom he was happy, but hereditary mental depression added to financial worry preyed on his mind and caused him to commit suicide by shooting himself in 1870.

The first Melbourne Cup was run in 1861 and ever since on the first Tuesday in November. A full national holiday is observed and all other activities cease. Melbourne Cup week at Flemington combines the festive atmosphere of Epsom on Derby Day with the quality and elegance of Royal Ascot.

The realization of a two-mile handicap worth £556,485 to the winner (1989) is unlikely to advance beyond imagination in the minds of English racegoers, at least in contemporary lifetimes.

A MIXED CARD

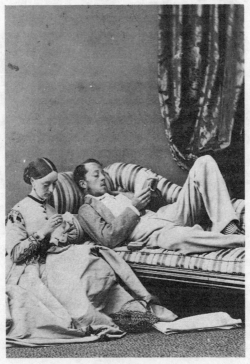

The Marquess and Marchioness of Hastings, c. 1864, at the start of their four
years of marriage.
(*National Horseracing Museum*)

Lady Florence Paget: The Pocket Venus

The turn of events whereby Hermit (1864) provided Henry Chaplin with a Derby winner and brought final ruin to his rival, Harry, 4th Marquess of Hastings, has often been told. The prelude to that sombre outcome may be less well known.

It was during the season of 1863, when their friendship – and their rivalry – had become established, that Harry Hastings and Henry Chaplin became fully aware of Lady Florence Paget. They may, it is true, have encountered her before, but it was her advent in Society during this season of 1863 which arrested their attention. She created a sensation on her début, and both – as befitted men of the world – were quickly alive to it.

During that season, both Harry Hastings and Henry Chaplin must have met Lady Florence fairly frequently; and it is possible that by the end of the season each was fascinated by her and possibly half in love with her. *The Queen* magazine, in its issue of 13 June 1863, describes a grand fancy-dress ball which was held at Willis's Rooms in aid of the Royal Caledonian Society and of the Royal Scottish Hospital. The highlight of this ball was a quadrille arranged by the Duchess of Roxburghe and the Countess of Seafield, in which those taking part represented the four seasons of the year. The four ladies representing spring were dressed in green, and they included Lady Florence Paget. Amongst the men dancing 'Winter' was Henry Chaplin.

It is not surprising to find that Harry Hastings' name was absent from most of these social functions. The solemnity of a fashionable ball in aid of charity was not his idea of entertainment; nor was he an enthusiastic devotee of the quadrille. He left such orthodox functions to Henry Chaplin, preferring to spend his evenings carousing in the East End.

However, his rivalry with Henry Chaplin was now being sharpened by their mutual admiration for 'the Pocket Venus'. Both were prominent in Society at this time, and both had won the reputation of being men of the world. Moreover Lady Florence Paget, as the most beautiful woman in London, constituted a prize such as the most highly bred young aristocrat might pursue with tenacity. It was not simply that she was desirable and beautiful and that she was also excellent company. The great attraction, for any young buck, was that once he entered a ballroom with so exquisite a partner on his arm he became the focus of all eyes and the envy of all male hearts.

Although Harry Hastings was a member of the Prince of Wales's set, he was never an intimate of the Prince, as was Henry Chaplin. For example, when in July of 1863 the Prince gave an entertainment at Marlborough House to a few of his close personal friends, it was noticeable that the guests included both Henry Chaplin and Lady Florence Paget, but not Harry Hastings. Bertie, with his eye for a beautiful woman, must have looked upon Lady Florence with undisguised admiration, and he no doubt congratulated Henry Chaplin privately on his good fortune at being chosen so frequently as her escort.

A few days previously – on Saturday, 20 June – Lady Florence had been presented to the Queen at St James's Palace. She had been generally admired, as on all other occasions, and the Queen herself had remarked on her grace and carriage. She had been dressed in a manteau of white imperial lace, brocaded with white flowers in terry velvet, and trimmed with bouillons of tulle. Her petticoat had been of white glacé silk, with skirt bouillonnée to the waist, and a tulle veil corsage to match, trimmed with chatelaines of white Lebanon flowers. Her head-dress had been a wreath of Lebanon flowers, with diamond ornaments in the centre and diamond stars. Her necklace had been composed of pearls and diamonds. She had looked magnificent – and had been fully conscious of the stir which she had caused.

But if Henry Chaplin and Harry Hastings both pursued Lady Florence with some eagerness, it is not surprising that Henry Chaplin at first claimed most of her attention.

But although Harry Hastings was apt to lose marks in the social graces he yet enjoyed several notable advantages. As a rebel, he was bound to appeal to that streak of Paget unorthodoxy which was as strong in Florence as in any of them. Moreover he held an immense asset over Henry Chaplin in Society, for Harry Hastings was already being listed by many matrons as dangerous, and young girls were being warned against him. Now there is nothing more attractive to an innocent young girl (especially if she be something of a rebel) than a young man with a bad reputation. A woman's curiosity, and her love of playing with fire, make any such man intriguing. While girls are young and in search of excitement, they are attracted by charming rogues; it is not until they begin to think seriously of marriage that they tend to consider the more solid virtues of a worthy and reliable suitor.

Thus the contest for Lady Florence's attentions, and ultimately for her hand, gradually developed between these two young men during the latter part of 1863. Those who were prepared to bet on the outcome (and it was an age that was much given to such wagers) were for the most part happy to place their money on Henry Chaplin, for he seemed the obvious choice on form. But some of the shrewder backers favoured Harry Hastings. It was not a question of his wealth or titles. It was his hidden assets as a suitor; and his unexpected abilities to attract a woman. Moreover a Paget was unlikely to adopt the safe and obvious course. Harry, they therefore maintained, was clearly a very live candidate for this most desirable prize.

It would therefore seem that Lady Florence Paget was in an ideal position for a young woman. She was the toast of London Society and had its two most eligible bachelors at her feet. She had only to make up her mind which of the two was the more desirable, and then to contract a highly successful marriage.

However, it was not quite as simple as that, for Harry Hastings was far too unreliable to be counted upon, while Henry Chaplin was invested by Nature with a streak of caution. Harry Hastings was too unstable to fall head over heels in love. Henry Chaplin was too matter-of-fact and too rational to do so. Young though she was, Florence probably realized that she might quite easily end up without either of them.

As the year of 1863 drew to its close, Henry Chaplin became more and more attentive to her. They were constantly in each other's company, and yet he still held back. He was still very

young, and the leisured life of a London bachelor, without cares
or responsibilities, was very attractive to him. Marriage, he probably felt, could wait for just a little longer.

Henry Chaplin's reaction was characteristic of him. Indeed he
followed what was almost a standard pattern for wealthy young
Victorian bachelors who were suffering from doubts. He denied
rumours, packed his bags and retired to the Far East in search of
big game, accompanied by his Oxford friend and confidant, Sir
Frederick Johnstone. This was a repetition of their withdrawal
from Christ Church, when they had gone buffalo-hunting together
in Canada. As men of the world, they believed that they were best
able to ponder on life while squinting down the barrel of a rifle.

Their big-game expedition took them to India, and here they
spent the winter. Henry returned in May of 1864, possibly with
his mind still not made up; but he at once sought out Lady Florence
and they again became inseparable. The memory of her beauty
may have dimmed whilst he was so far away, but the effect of it
upon him was once more quite overwhelming. She was now in the
prime of her early womanhood, and looking lovelier than ever.

One thing, however, soon became clear to Henry. Harry Hastings had not been wasting his time while his rival was at the other
end of the world. Henry Chaplin realized that Harry and Florence
were now much more intimate in their manner than they had been
before he left, and Harry's attitude to her had now become quite
proprietorial. She had been seen frequently in his company, and
Henry was warned by his friends that it would be unwise to remain
undecided for very much longer if he was seriously thinking of
asking Lady Florence to become his wife.

Meanwhile Harry himself had other interests to occupy his attention. The peak of the racing season was approaching, and while
he had nothing in his string that was good enough to compete in
the Classic races, he was already enjoying several encouraging
successes as an owner. Derby week arrived, and Harry threw himself with his customary abandon into all that this implied.

Harry, in short, would be enjoying himself far too much to be
troubled by thoughts of the entrancing Lady Florence; and this
was a fact of which the young lady herself would be fully aware.

Harry, she also realized, would not be wanting, amidst all these
revels, of charming young companions who would be only too
willing to offer him solace, especially when he adopted his air of
a little-boy-lost.

The Derby itself was won on this occasion by William l'Anson's
Blair Athol, a colt who had never seen a racecourse before, but
whom the Yorkshiremen in the crowd had backed to a man. The
Londoners had not shared in their enthusiasm, but amongst the
members of Society it had been known for some time that the
officers of two of Her Majesty's crack cavalry regiments had pooled
their resources to win a fortune over 'the bald-faced chestnut',
whose trainer had sworn he was invincible, and Harry Hastings
had been infected with some of their optimism. He had a good
wager on the winner and surveyed the finish of the race with a
half-suppressed smile of satisfaction.

Henry Chaplin, accompanied by Lady Florence, had watched
the race from the royal box, in company with the Prince and Sir
Frederick Johnstone. Like the majority of backers, he had sup-
ported the favourite, Lord Glasgow's General Peel. His Lordship
was never one to mince words, and he had told the royal party
that his bay colt was unbeatable. But Henry Chaplin's interest in
racing was still only a mild one, and his bets were moderate. His
attention was largely focused on the beautiful girl at his side, on
whom Bertie also cast an admiring glance from time to time. In
the betting over the Paget stakes, Henry was now generally thought
to be a certainty.

Perhaps wind of this reached Harry Hastings. Or it may have
been that Henry Chaplin was by now beginning to look com-
placent, and to treat Florence as his special property. Inevitably,
when she went racing, Florence preferred to go with Henry,
because this meant that she enjoyed the distinction of watching
from the royal box. Moreover Harry was always so busy betting
that he paid her scant attention, while Henry Chaplin ignored the
betting, and even the racing, and devoted all his attention to her.
Harry, however, had still one trump card up his sleeve after Epsom
was over, and now he played it.

He had already flattered Florence immensely by naming one of his two-year-olds after her. Now he informed her that it was his intention to allow the filly to make her racing début on the first afternoon of the Ascot meeting, which was, as always, one of the highlights of the London season and which took place a fortnight after the Derby meeting.

Florence was naturally delighted and excited. When Harry Hastings asked her if she would accompany him to the meeting, and go with him into the paddock to inspect the other Lady Florence, she at once accepted.

Henry Chaplin had assumed that she would be going with *him* to Ascot. Both he and Sir Frederick Johnstone would be members of the royal party and would be entertained by the Prince in the royal box, and he had never imagined that she would find Harry's company more desirable. He was more than a little put out.

The first day of the Ascot meeting was on 7 June. The weather was fine and the sun shone down on the enclosures with their brilliant flowers and on the cream of Society which paraded before the stands and in the paddock. When the time for the third race on the card approached, Harry Hastings entered the paddock with Lady Florence on his arm. They made a stirring picture, she so radiant and excited and he retaining with difficulty his customary air of casual nonchalance. It was a picture completed by the filly herself. The little chestnut by Newminster looked superb in her summer coat, and danced and pirouetted on her toes as she circled the ring. There was a large field, and she was not fancied to win; but in looks it was clear that she could more than hold her own with any of them. The two Lady Florences were the centre of attraction, and few could have said which looked the more beautiful.

Ascot ended in a blaze of sunshine, and the motley crowd dispersed. The swells and the acrobats, the carriage folk, the touts and the tipsters returned to their several ways of life and to their homes – to their love-making, their ambitions and their regrets.

Henry Chaplin returned to his rooms in Park Lane. Here he found it impossible to obliterate Florence from his thoughts. Any hesitancy which had previously existed in his mind was now rapidly disappearing in the face of this renewed competition from Harry Hastings.

He was in a position only too familiar with young lovers, for although the girl in whose company he had spent so much time appeared always to be both open-hearted in her affections and uncomplicated in her character, she yet remained mysterious and unpredictable. He could not say for certain what exactly she was thinking and what were the promptings of her heart. He knew that she had the warmest affection for him and that she both respected and admired him. But was she in love with him? And just what exactly was her attitude to Harry Hastings?

These were questions which could be answered in only one way. The time for uncertainty was past. He must settle the matter, once and for all, by asking her to marry him.

Proposals are sometimes premeditated and are sometimes made on the spur of the moment; but time and place play an important part. There seems little doubt that Henry Chaplin had decided to ask Florence to be his wife soon after her return from Ascot, and an admirable opportunity was soon to present itself.

The next major event in the London season was to be the dinner and ball which the Marquess and Marchioness of Abercorn were giving at Chesterfield House in honour of the Prince and Princess of Wales. It was to be held on the evening of Monday, 20 June, and everyone who was anyone in London Society had already been invited.

When Lady Florence arrived on the arm of her father, she looked radiant and serene. When Henry Chaplin arrived, immaculate and elegant as ever, he looked nervous and distrait. When Harry Hastings arrived, he wore his customary air of indifference and boredom, which suggested that he found such orthodox entertainments of little interest to him.

It has so far been possible to gauge with some degree of accuracy the emotions felt by each of these two young men. It is not so easy to assess what was going on in the mind of Florence herself.

It was not an easy situation for a young girl to face, especially for a young girl who was without a mother's guidance and without very much experience of the world. Had she been a little more prosaic in her outlook, a little less romantic and altogether less of a Paget, she might well have found the problem easy enough to solve. She must have realized that she could prevaricate no longer. It was now necessary for her to commit herself, one way or the other. It was the tragedy of these three young people that they had to make their decisions early, at a time when each would have been far happier sitting for a little while longer on the fence.

Harry Hastings was a stimulating and an amusing companion, and his lack of convention intrigued her. She shared his interest in the Turf and admired his determination to break the Ring. The courage with which he was setting about this task appealed strongly to the Paget in her.

She was also worried about him. He was drinking too much, gambling too much and burning his candle at both ends. His friends were for the most part unworthy of him and seemed bent on his destruction. His charm and his courage were indestructible, but each day he looked a little more forlorn. Battling with the Ring and winning or losing with panache, he was in his way a hero; but off-guard, in moments when she studied him covertly, he was still a little-boy-lost. He aroused the mother instinct, which was strong within her, and also the reforming instinct, which inspires so many women in their relationship to the male. Harry was beginning to go downhill fast, and she may well have decided that only the love of a woman who understood him could save him from his ultimate goal of self-destruction.

Henry was above all things a *man*. He was healthy, masterful and mature. The woman in her admired this male domination; but the Paget in her made her resentful of it. With her beauty, and her powers of persuasion, she believed that she could probably make Harry do anything she wanted. She was not so sure about Henry Chaplin.

So when Henry Chaplin finally achieved his moment of courage and asked her to marry him, she did not hesitate in her reply. Her answer was 'yes'. His boyish delight, his eagerness and his humbleness must have touched her deeply. She realized that she had made him supremely happy. This realization was strengthened by the events of the next two weeks. His pride in her was only equalled by his pride in the home which was soon to become her own. She was at once taken to Blankney to decide upon any alterations which she might care to make. She was proudly introduced to his staff as their future mistress, and it was obvious that they were as happy as their beloved master in his boyish enthusiasm. The house, the gardens, the stables and the kennels were each paraded before her eyes, and any alteration that she suggested was at once acted upon.

The young couple decided upon a relatively short engagement. A date early in August was tentatively decided upon, for the marriage would then come at the end of the season and shortly after the Goodwood meeting. Invitations were widely sent out and at once accepted.

The two lovers were constantly to be seen in each other's company, at balls, dinners and in the Park. Henry was the proud owner of a smart 'cab', and he would collect his fiancée in the afternoon and take her along 'the Ladies' Mile' from Apsley House to Kensington, with a little 'tiger' standing up behind and looking as proud as his master. And the single horse would be high-stepping in front, itself as proud as either of them. Not even 'Skittles' herself aroused more attention in the Park, and all eyes turned to watch Henry Chaplin and his Pocket Venus as they drove by. All the world loves a lover. There can have been few who did not wish them well.

On 14 July, Henry Chaplin, now as excited as a schoolboy, escorted his fiancée down to Blankney to show her the kennels and stables, which had recently been enlarged, and to inspect some further improvements which had been carried out at her request. His loyal staff welcomed their squire and his future wife with warmth and noted his obvious happiness with satisfaction.

They returned to London that night, for they were both looking forward to a special occasion on the following evening. This was their visit to the Opera House at Covent Garden, where Henry Chaplin had booked a box for a performance of *Faust*. It was the night of Friday, 15 July, and the occasion marked Mlle Adelina Patti's last appearance of the season. Henry, with characteristic generosity, had suggested to Florence that Harry Hastings should join them, and she had at once concurred. Opera-going, she knew, was not very much to Harry's taste, but she agreed with Henry that a quiet evening spent in gracious surroundings might make a pleasant change for him.

They sat together in the box, on either side of Florence, while Mlle Patti sang to a packed and appreciative house. During the performance, there were many in the stalls who looked up at the three figures in the box. Henry Chaplin was obviously enjoying himself. Lady Florence was silent and preoccupied with her thoughts. Harry Hastings sat moody and expressionless.

The events of the next day, Saturday, 16 July 1864, have been variously described, nearly always inaccurately, and have been variously interpreted, usually without any real understanding of the motives which inspired them. One point, at least, was afterwards agreed upon. These events constituted one of the most remarkable scandals of the Victorian era. The actions of the central characters appeared, at the time, to be inexplicable. And when they *were* explained, it was through the eyes of those who saw these events as some sort of inverted morality play of the period, in which sex, sin and selfishness momentarily triumphed over honour and integrity, while retribution waited in the wings.

The first main point of doubt concerns where Lady Florence spent the Friday night. It must either have been at the St George's Hotel in Albemarle Street or at her father's house at 70 Portland Place. *The Queen*, in its subsequent report, stated emphatically that it was at the hotel. The *Morning Post*, a trifle smugly, then printed a comment to the effect that they had been asked to correct a statement made by a contemporary which had said that she had stayed at the hotel; and that she had, in fact, stayed with her father.

This is probably correct, for Henry Chaplin's daughter, the Marchioness of Londonderry, in her biography of her father, states that on the Saturday morning Florence dressed up in her wedding dress, which had only that morning been delivered, and then showed herself to the Marquess. This is also probably true, but if it is, it seems to make nonsense of what happened next, for Lady Florence then announced that it was necessary for her to do some more shopping in connection with her trousseau. She either used her father's brougham (according to *The Queen*) or used a carriage which she had previously hired. *The Queen*, which maintained that she was at the St George's Hotel, said that she instructed the hall porter before she left to tell Mr Chaplin, if he should call, that she would not be returning to the hotel before two o'clock.

In either case she travelled alone, which was unusual for a young lady of her class. However, her destination is generally agreed upon by all who recounted her actions that morning. She went to the fashionable store of Messrs Marshall and Snelgrove in Oxford Street, arriving there shortly after ten o'clock.

Once inside, she was met by one of four people. The Marchioness of Londonderry, in her biography of her father, said it was Harry Hastings himself who was waiting for her. *The Queen* said that it was Harry's sister, Lady Edith Maud Hastings. Donald Shaw, in *London in the Sixties*, said that it was Harry's closest friend, Freddy Granville, who was there; and the *Morning Post* declared that it was Freddy's wife who was waiting. (The Granvilles had only recently been married.)

Whichever of the four it was, all accounts are agreed upon what happened next. After a short and hurried consultation, Lady Florence left by either the main or the Vere Street entrance and entered a cab.

She was driven down Bond Street into Hanover Square, to St George's church, and there she married Harry. By midday she was the Marchioness of Hastings.

When the ceremony was completed, the bridal party went to the Granvilles' lodgings in St James's Place, where the reception, such as it was, took place. Here the bride sat down and wrote a long letter to Henry Chaplin, which was at once dispatched to him at his rooms in Park Lane.

The bride and bridegroom then set off for King's Cross Station, where a special train had been ordered for them (not, in itself, such an unusual or costly method of travel in those days, when special trains were often used). This train took them to Loughborough, where Harry's travelling carriage, with its four horses and coachmen, was waiting to meet them, his staff having been notified of his arrival by telegraph.

Before describing the further events of this remarkable day, it is of interest to consider some of the other stories that were circulated at the time, and which some people still maintain to be true.

The chief one, which is believed by many people even today, is that Lady Florence actually took Henry Chaplin with her when she drove to Marshall and Snelgrove, and that she left him outside while she entered the shop. Assistants serving in the shop later declared that they had seen him enter in search of her and that he had grown increasingly alarmed and distraught; and that he had finally called for the manager and demanded that the premises should be searched.

This seems improbable for two reasons. In the first place, it is inconceivable to think that Lady Florence would have committed so heartless an act. She may have been thoughtless, but she was never cruel. And, in the second place, the story does not ring true because Henry, at that time, can have had no suspicion of what was about to happen, and if he had accompanied Lady Florence on a shopping expedition and she had disappeared into the shop, he would surely have assumed that he must have missed her and simply gone home without ever demanding to see the manager. Moreover such an action on her part would suggest that she was motivated by a sudden wild impulse when she chanced to meet Harry Hastings inside, but all the evidence proves that there was definite premeditation in the elopement, and that arrangements, both at the church and elsewhere, had already been made, albeit somewhat hurriedly.

Another version of this story, even more improbable than the first, was that she actually took Henry Chaplin into the shop with her, and that for a few minutes they stood together while she examined some beautiful lingerie for her trousseau which was laid out on the counter in front of them. Then she excused herself and disappeared.

One report of the affair which is intriguing is the statement that her unfortunate coachman waited for more than six hours outside the shop before finally deciding to go home.

The degree of premeditation in the whole affair is underlined by the ordering of a special train from King's Cross. This cannot have been done without some warning having been first given to the station staff. But the suggestion that Lady Edith Hastings was only told at the last minute, and only just reached the church in time, does imply that it may only have been decided upon very hastily.

And what of Henry Chaplin all this time, left almost at the altar without his bride? He was a proud young man, who valued his position in Society, and the heartbreak and the humiliation must have been extremely painful to him. It is not uncharitable to say that the latter may have been greater than the former. He was in love with Lady Florence, and he was in love with her beauty, and the loss he suffered must have left him momentarily beaten down and overwhelmed. But not fully heart-broken. The evidence of his previous hesitation, and of the time which it had taken him finally to make up his mind, does not suggest a wild and uncontrollable adoration. He was deeply hurt and greatly depressed; but not quite heart-broken.

His humiliation, however, must have been overwhelming. Suddenly, and without any previous warning, he was made the centre of a scandal that shook Society. The fact that he was the injured party, and that he had been shamefully treated by his fiancée and by one of his close friends, was no consolation to his pride. He was left with the need for cancelling all his wedding arrangements, returning all the presents and notifying everyone that his marriage would not take place. He was a proud man, and he found himself the object of pity. He was a self-important man, and he found himself an object of ridicule. The world looked upon him as a cuckold – a man who had put his trust in a woman who was in reality the property of someone else.

There is no evidence to suggest that Lady Florence had ever been Harry Hastings' mistress, but the gossips of any community can always be relied upon to conjure up fire from smoke. It was soon being suggested that she *had* been his mistress; and that she had never really intended to become Henry Chaplin's wife.

It has always been the custom, in yellow journalism, to arouse malicious gossip by suggesting that an issue is one of rich versus poor, or of class distinction. Lady Florence was promptly branded on both counts. She had given herself to the richer man, and the man with a title. She was therefore considered to be worthless and despicable.

More than a hundred years have now passed since Lady Florence came to the decision which made her forsake one man and turn to another. In this time, her action has frequently been referred to in newspaper articles and in biographies. And during this time no one seems to have made any serious attempt to analyse her decision, or indeed to do anything but to condemn her for it. It is so simple to brand her action as that of a fickle and selfish young woman, without heart or principle. But this must be unlikely because none of the evidence available ever suggests that she was such a woman. This was not 'Skittles', selling herself to the highest bidder. This woman was a Paget, whose menfolk were heroes and whose women were angels.

Lady Florence may not have been an angel, but she was certainly not a trollop. Her motives may have been misguided, but that is not to say they were ignoble.

The most informative piece of evidence is the note which she wrote in haste at the Granvilles' lodgings in St James's Place before she hurried away with her husband to catch the special train which was to take them north to Castle Donington.

This is what Henry Chaplin read in what must have been a mood of utterly bewildered incomprehension when it was delivered to him on the afternoon of 16 July, the night after he had taken his fiancée to the Opera and but forty-eight hours after she had spent the day with him going over their future home at Blankney Hall.

July, 1864, Saturday

Henry – To you whom I have injured more deeply than any one, I hardly know how to address myself. Believe me, the task is most painful and one I shrink from. Would to God I had moral courage to open my heart to you sooner, but I could not bring myself to do so. However, now the truth must be told. Nothing in the world can ever excuse my conduct. I have treated you too infamously, but I sincerely trust the knowledge of my unworthiness will help you to bear the bitter blow I am about to inflict on you. I know I ought never to have accepted you at all, and I also know I never could have made you happy. You must have seen ever since the beginning of our engagement how very little I *really* returned all your devotion to me. I assure you I have struggled hard against the feeling, but all to no purpose. There is not a man in the world I have a greater regard and respect for than yourself, but I do not *love* you in the way a woman ought to love her husband, and I am perfectly certain if I had married you, I should have rendered not only *my* life miserable, but your own also.

And now we are eternally separated, for by the time you receive this I shall be the wife of Lord Hastings. I dare not ask for your forgiveness. I feel I have injured you far too deeply for that. All I can do now is to implore you, to go and forget me. You said one night here, a woman who ran away was not worth thinking or caring about, so I pray that the blow may fall less severely on you than it might have done. May God bless you, and may you soon find someone far more worthy of becoming your wife than I should ever have been – Yrs.

Florence

Two points emerge clearly from this letter. Lady Florence had been trying to tell Henry Chaplin for some time that she could not marry him; and secondly she had been trying to tell him that she was not in love with him.

There is not a man in the world I have a greater regard and respect for than yourself, but I do not *love* you in the way a woman ought to love her husband . . .

This is possibly the essence of the whole sad affair. A warm, vital and probably a passionate young woman found to her dismay that she was not physically attracted to the man whom she had agreed to marry. He was so suitable in every other way that she tried to convince herself that such a feeling could in the course of their marriage be overcome; and he was so kind and so sympathetic to her that she had not the heart to tell him something so intimate – and so wounding.

Henry may well have been insensitive and unobservant of her moods. The fact that he did not attract her physically may not have registered with him, or he may have mistaken her reluctance for maidenly modesty. On the other hand, he may have been slow in showing any emotion or passion himself, so that she began to suspect that he was not really experiencing any. Possibly this was because he did not, in fact, experience any. He may well have belonged to that Victorian school of thought which considered passion to be something that one shared with one's mistress, whilst it was affection which one shared with one's wife. One did not subject a gentlewoman to the lustful enthusiasm which motivated one in profane love. Genteel women were not passionate, and Florence was so evidently genteel (and the word had a far higher meaning then than it has today). Henry Chaplin was a perfectly normal, virile and gentlemanly young Englishman of his period, which is to say that he probably knew nothing about women at all.

These are all suppositions, but they are ones that fit the facts. They may appear to be a defence of Florence, but she is a woman who has always been in need of defenders, for her own generation condemned her without pity.

Whatever may be said of her conduct, the weight of evidence about her character does not for one moment suggest that Lady Florence was ever either calculating or materialistic in her attitude to life and certainly not to marriage. She was never a young woman who would marry for money or a title. It is true that she had known the embarrassment of comparative poverty, with a father who was frequently in debt and hounded by his creditors, but there is no suggestion that she was wildly extravagant. Therefore Henry Chaplin's more than liberal endowment, and his great generosity, would have provided her with everything she needed. He had no title, it is true, but he was a close friend of the Prince of Wales. Moreover Florence was the daughter of a Marquess – she was not some cheap upstart or snob, eager to better herself in the social sphere.

Was she a romantic? No doubt she was. But the popular view that she forsook a dull and worthy man, the stuffy son of a country parson, in favour of a dashing young gallant, simply does not hold water.

The answer, surely, is that Harry Hastings needed her and Henry Chaplin did not. In the eyes of the world, Harry had everything and Henry had nearly everything, but this would not deceive a sensitive woman. It was Henry Chaplin who had everything, because he had health, self-confidence and security. He was the product of a happy home and was without complexes or inhibitions.

But Harry Hastings – the rake, the gambler, the little-boy-lost – was in desperate need of both pity and understanding. He was going downhill fast, and only a woman's love could save him. A woman does not love a man for his virtues but for his weaknesses, and Harry was weak, foolish and urgently in need of reformation. A woman who married Harry might achieve something. She might save a soul. A woman who married Henry Chaplin would not be required to save him. He was perfectly capable of looking after himself.

It is suggested that these are the factors which motivated Florence when she suddenly decided to elope. Of course, she behaved foolishly and irresponsibly. Faced with a situation which was untenable, she did nothing about it until it was too late. Then she acted precipitously and betrayed a man who had never shown her anything but kindness. For this she cannot be excused. She failed to live up to the Paget tradition of courage and honour.

But she was not yet twenty-two. It is scarcely an age of sober judgement and considered action.

The one person who came out really badly from this whole affair was Harry Hastings. Throughout he behaved like a cad. He continued to share Henry's hospitality and friendship at a time when he was scheming to steal his future wife; and he showed no compunction at any time. When he found that his own weaknesses, his gambling and his ill health each combined to arouse Florence's sympathy and affection, he played these cards to their fullest effect, for he knew well enough the power he held over her when he looked pathetic. His behaviour was unforgivable, and yet he has constantly been forgiven for it, especially by women.

One thing is certain. The stimulus to his ego must have been immense. Here was dashing Harry Hastings, the irresistible Don Juan, running off with another man's betrothed right under his nose – and she the most beautiful woman in Society! At Donington, where they cheered him with gusto, and on his visits to the haunts of vice and dissipation which he had no intention of giving up, he was the hero of a sparkling enterprise. He probably did not suffer a moment of remorse.

Henry Blyth (1966)

The Derby of 1867 provided an ironic sequel to the story. Hastings had laid against Chaplin's colt Hermit 'as if he were dead', including a bet of £20,000 with Chaplin, despite the latter's warning that Hermit had an excellent chance. This advice was ignored, and though, having broken a blood vessel, his chance seemed remote, Hermit triumphed on the day.

Harry Hastings died aged twenty-six, broken in health and financially ruined by absurd extravagance. His widow was no luckier in her second marriage, having chosen another compulsive gambler, Sir George Chetwynd of Grendon, Warwickshire, a former Steward of the Jockey Club who retired from racing after an unsuccessful libel action against Lord Durham, a fellow Steward.

The Pocket Venus must remain an enigma although there is evidence to suggest that she was at least kind and forbearing. She died at Long Walk House, Windsor in 1907 at the age of sixty-four. Her eldest son became the fifth Baronet on the death of his father in 1917; the eldest of her three daughters married the fifth Marquess of Anglesey.

By the time of his death in 1923, Henry Chaplin (now Viscount), had spent his huge inheritance and sold the Blankney estate but he had enjoyed to the full the grand way of life.

The Changing Pattern of Racing

Since racing emerged from the early days of four-mile heats and began to assume its present shape, it has changed greatly. Its modern form can be said to have started in 1814, the first year in which all five Classics were run. Apart from riding styles, training methods and technical innovations, the most noticeable difference has been in fashion respecting the distance of races. This affects the breed through natural selection: if every race was two miles a breed of pure stayers would result, if the longest race was five furlongs the outcome would be a strain of sprinters. Such extremes have not occurred because the Classics, around which the racehorse has evolved, have remained constant – it would be a grave error to interfere with them – but the introduction of new, valuable races and the debasement of some old-established ones has left a mark.

For many years the most esteemed prizes were the Classics and the Ascot Gold Cup, while long-distance races such as the Goodwood Cup and Doncaster Cup carried much prestige. Also favoured by the racing public and owners were the important handicaps, which were the most valuable after the Classics and the Cups and often attracted Classic winners.

Against the emphasis on stamina in races for three-year-olds and up was the popularity of two-year-old racing at five and six furlongs. These two contrasting influences of speed and stamina created a sound balance in the breed: the *via media* has always provided a successful precept in all aspects of English life.

Between the two wars the Ascot Gold Cup drew horses of the highest calibre, even Derby winners, the last of these to win the Gold Cup being Ocean Swell as a four-year-old in 1945. From then on a gradual transition has occurred. First, the Derby no longer stands alone amongst races at a mile and a half for three-year-olds: both the Irish Derby and the French equivalent, the Prix du Jockey Club, are comparable prizes. Though these do not have the status of the Derby, they offer alternatives to possibly sterner opposition at Epsom and take some of the spice out of the Derby itself.

Second, the lack of enthusiasm of owners and breeders for stayers has downgraded the runners in the Ascot Gold Cup. This is due to the international trend of devaluing long-distance races and shortening them, the most notable example being the Grand Prix de Paris, traditionally one mile and seven furlongs and once worth more than the Derby, but now ten furlongs carrying a fairly modest reward. In the first half of the century some great horses won the Ascot Gold Cup and became influential sires, including Bayardo,

Prince Palatine, Solario, Foxlaw, Precipitation and Alycidon, also the wartime Derby winners, Gainsborough, Gay Crusader and Owen Tudor, who won substitute Gold Cups run at Newmarket.

One of the chief attractions of English racing is its variety, including tests at all distances, which appeals to the public and benefits the breed: English racegoers would not tolerate the stereotyped boredom of American racing and, as the famous Italian owner-breeder Federico Tesio declared, the pedigree of a champion racehorse contains top-class representatives at all distances. It is therefore imperative that breeders should produce stayers as well as fast horses if the merit of the thoroughbred and variety in racing programmes is to be maintained. Subservience to fashion dictated by financial pressures can only prove derogatory.

Many years ago, an experienced and successful owner-breeder remarked to me, 'In racing and breeding, take a look around at what everyone else is doing and do the opposite.' There is wisdom in this philosophy. The Turf is an area of fierce competition and to 'follow the table' in it is costly and can lead to mediocrity rather than superiority.

The spate of French victories in our important races immediately after the 1939–45 war caused a change in two-year-old races in England. Some of them were lengthened, the value of those early in the season was reduced and fresh, richly endowed events beyond six furlongs were brought in. The theory behind this was to discourage racing prospective Classic horses too soon and to encourage middle-distance runners and stayers as opposed to sprinters. Racing two-year-olds too soon and too often can be detrimental, though much depends on the individual – the Derby winner Donovan won the Brocklesby Stakes at two years in the first week of the season, and The Bard, second to Ormonde in the Derby, won all his sixteen starts the previous year. On the other hand, the further a two-year-old is raced the greater the strain imposed, and the later it is in the season the longer recovery takes.

While allowing that two-year-olds devoid of speed will do better racing beyond six furlongs than over short distances, the late Fred Darling, one of the greatest trainers of modern times and responsible for seven Derby winners, was adamant that horses with valid

Classic pretensions should never go beyond six furlongs as juveniles – had the Champagne Stakes at Doncaster been run at seven furlongs in his day, neither the subsequent Derby winner Coronach nor Fair Diana and Myrobella, all trained by Darling to win the race, would have run in it. He opined that, at two, horses are immature and if severely exerted beyond six furlongs are prone to damage and having their speed blunted. Only one of Darling's Derby winners raced beyond six furlongs as a two-year-old, Pont l'Évêque, a pure stayer and second string in the Derby to Tant Mieux, who failed to stay and finished fourth.

Until recently, the Middle Park Stakes of six furlongs was the main target for two-year-olds in the second half of the season, rather than the seven-furlong Dewhurst Stakes a fortnight later and now the preferred choice. This goes against Darling's principle and does not allow for horses training off towards the end of the year, when a candidate for the Dewhurst may have passed his best, particularly in an early autumn. Since a true Classic contender must have the speed to win at six furlongs as a two-year-old, there is no point in racing him or her further at this stage. It is a fact that the champion sprinter is not necessarily the fastest horse in training, as this may be running in the Classics or other races at longer distances – the fastest horse the late Tommy Weston ever rode was the St Leger winner Fairway.

The old order changeth, but not always for the better. While support for stayers must not lapse, there is a case for the Champagne Stakes at Doncaster reverting to six furlongs and fashion moving from the Dewhurst back to the Middle Park.

John Hislop (1988)

Making a Handicap

The whole set-up of handicapping has completely changed since I started in 1932. Before 1935, a handicapper was not appointed by the Jockey Club Stewards. He had to find his own work and, having once made a start, the better he did his job the more likely he was to get more work.

The first appointment was obviously the most difficult, for the Stewards would not grant the necessary licence until the prospective handicapper could show that he had been promised some meetings. Since a race, possibly one to which the executive had added a big stake, could – and indeed still can – be ruined by careless handicapping, no racecourse management was likely to chance employing anyone without a long racing background. The budding handicapper had definitely to start on the bottom rung of the ladder.

Personally, I was lucky to have had the help of my uncle, Thomas Dawkins, who had retired at the end of the 1931 season after thirty years as a senior handicapper. He was at that time managing director at Warwick and, to help me over the first hurdle, he promised me the job of handicapping at that meeting – somewhat reluctantly, I may say, for he was always critical of nepotism in any form. However, this enabled me to apply for a licence and I was able to make a start. No major disaster occurred in the early days of my career as a handicapper and having already been a regular racegoer for over twenty-five years – and in consequence known to many people, who kindly gave me all the help they could – I managed to make steady progress and gradually got more work. I should say this was typical of how a racecourse official got a start in those days, the one essential qualification being the knowledge that can be gained only on the racecourse.

In 1934, the year before the Jockey Club took over the appointment of handicappers, there were ten handicappers licensed to work under Jockey Club rules. At that time there were only two instructions that went with the licence – firstly, not to handicap at two meetings in the same week, and secondly, to attend the meeting at which one had made the weights. At that time some handicappers worked only under Jockey Club rules and some only under National Hunt rules. But in 1935, when the Jockey Club Stewards appointed the handicappers to the different meetings, the number of handicappers under Jockey Club rules was reduced to seven, with one assistant or learner handicapper. It was not until some years later that the National Hunt Stewards followed this lead and allotted the fixtures to the handicappers. In my case it seemed to make little difference: I was given rather fewer days and received slightly less cash.

But the stewards had taken on the task of finding and training their handicappers – a job which had always been done for them. For some years this did not present any great difficulties, as they already had a reliable team to hand. In fact it was not until after the war, when new handicappers were needed, that it became apparent that it was going to be difficult to find the chap with the necessary racing background, the one who had spent – or, as some might say, wasted – long years on the racecourse. And for financial reasons this difficulty was likely to become more acute.

Lately there seems to have been a tendency to take on younger people with less and less racing experience – thus disregarding the one really essential qualification, without which it is difficult to see how anyone could succeed as a handicapper. For surely someone who has learnt racing the hard way, as an owner or backer of horses, must have a great advantage. Anyway, he will have realized that even the greatest certainties get beaten, and always will, and that without any sinister happenings. Probably all handicappers gain experience as time goes on, but in the old days they had bought experience at their own expense. As it is seldom that a handicapper lasts twenty-five years, there seems little reason for not looking for greater age and more experience.

Before handicappers were put on a salary, they were of course paid a fee by the racecourse employing them. The reward for the better meetings was around 35 guineas for a two-day Flat meeting and 30 guineas for a two-day steeplechase meeting. This fee had to cover all expenses and the free lunch for officials had not yet arrived. A much appreciated variation to this scale of payment occurred at Uttoxeter, where the handicapper was paid 2s. 6d. per entry and a further 2s. 6d. per runner, the idea being presumably that the more confidence owners and trainers had in the handicapper, the greater should be his reward.

I am often asked how a handicap is made. It is not a question to which there is a pat answer. The Stewards of the Jockey Club through the ages have said in their wisdom no more than this: 'A handicap is a race in which the weights to be carried by the horses are adjusted by the handicapper for the purpose of equalizing their chances of winning.' As simple as that. No handicapper can complain that his task has been made more difficult by complicated instructions.

The book of form is the handicapper's bible and he would be wise to stick to it as closely as he can – although on occasions he and the connections of the horse are inclined to be influenced by different pages of the book. But if the handicapper will use his racecourse knowledge and ordinary common sense, and if he has allowed himself time to do the job in an unhurried frame of mind, he should not be very far wrong at the finish. This part of handicapping is impossible to teach; the handicapper either picks up the know-how, or would be wise to take to something else to occupy his time.

But perhaps it would be possible to point out how some errors can be made. A common fault is to take into consideration only the horses actually entered in the handicap in question, and to ignore the form of horses who could just as well have been entered. In this way you are inclined to use the race results where the horses entered have largely run amongst themselves and take no account of collateral form with horses who are not entered in that particular race. I have often heard a handicapper say what a good thing it was that some particular horse had not been entered, as it would have messed up the whole handicap. Well, perhaps next week this horse is entered in such a handicap, which means that the handicapper has to make some drastic alteration to his previous handicap. He would have been wiser to do all this in the first instance, for even though he may not be optimistic enough to expect everyone to agree with him, obviously he should try to agree with himself.

Sometimes one wonders if the handicapper has paid sufficient regard to the official weight-for-age scale. Although this scale has not been altered since 1880, it still seems to be wonderfully correct, and is a great safeguard in making handicaps for three-year-olds and upwards. As an instance of how well it works even to this day it is only necessary to look at the results of the King George VI and Queen Elizabeth Stakes, run at Ascot's July meeting. In the sixteen years since it was inaugurated this race has attracted 168 runners – 76 three-year-olds, 66 four-year-olds and 26 five-year-olds and over. Three-year-olds have won seven times, been second eight times and third seven times. Four-year-olds have won eight times, been second six times and third six times. Five-year-olds and over have won once, been second twice and third three times.

In any handicap, and especially one including good-class horses, it is very dangerous to ignore this scale. By extending one's handicap to include the best horses of the different ages, over that distance, one can often avoid making the sort of mistake that by the day of the race has shown up as an obvious error.

Last year [1966] it was decided that any horse who had won a race under Jockey Club rules could be given a weight in a handicap. Possibly this instruction has not been thoroughly understood. It was meant to allow the horse to run and to save the trouble and expense often caused by the difficulty of finding a race in which a winner that had not run the previously required three times could be entered. It was obviously not intended that the handicapper should assess this horse strictly on his very limited form. Once again the handicapper's racing experience should come to his rescue.

One more point – it is no good trying to make a handicap that nothing can win. Rather try to give everything a chance. This usually means taking off the odd pound rather than adding it on. The object is a good acceptance – and a good betting race – the rest is in the lap of the gods and it would be unwise to get unduly elated if the race results in a close finish, or too depressed if they come home like a lot of ducks.

There has been much talk of handicapping by committee and of the possible assistance a computer could give. When the senior handicapper of the day retired after the 1900 season, his job was taken on by a triumvirate – Dawkins, Keyser and Lee – three very experienced racegoers. This arrangement actually lasted twelve years, but the three were in a constant state of disagreement amongst themselves and did not give any great satisfaction to the racing fraternity either.

As regards the computer, I believe that it can tell you only what you have told it – that is marshal the facts fed to it. So it would be to a great extent under the influence of the official detailed to supply the information. But whatever its merits – and obviously it must be given credit for accuracy and speed – the computer would always lack the one essential quality – racing experience.

Geoffrey Freer (1967)

GEOFFREY FREER (1887–1968) was an outstanding Jockey Club handicapper, a post he held from 1945 till 1962. Much wisdom is contained in these few pages and a good deal more can be extracted from between the lines, in particular those referring to the handicapping of a horse which wins before he has run three times.

Whether ratings are held in a computer or handicaps are compiled from entries (as they were when this article was written), exactly the same principles apply.

Many methods have been employed in attempting to pull wool over handicappers' eyes. The only tried and sure way of beating them is with a good horse that keeps on improving.

———

Rule 153

This letter was published in the Sporting Life on Thursday, 30 October 1986, following the disqualification of Forest Flower in the Tattersalls' Cheveley Park Stakes.

The misfortunes of Forest Flower seem to have been seized upon as a heaven-sent platform by those who seek to separate the fate of a guilty jockey from that of his innocent mount.

The fact that some good judges considered that the courage and determination of the filly was more responsible for the fracas at Newmarket than the conscious decision of her jockey hardly adds stability to this particular platform.

However, my interest, like that of the reformers, lies in the general application of the Rule, so I do not wish to take advantage of specific aspects of the Cheveley Park itself. Rather, I want to submit my pennyworth in support of the present united treatment of horse and jockey when it comes to a misdeed on the part of a jockey.

I accept that the reformers' appeal to the Stewards of the Jockey Club to punish the guilty jockey but to leave his mount with the spoils is well meant. However, when you boil it down, it is no more than a plea for a foul to be disregarded in deciding the outcome of a race.

Ever since the eighteenth century, the rulers of racing have taken the view that someone who commits a foul to gain a prize should be deprived of it.

On one basis or another I have seen the inner workings of panels of Stewards for over thirty years and I am certain beyond anything else that they simply could not operate properly with that principle seriously undermined: it is the very linchpin of our system.

If you want to look into the abyss represented by the proposed changes you need to go no further than to football and its 'professional fouls'.

It must never become a matter of who would or would not have won but for the foul; once the fact is proven, that is, always has been and always should be the end of the matter in racing.

Proper justice, as I see it, can only be dispensed on that principle. If, occasionally, the result is felt to produce rough justice for some punters then that, in my view, is the price that must be paid for the general integrity, on the racecourse, of the sport itself.

Thus it is on a central principle that I rest my case, namely that a misdeed is something that no proper rules should allow to be rewarded. Both for myself and, to my knowledge, some members of the Jockey Club, the standard defence of the present arrangement, to the effect that any change would encourage dangerous riding, while valid in itself, is too narrow and legalistic in character to be a defence on its own.

I would ask a question of those who wish to reform Rule 153. What would be the destination of the jockey's percentage of, say, the Derby stakes if he were adjudged to have fouled but not, thereby, to have affected the result?

A worthy charity perhaps, but not, presumably, a fund from which to pay his fine.

Assuming that the answer follows these lines, I would ask a supplementary question of the reformers. What would happen to the breeding right which the jockey might expect to receive a year or so later, worth perhaps ten times as much as his percentage? Surely, while the suggested reform of Rule 153 may be superficially attractive and entirely well me... it is, in fact, ill-conceived and unworkable.

If the sport of racing is going to become subservient to the interests of punters (or, for that matter, to those of multi-millionaire owners, or breeders, or the professional element represented by trainers and jockeys, or to those of anyone else, come to that) then I could have spent my twenty-seven years as a handicapper with more advantage serving some other activity.

Racing means many different things to different people but, above all else, it is a sport and it must be conducted as a sport.

DAVID SWANNELL
Yardley Hastings
Northamptonshire

Before and since this letter was written in October 1986, Rule 153 has had many opponents and few friends. A strong head of steam erupted at Royal Ascot 1988 following the disqualification of Royal Gait. His demotion was no less controversial than that, say, of Vacarme (Richmond Stakes, Goodwood 1983) and Nureyev (Two Thousand Guineas, 1980).

The crux of the rule lies in the interpretation of 'careless', an unsatisfactory word only finely removed from 'accidental' and clearly, like racing itself, meaning different things to different people. Lester Piggott's part in the Vacarme affair may not have been 'accidental', but whatever else it was it was not 'careless': it was premeditated and carefully executed. Unlike the Nureyev case, it affected nobody's chance, it caused neither damage nor danger, and in equity and common sense the result should have stood. It is a strongly held view that the Stewards were mesmerized by Piggott's manoeuvre, but they had to be seen to do something and

*did the wrong thing. Life would be so much duller, though, if
everybody was infallible, and all rules were perfect. This rule will
come to the aid of journalists for many years to come and we shall
continue to defend the principle for which it stands.*

Selling Races, 1884

At the meeting of the Jockey Club I brought forward a motion to
abolish selling handicaps, simply because I think it ridiculous that
one horse should be called on to give another of the same age
perhaps 2 st., when both are entered to be sold for the same price;
and because it encourages people to keep worthless animals in
training, in hopes they may get them through some wretched little
selling handicap with the best of the weights. The motion did not
meet with the favour I anticipated, several members of the Jockey
Club protesting that some little northern meetings would cease to
exist if selling handicaps were abolished, and I agreed to postpone
the subject on the understanding that the Stewards would under-
take to deal with the matter at once; which, by the way, they never
did.

                                        Sir George Chetwynd, Bt (1891)

Sir George Chetwynd, Bt (1849–1917)

*It is over 100 years since this relevant aspect of selling races was
brought up by Sir George and it is still 'ridiculous' that two horses,
of the same age, 28 lb. apart in the weights, should be entered to
be sold for the same price. Selling races still of course encourage
owners to keep bad horses in training but improvement in the
conditions of auction and claiming races, and their increased popularity, will, it is to be hoped, eventually exclude them.*

*Sir George understood racing in all its aspects and although he
was a Steward of the Jockey Club, he was, to all intents and
purposes, a professional backer. He controlled Sherrard's yard in
Newmarket which had first claim on Charles Wood, a jockey of
undoubted ability but of dubious integrity. The activities of 'a
certain yard' were referred to by Lord Durham in his speech at*

the Gimcrack Dinner of 1887; in the libel action which followed,
Chetwynd was awarded one farthing in damages, resigned from
the Jockey Club and retired from racing.

———

The Time Factor

The time of any race naturally depends on how it is run. In the
case of 1936 Derby, Charlie Smirke, who had originally planned
a waiting race on Mahmoud, saw, as he came into the straight,
that Thankerton had taken a long lead and thought he had better
get closer to him.

Much to his surprise he found himself in the lead two furlongs
out, and almost wrote off his chances.

However, he kept at his mount and Mahmoud ran on to win
by three lengths from the same owner's Taj Akbar, ridden by
Gordon Richards, with Tommy Burns on the half-bred Thankerton
a length away, third. When a record time of 2 minutes 33.8 seconds
was announced, Smirke was in for another surprise.

With Knockroe's new record,* the course best times for all
distances at Epsom stand to the credit of post-war horses. And
much the same can be said of all other racehorses, here and abroad.
So there can be little, if any, doubt that the racehorse as a breed
is improving.

Regarding the Derby course, it might be as well here to repeat
the facts and the opinions of those most qualified to express them.
A few years ago, when the subject was being discussed in the
Sporting Life, Mr J. D. Watts, for ten years Clerk of the Course
at Epsom up to 1964, and before that Assistant Clerk for eight
years, wrote to the paper as follows:

Various views have been expressed on the time taken for the Derby course
today compared with twenty-five or more years ago. Readers may wish
to consider the following points:

Mahmoud ran on a course which had a very much greater percentage

———

* Now held by Bustino, 4 yrs, Coronation Cup, 7 June 1975, 2 minutes 33.1
seconds.

of the tough fescue grasses and weeds in its turf than today. This natural
downland turf gave splendid going in most weathers and the turf was
scarcely broken.

With the use of fertilizers, which were necessarily applied to the Epsom
course, the course lost its fescues and finally became good meadow grass
which cut up badly, especially with bigger fields and more racing.

Repair work has become increasingly difficult and tons of imported soil
have been used to restore the course and keep it even.

At the insistence of owners, trainers and the Press, the policy was
followed of avoiding jar in the ground in a dry summer. Sedge peat and
peat moss have been applied during the past twenty years. Quantities?
Not less than 1,500 tons of imported soil and peat since the war.

This material has been used on the running part of the course – a total
of approximately eight acres, or nearly 200 tons an acre.

What purpose can there be in comparing Mahmoud's time for the course
with those recorded today? They're running on a different going, they're
running on a different course.

We have recently seen winners coming on the stands side at Epsom in
soft conditions. The reason is obvious. The stands side has not had the
treatment given to the running side and the going there is five or six
lengths faster – more like Mahmoud's course.

What does all this boil down to? This: there is no true basis for comparison between performances in the same or different years unless the going
is accurately measured.

While Clerk of the Course at Epsom, I had the advantage of using an
instrument for this purpose. This proved that the Derby course going was
extremely even, longitudinally, but from side to side the difference was
disturbing.

'Donovan' (1974)

*Thousands of words, many of them meaningless, have been written
on the subject of race timing. Horses race to beat other horses and
if, coincidentally, they beat the clock it is due to inconstant factors:
going, wind direction and the widely varying conformation of
English racecourses.*

*The observations of Mr J. D. Watts are extremely interesting
but an opinion formed over many years of experience has proved
useful: the stands side, on any racecourse, will ride some lengths
faster when the ground is 'soft' or 'heavy'. The machinery used on
the course is invariably housed under or behind the stands. It
moves down the course on the stands side, the footborne labour*

likewise. The effect of this traffic, over a period of time, has consolidated the ground to a disproportionate extent, compared to other parts of the course.

The opinion expressed that the post-war breed of racehorse is improving, is a matter for conjecture if based upon time. Quite moderate racehorses record fast times and break records.

———

A Pacemaker

One day I heard from Mullins, telling me my horse was fit and that it had been entered in a race. Would I come over about a week before as he had news for me? I went, and over breakfast Mullins told me that the true reason why the horse had been sold to me was that it couldn't stay more than a mile and a half. It was a front runner and would hold this position for that distance, thereafter it would run out of 'puff' and be tailed off. However, it was useful to him as a pacemaker and this was to be the plan for the forthcoming race.

Mullins had two horses entered in the same race at Mullingar; both their chances he estimated to be good, more particularly as the other entries were not up to much in his opinion and half of them would be ridden by their owner-riders, 'bumpers' like myself. Cnamh was to go into an immediate lead, and stay on the rails, where they existed. As he ran out of steam I was to look round and see what horse was tracking me. If it was one of ours, I was to leave the rails and let it through, impeding the opposition by 'dying' in front of them, if necessary meandering about the course to render this operation more effective. If, on the other hand, it was not one of our pair, I was to stay where I was and deny our rivals the inner position.

This event was to be a big coup for one and all connected with the operation. Our two horses opened up the betting, one at 6–4 favourite and the other at 5–2 second favourite. Our connections backed the second horse down to even money, allowing the other horse to drift out to 9–2, since everyone concluded that it was a non-trier. Then they proceeded to plunge on the other horse. The final result of these manoeuvres was that the horses ended up at 6–4 each of two. My reward, for my part in the affair, was to be on the odds to a 'pony', a great deal of money at that time. But being over-confident as to the outcome of this stone-wall certainty, I threw my total wealth into the gamble.

The race started in pouring rain. I got a 'flyer' and took up my position. Once off, the going was like Fowler's Black Treacle, the rain deluging down. I was doubtful if I could hold my position long enough to be of any use. My horse hated the wet.

If the reader has ever galloped in porridge-like mud he will know that the thrash of the horse's hooves makes an infernal noise. Despite this, passing the stand on the first circuit, I could hear a lot of shouting from the patrons. This caused me to look around before the appointed moment, when I made the horrifying discovery that I was the only one out of the eleven runners left standing. Two had fallen early on, bringing down half the field. Running out and slipping up had accounted for the rest. For my own personal safety I slowed down and miraculously kept Cnamh on his feet until the last fence. He trotted up to it, slid over, landed safely, and ambled past the post, the winner.

It was well known that his chances were nil, all things being equal, and anyone could have had 200–1 on him had they wanted. As I unsaddled my horse in solitude – the trainer and stable connections were out in the country picking up the pieces, and probably had no intention of showing up in order to avoid financial embarrassment – a little old woman came up to me waving a ticket, and congratulated me on my performance. She was the only person who had backed Cnamh, and I could have killed her. Cnamh was sold immediately. In his first race in new ownership he fell and broke his neck, thus ending this tragic story.

John Skeaping, RA (1977)

John Skeaping, RA (1901–80)

John Skeaping was first and foremost a sculptor, winner of the Rome Prize. He was a contemporary of Henry Moore, but as he admits in his autobiography, Drawn from Life, *he lacked the former's dedication to his profession, having wide interests, among them racing. This is reflected in his work, which includes the life-size statues of Hyperion, Chamossaire and Brigadier Gerard at Newmarket.*

———

The Gentle Art of Tipping

One of the things which I have always found most difficult in life is to throw away racing articles I have written and photographs I have taken. As I have been writing regularly for forty-six years and have been taking photographs for sixty-six years, it will be gathered that it is lucky we have a large number of outhouses. Sometimes I embarrass myself by fetching an old cutting book and reading the articles I used to write over forty years ago. The reason for my embarrassment is that one article after another shows how much I thought I knew and how little I did know.

There is one thing though which delights me and which reminds me of my favourite story of the Chelsea Pensioners. One of them said to the other, 'You remember those tablets they gave us in the Boer War to take our thoughts off the ladies? Well, I believe mine are beginning to work.' In my articles I was full of ideas for the improvement of racing. Some of them took only a few years to work, but others are only just beginning to work now. The most important was to do with the Tote, and the second most important was the suggestion, made almost week after week, that we should have paid stewards.

I have often told the story of the unpardonable offence I committed when, for a short time, I wrote as Larry Lynx for the *People*. When I was approached by the all-highest of Odhams Press, Mr Elias, I stipulated that I must be allowed to write what I thought was in the interests of racing. My start was a very good one. When I joined the paper I had just returned from a month's skiing in Switzerland and, as I was right out of touch with racing, I suggested that it would be better if I didn't give selections. I was told that I must give selections, so I did so. I had seventeen runners and eleven of them won, some at quite good prices. I was billed on the buses as the world's greatest racing writer. All went well until the Sunday before the Chester meeting. I have always said that no one enjoys reading my racing articles more than I do. My horror can be imagined when I opened the paper and saw that not one word of my article had been printed, and that some stuff about the ancient history of Chester racecourse had been substituted under my *nom de plume*.

On Monday, full of indignation, I hurried to Odhams to see Mr Elias. When I was shown into his office I found that he was not just full of indignation, but overflowing with it. He had apparently issued orders for me to go and see him at once. If I had set fire to the building he couldn't have been more furious with me for writing words which he said would have ruined his firm had they not been taken out of the *People* after the first edition. I hadn't the foggiest idea what he was talking about. When I explained my bewilderment, he asked me whether I had neglected to study the policy of the *Sporting Life*, which was, of course, another Odhams publication. It did not improve matters when I said that although I was a great *Sporting Life* reader it had never dawned on me that it had a policy. It gradually got home to me that my terrible offence had been to write that I felt strongly it would be for the good of racing if the Tote were tried out in this country. I said that I hoped I should live to see it. Mr Elias calmed down a little when I said that although I personally thought we should have the Tote one day I was sorry to have so nearly ruined him. He said, 'A few nights ago I was dining with the Prime Minister and he assured me that we shall never have the Tote in this country.'

Ramsay MacDonald was the Prime Minister at the time, but he was not the only politician to have made an incorrect prophecy. Joseph Toole, the Labour Member of Parliament, wrote a most entertaining book called *Fighting through Life*. Toole wrote that Winston Churchill, whom he greatly admired, was quick, lively, cultured, a master of procedure and a great debater with a grip of world problems, demanding the respect of everybody. He then went on to say that the one thing Churchill could never command was confidence. He wrote, 'Whatever changes this nation may see, there can never again be a high place in the state for this most distinguished statesman.' The book was published in 1935.

No prophet could ever have been as far out as Ramsay MacDonald and Joe Toole were. It must not be thought that I claim to have been gifted with second-sight. I have had some fantastic prophecies come true, but I realize that the fantastic ones have been flukes. I made my first prophecy at the age of six. At that time we had a huge garden with innumerable gardeners and an estate carpenter. One day, when walking in the garden with the under-nurse, we met Mr May the carpenter. I was always a nosy little boy and I said, 'Mr May, how many children have you got?' 'Eight,' said Mr May. 'Count tomorrow,' I said, 'and you will have one more.' This is a true story. Next day my nurse told me that Mr Stork had brought a new little baby to Mr and Mrs May. The under-nurse, who was a great follower of Old Moore, and who consulted his almanac every day, was enormously impressed with my prophecy. I am sure she had hopes that I might be a young Moore when I was a little older. The words were not so clever as they sound, however, as for eight consecutive years Mr Stork called on the Mays, so it was only 365–1 against my prophecy coming true. (Clever mathematicians needn't trouble to point out that the true odds should be 364–1. It was a leap year.)

Every year I hear from readers who have never forgotten my start to the flat-race season in 1922. The first race was the five-furlong Brocklesby Trial Stakes, a handicap. There were twenty-seven runners. When the horses were on their way to the post, I wondered why I had selected Gentleman, a moderate three-year-old with 7 st. 7 lb. No other writer had mentioned his name. Gentleman had won his first race as a two-year-old at Kempton on the day before the Jubilee by a short head and had survived an objection, but he had later descended to selling races without further success. I remember saying to a friend, 'It would be a miracle to give a winner today.' I thought I was going to wake up when I saw Gentleman winning at 33–1. Three races later there was an even greater miracle. I had been obliged to nap something and I had read that Bethersden Marble, a gelding trained by Jack Jarvis, had been going well at Newmarket. Horses who go well at Newmarket have not always gone well at Lincoln, but Bethersden Marble was the exception. Ridden by Charlie Elliott, he won the

Welbeck Handicap by two lengths. When my friend who returned the s.p. came into the press room, I said, 'I suppose that was a hot favourite.' He said, 'There wasn't a penny for him. He started at 20–1 others.' The *Sunday Express* was so carried away that I was sent a telegram of congratulations. There is one thing I do particularly remember about those selections. It was the number of people who would not believe it when I told them that I had no inside information and that it was just a staggering fluke. One man was so persistent and kept saying to me, 'If you tell me where you got the information I promise you I won't tell anyone else,' that eventually I said, 'On the day before I did my selections I went into a cloakroom duly labelled outside, and I found it was made of Bethersden marble.' He used some very bad language.

Geoffrey Gilbey (1966)

When Geoffrey Gilbey wrote this piece a quarter of a century ago, racing journalists took life (and themselves) a good deal less seriously than they do now; perhaps, in fairness, life generally was less serious. Racing, certainly, was much more fun, if somewhat less hygienic than it is today.

———

Ecclesiastical Wrath

The Revd Mr King – though it was only under the *nom de course* of Mr 'Launde' that the highly respected vicar of Ashby-de-la-Launde was familiar to the sporting world, and then as the owner of the whilom Derby favourite, Holy Friar, and the Oaks and St Leger heroine, Apology – died on Sunday afternoon, 9 May 1875. Though he had been ailing for a long time, the more immediate cause of death arose from the fracture of the thigh which befell him nearly twelve months previously. After Mr King won the St Leger of 1874, the then Bishop of Lincoln, within whose see Ashby-de-la-Launde was situate, addressed a somewhat serious remonstrance to Mr King against him associating himself with Turf matters, to which the reverend gentleman responded by resigning his living, addressing in reply a most caustic, gentlemanly reminder to his lordship, of which the following is an extract:

It is true that now for more than fifty years I have bred, and have sometimes had in training, horses for the Turf. They are horses of a breed highly prized, which I inherited with my estate, and have been in my family for generations. It may be difficult, perhaps, to decide what constitutes a scandal in the Church, but I cannot think that in my endeavours to perpetuate this breed, and thus improve the horses in the country – an object of general interest at the present moment – I have done anything to incur your lordship's censure. I am fully aware – as I think your lordship must be, too, by this time – that legal proceedings upon your part would be powerless against me, and if, therefore, I resign the living which I hold within your lordship's diocese, it will not be from any consciousness of wrong, or from fear of any consequences which might ensue in the ecclesiastical Courts, but simply because I desire to live the remainder of my days in peace and charity with all men, and to save your lordship the annoyance, and the Church the scandal of futile proceedings being taken against one who has retired for some time from parochial ministrations, and is lying on the bed of sickness at this moment.

Mr 'Launde' in his time possessed first-class racehorses, but he failed to carry off the big three-year-old events until the year when, with Apology, he won the One Thousand, the Oaks, the Coronation Stakes at Ascot, and the St Leger.

John Radcliffe (1900)

Apology (1871), by Adventurer-Mandragora (Rataplan), was one of the outstanding mares of nineteenth-century racing. So popular was her St Leger win that the cheering from Doncaster was said to have been audible in York.

———

A Racing Bore

'What a racing bore you must be,' remarked a critic to me at Ascot after he had read my article in the *Racehorse* last week. He imagined that anyone who came to my house would hear nothing but racing talk.

I must confess that, forty years ago, I was a dreadful racing bore – but I was cured.

One night, when we were living at Windlesham on the edge of Sunningdale golf course, we were invited to dine with a man I had met because he had sliced a ball at the seventh hole and it had landed in our garden.

If anyone ever says that he likes children or dogs 'in their place', you will know that he dislikes them. His 'place' for dogs will be the kennel and his 'place' for children school or the nursery. It must not be thought, though, that I dislike golfers when I say that I like them 'in their place'. I like them so long as when they have finished their rounds they remember that the place for golf talk is the clubhouse.

As we sat down to dinner, my host said: 'You're a keen golfer, Gilbey; you'll be interested in the round I played this morning.'

That sentence contained two lies.

Before I could protest, though, he so-to-speak straightway teed up for the first drive. He didn't miss one shot. We did the whole eighteen holes and by the time he had sunk his last putt and had won a magnificent victory the ladies had departed and the port was going round for the second time.

I don't drink port but I was relieved that the golf round was over. My horror can be imagined when my host said: 'You enjoyed that round, Gilbey, but you will enjoy even more the foursome we played in the afternoon.'

These two lies were even bigger than the first two.

It was eleven o'clock before we completed the second round.

The next day, I was telling a friend of the miserable evening I had spent.

He said: 'It should be a lesson to you: you apparently don't realize that you bore the pants off everyone who comes to your house by talking of racing.'

This pulled me together with a bang. I remembered that, only the day before, a dear old lady who came to lunch had not seemed to share in my joy when I had told her of the five winners I had backed two days before, describing the races in detail. Not being observant and not having looked under the table, I hadn't any idea

of the indignity my friend said I had inflicted on her. From that
moment, I was no longer a racing bore.

Geoffrey Gilbey (1963)

*Geoffrey Gilbey's recollections (and cure) may prove helpful to
some who suffer misery from the gratuitous reminiscences of those
who feel that a connection with racing is of absorbing interest to
others whose tastes in entertainment lie elsewhere. Bores will be
bores in any company but golf probably provides the greatest
scope.*

A Cautionary Tale, c. 1890

Early on the morning of the Monday before a very recent Goodwood, a very well-known Nottingham bookmaker left the strong-
hold of doilies and dollymops on his annual pilgrimage to Chiches-
ter. In the inside pocket of his waistcoat he carried the principal
implements of warfare: banknotes in the original lump. They were
clean, fresh notes, straight from the bank, and the value of the roll
was £2,500.

As he had a little business to transact in crossing the metropolis,
he found he could not get down to Sussex in comfortable time to
dine, so he had a cut from the saddle at Simpson's, and reserved
a bedroom at a certain palatial hotel within easy reach of Victoria
Station.

On the following morning, oversleeping himself somewhat, and
starting in no end of a hurry, he had travelled as far as Midhurst
– some sixty-four miles – ere he made the discovery that he had
left his boodle behind, tucked snugly beneath his pillow, at the big
hotel.

He was out of that train at the next station, and agitating the
wire, and, much later in the day, he literally burst into the manager's room at the huge caravansery.

'It's all right, sir, it's all right!' cried the hotel manager, who had
no difficulty in divining the cause of his late guest's reappearance;

'the chambermaid found 'em when she went up to strip the beds, and they're now in the safe in my office!'

And they were – but one fiver was missing. In the moment of temptation the poor girl, like the clergyman who sat down on the fish-hook (who was too good to swear, but felt too bad to let it alone), could not resist the temptation of swiping just one little fiver – it meant such a deal to her – and though the rejoicing bookie freely gave her four more to go with it, she lost her place; which made up a combination of as hard and as soft luck as ever I heard of.

Arthur M. Binstead (1898)

The 'implements of warfare' entrusted to the waistcoat pocket represented about £100,000 in today's currency. Having touched for the modern equivalent of a 'grand', it is hard not to hope that the chambermaid put the 'pony' to good use.

The curious jocular style of the period contrasts strangely with the turgidity of the serious writing.

———

The Thoroughbred Sportsman: George Osbaldeston

Strange to say, none of the obituary notices in the sporting papers, following the death of Mr Osbaldeston (the Squire), so far as we have seen, have given any particulars of the famous match against time, which is thus briefly recorded in the *Calendar:*

Newmarket Houghton Meeting, 1831 – Saturday, November 5: Mr Osbaldeston having made a wager of 1,000 guineas that he would ride 200 miles in 10 hours, and the ground forming a circle of four miles having been marked out on and about the racecourse, he started about seven o'clock this morning, and performed the distance in 8 hours and 42 minutes. He changed his horse every four miles, and rode twenty-nine different horses. A bet – 1,000 to 100 – was laid that he did not perform the distance in 9 hours.

The Squire rode it at 11 st.

Anon, *The Sporting Magazine* (1866)

GEORGE OSBALDESTON (1786–1866) scaled heights in sporting achievement which in a more mundane age are never likely to be surpassed. He was a brilliant shot, an outstanding whip, the best amateur rider of his time and probably the best amateur huntsman of his or any other time. Racing and betting were his downfall. His hounds, horses and estates sold, he died in reduced circumstances in St John's Wood, by then no longer a fox covert.

Even by the Squire's standards, the Newmarket ride was a remarkable performance. After the first hundred miles, in 4 hours 19 minutes 52 seconds, he stopped and 'took a mouthful of bread and some brandy and water'. After 120 miles, 'Mr Osbaldeston rested six minutes and a half, and lunched upon a cold partridge and brandy and water in the stand, but although wet to the skin refused to put on dry clothes.' The 200 miles was 'covered in 7 hours 19 minutes 4 seconds at the rate of 26 miles per hour, the horses whilst running covering the ground at the rate of 27⅓ miles per hour.' At four o'clock p.m. the Squire was home in Newmarket, had a bath, changed and went out to dinner.

———

Rainbow's Race

The piece which follows is taken from Robbery under Arms, a classic of Australian literature, first published in 1888. Its author was an Englishman named Thomas Alexander Browne, who emigrated to Australia and chose the pen-name of Rolf Boldrewood. The hero of the story, which the author describes as 'an 'ower true tale' of the wilder aspects of Australian life, is 'Captain Starlight', an English gentleman turned bushranger.

We hadn't been long at home, just enough to get tired of doing nothing, when we got a letter from Bella Barnes, telling us that she was going to get married the day after the Turon races, and reminding Starlight that he had promised to come to her wedding. If he didn't think it was too risky, she hoped he'd come. There was going to be a race ball, and it was sure to be good fun. It would be a good wind-up, and Maddie was coming out a great swell. Sir Ferdinand would be there, but there'd be such a crowd anybody would pass muster, and so on.

'Yours sincerely,
'ISABELLA BARNES.

'P.S. There was a big handicap, with 500 added; hadn't we a good horse enough?'

'Well done, Bella!' says Starlight. 'I vote we go, Dick. I never went to a hop with a price on my head before. A thousand pounds too! Quite a new sensation. It settles the question. And we'll enter Rainbow for the handicap. He ought to be good enough for anything they're likely to have.'

'And who was to enter Rainbow and look after him?'

'Couldn't we get old Jacob Benton; he's the best trainer I've seen since I left home? Billy the Boy told us the other day he was out of a job, and was groom at Jonathan's; had been sacked for getting drunk, and so on. He'll be all the more likely to keep sober for a month.'

'The very man,' I said. 'He can ride the weight, and train too. But we can't have him here, surely!'

'No; but I can send the horse to him at Jonathan's, and he can get him fit there as well as anywhere. There's nearly a month yet; he's pretty hard, and he's been regularly exercised lately.'

Jacob Benton was a wizened, dried-up old Yorkshireman. He'd been head man in a good racing stable, but drink had been the ruin of him – lost him his place, and sent him out here. He could be trusted to go right through with a job like ours, for all that. Like many men that drink hard, he was as sober as a judge between one burst and another. And once he took over a horse in training he touched nothing but water till the race was run and the horse back in his box. Then he most times went on an awful perisher – took a month to it, and was never sober day or night the whole time. When he'd spent all his money he'd crawl out of the township and get away into the country more dead than alive, and take the

first job that offered. But he was fonder of training a good horse
than anything else in the world; and if he'd got a regular flyer, and
was treated liberal, he'd hardly allow himself sleep or time to eat
his meals till he'd got him near the mark. He could ride, too, and
was an out-and-out judge of pace.

When we'd regular chalked it out about entering Rainbow for the
Grand Turon Handicap, we sent Warrigal over to Billy the Boy,
and got him to look up old Jacob. He agreed to take the old horse,
the week before the races, and give him a last bit of French-polish
if we'd keep him in steady work till then. From what he was
told of the horse he expected he would carry any weight he was
handicapped for and pull it off easy. He was to enter him in his
own name, the proper time before the races. If he won he was to
have ten per cent on winnings; if he lost, a ten-pound note would
do him. He could ride the weight with some lead in his saddle,
and he'd never wet his lips with grog till the race was over.

So that part of the work was chalked out. The real risky business
was to come.

. . . Next day was the great excitement of the meeting. The 'big
money' was all in the handicap, and there was a big field, with
two or three cracks up from Sydney, and a very good local horse
that all the diggers were sweet on. It was an open race, and every
man that had a note or a fiver laid it out on one horse or another.

Rainbow had been entered in proper time and all regular by old
Jacob, under the name of Darkie, which suited in all ways. He was
a dark horse, sure enough; dark in colour and dark enough as to
his performances – nobody knew much about them. We weren't
going to enter him in his right name, of course.

Old Jacob was a queer old fellow in all his ways and notions,
so we couldn't stable him in any of the stables in Turon, for fear
of his being 'got at', or something. So when I wanted to see him
the day before, the old fellow grinned, and took me away about
a mile from the course; and there was old Rainbow, snug enough
– in a tent, above all places! – but as fine as a star, and as fit as
ever a horse was brought to the post.

'What's the fun of having him under canvas?' I said. 'Who ever heard of a horse being trained in a tent before? – not but what he looks first-chop.'

'I've seen horses trained in more ways than one,' says he, 'and I can wind 'em up, in the stable and out of it, as mighty few in this country can – that is, when I put the muzzle on. There's a deal in knowing the way horses is brought up. Now this here's an excitable hoss in a crowd.'

'Is he?' I said. 'Why, he's as cool and steady as an old trooper when – '

'When the powder's burning and bullets is flying,' says the old chap, grinning again; 'but this here's a different crowd. When he's got a training saddle and seven or eight stone up, and there's two or three hundred horses rattling about this side on him and that, it brings out the old racehorse feeling that's in his blood, and never had a chance to show itself afore.'

'I see, and so you want to keep him quiet till the last minute?'

'That's just it,' says he; 'I've got the time to a second,' – here he pulls out a big old turnip of a silver watch – 'and I'll have him up just ready to be weighed out last. I never was late in my life.'

'All right,' I said, 'but don't draw it too fine. Have you got your weight all right?'

'Right to a hounce,' says he, 'nine stun four they've put on him, and him an untried horse. I told 'em it was weighting him out of the race, but they laughed at me. Never you mind, though, he can carry weight and stay too. My ten per cent's as safe as the bank. He'll put the stuns on all them nobs, too, that think a racehorse must always come out of one of their training stables.'

. . . The course had 20,000 people on it now if there was one. About a dozen horses stood stripped for the race, and the betting men were yelling out the odds as we got close enough to the stand to hear them. We had a good look at the lot. Three or four good-looking ones among them, and one or two flyers that had got in light as usual. Rainbow was nowhere about. Darkie was on the card, but no one seemed to know where he was or anything about him. We expected he'd start at 20 to 1, but somehow it leaked out that he was entered by old Jacob Benton, and that acted as a damper on the layers of the odds.

'Old Jake's generally there or thereabouts. If he's a duffer, it's the first one he's brought to the post. Why don't the old varmint show up?'

This was what I heard about and round, and we began to get uneasy ourselves, for fear that something might have happened to him or the horse. About 8 or 9 to 1 was all we could get, and that we took over and over again.

As the horses came up the straight, one after the other, having their pipe-openers, you'd have thought no race had been run that week, to see the interest all the people took in it. My word, Australia is a horsy country, and no mistake. With the exception of Arabia, perhaps, as they tell us about, I can't think as there's a country on the face of the earth where the people's fonder of horses. From the time they're able to walk, boys and girls, they're able to ride, and ride well. See the girls jump on barebacked, with nothing but a gunny-bag under 'em, and ride over logs and stones, through scrub and forest, down gullies, or along the side of a mountain. And a horse race, don't they love it? Wouldn't they give their souls almost – and they do often enough – for a real flyer, a thoroughbred, able to run away from everything in a country race. The horse is a fatal animal to us natives, and many a man's ruin starts from a bit of horse-flesh not honestly come by.

But our racing ain't going forward, and the day's passing fast. As I said, everybody was looking at the horses – coming along with the rush of the thoroughbred when he's 'on his top' for condition; his coat like satin, and his legs like iron.

. . . There was a stir in the crowd, and old Jacob came along across the course leading a horse with a sheet on, just as easy-going as if he'd a day to spare. One of the stewards rode up to him, and asked him what he meant by being so late.

The old chap pulls out his watch. 'You'll stick to your advertised time, won't you? I've time to weigh, time to pull off this here sheet and my overcoat, time to mount, and a minute to spare. I never was late in my life, governor.'

Most of the riding mob was down with the racehorses, a distance or so from the stand, where they was to start, the course being over two miles. So the weighing yard and stand was pretty well empty, which was just what old Jacob expected.

The old man walks over to the scales and has himself weighed all regular, declaring a pound overweight for fear of accidents. He gets down as quiet and easy as possible to the starting-point, and just in time to walk up steadily with the other horses, when down goes the starter's flag, and 'Off' was the word. Starlight and the Dawsons were down there waiting for him. As they went away one of the ringmen says, 'Ten to one against Darkie. I lay Darkie.' 'Done,' says Starlight; 'Will you do it in tens?' 'All right,' says the 'book'. 'I'll take you,' says both the Dawsons, and he entered their names.

They'd taken all they could get the night before at the hotel; and as no one knew anything about Darkie, and he had top weight, he hadn't many backers.

. . . We were close by the winning-post when they came past; they had to go another time round.

The Sydney horses were first and second, the diggers' favourite third; but old Rainbow, lying well up, was coming through the ruck hard held and looking full of running. They passed close by us. What a sight it is to see a dozen blood-horses in top condition come past you like a flash of lightning! How their hoofs thunder on the level turf! How the jockeys' silk jackets rustle in the wind they make! How muscle and sinew strain as they pretty near fly through the air! No wonder us young fellows, and the girls too, feel it's worth a year of their lives to go to a good race. Yes, and will to the world's end. 'O you darling Rainbow!' I heard Aileen say. 'Are you going to win this race and triumph over all these grand horses? What a sight it will be! I didn't think I could have cared for a race so much.'

It didn't seem hardly any time before they were half-way round again, and the struggle was on, in good downright earnest. One of the Sydney horses began to shake his tail. The other still kept the lead. Then the Turon favourite – a real game pebble of a little horse – began to show up.

'Hotspur, Hotspur! No. Bronzewing has it – Bronzewing. It's Bronzewing's race. Turon for ever!' the crowd kept yelling.

'Oh! look at Rainbow!' says Aileen. And just then, at the turn, old Jacob sat down on him. The old horse challenged Bronzewing, passed him, and collared Hotspur. 'Darkie! Darkie!' shouts everybody. 'No! Hotspur – Darkie's coming – Darkie – Darkie! I tell yer Darkie.' And as old Jacob made one last effort, and landed him a winner by a clear head, there was a roar went up from the whole crowd that might have been heard at Nulla Mountain.

Starlight jumps off the drag and leads the old horse into the weighing yard. The steward says 'Dismount.' No fear of old Jacob getting down before he heard that. He takes his saddle in his lap and gets into the scales. 'Weight,' says the clerk. Then the old fellow mounts and rides past the judge's box. 'I declare Mr Benton's horse Darkie to be the winner of the Turon Grand Handicap, Bronzewing second horse, Hotspur third,' says he.

Well, there was great cheering and hollering, though none knew exactly whose horse he was or anything about him; but an Australian crowd always likes to see the best horse win – and they like fair play – so Darkie was cheered over and over again, and old Jacob too.

Aileen stroked and petted him and patted his neck and rubbed his nose, and you'd really thought the old horse knew her, he seemed so gentle-like. Then the Commissioner came down and said Mrs Hautley, the police magistrate's wife, and some other ladies wanted to see the horse that had won the race. So he was taken over there and admired and stroked till old Jacob got quite crusty.

'It's an odd thing, Dawson,' says the Commissioner, 'nobody here knows this horse, where he was bred, or anything about him. Such a grand animal as he is too! I wish Morringer could have seen him: he's always raving about horses. How savage he'll be to have missed all the fun!'

'He's a horse you don't see every day,' says Bill Dawson. 'I'll give a couple of hundred for him right off.'

'Not for sale at present,' says old Jacob, looking like a cast-iron image. 'I'll send ye word when he is.'

'All right,' says Mr Dawson. 'What a shoulder, what legs, what loins he has! Ah! well, he'll be weighted out now, and you will be glad to sell him soon.'

'Our heads won't ache then,' says Jacob, as he turns round and rides away.

'Very neat animal, shows form,' drawls Starlight. 'Worth three hundred in the shires for a hunter; if he can jump, perhaps more; but depends on his manners – must have manners in the hunting field, Dawson, you know.'

'Manners or not,' says Bill Dawson, 'it's my opinion he could have won that race in a canter. I must find out more about him and buy him if I can.'

'I'll go you halves if you like,' says Starlight. 'I weally believe him to be a good animal.'

Just then up rides Warrigal. He looks at the old horse as if he had never seen him before, nor us neither. He rides by the heads of Mr Dawson's team, and as he does so his hat falls off, by mistake, of course. He jumps off and picks it up, and rides slowly down towards the tent.

It was the signal to clear.

Rolf Boldrewood (1888)

———

The Joys of Multiple Ownership

Judged purely on the figures, I appear to be a candidate for Twit of the Year. In the spring of 1987, I bought two shares in a company called Newmarket Thoroughbred Racing & Chasing (NTRC) at a cost of £395 each. The company's aim had been to sell 2,000 shares, producing £790,000 with which to buy up to twenty-five racehorses and pay for their training and racing. What it actually sold was 783 shares, producing £309,285 – a drop in the oil well to a horse-mad racing sheikh but still a worthwhile sum to the likes of you or me.

The plan was for NTRC to cease trading on 30 November 1988, and to redistribute any cash left in the kitty. It did indeed cease trading. It has now been put into formal liquidation. In the weeks ahead, I expect to receive a cheque. It will not be a large cheque because the final distribution from NTRC is expected to be between £15 and £20 a share. Let us call it £17.50.

In summary, my outlay was £790, of which I will recover £35. Call me Super Twit. But I am not downcast. I am not particularly upcast, come to that – but at least I approached the venture with my eyes open, well knowing what a hazardous investment racing can be.

It is an axiom of British racing that – except in rare instances – your money starts to whoosh away with a deafening roar from the moment you have anything to do with ownership. Do not speak to me about cocoa, soya beans, platinum or pork bellies because the whackiest commodities roller-coaster of the lot is buying, selling and racing horses. I *knew* this was so. Moreover, because NTRC was managed very properly and has produced detailed accounts for the brief period of its existence, I am now in a position to see precisely where the money went with such a whooshing roar.

The company was set up by Newmarket trainer Patrick Haslam and racing entrepreneur Anna Ludlow. In total, seventeen horses passed through its hands, yielding nine wins and seventeen places from eighty runs. As the trainer said at the recent winding-up meeting in Newmarket (a quiet affair attended by just seven shareholders): 'We haven't made a lot of money but we've had some successes and fulfilled our objectives.'

Where did the money go? Remember that the sale of shares attracted a start-up sum of £309,285. Purchases of bloodstock accounted for £147,149. When sold, these horses recouped £65,300, so that the deficit on buying and selling horses was £81,849. Prize-money yielded just £17,198 from eighty races.

One of the biggest items of expenditure was training fees, which totalled £69,017. Other items included: race manager's fees, £16,400; horse transport £10,376; entry fees and expenses, £14,135; VAT, £12,576; secretarial and office expenses, £15,739;

printing, advertising, etc., £13,985; legal and professional charges, £11,484; and on and on.

Given the scale of the trading losses (£253,874), plus the heavy start-up costs involved in forming and publicizing such a company (£34,408), it is easy to see how the initial capital sum of £309,285 was boiled down rapidly to the amount that is now left in the kitty (£21,003) from which various expenses are yet to be deducted.

I have always known that training and racing costs were hard to recover. Even the Maktoum family of Dubai, which is enjoying an enormously successful season on the racetracks of Europe, must find it hard to recoup its basic racing expenses which, in its case, run to many millions. What I had not realized was how few racehorses are resold at a profit or break-even, at least at the bottom of the market where NTRC operated. Let us take a look at a few of the horses that passed through its ownership. The sound you can hear is that of money whooshing.

Elegant Stranger   This was NTRC's one big success. He was bought at the Doncaster sales for 5,000 guineas plus VAT (£6,037.50), won two races as a two-year-old and was placed second four times as a three-year-old. He was resold for £11,550.

Baxtergate   A real blot on the landscape. He cost £15,784.50 and was described as a top-class potential hurdler. When they got him to Newmarket, he did not appear sound and had a swelling on his tendon. A veterinary scan showed him to be useless for NTRC's requirements. There were heated exchanges between NTRC, the sales company and the horse's previous trainer. Finally, NTRC was given a £5,001 credit by the sales company.

Stormy Eve   An appalling little madam. You might have seen her on the telly, behaving like a cow at Sandown and refusing to go down to the start, a performance which sent her value crashing. She had cost us £3,622.50. Eventually, she was exported to Italy for 800 guineas. Some Italians spend that much on a sweater. I hope that she is safe and well and minding her p's and q's.

Zarafion   Cost £6,300. Not a lot was thought of him. Sold to Sweden for £1,500.

Pertain   Cost £2,500. He won a seller and was bought in for 3,750 guineas. On one occasion, was ridden by Steve Cauthen. Eventually sold to Sweden for £3,800.

Andartis   NTRC bought 65 per cent of him for £10,000. Thought to have been a promising hurdler but developed tendon trouble. Stake sold for £496.74.

Llanpadrig   A steeplechaser. Cost £16,834.50. Suffered various troubles. Finally sold privately to go point-to-pointing for £4,000.

Howhus   Another very expensive failure. He cost £5,704.50 but was sold for £400.

Easy Line   Cost £9,660, and actually won twice on the Flat. Sold privately for £3,000.

Lucayan Gold   Cost £16,800. He had two runs over hurdles and several runs on the Flat without success, although he was thought to have run an excellent race against top-class hurdlers at Huntingdon on one occasion. Sold for £7,560.

And so it went.

Naturally, the people who sell and train racehorses always insist that there is more to the sport of kings than dollars and cents. There is the matter of 'psychic payout' – that ecstatic glow of pleasure and satisfaction that is reckoned to descend on you, bringing tears of happiness to your eyes, even while the horse that you own, or are associated with, is finishing last or savaging its stable lad or behaving generally in a manner bound to send its value plummeting.

I do not envy the Maktoums. At present, they are winning everything in sight. The money is rolling in. But that cannot drown the vast roar of the money that is whooshing out.

Michael Thompson-Noël (1989)

Racing has been called many things; 'a rich man's sport' is at least accurate, and this aspect is entertainingly confirmed. Above all else, there is nothing like a winner, whether it's a Classic at New-market or a claimer at Southwell in February. Without that fact there would be no racing and given a bit of luck and good management the syndicates can achieve the 'psychic payout', without, normally, serious financial injury and, generally, with considerable enjoyment.

———

How to Bet

There is no doubt that Barnum was not exaggerating when he said a mug was born every minute. In ninety-nine towns out of a hundred it is the bookmaker who owns the longest, most powerful and most luxurious car, smokes the best cigars, drinks the most champagne and is about the only person who knows where the next pot of caviare is coming from. Everybody can see this, but nevertheless the majority will keep on betting.

Of course, the money they lose (and they nearly all do lose in the long run) is not all thrown away. They get a tremendous lot of pleasure in trying to pick winners and waiting for the results. However, that doesn't mean that they are not mugs – maybe not as big mugs as the people who put sixpences and shillings into one-armed bandits, but mugs just the same. Having a system or going strictly on form generally saves most punters money throughout the season. They don't lose as much as those who bet indiscriminately, or those who must have a bet even if they have to resort to the old pin business. There are certain people with whom gambling is a mania, and it is the most difficult of diseases to cure. I have only known one dyed-in-the-wool gambler who was cured and that is Rae Johnstone, the jockey; Rae cured himself.

Even Rae was not as bad as the man in a certain town who, when asked by a bartender where he was going to spend the evening, said he was going to So-and-So's Club to play roulette. When the bartender said, 'Good God, don't you know the wheel is crooked?' the gambler replied, 'Of course I do, but it's the only one in town.'

The best way for a novice who only goes racing occasionally to find a winner is first of all to study the form book carefully. Form works out right more often than not.

However, there are lots of things to be taken into account, and so it is a very good idea to watch the horses in the paddock before the race and cantering down to the start.

The adage 'Never bet on a handicap; but if you must, back the top weight', is still a very good maxim for the simple reason that only a good horse is given top weight. Another thing about a handicap: back a horse that has run well in a Classic race, no matter what weight it has been allotted. Maybe you will find it is top weight anyway. Nearly every spring, almost blinded by tears, I read how the bookmakers, murdered by the winner of the Lincolnshire Handicap, will need extreme luck in the Grand National to recover their enormous losses. Just the same, I still think you'd be better off playing roulette – providing the wheel isn't crooked – than betting in a handicap.

Bet on horses that have won before, even if they have to carry a penalty. Winning horses so often win again. That is why it's a good idea to follow a winning two-year-old until it gets beaten, and then back the one that beats it.

A good jockey, a good horse, a good bet. Follow a stable or a jockey in form. Pick out a good looker; you very seldom see a bad looker in the winning enclosure after the race. So much the better if the one you pick is a good resolute walker, and moves well cantering down. Moving well means a perfectly balanced rhythmic stride – it's all in the rhythm.

Now for the don'ts. Don't back an animal that's sweating a lot, unless you know it has been like this before and won, or if it is a characteristic of the breed, or if it is a hot day.

Don't bet on a horse wearing ankle boots in flat racing: even the best-fitting and lightest of them weigh too much on the wrong place. And bet very seldom on one wearing bandages, unless you know the whys and wherefores. Don't bet on one that looks as if it is 'turning it up' when being led around – laying its ears back, switching its tail round, or kicking in a nasty way with one leg.

On the other hand you can back one that gives a squeal and good old-fashioned jump and kick; that just means it's feeling well.

Don't bet on a horse that has got a long winter coat, especially a filly; it generally means, in the spring, that it is not yet ready, and in the autumn that it has gone off.

Don't bet on one that looks very light and has to wear a breast girth to keep the saddle from slipping back. The very light ones often have what is known as the Danebury mark ('poverty lines', to hunting people) a deep mark running down the quarters from either side of its tail.

Don't underrate horses from abroad or, for that matter, any horse that has travelled a long way to the meeting: they wouldn't have sent him if he hadn't got a chance. Don't underestimate a horse that wins any type of race easily – if the opposition is bad it isn't the winner's fault.

Last, but certainly not least, when you have made your selection, don't be talked out of it by anybody; it's so easily done because most of us are inclined to listen to other people's opinions too much.

Jack Leach (1961)

JACK LEACH (1901–72), *a popular member of a long-established Newmarket racing family, rode with great success until increasing weight caused him to relinquish his licence in 1931 and start training. On retirement in the early fifties he became a widely read writer and journalist.*

_____

The Charms of Newmarket

So long as horse-racing remains our national sport, Newmarket will stand unrivalled as the place where it can be best enjoyed and where its attraction can best be appreciated. At many of the great race gatherings of the year the racing is quite of a secondary matter.

The Derby is a monster picnic, Ascot a full-dress parade at the height of the season, and, at Goodwood, Society displays its glitter in public for the last time before betaking itself to the pleasures of yachting and shooting, of country life, or continental travel. Doncaster indeed would be a formidable rival to Newmarket were it not for the imperfections of its course. The North of England loves a horse for the horse's own sake: the South for the sake of what can be made out of him. Yorkshiremen are roused to an extraordinary pitch of enthusiasm by a genuine contest between thoroughbreds of real merit, for they know the points of a horse, are shrewd judges, care little for mediocrities, and give the second place in their thoughts to pecuniary considerations. We fear many of their southern fellow countrymen, on the other hand, care not a button what the merits of a horse may be as long as they win their money.

But the nature of the course at Doncaster effectually prevents it from taking equal rank with Newmarket. There is a very awkward turn – not so bad as the dreaded Tattenham Corner at Epsom, but still the cause of much anxiety and many disappointments – just at the most critical point of the course, which has to be safely negotiated. In the short-distance races there is a fearful rush from the start to get the inside place at the bend, and it is a mere lottery which horses get through and which get shut in; and moreover the course is hardly wide enough for a large field.

At Newmarket the state of affairs is very different. There is no fear of jostling or of disappointment on the matchless Rowley Mile; and when, in the waning light of an October afternoon, forty horses thunder abreast up the Cambridgeshire hill you can see that even if the field was half as large again there would be room and to spare. Then there is every variety of course to suit all kinds of horses. There are courses for such as cannot go down a hill, for such as cannot go up a hill, for such as are quick on their legs and love a short and speedy journey, and for such as are slow beginners and require a distance of ground to show their real powers; courses of every variety of gradient and every variety of length (from the time-honoured Beacon, which Osbaldeston traversed fifty times in a single day, to the short and easy last half of the Abingdon Mile, or the now disused yearling course of two furlongs only).

The turf, too, on Newmarket Heath is of a luxuriant quality that neither the droughts of spring nor the 'branding summer suns' can seriously affect; and on the other side of the Ditch – that paradise of racing men where the July meeting is held – the running ground is like a carpet of velvet, and you can either lounge on a bank of thyme, or, screening yourself from the sun's rays under the shelter of the plantation, survey the racing at your leisure.

But above all the charm of Newmarket is its quiet and its perfect freedom. After a week at Ascot or Epsom, a visit to Goodwood, or a trip to Liverpool, what are one's experiences? A struggle at railway stations to obtain a seat, a struggle up dusty hills leading to the scene of the sport, almost a hand-to-hand fight to get into or out of the ring, into or out of the saddling paddock, up to the top of the stand or down again; while all the time one's ears are dinned by the never-ceasing Babel of voices from which there is no escape; or the most desperate struggle of all, to get home at the end of the day, remains to be undergone. In fact, at the close of an ordinary race week the visitor finds himself reduced to the last stage of physical exhaustion, but at Newmarket he can enjoy racing without the necessity of exertion and without incurring fatigue.

He can drive – or better still ride – pretty much where he likes. The Heath is open to him, and he can suit his own tastes. He can gallop down to see the start, or station himself at the Bushes or some favourite point where racing veterans say they can always pick out the winner as the horses flash by, or he can remain near the judge's chair and enjoy the excitement of a well-contested finish. There is no mob of excursionists, with their ginger-beer bottles and sandwich bags; there are no nigger minstrels, no acrobats, no comic singers with their knee-breeches and shillelaghs, and no army of policemen shouting out that the course must be cleared. The few hundred spectators know very well when to get off the course without being told, the numbers go up at the appointed moment with military punctuality, the horses canter past you to the starting-post, each accompanied by his own select following of admirers or critics, the white flag – they always use a white flag at Newmarket – is elevated for a moment and then falls, for the starter's patience is rarely taxed, the horses sweep by, and the race is over without any fuss, disturbance or difficulty.

It is true there are great days at Newmarket when the neighbouring countryfolk come out in full force, and when the sporting

Cambridge undergraduate is painfully conspicuous. The last is the special nuisance of the Two Thousand and Cambridgeshire days, and his semi-barbarous antics vex the soul of the Admiral, and cause the veterans of the racing world to indulge in expressive but uncomplimentary language. Either he careers wildly over the sacred Heath, half on and half off the back of a fearfully and wonderfully made screw, or he drives a pair of such animals in a tandem – at least we should say he is drawn along by them, for he is innocent of the arts of driving, and the leader turns round and looks the wheeler pleasantly in the face whenever he pleases. He brings great store of provisions, and may be seen at any moment eating chicken and college pies. He drinks copious draughts of effervescent liquor, which has been retailed to him as champagne, and then he throws the bottles away among the carriages, and they get broken and horses cut their feet – all of which is very unpleasant. Towards the end of the afternoon he gets very noisy and occasionally quarrelsome, and his return journey to Cambridge is marked by a series of hair-breadth escapes of which he has probably only a confused remembrance on the morrow. Everyone is thankful when these days are over, and Newmarket resumes its peaceful serenity. It is in the meetings that have no great days – the First October, July, the Craven – that the real charms of Newmarket are apparent.

'There is an end to everything,' a great diner-out remarked, 'except to Upper Wimpole Street,' and the altered tastes and habits of the present day bid fair to put an end before long to many of the peculiarly distinguishing features of Newmarket. The old stand – half barn, half barracks – on the July course, from whose quaint windows the Merry Monarch, with Rochester and Arlington at his side, witnessed the beginnings of our national sport, has passed away and a brand new one will be erected in its place. At the end of the Rowley Mile, also quite an imposing structure is well-nigh completed, with refreshment rooms, enclosures and the whole paraphernalia of indispensables for modern racegoers. Our fathers thought little of the torrents of rain that so often sweep across the Heath, and they were capable of galloping about three or four hours without feeling a constant urge for bottled beer and brandy and soda. Their descendants feel differently and I am sorry for it.

A circular course also is to be made so that languid spectators may see a race in its entirety without troubling themselves to move an inch from their snug positions on the stand; and as I utterly hate and detest circular courses I am sorry for this innovation also. Orthodox white posts and rails are rapidly supplanting the cords which used to be sufficient to mark out the finish of the different races; and soon the Jockey Club donkey will be one of the few relics of the past. His day, too, will come; and then the judge's chair will travel, I suppose, along a tramway from one winning-post to another.

Well, we must not repine that the inevitable law of change should make itself felt at Newmarket as elsewhere: while we remember the past with fondness, we may still hope that the fortunes of the greatest racecourse in the world will continue to flourish under altered circumstances.

Newmarket Journal (1875)

Idyllic as Victorian racing at Newmarket may have been for some, it was not, it seems, without its ration of hooligans, albeit of a different source from today's. Undergraduates now appear to have less time to devote to the Turf.

Both racecourses at Newmarket were laid out before the interests of the public entered into Jockey Club calculations. In recent years, under enlightened and progressive management, much has been done to improve the lot of spectators. When once acquired, a taste for racing at Newmarket is usually permanent.

As We are Now

The end of the decade finds the Turf in a new guise. At no time has the overall standard of competition been higher. From the immediate post-war years, when French horses dominated our important middle-distance and staying races, we can now take on the world, as shown by the successes of English-trained horses abroad. Notable among them was the victory in the Prix de l'Arc de Triomphe of Carroll House; his form here does not entitle him to be rated higher than a top second-class performer.

That is not to say that the great horses of the past were inferior to their modern counterparts, but that class below the top fell more sharply in those days. Formerly it was possible to gauge the opposition fairly accurately by the status of different racecourses; one would have been unlikely to meet an Ascot horse at Leicester, or a Kempton horse at Carlisle. Today, anyone thinking of finding a pushover at Folkestone or Hamilton could be disillusioned. This change has come about through the vast Arab investment in English racing and breeding, by buying the cream of international bloodstock and having an unprecedented number of horses in training.

The behaviour of the Arabs is impeccable. They are excellent employers, race their horses openly and competitively, are modest in victory, uncomplaining in defeat and understand and appreciate horses. The only snag to their involvement is that its size unbalances racing as a whole. Having so many high-class horses, the Arabs mop up many small races with better horses than ran in them in the past, making it difficult for others to win anywhere with a moderate performer nowadays.

But in the excellence of the horses competing the racing public has never had it so good, and since the essence of the sport is the survival of the fittest, the Arabs can hardly be blamed for the strength of their support. In any case, the most expensively bred or bought horses do not always win the best races, and the Arabs have yet to produce a stallion of consequence. At the same time, some adjustment to the pattern of racing below top level seems desirable. Races for horses bought under a certain sum or sired by stallions standing at comparatively modest fees, would encourage less affluent owners and breeders, some of whom are drifting out of racing through the power of the opposition.

Below the veneer of top-class racing and horses, the English Turf leaves something to be desired. It is suffering from having grown too big, so that standards in racing stables have dropped owing to a shortage of good labour. While the best horses may be properly looked after, many of the lesser ones are not. Ask any experienced stableman, and he will confirm this.

To some extent this is a problem of wages. Though these may be adequate in the best stables, where large bonuses are also paid, lower down the scale and at the bottom there is hardship.

If the labour in stables and on studs is to improve, there must be an appreciable increase in the minimum wage and a reduction in the number of horses bred and in training. This will produce a demand for higher prize-money in minor races which, though desirable, may not be the panacea hoped for, since costs will rise too, and rich owners will continue to win many of the smaller races.

Racing and breeding is expensive and cannot be approached as if it were part of the Welfare State; there is money to be made out of it, though more likely lost. However, the comparatively new introduction of group ownership offers the chance of active involvement for a reasonable outlay.

Accommodation for horses, upon whom the whole enterprise depends, is inadequate on some racecourses, as is that for stable staff. This was revealed in a survey made by the *Sporting Life*, which has produced some improvement. Amenities for racegoers fall below those in other main racing countries. Most of the stands built since the war are flawed, others obsolete. With rare exception, racecourse catering varies between fairly good and frightful, and is expensive.

Much of all this is due to lack of money, but complacency and bad planning have contributed. The problem of finance is ever present. It stems from failure in the past to take advantage of the change in the betting laws to benefit racing, and from the way in which the need for finance was presented later.

Betting has always been an integral part of racing, and course bookmakers are part of the scene, which would be duller without them. While a Totalisator monopoly would bring in more money, the public prefer a choice of the two systems. However, the taking-over of many of the small firms by large combines has resulted in the public being exploited through penal restrictions, deceptive advertising and chicken-hearted trading, with too much money being channelled into the big firms' outside investments.

Gone is the individuality, gambling spark and character of old-time bookmaking. The whole system needs reviewing and putting under stricter control to protect the punter and benefit racing as a whole. Adoption of the method of betting in Victoria, Australia, might be the answer. There the course bookmakers operate under rules giving the punter a fair deal, and all off-course money goes through the Tote.

Any change needing legislation should be presented in such form as to make it clear that money so produced goes to improvement in matters such as safety, medical and veterinary facilities, amenities for the racing public and those who work in the sport. Men, women and horses take priority before prize-money. The begging-bowl attitude of the past must be shunned.

The conduct of racing is stricter and fairer than in the days before the patrol and video cameras, when many infringements went undetected. While no authority is beyond criticism, much aimed at the Jockey Club is undeserved. Training has advanced with new techniques such as all-weather surfaces and swimming, and horses with a future are given more time to develop than in former days.

Jockeyship suffers from the fashion of riding with exaggeratedly short stirrup leathers, and too frequent use of the whip in the wrong hand, resulting in unnecessary falls and failure to keep horses straight. Excessive use of the whip is diminishing. At the time of writing the final trials for all-weather racing have taken place, and racing on these surfaces on the flat and over hurdles has gone forward at Lingfield and Southwell. The object is to increase betting turnover, provide scope for moderate horses and offset loss of meetings from bad weather. Whether this will enhance the sport remains to be seen.

The fault of policy in general is that quality and standards are being sacrificed to quantity and money, regardless of what is entailed, and insufficient attention is given to the needs of genuine racegoers. Private boxes bring in revenue, but too often have prefer-ence over accommodation for the true racing public. The traditional features and values of the sport are being edged out by the demands of sponsors. Programmes are manipulated to suit these and television coverage.

Most owners are in the game for pleasure and not profit, and the vulgarization and *ennui* attached to some sponsored races removes much of the enjoyment of winning them.

The public go racing primarily to see good horses and good racing. Their chief requirements are good viewing of the racing and horses in the paddock; protection from the weather and dry footing; satisfactory betting facilities; decent, simple food and drink, at reasonable prices, served quickly; efficient car-parking, at fair prices or free. There is room for improvement in these items. All possible steps are being taken to cope with hooliganism and drunkenness on racecourses, and seem to be succeeding.

The health of the Turf is best measured from the grass roots upwards, not by the growth of the lushest area. By the same token, planners should make and apply that well-proved precept of horsemastership: 'no foot, no horse'.

John Hislop (1989)

SOURCES

Books

Astley, Sir John, Bt, *Fifty Years of My Life*, Hurst and Blackett, 1894, p. 221

Beasley, P. T. (Rufus), *Pillow to Post*, privately published, 1981, p. 33

Binstead, Arthur M., *A Pink 'Un and a Pelican*, Buss Sands, 1898, p. 318

Boldrewood, Rolf, *Robbery under Arms*, Remington, 1881, p. 320

Briscoe, Basil, *The Life of Golden Miller*, Hutchinson, 1939, p. 244

Brown, Harry, *Steeplechasing*, Lonsdale Library, Vol. XXXII, Seeley Service, 1954, p. 212

Blyth, Henry, *The Pocket Venus*, Weidenfeld and Nicolson, 1966, p. 280

Chetwynd, Sir George, Bt, *Racing Reminiscences*, Longman, Green, 1891, p. 307

Chifney, Samuel, *Genius Genuine*, privately published, 1792, p. 187

Davy, Colin, *Ups and Downs*, Collins, 1939, p. 240

Gallier, Susan, *One of the Lads*, Stanley Paul, 1988, p. 112

Gilbey, Quintin, *Fun Was My Living*, Hutchinson, 1970, pp. 51, 192

Gordon, Adam Lindsay, *Collected Poems*, Foulis, 1912, p. 272

Graham, Clive, Introduction by the 18th Earl of Derby, *Hyperion*, J. A. Allen, 1967, p. 147

Herbert, Ivor, *Arkle*, William Luscombe, 1966, p. 265

Hewitt, Abram S., *Great Breeders and Methods*, The Thoroughbred Record, 1982, p. 106

Hislop, J. L., *Anything but a Soldier*, Michael Joseph, 1965, p. 252

——*The Brigadier*, Secker and Warburg, 1973, p. 149

Lambton, The Hon. George, *In My Opinion*, Constable, 1928 (edited by Major W. E. Lyon), p. 68

——*Men and Horses I Have Known*, Thornton Butterworth, 1924, pp. 6, 191, 225

——*Scapa Flow*, privately published, 1937, p. 135

Leach, Jack, *Sods I Have Cut on the Turf*, Victor Gollancz, 1961, p. 331

Lehndorff, Count, *Horse Breeding Recollections*, Horace Cox, 1883, p. 65

Lyle, R. C., *Brown Jack*, Putnam, 1934, p. 239

Mellon, Paul, *Address at 200th Anniversary of the York Gimcrack Club*, 1970 The Spiral Press, New York, 1971, p. 129

Mortimer, Roger, *Anthony Mildmay*, MacGibbon and Kee, 1956, p. 248

——*The Flat since 1939*, George Allen and Unwin, 1979, p. 259

——*The Jockey Club*, Cassell, 1958, p. 1

——*More Great Racehorses of the World*, Michael Joseph, 1972 (with Peter Willett), p. 165

——*Twenty Great Racehorses*, Cassell, 1967, p. 159

Munnings, Sir Alfred, *The Second Burst*, Museum Press, 1951, p. 142

Murless, Sir Noël, *The Golden Post, Richard Stone Reeves and Patrick Robinson*, Fine Art Enterprises, 1985, p. 89

Onslow, Richard, *Headquarters*, Great Ouse Press, Cambridge, 1983, p. 6

O'Sullevan, Peter, *Calling the Horses*, Stanley Paul, 1989, p. 96

Paterson, A. B., *Collected Verse*, Angus and Robertson, 1953, p. 215

Persse, H. S., *Flat Racing*, Lonsdale Library, Vol XXVIII, Seely Service, 1940, p. 72

Radcliffe, John B., *Ashgill, The Life and Times of John Osborne*, Sands, 1900, p. 315

Ramsden, Caroline, *Ladies in Racing*, Stanley Paul, 1973, p. 43

Richards, Sir Gordon, *My Story*, Hodder and Stoughton, 1955, p. 28

Rous, The Hon. Captain H. J., RN, *The Laws and Practice of Horseracing*, Bailey Brothers, 1850, p. 125

Seth-Smith, Michael, *A Classic Connection*, Secker and Warburg, 1983, p. 226

——*Bred for the Purple*, Leslie Frewen, 1969, p. 15

Skeaping, John, *Drawn from Life*, Collins, 1977, p. 310

Spenser, Edward, *The Great Game*, Grant Richards, 1900, p. 210

Sutherland, Douglas, *The Yellow Earl*, Cassell, 1965, p. 12

Thormanby, *Kings of the Turf*, Hutchinson, 1898, p. 188

Welcome, John, *Infamous Occasions*, Michael Joseph, 1980, p. 229

Willett, Peter (with Roger Mortimer), *More Great Racehorses of the World*, Michael Joseph, 1972, p. 165

Other Sources

Bloodstock Breeders' Review, Vols. I, XXXVII, The British Bloodstock Agency, 1912, pp.127, 145

The British Racehorse
  John Hislop, 1974, p. 18

The Daily Telegraph and Morning Post
  'Marlborough' (Lord Oaksey), 18 June, 1962, p. 262

The European Racehorse
  H. J. Joel, 1983, p. 36

The Field
  William Douglas-Home, 1987, p. 59
  John Hislop, December 1989, p. 337

The Financial Times
  Michael Thompson-Noel, 12 August 1989, p. 327

Flat Racing
  The Badminton Library, 1885, p. 211

Horse and Hound
  Donovan, 31 May, 1974, p. 308
  John Oaksey, 12 November, 1987, p. 204

The Newmarket Journal
  Anon., November 1875, p. 337

The Observer
  Lester Piggott (with Kenneth Harris), 7 June, 1970, p. 199

The Racehorse
  Geoffrey Gilbey, 1963, p. 316

Racehorses of 1986
  Timeform Ltd, 1986, p. 268

Racing Post
    Tony Morris, 1 June, 1989, p. 109
The Royal Hong Kong Jockey Club (Racehorse Owners' Dinner)
    Henry Cecil, 1988, p. 100
A Selection of Essays
    Portway Press, Timeform Ltd, 1982
The Sporting Life
    John Hislop, November 1985, p. 195
    David Swannell, 30 October, 1986, p. 304
The Sporting Magazine
    Anon., 1866, p. 319
The Times
    Simon Barnes, 16 March, 24 July, 1989, p. 151
    John Hislop, p. 153, 296, 336
    Michael Seely, 7 October, 1989, p. 52
    Alan Lee, 20 November, 1989, p. 207
The Tote Annual
    Peter Burrell (with Kenneth Harris), 1966, p. 83
    Geoffrey Freer, 1967, p. 299
    Geoffrey Gilbey, 1966, p. 312
    Peter Willett, 1966, p. 131

ACKNOWLEDGEMENTS

For permission to reprint copyright material the publishers gratefully acknowledge the following. Where the copyright-holder is other than the original publisher, the latter's name is given in brackets. Faber and Faber apologizes for any errors or omissions in this list and would be grateful to be notified of any corrections that should be incorporated in any future reprint of this volume. Sources are listed alphabetically by author.

'Admiration for Horse of the Decade' by Simon Barnes (*The Times*, 1989), The Author; 'Dessie in World without Subtitles' by Simon Barnes (*The Times*, 1989), The Author; *Pillow to Post* by Rufus Beasley (1981), published privately; *The Pocket Venus* by Henry Blyth (Weidenfeld & Nicholson, 1966), Anthony Shiel Associates Ltd; *The Life of Golden Miller* by Basil Briscoe (Hutchinson & Co Ltd, 1939), Random Century Group; 'Breeding to Win the Derby' by Peter Burrell (1966), *The Tote Racing Annual*; 'Address to Racehorse Owners' Dinner', RHKJC, by Henry Cecil (1988), Henry Cecil; *Ups and Downs* by Colin Davy (Collins, 1939), David Higham Associates Ltd; 'Making a Handicap' by Geoffrey Freer (1967), *The Tote Racing Annual*; *One of the Lads* by Susan Gallier (1988), Stanley Paul; 'A Racing Bore is Cured' by Geoffrey Gilbey (*The Racehorse*, 1963), Raceform Ltd.; 'The Gentle Art of Tipping' by Geoffrey Gilbey (1966), *The Tote Racing Annual*; *Fun was my Living* by Quintin Gilbey (Hutchinson & Co, 1970) Random Century Group; 'L. Piggott, An Interview' by Kenneth Harris (1976), *The Observer*; *Arkle* by Ivor Herbert (William Luscombe, 1966), The Author; *Great Breeders and Their Methods* by Abram Hewitt (1982), Thoroughbred Publications Inc.; *Anything But A Soldier* by John Hislop (1965), Michael Joseph Ltd; *The Brigadier* by John Hislop (1973), Martin Secker & Warburg; 'Piggott & Sir Gordon' by John Hislop (1985), *The Sporting Life*; 'The Sixth Earl of Rosebery' by John Hislop (The British Racehorse, 1974), Turf Newspapers Ltd.; 'Turf's Whip Hand' by John Hislop (1989), *The Field*; 'The Derby Horse with a Rum Idea of Nap' by William Douglas Home (1987), *The Field*; 'Racing Reminiscences' by H. J. Joel (1983), *The European Racehorse*; *Men and Horses I Have Known* by Hon George Lambton (Thornton Butterworth, 1924), J. A. Allen & Co; *Scapa Flow* by Hon George Lambton (1937), published privately; *Sods I Have Cut on the Turf* by Jack Leach (Gollancz, 1961), Executors of the Author's Estate; *Conquering Hero Driven by Obsession for Winners* by Alan Lee (1989), *The Times*; *Brown Jack* by R. C. Lyle (Putnam, 1934), The Bodley Head Ltd.; 'Two Hundredth Dinner of the York Gimcrack Club', Extract from an Address by Paul Mellon (1970), The Author; 'Unique Problems Beset-ting The Royal Operation' by Tony Morris (1989), *Racing Post*; *The Flat Since 1939* by Roger Mortimer (George Allen & Unwin, 1979), Unwin Hyman Ltd.; *The Jockey Club* by Roger Mortimer (Cassell, 1958), Mac-millan Inc.; *More Great Racehorses of the World* by Roger Mortimer and Peter Willett (1972), Michael Joseph Ltd.; *Twenty Great Horses* by Roger Mortimer (Cassell, 1967), Macmillan Inc.; *The Second Burst* by Sir Alfred Munnings (Museum Press, 1951), The Alfred Munnings Art Museum, Dedham; 'Cauthen Takes Title' by Audax (Lord Oaksey) (1987), *Horse And Hound*; 'Heroic Mandarin' by Marlborough (Lord Oaksey) (*Daily Telegraph and Morning Post*, 1962), The Author; *Headquarters* by Rich-ard Onslow (Great Ouse Press, 1983), The Author; *Calling The Horses* by Peter O'Sullevan (1989), Stanley Paul; *Ladies in Racing* by Caroline Ramsden (1973), Stanley Paul; *My Story* by Sir Gordon Richards (1955), Hodder and Stoughton; 'The Maktoum Family Business' by Michael Seely (1989), *The Times*; *A Classic Connection* by Michael Seth-Smith (1983), Martin Secker and Warburg; *Drawn From Life* by John Skeaping (1977), Collins (UK & Commonwealth), Toby Eady Associates (USA); *The Yellow Earl* by Douglas Sutherland (Cassell, 1965), Macmillan Inc.; 'Rule 153' by David Swannell (1986), *The Sporting Life*; 'That's Not Niagara' by Michael Thompson-Noel (1989), *Financial Times*; *A Selection of Essays* by Timeform (1982), Timeform; *Infamous Occasions* by John Welcome (Michael Joseph, 1980), John Johnson Ltd.; 'St Simon' by Peter Willett (1966), *The Tote Racing Annual*.

INDEX

Abbot's Trace, 229
Abdulla, Prince Khaled, 52, 57, 206
Abelia, 171
Abercorn, Marquess and Marchioness
   of, 285
Abernant, 90, 93, 165, 260
d'Abernon, Lord, 21
Aboukir, 81
Aboyeur, 227
Absurdity, 42, 43
Acropolis, 160
Adventurer, 316
Afterthought, 23
Aggressor, 174
Airborne, 162
Alcide, 36, 164
Aldborough, 163
Aldby Park, 128
Alexanders, owners of Lexington, 106,
   108
Alexandra, Queen, 228
Alibhai, 89
Allenby, Field Marshal, Lord, 20
Almagest, 149, 150
Alston, Walter, 135–6
Altesse Royale, 94
Alycidon, 107, 159–64, 298
Amour Drakè, 261, 262
Amuse, 42, 43
Anchora, 136
Andartis, 330
Angelica, 133
Anglesey, 5th Marquess of, 296
Anmer, 226, 227, 228
l'Anson, William, 283
Anthony, Ivor, 239
Anthony, Jack, 145, 146, 213
Anthony, Owen, 246
Apelle, 82, 172, 173
Apology, 315, 316
April the Fifth, 22
Arab Maid Family, 146

Arbar, 162
Archer, F., 10–12, 60, 132, 134,
   189–90, 191, 198, 199, 203, 207,
   210, 221, 222, 223, 231
Ard Patrick, 32
Arden, 208, 210
Ardross, 91, 92
Aristophanes, 89
Arkle, 146, 248, 265–8
Armada, 268
Arousal, 160
Ascot, 333, 335
Ascot Gold Cup, 22, 42, 92, 133, 134,
   136, 140, 141, 155, 159, 162–3,
   297
Asquith, Raymond, 16
Astley, Sir John, 222, 224, 225
Astley Institute, The, 224
Astor, Sir John, 61, 107, 253
Atlantic, 11
Atmah, 39
'Audax' (Lord Oaksey), 176
Aurelius, 92
Aureole, 159
Aurora, 159
Avenger, 248, 249

Bachelor's Button, 42
Bahram, 94, 141, 178
Baillie, Lady, 50
Bakharoff, 268
Balding, Ian, 130, 181
Ballymoss, 94, 149
Banstead Selling Plate, 27
Barbour, Frank, 146
Barbs, The, 125
Barcaldine, 222
Bareed, 241, 242, 243
Barnes, 241, 243
Barnes, Simon, 152, 272
Barnes Park, 169
Barry, R., 209
Bartlet's Childers, 129

Bashful, 23
Basto, 126
Bates Motel, 95
Batthyany, Prince, 132, 133
Baxtergate, 329
Bayardo, 155, 297
Baytown, 259
Beary, M., 195
Beasley, H., 196, 247
Beasley, P. T., 33–6, 196
Beatty, Mrs Chester, 241
Beatty, Peter, 193
Beaver II, 263
Beckhampton, 28, 165, 166, 168, 231, 234
Bedford Lodge, 6, 7, 221
Bedford Stakes, 166
Beech House Stud, 54
Beechwood House, 246, 247
Bella Paola, 97
Bellini, 173
Belper, Lord, 22
Bend Or, 37
Bendir, Arthur, 26
Bennet, Captain G. H., 242
Benny Lynch, 162
Beresford, Hon. Caroline Agnes, 6
Beresford, Lord William, 191
Bertie, Norman, 30
Bethersden Marble, 314
Biddlecombe, T. 209
Big Game, 15
Billy Barton, 145
Bisgood, Cdr John, 194, 195
Bismarck, Prince, 61
Black Jester, 37
Black Tarquin, 161, 162, 163, 164
Blair Athol, 283
Blakeney, 179
Blandford, 107, 164, 233
Blankney Stud, 67
Blenheim, 159
Bleu Azur, 94
Blue Peter, 22, 23, 141
Blue Prince, 245, 249
Blushing Groom, 95, 109, 112, 151
Bob and Peter, 61
Bobette, 192

Bois Roussel, 174, 192, 193, 194, 260
Bold Ruler, 92
Boldrewood, Rolf, 320
Booklaw, 139
Borealis, 160
Bostwick, G., 248
Bosworth, 140–1
Boussac, Marcel, 107, 159, 168
Boyd-Rochfort, Captain Sir Cecil, 33–6
Brave Cry, 245
Breasley, A. E., 98, 176, 199, 206
Breeder's Cup, 269
Brickfields Stud, 159
Bridges, Hon. and Revd Henry, 128
Brigadier Gerard, 149–50, 155, 180, 181, 182, 182–4, 269, 312
Briscoe, Basil, 247
Britt, E., 163
Brocklesby Stakes, 298
Brocklesby Trial Stakes, 314
Bronzino, 37
Brooks, Charles, 208
Brookshaw, T., 209
Brown, Harry, 215
Brown, Jack, 233, 240
Browne, Liam, 206
Browne, Thomas A., 320
Bruce, Hon. Eva, 23
Buckle, F., 198, 204
Buckpasser, 92
Bullock, Frank, 195
Bunbury, Sir Charles, 126, 130
Burns, T. P., 308
Burpham, 167
Burrell, Peter, 83–9
Busted, 90, 93, 94
Bustino, 134
Busybody, 134
Butters, Frank, 94–5, 137, 138, 139, 141
Byerly Turk, The, 125, 129

Caergwrle, 90, 91, 92, 94, 171
Caldwell, J., 239
Call Boy, 133
Calumet Farm, 106
Cambridgeshire Stakes, 7, 12, 336
Cannon, H., 35

Cannon, J., 11
Cannon, T., 12
Captain Cuttle, 229
Carnarvon, 7th Earl of, 111
Caro, 180
'Carrie Red', 6
Carroll House, 338
Carslake, B., 35, 40, 80, 195
Carson, W. 199
Castle Irwell, 245, 248
Cauthen, S., 199, 204, 206, 207, 330
Cavaliere d'Arpino, 173
Cavalry Open Cup, 244
Cazalet, Peter, 248, 250
Cecil, Henry, 106, 205, 206
Cecil, Mrs Julie, 171
Cecil, Lady Robert, 17
Celina, 94
Cesarewitch, 7, 81, 164
Chamossaire, 312
Champagne Stakes, 37, 40, 167, 137,
    260, 299
Champion Chase, 246
Champion Hurdle, 240, 265
Champion Stakes, 89, 94, 140, 146,
    149, 150, 155, 181, 183
Chandoes, Lord, 128
Chaplin, Henry, Viscount, 279-96
Charles I, 125
Charles II, 125
Charlton, Ruth, 44-50
Chaucer, 107, 136, 141, 148
Cheltenham Gold Cup, 145, 146, 246,
    247, 263, 264, 265, 266, 267, 270,
    272
Chesham Stakes, 166
Chester Vase, 160, 233
Chetwynd, Sir George, 296, 307, 308
Cheveley Park Stakes, 58, 159
Cheveley Park Stakes, Tattersalls', 304,
    305
Chifney, S., 188
Childs, J., 195
Childwick Stud, 36, 40
Christopher Wren Stakes, 160
Chumleigh, 198
Church, Charles, 241
Churchill, Sir Winston, 3, 148, 313

Cicero, 19, 22, 226
Citation, 92
City and Suburban, 36, 37
Clairvoyant, 159
Clarence House Stakes, 167
Clarissimus, 159
Classic Trial Stakes, 160
Classics, The, 296-9
Closeburn, 166
Cnamh, 310-11
Coe, Sebastian, 103
Cochrane, Sir William, 18
Colling, George, 259-60
Colling, Jack, 33, 35
Colombo, 230-8, 269
Colorado, 149
Commando, 107
Connaught, 90, 93
Conquistador Cielo, 95
Cool Customer, 9
Cork and Orrery Stakes, 170
Coronach, 299
Coronation Cup, 155, 160, 182, 308,
    316
Coronation Stakes, 93, 174, 175
Corrie Roy, 7
Costa, 222
Cottage Rake, 146
County Hurdle, 265
Coupe de Chapeau, 146
Coventry Stakes, 37, 137, 167, 180,
    259
Craganour, 227, 228, 229, 236
Craven Stakes, 37, 233
Crepello, 94, 95, 159, 165
Cripple, 129
Cromwell, 251
Crown Prince, 22
Crump, Neville, 265
Cunningham, Helen Monica Mabel, 25
Cureton, Lionel, 197
Curwen's Bay Barb, 126
Custance, H., 188
Cydonic, 139
Cyllene, 42
Cypria, 164

Dalham Hall Stud, 53, 54

Dalmeny, Lord, 23
Damascus, 92
Dan Cupid, 175
Dancing Brave, 53, 54, 89, 151, 238, 268, 269
Danzig, 109
Darby Dan Farm, 111
Darley Arabian, The, 125, 127–9
Darley, Thomas, 128
Darling, Fred, 28–33, 99, 165, 166, 193, 229, 233, 234, 298
Darling, Sam, 32
Dastur, 22
Daumas, M. 263
Daumier, 172
Davy, Major Colin, 244
Davies, R., 209
Davison, Miss Emily, 226, 227, 228
Davy Jones, 214, 248–52
Dawkins, Thomas, 300
Dawson, Joe, 6, 221
Dawson, Mathew, 11, 132, 133, 135
Day, Mr., 8
Dean Swift, 36, 38
Deban, 242
Decidedly, 90
Decies, Lord, 6
Decorum, 168
Delaneige, 249
Delleana, 159
Derby, The, 6, 11, 18, 22, 23, 30–3, 34, 36–43, 53, 60, 73, 83–9, 90, 91, 93, 94, 98, 100, 102, 109, 133, 134, 136, 138, 141, 142, 143, 144, 148, 151, 155, 159, 160, 161, 162, 164, 168, 170, 172, 173, 175, 177, 179, 180, 193, 194, 226, 227, 228, 229–38, 260, 283, 297, 298, 308, 333
Derby, 17th Earl of, 37, 38, 41, 53, 59, 72, 89, 107, 136, 138, 139, 140, 141, 148, 159, 160, 162, 229
Stud of, 108
Derby, 18th Earl of, 148, 260
Desert Orchid, 151, 270–2
Desmond, 74
Dewhurst Stakes, 37, 40, 155, 168, 299
Diadem Stakes, 170

Diamond Jubilee, 134, 154
Dick, D. V., 264, 267
Dictus, 181
Dillon, B., 225
Diminuendo, 53
Disraeli, Benjamin, 61
Djebel, 107
Djeddah, 162
Domino, 107
Donatello, (artist), 172
Donatello II, 42, 159, 164
Doncaster, 333, 334
Doncaster Cup, 163, 297
Donoghue, S., 11, 33, 41, 52, 60, 142–3, 193, 195, 198, 205, 227, 229–238, 239, 240
Donovan, 298
Double Crossed, 249
Douglas Home, J., 61
Douglas Home, Hon. William, 62
Doyle, E., 242
Dreaper, T., 267
Dudley, 212
Duke of Normandy, 111
Duke of Richmond, 134, 135
Duller, G., 155
Durham, 3rd Earl of, 296, 307

Earl, Walter, 160
Easter Hero, 145–7, 268
Easter Week, 146
Easton, 233–7
Easy Line, 330
EBF Armistice Stakes, 206
EBF Nursery Stakes, 206
EBF Remembrance Stakes, 206
Eccles, S. Smith, 209
Eclipse, 90, 126, 127, 131, 132
Eclipse Stakes, 23, 37, 53, 90, 93, 139, 140, 155, 180, 181, 182, 183, 225
Eddery, Patrick, 199, 204, 206, 207
Edward VII, 36, 228
Edwardes, George, 136
Egerton, Major, 9
Egerton Stud, 171
Ego, 250
Egypt, King of, 241
El Barq, 167

El Gran Senor, 91
El Greco, 172, 173
Elder, T., 248
Elegant Stranger, 329
Elias, Mr., 312
'Ellangowan', 22
Elliott, E. C., 169, 193, 195, 205, 260, 314
Ellis, Terence, 206
Elizabeth II, HM Queen, 109–12
Emancipator, 245, 248, 249, 250
Enthusiast, 146
Epsom, 334, 335
Equitrack, 105
Eryholme, 136
Escape, 188
Esmond, E., 159
Estes, Joseph, 177
Exbury, 181

Fair Diana, 299
Fair Ellen, 125
Fairfax-Ross, Brigadier T., 160
Fairway, 89, 136–41, 299
Falmouth, 6th Viscount, 11, 107, 108
Faraway Dancer (USA), 89
Faraway Son, 183
Farncombe Down Stud, 57
Farquhar, Sir Horace, 191
Favorita, 171
Fawcus, Captain Jack, 9
Feakes, M., 252, 254
Felizande, 227, 228
Feola, 111
Fergusson, Mr, 241, 244
Flaming Page, 177
Flamingo, 138
Flares, 163
Fleet, 93
Flush Royal, 162
Flying Childers, 126, 129
Foliation, 140
Fordham, George, 11, 205
Forego, 89
Forest Flower, 304
Forli, 89
Formidable, 152
Foster, 'Mush', 264

Fouquet, 245
Fox, F., 196, 199, 205, 237
Foxhall, 221
Foxhall Stakes, 33
Foxlaw, 298
Francome, J., 208, 209, 210
Franklyn, Robert Alan, 98, 99
Fraser, Donald, 142
Free Handicap, 37, 166, 168, 231
Freeman, William, 141
Freemason Lodge, 33, 35, 36
Freer, Geoffrey, 304
French Derby, 97
French St Leger, 178
Fulmen, 132

Gainsborough, 148, 298
Galbreath, John, 111
Galcador, 238
Galopin, 133, 135
Galtee More, 32
Galwex Lady, 208
Gantry, James, 26
Gaselee, Nicholas, 61
Gay Crusader, 198
Gee, Mr, 221
General Peel, 283
Gentleman, 314
George V, 226, 227, 230
Gesture, 42
Gibson, Mr, 241, 243
Gifford, J., 209
Gilbey, Geoffrey, 315, 316–18
Gilbey, Quintin, 175, 195, 237
Giles, Mr, 223
Gimcrack, 129, 130
Gimcrack Club, The, 129–30
Gimcrack Dinner, 308
Gimcrack Stakes, 168, 180
Gladiateur, 65
Glanely, Lord, 230–7
Glasgow, Lord, 283
Glenister, Henry A., 259, 260
Glennon, T. P., 176, 177
Glorious Devon, 205
Goblin, 60, 61
Godiva, 89
Godolphin Arabian, The, 126, 129

Goha, 241, 242
Gold Finder, 126
Gold Rod, 181, 183
Golden Miller, 50, 146, 244–7, 248, 249, 265
Golding, Mr, 8
Gollings, William, 267
Gondolette, 135
Goodwill, A. W., 149
Goodwood, 333, 335
Goodwood Cup, 40, 133, 163, 297
Goodwood Mile, 183
Gordon, Adam Lindsay, 217, 256, 274
Gorytus, 151
Graded Races, 148
Grakle, 145
Grand Criterium, 97
Grand National, 145, 146, 211, 213, 215, 244–8, 249, 250, 265, 332
Grand Parade, 230
Grand Prix de Paris, 159, 164, 192, 193, 194, 232, 297
Grand Prix de Saint-Cloud, 98, 175
Grand Prize, 221
Grand Steeplechase de Paris, 72, 146, 262
Grande Course de Haies, 263
Granville, Frederick, 289
Graustark, 111
Graves, Lord, 26
Gray, Mr, 8
Great Sport, 227
Great Surrey Foal Stakes, 36
Great Yorkshire 'Chase, 9
Green, Frederick, 16
Greenham Stakes, 37, 168
Gregalach, 145
Gregarious, 111
Gregson, Mrs Mollie, 252
Grey, W., 205
Grey Lag, 97
Grosvenor, 1st Earl, 130
Grosvenor, Lady Dorothy, 24
Gugenheim, Jean-Marc, 27
Gwen, 23, 171
Gyr, 100, 179

Hadden, Mr, 241

Hakim, 137
Hambleton, 165, 166
Hamilton, 12th Duke of, 10
Hampton, Jack, 26
Hancock, A. B., 95
Hanmer, John, 206
Hardwicke Stakes, 92, 134, 223
Harris, Kenneth, 83–9, 199–204
Hartigan, Martin, 242
Harvester, 134
Harvey, Brigadier, C. B., 197, 240–3
Harwood, Guy, 268
Harwood, Leo, 39
Haslam, Patrick, 328
Hastings, Lady Edith Maud, 289, 291
Hastings, 4th Marquess of, 279–96
Hastings-Bass, Peter, 148
Hatta, 55
Hazelhatch, 136
Height of Fashion, 109, 112
Henderson, Nicholas, 61
Hennessy, Madame K., 262, 264
Hennessy Gold Cup, 263, 267
Henschel, Count, 188
Herbert, Ivor, 267
Hermit, 104, 221, 279
Hern, Major W. R., 57, 112, 149, 184
Hewitt, Abram S., 108
Higgins, R., 97
High Top, 56
High Veldt, 172
Highclere, 109, 112
Highflyer Sale, 54
Highland Spring Derby Trial, 268
Hill, William, 259
Hill Shade, 90
Hillary, 90
Hillingdon, Lord, 15
Hippius, 89
Hislop, John, 12, 195, 197, 198, 252
Hobbs, Bruce, 20
Hobbs, Sir Jack, 19
Hogg, Captain T., 230
Holliday, Major Lionel, 98
Holy Friar, 315
Hore-Belisha, L., 244
Horner, Cicely, 16, 18
Horner, Sir John, 16, 17

Howhus, 330
Huby, John, 134
Huic Holloa, 245
Humble Duty, 171
Humorist, 40-2, 142-4, 229
Hunt, Nelson Bunker, 98
Huxtable, H., 8
Hycilla, 89
Hypericum, 89
Hyperion, 59, 72, 89, 90, 92, 93, 107,
    131, 132, 136, 147, 155, 159, 181,
    229, 312
Hypnotist, 34

Icy Wonder, 265
Imperial Produce Stakes, 213
Imperial Stud Germany, 67
International Classification, 268
Irish Cambridgeshire, 92
Irish Derby, 92, 93, 297
Irish Oaks, 33, 94, 233
Irish One Thousand Guineas, 233
Irish St Leger, 56
Irish Two Thousand Guineas, 89, 170
Ismay, C. B., 227
Isonomy, 131
Italian Derby, 173
Italian St Leger, 173

J. O. Tobin, 90
Jackdaw, 240
Jackson, Harry, 45
James I, 125
James II, 126
Jarvis, Sir Jack, 20, 24, 106, 260, 314
Jarvis, Paul, 151
Jelliss, H., 229
Jersey Stakes, 93
Jest, 40, 42, 144
Jockey Club, The, 3-5, 187, 300, 307,
    308, 340
Jockey Club Cup, 140
Jockey Club Stakes, 136, 140, 161
Jockey Club Stewards, 4, 299-304,
    305, 306
Joel Family, 52
Joel, H. J., 43, 92
Joel, J. B., 40, 43, 142-4, 229

Joel, S. B., 40, 42, 78
Joel, Stanhope, 92
Johnstone, Sir Frederic, 282, 283, 284
Johnstone, W. R., 97, 231-8, 261, 331
Jones, H., 154, 226, 227, 228
Jones, Richard, 260
Jones, R. A-., 195
Joyner, Andrew, 225
Jubilee Stakes, 191
July Course, 42
July Cup, 93, 170
July Sales, Keeneland, 54, 55
July Stakes, 40, 137
Justification, 31

Karabas, 204
Keen Blade, 248, 249, 250
Keene, James, R., 106
Kelso, 89
Kenmare, 111
Kentucky Derby, 90
Kerrera, 56
Keyser, Mr, 303
Khaled, 89
Khan, The Aga, 52, 53, 94, 108, 160
Khan, Prince Aly, 51-2, 94, 192
Kildangan Stud, 53
Kiltoi, 249
King George VI and Queen Elizabeth
    Diamond Stakes, 53, 93, 97, 102,
    151, 159, 160, 162, 164, 170, 172,
    174, 180, 181, 182, 183, 303
King Edward VII Stakes, 161
King, L., 146
King, Revd Mr, 315
King Tom, 135
King's Nephew, 265, 266, 267
King's Stand Stakes, 93, 170
Kingcraft, 132
Kinlochewe, 168
Kinsky, Count Charles, 16
Knight of the Thistle, 191
Knockroe, 308
Kong, 259
Kris, 111
Kroonstad, 140

La Fleche, 134

La Paiva, 182
Ladas, 19, 22, 132
Ladbrokes, 26, 27
Lady Florence, 284
Lady Josephine, 168
Lady Masham, 221
Lady Nairne, 230
Laing, Ray, 206
Lambton, Lady Anne, 17
Lambton, Hon. George, 9, 12, 15–18, 41, 59, 72, 83, 108, 147, 148, 229
Lambton, Jack, (3rd Earl of Durham), 16
Larkspur, 160
'Launde', Mr, 315, 316
Lauraguais, Count, 129, 130
Lavandin, 238
Lawrence, John (Lord Oaksey), 176
Le Landy, 27
Leach, Jack, 333
Leader, Thomas, 149
Lee, Mr, 303
Leeds, Duchess of, 17
Lefevre, C. J., 7
Lehndorff, Count, 67
Lemberg, 37, 225
Lewis, G., 130
Lexington, 107, 108
Liberal Lady, 171
Lincolnshire Handicap, 332
Linden Tree, 180
Lingfield Derby trial, 236
Lingfield Park, 92
Lister, C., 241, 243
Liverpool, 335
Llanpadrig, 330
Llewellyn, Sir H., 250
Loewenstein, A., 146
Londonderry, Marchioness of, 288, 289
Longriggan, 33
Lonsdale, 5th Earl of, 12–15
Louvier, 227
Louvois, 227, 228
Love Wisely, 136
Lovely Cottage, 146
Lowrey, T., 161
Lowther, Hugh Cecil, 12–15

Lubbock Sprint, 170
Lucayan Gold, 330
Ludlow, Anna, 328
Lumino, 264
Lycaon, 38, 40
Lynx, Larry, 312
Lyphard, 109

McCall, D., 34, 35
McCall, P., 34, 35
McCreery, Robert, 56, 57
MacDonald, Ramsay, 313, 314
Macdonald-Buchanan, Lady, 168, 171
Macdonald-Buchanan, Major Sir Reginald, 165
McGowan, Desmond, 173
McHarg, Colonel W. W., 24
Machell, Captain J., 222
Mah Iran, 94
Mah Mahal, 94
Maher, D., 23, 37, 38, 80, 225, 226
Mahmoud, 94, 308
Maiden, William, 255
Maidment, C., 205
Mail Fist, 239
Mainwaring, Reginald, 9
Maktoum Family, 52–9, 329, 330
    Maktoum Al-Maktoum, 52, 56
    Ahmed Al-Maktoum, 52, 54
    Hamdan Al-Maktoum, 52, 53, 57
    Mana Al-Maktoum, 56
    Sheikh Mohammed, 52–9
Malton, 36
Man O'War, 92
Manchester Cup, 211, 222
Manchester November Handicap, 205, 206
Mandarin, 262, 263, 264
Mandragora, 316
Manila, 269
Manna, 230
Mannicka, 127
Manton, 6
'Manton', Mr, 6, 9
Marchetta, Family, 159
Markham, Mr, 125
'Marlborough', (Lord Oaksey), 262
Marsden, Mr, 241

Marsh, Marcus, 233
Marsh, Richard, 8
Marshall, B., 209, 263
Martini, 7
Masson, Thomas, 252, 254, 255, 257, 259
Mathet, Francois, 96, 97
Meadow Court, 177
Mediaeval Knight, 234-6
Melbourne Cup, 272-5
Meld, 33, 164
Mellon, Paul, 129, 130
Mellor, S. 208, 209
Melton, 42, 132
Mentmore Stud, 22, 23
Mercer, J., 155, 199
Merry, James, 188
Michelozzo, 56
Middle Park Plate, 40
Middle Park Stakes, 37, 58, 155, 167, 183, 252, 299
Middleham, 9
Milan Mill, 179
Mildmay, Lord, 251
Mildmay, Anthony Bingham, 214, 248, 249
Mill House, 265, 266, 267
Mill Reef, 42, 111, 129, 130, 179-82, 182, 269
Milner, Henry, 9
Minoru, 36
Miracle, 22
Miss Dan, 178
Miss Elliott, 129
Mitchells, 252
Molecomb Stakes, 40
Moller, The Brothers, 55
Molony, M., 214
Molony, T., 209
Montrose, Caroline, Duchess of, 6-9
Montrose, 4th Duke of, 6
Moore, Henry, 311
Morris, Anthony, 112
Morriss, H. E., 229
Mortimer, Roger, 5
Morton, Charles, 38-42, 142-5
Mr Jinks, 83
Mr Prospector, 95, 109

Mtoto, 52, 53
Mullins, Mr, 310
Mumtaz Mahal, 93, 94, 168
Mundy, Mrs, 248
Munnings, Sir Alfred, 143, 145
Murless, Sir Noël, 59, 95, 96, 165, 166, 168, 169, 170, 175
My Love, 161, 238
My Prince, 146
My Swallow, 180
Myrobella, 15, 299
Mysterious, 94

Nance colt, 35
Nashkour, 268
Nashua, 92
Nashwan, 52, 53, 54, 56, 58, 109, 151
Nasrullah, 95, 107
Nathoo, 160
National Breeders Produce Stakes, 37, 167
National Hunt 'Chase, 22, 72, 214
National Hunt Stewards, 301
National Stud, The, 88
Nearco, 42, 92, 107, 141, 172, 193, 194, 259
Nearctic, 90
Neil Gow, 37, 225
Never Bend, 179
Nevett, W., 196
New Astley Club, 225
Newmarket, 57, 189, 333-7
Newmarket Heath, 90
Newmarket Stakes, 37, 138, 233
Newmarket Thoroughbred Racing and Chasing, 327-30
Newminster, 284
New Stakes, 37
Niccolo dell'Arca, 172
Nickalls, Lt.-Col. Tom, 176
Night Pass, 206
Nijinsky, 42, 100, 149, 177-9, 269
Nimbus, 93, 167, 169, 170, 259, 260, 261
Norrie, Colonel Willoughby (Lord), 244
Northern Dancer, 89, 90, 92, 109, 177
Nunthorpe Stakes, 93, 170

Nureyev, 306
Oaks, The, 6, 11, 22, 33, 40, 43, 58, 94, 97, 134, 155, 164, 233, 238, 316
Oaksey, J., 61
Obliterate, 23
O'Brien, Vincent, 178, 179
Observer Gold Cup, 98
Ocean Swell, 22, 23, 297
Oh So Sharp, 53, 58
Old Vic, 52, 54, 56, 58
Oncidium, 176
O'Neill, F., 194
O'Neill, J., 209
One Thousand Guineas, The, 6, 22, 23, 33, 39–42, 90, 93, 94, 97, 98, 155, 164, 170, 316
Orban, 207
Orme, 133
Ormonde, 131, 132, 298
Oros, 92
Ortello, 172
Osbaldeston, George, 319, 320, 334
Osgood, Frank, 149
O'Sullevan, Peter, 97, 99, 265, 267
Oswald, Michael, 111
Ottoman, 161
Outbreak, 146
Overseas, 252, 254, 255, 256, 257, 258
Owen Tudor, 89, 93, 165, 168, 298

Paget, Hon. Dorothy, 43–50, 230, 245, 246, 279–96
Paget, Lady Florence, 279–96
Palais Royal, 140
Palmer, F., 173
Papyrus, 41, 173, 229
Paradoxical, 42
Park, James, 171
Parkes, P., 23
Parthia, 36
Pasch, 193
Pas Suel, 265, 266, 267
Pattern Races, 148
Pattern System, 153
Peace, Mr, 8
Peck, Charles, 42
Peel, General, 221

Pella, 74
Pembroke, Countess of, 17
Penco, U. V., 174
Persimmon, 134, 163
Persse, H. S., 33–5, 83
Pertain, 330
Peter, 221, 222, 223, 224
Petite Étoile, 52, 94, 165, 174
Petition 92, 94, 174
Phalaris, 42, 107, 136, 137, 139, 141
Pharamond, 138
Pharis II, 141
Pharos, 107, 141, 173
Phil Drake, 97
Phoenix Stables, 90
Picture Play, 42, 159
Piggott, L., 60, 174, 175, 178, 179, 195–9, 200–4, 206, 210, 231, 306
Piggott, Susan, 200
Pinza, 30, 33, 159
Pipe, Martin, 208
Plack, 22
Pleasant Colony, 95
Polish Precedent, 52, 54, 56
Pollet, Étienne, 97–8, 177
Polymelus, 42, 137, 144
Pommern, 42
Pont L'Evêque, 299
Pony Derby, 147
Pope, George, 90
Portland, 6th Duke of, 32, 131, 132
Portvaso, 206
Poule d'Essai des Pouliches, 98
Pratt, William, 164
Precipitation, 298
Premio Roma, 207
Prendergast, Paddy, 98
Pretty Polly, 42, 131, 155, 159, 174
Primera, 176
Primrose, Hon. Neil, 19
Prince Chevalier, 182
Prince Palatine, 40, 297
Prince Regent, 146, 268
Prince of Wales's Nursery Stakes, 133
Prince of Wales's Stakes, 155
Princely Gift, 174
Princequillo, 92
Princess Dorrie, 40

Princess of Wales's Stakes, 109, 140, 161
Prix de l'Arc de Triomphe, 56, 91, 98, 102, 151, 173, 174, 175, 176, 178, 180, 269, 337
Prix des Drags, 146
Prix Foy, 93
Prix Ganay, 182
Prix Greffulhe, 175
Prix de Guiche, 98
Prix de Jockey Club, 297
Prix Lupin, 98, 175
Prix Robert Papin, 180
Probyn, General Sir Dighton, 228
Proud Crest, 205
Prue, 23
Pyramus, 125

Queen Elizabeth Stakes, 149
Queen Elizabeth II Stakes, 56, 183
Queenborough, Lord, 43
Queenpot, 170
Queen's Hussar, 182
Queen's Vase, 223
Querquidella, 240

Radiancy, 39
Radium, 142
Ragusa Stud, 53
'Rainbow', 320-7
Rainbow Quest, 53
Rajpipla, Maharaja of, 233
Rank, J. V., 193
Rank, Mrs J. V., 193
Raphael, Walter, 81
Rataplan, 316
Really True, 245
Recruit, 125
Red Rum, 151
Rees, L. B., 240
Reeves, Richard Stone, 90, 91
Reference Point, 102, 106, 151
Relko, 97
Resplendent, 233
Rest Assured, 255, 258
Reynoldstown, 248, 249, 250, 251
Rhodes Scholar, 162
Ribocco, 93

Ribot, 92, 132, 172-4, 269
Richards, Sir G., 23, 50, 94, 155, 166, 167, 169, 170, 171, 192-5, 196-9, 199, 205, 206, 207, 214, 230, 231, 234, 236, 308
Richmond Stakes, 159, 230, 306
Ridge Wood, 92
Riding Mill, 163
Right Away, 98
Right Boy, 174
Right Royal, 97, 98
Rigolo, 162
Rimell, F., 248
Rivalry, 205
Roberto, 111
Robinson, G. W., 266, 267
Robinson, J., 198
Robinson, Patrick, 91, 93
Rob Roy, 146
Rock Sand, 226
Rogerson, John, 267
Romanella, 172, 173
Ronaldshay, Lord, 58
Rosebery, 6th Earl of, 18-24, 53, 106, 248
Rose Red, 159
Rossetti, Dante Gabriel, 60
Rothschild, Hannah, 19
de Rothschild, James, 37, 39
de Rothschild, Leopold, 227
de Rothschild, Baron Meyer, 19
Rous, Vice Admiral the Hon. Henry, 126
Rous Memorial Stakes, 140
Rowley Mile, The, 7, 170, 226, 334, 336
Roxburghe, Duchess of, 279
Royal Ascot, 306
Royal Forest, 167, 168
Royal Gait, 306
Royal Hunt Cup, 221, 222, 223, 224
Royal Lancer, 15
Royal Mares, The, 125
Royal Minstrel, 138, 139, 140
Royal Palace, 43, 92, 93, 95, 149, 165
Royal Standard Stakes, 160
Royal Studs, 109, 112
Rustom Mahal, 93

Rustom Pasha, 165, 168

Sadler's Wells, 54, 89
Sailor Prince, 12
St Angela, 133, 135
St Chad, 93
St Frusquin, 136, 233
St George, Charles, 56
St George Stakes, 161
St James's Palace Stakes, 37, 183, 252
St Leger, The, 8, 11, 22, 33, 34, 36,
    37, 40, 41, 42, 56, 93, 102, 133,
    139, 140, 147, 155, 160, 161, 162,
    164, 172, 177, 198, 315, 316
St Martin, Y., 97
St Medard, 134
St Mirrin, 12
St Paddy, 93, 95, 165
St Simon, 107, 131–5, 148
St Simon Stakes, 135
Sanctum, 81
Sandwich, 22
Sansovino, 72, 135, 229
Sassafras, 178
Sassoon, Sir Victor, 91, 93, 94
Saxby, W., 228 , 229
Sayajirao, 161
Scapa Flow, 135, 136, 141
Sceptre, 131, 155
Scottish Union, 193
Scrope, Colonel Adrian, 147
Scudamore, Marilyn, 207
Scudamore, P., 207–10
Sea-Bird II, 98, 175–7, 182, 269
Seafield, Countess of, 279
Seattle Slew, 95
Secretariat, 95
Secreto, 91
Sefton, 6, 7
Sefton Lodge, 7, 8, 42
Sefton Stud, 9
Selene, 136, 148
September Stakes, 42
Shaadi, 52
Shadwell Stud, 53, 54
Shahrastani, 89, 268, 269
Sharp, J., 188, 189
Sharp Reminder, 206

Shaw, Donald, 289
Shaw, R., 160
Shergar, 151, 269
Sherrard, Richard, 6, 211, 307
Sherwood, S., 272
Shirley Heights, 60, 61, 95, 111, 152
Shoemaker, W., 200
Shreiber, Captain A., 241
Sicalade, 175
Sicambre, 175
Side Hill Stud, 147
Silvio, 132, 262
Simmons, Alfred, 28
Sir Ivor, 90, 204
Sir Visto, 19, 22, 132
Skeaping, John, 148, 311
Slater, 245
Sleeping Partner, 22
Slew o 'Gold, 95
Slip Anchor, 106
Sloan, J. F. 'Tod', 60, 191–2
Smirke, C., 195, 234, 235, 236, 308
Smith, D., 20, 33, 160, 161, 163, 196,
    199, 261
Smith, Eph, 160, 196
Smyth, R. V., 255
Smyth, Victor, 35
Snaafi Dancer, 55
Snow, Donald, 246, 247
Snowden, J., 11
Solar Slipper, 161
Solario, 298
Solatium, 239
Solonaway, 170
Somerset Stakes, 168
Southcourt Stud, 142
Southern Hero, 245
Souverain, 162
Spanish Prince, 38
Sparkler, 183
Spearmint, 226
Speck, W., 214
Spion Kop, 194
Spring Stakes, 166
Stalker, C., 254, 258, 259
Stanley family, 59, 160
Stanley House, 9, 18
Stanley House Stud, 135, 136, 159

Starkey, G., 238, 268, 269
Star of Iran, 94, 174
Star King, 167, 168, 169
Star Kingdom, 168
'Starlight', Captain, 320–7
Stedfast, 38
Stephenson, W., 33
Stern, G., 39–40
Stewards' Cup, 166
Stirling Crawfurd, William Stuart, 6–8
Stirling Stuart, Major, R., 9
Stockbridge, 162
Stockwell, 107, 132
Stormy Eve, 329
Stroud, Anthony, 55
Stubbs, George, 90, 130
Sucaryl, 93
Sun Castle, 89
Sun Chariot, 89, 155, 174, 175
Sun Prince, 60
Sunspot, 38
Sunstar, 38–42, 144
Sun Stream, 89
Supertello, 159
Sussex Stakes, 94, 183
Swale, 95
Swallow Tail, 261
Swannell, David, 306
Swaps, 89
Swynford, 37, 107, 159

Taaffe, P., 266, 267
Tabor, Victor, 255
Taillefer, 263
Taj Akbar, 308
Taj Dewan, 93
Tangle, 170
Tant Mieux, 299
Targui, 168
Tatem, William James (Lord Glanely), 230
Taylor, Alec, 6, 136
Teenoso, 55
Templeton, Mr, 30
Tenerani, 172, 173
Tesio, Signor Federico, 107, 159, 172, 173, 193, 298
Tetratema, 83

Thankerton, 308
Thebais, 6, 7
The Bard, 298
The Bore, 215
The Cobbler, 169
The Potentate, 166
Theras, 245
The Story, 38
The Tetrarch, 83, 94, 164, 168
The White Knight, 74
Thirsk Classic Trial, 260
Thomas, Joe, 90
Thomond II, 245, 247
Thormanby, 132, 188
Thorne, John, 61
Thornton, Spencer, 25
Thoroughbred Breeders Association, 21, 58
'Tinman', 190
Tipperary Tim, 145
Todrai, 172
Tolarra, 35
Toole, Joseph, 313, 314
Totalisator, The, 27, 339
Tourbillon, 107
de Trafford, Sir Humphrey, 15, 35
Tranquil, 41, 136
Tree, Jeremy, 59
Trespasser, 155
Triple Crown, 154, 163, 178, 231
Tristan, 134
Troytown, 213, 214
Tudor Minstrel, 168, 182, 183
Turks, The, 125
Turnell, R., 267
Twelve Pointer, 82
Two Thousand Guineas, The, 11, 22, 23, 37, 38, 40, 41, 42, 43, 53, 93, 94, 133, 134, 136, 138, 141, 168, 169, 177, 180, 183, 193, 232, 233, 234, 236, 237, 260, 268, 306, 336

Umidwar, 236
Underdown, E., 12
Unfuwain, 109
Usher, 161

Vacarme, 306

Vague Discretion, 206
Vaguely Noble, 98, 99
Valour, 222, 224
Vergette, George, 198
Vermont, 65
Vernet, Helen, 25–8
Vernet, Robert, 25
Victoria, Queen, 280
Vienna, 98
Vilusi, 206
Vivian-Smith, Lady Helen, 24
Volterra, M. Leon, 192, 261
Voltigeur, 131
Vuillier, Lt.-Col. J. J., 108

Wake Up, 160
Waklin, Captain William, 128
de Walden, Lord Howard, 210
Wales, Prince of, (Prince Regent), 129,
    188, 280, 283, 285, 294
Wales, Princess of, 285
Walker, Daisy, 44
Walker, Stella, 129
Wallis, Reverend Colville, 8
Walnut Way, 208
Walwyn, F., 248, 250, 264, 265
Warren Place, 166
Washington International, 159
Watson, Geoff, 96
Watts, J. D., 308, 309
Watts, J. W., 20
Webb, F., 12
Welbeck Handicap, 315
Welbeck Stud, 134
Welcome Gift, 234
Wellesley Arabian, The, 125
Wernher, Sir Harold, 140
Wertheimer, M. Pierre, 27, 232
West Ilsley Stables, 109, 112
Westminster, Anne, Duchess of, 267
Weston, T., 60, 137, 138, 139, 140,
    141, 196, 199, 299

West Side Story, 43
Whalley, A., 227
Whisk Broom, 225
White Lodge Stud, 54, 55
White Star, 40
White, 'Tiny', 12
Whiteway, 164
Whitney, H., 225
Whitney, J. H., 145, 147
Wicks, Darrell M., 198
Wightman, William, 60, 61
William Hill Futurity, 268
Williams, E., 248
Wills Mile, 93
Wilson, G., 245, 246, 247
Wilwyn, 159
Windsor, Lad, 233–6
Wingman, 214
Winter, F., 209, 262, 263, 264
Wishard, Enoch, 68
Wokingham Stakes, 259
Wood, C., 12, 134, 211, 222, 307
Woodcote Stakes, 40
Wood Ditton Stakes, 268
Woodlands Stud, 148
Woodlark, 160
Woodpark Stud, 164
Woodward, William, 107, 161
Woolavington, Lord, 229, 234
Wragg, A., 196
Wragg, H., 195, 198, 199, 236
Wragg, S., 167, 196

Yank, Albert, 98
Yorkshire Oaks, 94

Zanoni, 223
Zarafion, 329
Zarco, 171
Zetland, 4th Marquess of, 58
Zetland Stud, 58
Zilzal, 52, 56